THE WORLD BOOK ENCYCLOPEDIA OF
PEOPLE AND PLACES

THE WORLD BOOK ENCYCLOPEDIA OF
PEOPLE AND PLACES

1/A-C

WORLD BOOK, INC.

a Scott Fetzer company

CHICAGO

Acknowledgments:

Front cover
large photo, © H. P. Merton, Corbis Stock Market
left inset, © Stefano Cellai, Corbis Stock Market
center inset, © Lindsay Hebberd, Woodfin Camp, Inc.
right inset, © Danielle Hayes, Bruce Coleman Inc.

Back cover
© H. P. Merton, Corbis Stock Market

For information on other World Book publications, visit our Web site **http://www.worldbook.com** or call **1-800-WORLDBK (967-5325).** For information on sales to schools and libraries, call **1-800-975-3250 (United States); 1-800-837-5365 (Canada).**

World Book, Inc.
233 North Michigan Avenue
Chicago, IL 60601

Library of Congress Cataloging-in-Publication Data

The World Book encyclopedia of people and places.
     p. cm.
  Includes bibliographical references and index.
  ISBN 0-7166-3755-3
   1. Encyclopedias and dictionaries. [1. Geography—Encyclopedias.] I. World Book, Inc.

AE5 . W563 2005
031—dc21

                              2004023271

Printed in the United States of America

16 17 18 19 09 08 07 06 05

Staff

Editor in Chief, World Book, Inc.
Dale Jacobs

Managing Editor, World Book Publishing
Paul A. Kobasa

Editorial

Managing Editor, General Publishing and Annuals
Maureen Mostyn Liebenson

Associate Editor
Shawn Brennan

Writers
Pamela Bliss
Kathy Klein
Susan Messer
Rita Vander Meulen

Permissions Editor
Janet T. Peterson

Cartographic Services
H. George Stoll, Head
Wayne K. Pichler
John M. Rejba

Indexing Services
David Pofelski, Head

Consultant
Kempton Webb
Prof. Emeritus of Geography,
Columbia University

Research Services

Manager
Loranne Shields

Researchers
Madolynn Cronk
Lynn Durbin
Cheryl Graham
Karen McCormack

Librarian
Jon Fjortoft

Art

Manager, Graphics and Design
Sandra Dyrlund

Designer
Kimberly Saar

Contributing Designer
Lucy Lesiak

Photographs Editor
Sylvia Ohlrich

Production and Administrative Support
John Whitney

Cover Design
Carol Gildar

Production

Director, Manufacturing and Pre-Press
Carma Fazio

Manager, Manufacturing
Steven Hueppchen

Senior Production Manager
Madelyn Underwood

Production Manager
Anne Fritzinger

Proofreader
Anne Dillon

Text Processing
Curley Hunter
Gwendolyn Johnson

Contents

How to Use This Series

There are six volumes in the *World Book Encyclopedia of People and Places:* volume 1, A-C; volume 2, D-H; volume 3, I-L; volume 4, M-R; volume 5, S-T; and volume 6, U-Z, the cumulative index, and Web site links for all countries.

Each book presents individual nations and other political or geographic units through articles that are at least two pages long. The countries are arranged in alphabetical order, beginning with the article on Afghanistan in Volume 1 and ending with Zimbabwe in Volume 6.

Articles about a specific place provide an overview of its history, geography, economy, people, culture, and current political situation. You will also find descriptions of the features that make that place unique.

Articles for countries with large populations or great prominence in world affairs generally cover several pages. In such cases, the article is divided into sections covering a particular topic relating to that country, such as History, Environment, People, and Economy. These sections are always covered within two facing pages. An example of an article with several sections is shown below.

A look at the articles

Coverage of each country includes a section that features a physical/political map and fact box. The fact box provides key information about government, economy, and people. For example, life expectancy and languages spoken are given, as is the percentage of the population entering various levels of schooling.

Another feature of this series is the timelines. Timelines found in articles including a history section list significant events in a country's past. For easy reference, color bars in the timeline signify different centuries or other periods of time.

In addition to the physical/political maps, a variety of thematic maps are included in the set. Diagrams and charts provide other information in graphic formats.

A comprehensive index

All the articles are referenced in the cumulative index at the end of volume 6. The index is an invaluable aid in finding specific information quickly.

Article titles are underlined.

Photographs in full color complement the text.

Section titles provide quick reference points.

Fact boxes contain key information for quick look-ups.

Flags shown for each country.

Locator maps show the location of a country on the globe.

Thematic and **historical maps** provide additional information.

Timelines list significant dates in a country's history.

The Canadian Wilderness

Canadian Cities

Economy and Resources

Conflict and Opportunity

History

The First Canadians

Environment

Canada Today

Canada

The article on Canada in volume 1 contains nine sections.

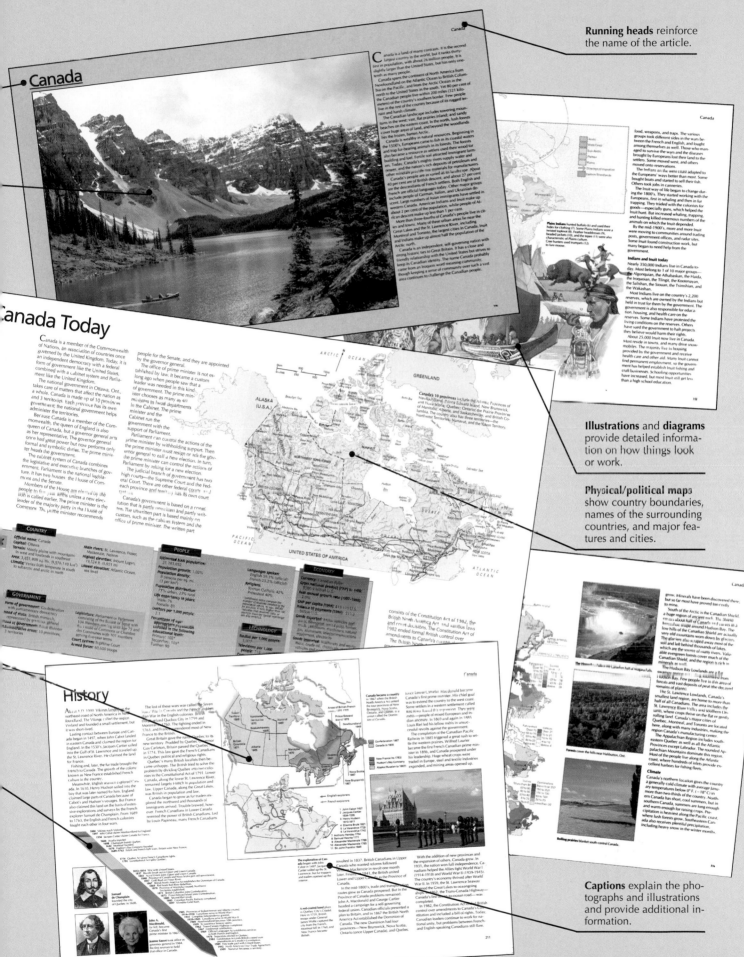

Running heads reinforce the name of the article.

Illustrations and **diagrams** provide detailed information on how things look or work.

Physical/political maps show country boundaries, names of the surrounding countries, and major features and cities.

Captions explain the photographs and illustrations and provide additional information.

Political World Map

The world has 193 independent countries and about 40 dependencies. An independent country controls its own affairs. Dependencies are controlled in some way by independent countries. In most cases, an independent country is responsible for the dependency's foreign relations and defense, and some of the dependency's local affairs. However, many dependencies have complete control of their local affairs.

By 2000, the world's population surpassed 6 billion, and the yearly rate of population growth was about 1.4 per cent. At that rate, the world's population would double in about 49 years. Almost all of the world's people live in independent countries. Only about 10 million people live in dependencies.

Some regions of the world, including Antarctica and certain desert areas, have no permanent population. The most densely populated regions of the world are in Europe and in southern and eastern Asia. The world's largest country in terms of population is China, which has more than a billion people. The independent country with the smallest population is Vatican City, with only about 1,000 people. The Vatican City, covering only 1/6 square mile (0.4 square kilometer), is also the smallest in terms of size. The world's largest nation in terms of area is Russia, which covers 6,592,850 square miles (17,075,400 square kilometers).

Every nation depends on other nations in some ways. The interdependence of the entire world and its peoples is called *globalism*. Nations trade with one another to earn money and to obtain manufactured goods or the natural resources that they lack. Nations with similar interests and political beliefs may pledge to support one another in case of war. Developed countries provide developing nations with financial aid and technical assistance. Such aid strengthens trade as well as defense ties.

Nations of the World

Name	Map key	Name	Map key	Name	Map key
Afghanistan	D 13	Bulgaria	C 11	Dominican Republic	E 6
Albania	C 11	Burkina Faso	E 9	East Timor	F 16
Algeria	D 10	Burundi	F 11	Ecuador	F 6
Andorra	C 10‡	Cambodia	E 15	Egypt	D 11
Angola	F 10	Cameroon	E 10	El Salvador	E 5
Antigua and Barbuda	E 6	Canada	C 4	Equatorial Guinea	E 10
Argentina	G 6	Cape Verde	E 8	Eritrea	E 11
Armenia	C 12	Central African Republic	E 10	Estonia	C 11
Australia	G 16	Chad	E 10	Ethiopia	E 11
Austria	C 10	Chile	G 6	Federated States of Micronesia	E 18
Azerbaijan	C 12	China	D 14	Fiji	F 1
Bahamas	D 6	Colombia	E 6	Finland	B 11
Bahrain	D 12	Comoros	F 12	France	C 10
Bangladesh	D 14	Congo (Brazzaville)	F 10	Gabon	F 10
Barbados	E 7	Congo (Kinshasa)	F 11	Gambia	E 9
Belarus	C 11	Costa Rica	E 5	Georgia	C 12
Belgium	C 10	Côte d'Ivoire	E 9	Germany	C 10
Belize	E 5	Croatia	C 11	Ghana	E 9
Benin	E 10	Cuba	D 5	Great Britain	C 9
Bhutan	D 14	Cyprus	D 11	Greece	D 11
Bolivia	F 6	Czech Republic	C 11	Grenada	E 6
Bosnia-Herzegovina	C 11	Denmark	C 10	Guatemala	E 5
Botswana	G 11	Djibouti	E 12	Guinea	E 9
Brazil	F 7	Dominica	E 6	Guinea-Bissau	E 9
Brunei	E 15				

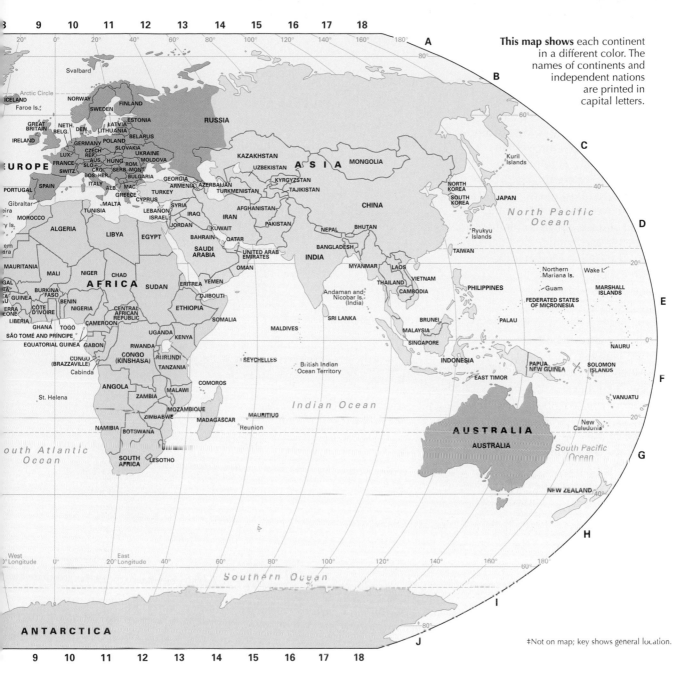

This map shows each continent in a different color. The names of continents and independent nations are printed in capital letters.

‡Not on map; key shows general location.

Physical World Map

The surface area of the world totals about 196,800,000 square miles (509,400,000 square kilometers). Water covers about 138,800,000 square miles (359,200,000 square kilometers), or 71 per cent of the world's surface. Only 29 per cent of the world's surface consists of land, which covers about 58,000,000 square miles (150,200,000 square kilometers).

Oceans, lakes, and rivers make up most of the water that covers the surface of the world. The water surface consists chiefly of three large oceans—the Pacific, the Atlantic, and the Indian. The Pacific Ocean is the largest, covering about a third of the world's surface. The world's largest lake is the Caspian Sea, a body of salt water that lies between Asia and Europe east of the Caucasus Mountains. The world's largest body of fresh water is the Great Lakes in North America. The longest river in the world is the Nile in Africa.

The land area of the world consists of seven continents and many thousands of islands. Asia is the largest continent, followed by Africa, North America, South America, Antarctica, Europe, and Australia. Geographers sometimes refer to Europe and Asia as one continent called *Eurasia*.

The world's land surface includes mountains, plateaus, hills, valleys, and plains. Relatively few people live in mountainous areas or on high plateaus since they are generally too cold, rugged, or dry for comfortable living or for crop farming. The majority of the world's people live on plains or in hilly regions. Most plains and hilly regions have excellent soil and an abundant water supply. They are good regions for farming, manufacturing, and trade. Many areas unsuitable for farming have other valuable resources. Mountainous regions, for example, have plentiful minerals, and some desert areas, especially in the Middle East, have large deposits of petroleum.

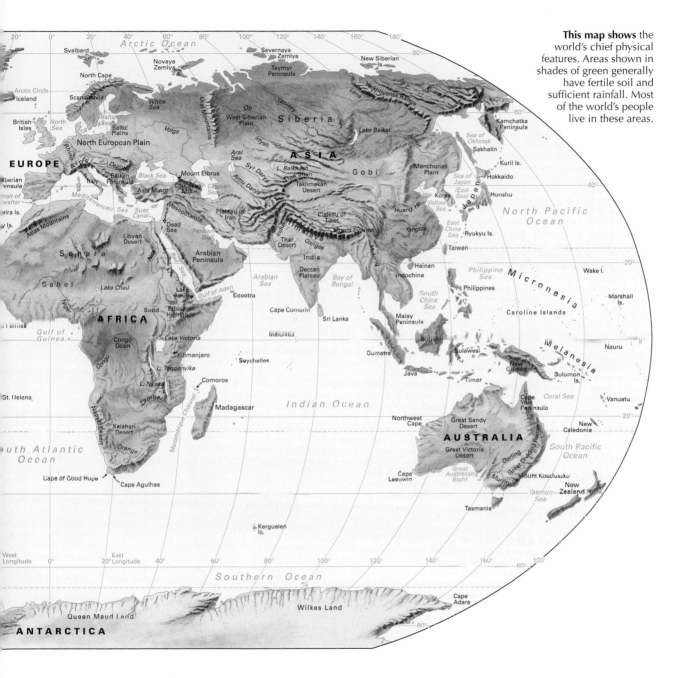

This map shows the world's chief physical features. Areas shown in shades of green generally have fertile soil and sufficient rainfall. Most of the world's people live in these areas.

Arctic Ocean

20° 0° 20° 40° 60° 80° 100° 120° 140° 160° 180°

Svalbard
North Cape
Scandinavia
Iceland
Arctic Circle
British Isles
North Sea
Baltic Sea
Baltic Plains
North European Plain
Rhine
Alps
Danube
Italy
Balkan Peninsula
Black Sea
Caucasus Mts.
Asia Minor
Caspian Sea
Mediterranean Sea
Suez Canal
Dead Sea
Persian Gulf
Mesopotamia
Plateau of Iran
Arabian Peninsula
Atlas Mountains
Libyan Desert
Sahara
Sahel
Lake Chad
Niger
Sudd
Ethiopian Highlands
Lake Assal
Gulf of Aden
Socotra

EUROPE

Siberian Peninsula
Strait of Gibraltar
Madeira Is.
Canary Is.

Novaya Zemlya
Severnaya Zemlya
Taymyr Peninsula
New Siberian Is.
White Sea
Ob
West Siberian Plain
Ural Mountains
Volga
Irtysh
Aral Sea
Syr Darya
Amu Darya
Yenisey
Siberia
Lake Baikal
Verkhoyansk Range
Lena
Amur
L. Balkhash
Tian Shan
Taklimakan Desert
Gobi
Manchurian Plain

ASIA

Plateau of Tibet
Mount Everest
Himalayas
Indus
Ganges
Thar Desert
Deccan Plateau
India
Arabian Sea
Bay of Bengal
Cape Comorin
Sri Lanka
Maldives
Mekong
Yangtze
Huang He
Hainan
Indochina
South China Sea
Malay Peninsula
Borneo
Sumatra
Java
Timor
Sulawesi

Kamchatka Peninsula
Sea of Okhotsk
Sakhalin
Kuril Is.
Hokkaido
Sea of Japan (East Sea)
Honshu
Japan
Korea
Yellow Sea
East China Sea
Ryukyu Is.
Taiwan
Philippine Sea
Philippines
Caroline Islands
Wake I.
Marshall Is.
Nauru

North Pacific Ocean

Micronesia
Melanesia

New Guinea
Solomon Is.
Vanuatu
New Caledonia

80°
60°
40°
20°

AFRICA

Gulf of Guinea
Congo Basin
Congo
Kilimanjaro
Lake Victoria
L. Tanganyika
L. Nyasa
Zambezi
Seychelles
Comoros
Madagascar
Mozambique Channel
St. Helena
Namib Desert
Kalahari Desert
Orange
Cape of Good Hope
Cape Agulhas

Indian Ocean

Kerguelen Is.

South Atlantic Ocean

West Longitude 0° East 20° Longitude 40° 60° 80° 100° 120° 140° 160° 100°

Northwest Cape
Great Sandy Desert
Great Victoria Desert
Cape Leeuwin
Great Australian Bight

AUSTRALIA

Cape York Peninsula
Coral Sea
Darling
Murray
Great Dividing Range
Mount Kosciuszko
Tasman Sea
New Zealand
Tasmania

South Pacific Ocean

20°

Southern Ocean

Queen Maud Land
Wilkes Land
Cape Adare

ANTARCTICA

80°
60°

Afghanistan

Afghanistan is a completely landlocked nation, bordered by China on the far northeast, Pakistan on the east and south, Iran on the west, and Turkmenistan, Uzbekistan, and Tajikistan on the north. It is a country of rugged terrain and harsh, dry climate.

Because of its location, Afghanistan has long been a crossroads for migrating people and conquering armies. For centuries, it was the site of great empires and trading routes. All of these ancient people and empires left their mark on the culture of Afghanistan, creating a large number of ethnic groups who live in the country today.

Yet Afghanistan remains one of the least developed countries in the world. Most of its people still live in small, tribal villages and work the land using old-fashioned farming tools. The country's history has been long and troubled, filled with foreign invasions, political revolt, and civil war. Centuries of conflict have slowed the development of Afghanistan.

Ancient kingdoms

The region that is now Afghanistan was first inhabited by prehistoric hunting people 100,000 years ago. About 1500 B.C., Aryans invaded Afghanistan. In the mid-500's B.C., Persians conquered an area of Afghanistan called Bactria. The Persians ruled Bactria until Alexander the Great invaded Afghanistan in 330 B.C.

About 85 years later, the Bactrians revolted against Greek control and regained their land. Their kingdom lasted until the Kushans seized the country about 150 years later.

The Kushan Empire was founded in the A.D. 50's when Kujala Kadphises united five central Asian tribes. Soon the empire stretched to the Indus Valley and the western Ganges Valley.

The rulers of the Kushan Empire opened and protected the Silk Road, the major trade route between China and the Middle East. Huge caravans traveled the Silk Road, bringing silk, spices, and ointments to India and the Middle East. From there, these luxury goods were loaded onto ships bound for the Roman Empire. In turn, the Romans sent back gold coins and Greek wine. New ideas

and customs were also shared along these routes.

The Kushans were Buddhists. Twin statues of the Buddha, 174 feet (53 meters) high, once stood in central Afghanistan. They were carved into a sandstone cliff at Bamian. The Taliban, a military group, destroyed the statues in 2001.

The arrival of Islam

In the late 600's, Arab conquerors swept into Afghanistan, defeating the Sassanians and the White Huns, who by then ruled the country. The Arabs brought with them the religion of Islam.

From the time of the Arab conquest until 1747, many armies fought over Afghanistan. Turkic-speaking people from eastern Persia and central Asia ruled from about 900 to 1200. The country was conquered by the Mongols, led by Genghis Khan, in the 1200's, and then by the Timurids in the 1300's. The magnificent Blue Mosque at Mazar-e Sharif dates from the Timurid period.

From the mid-1500's to the early 1700's, Safavids from Persia and Mongols from India struggled for control. In 1747, Afghan tribes became united for the first time in history under the leadership of Ahmad Shah Durrani. He established a monarchy that remained in power until 1973, when Afghanistan became a republic.

Even unified under a monarchy, Afghanistan still suffered from civil war between rival tribes. Foreign interference led to more wars on Afghan soil, as Great Britain and Russia fought for control of the country. Great Britain wanted to protect its empire in India, and Russia wanted an outlet to the Indian Ocean.

Early in 1919, Great Britain ended its involvement, and Afghanistan became fully independent in August of that year.

The Soviet Union sought to occupy Afghanistan in a war that lasted from 1979 to 1989. In the mid 1990's, a conservative Islamic group called the Taliban came to power. They allowed international terrorist organizations to create training camps in Afghanistan. Following devastating terrorist attacks against the United States in 2001, the United States and anti-Taliban within Afghanistan drove the Taliban from power.

Afghanistan Today

In recent years, Afghanistan has suffered bitter internal conflict. The current struggle began in 1973, when prime minister Muhammad Daoud led a revolt against King Muhammad Zahir, who was his relative. Military leaders took control of the government and established the Republic of Afghanistan. Daoud became president and prime minister.

Five years later, Daoud was killed when rival left wing military leaders and civilians revolted against the new government. This group had received a great deal of military and financial aid from the Soviet Union. When they took over the government, they established many Communist policies.

Civil war begins

Many Afghans disagreed with the Communist policies, claiming they violated Islamic teaching. They were also angered by the Soviet Union's influence on their government. These resistance fighters began to call themselves *mujahideen* (holy warriors). Fighting broke out between the mujahideen and the government. The Soviet Union sent troops into Afghanistan to help the government fight the mujahideen. The United States sent weapons to the mujahideen.

This conflict caused much death and destruction in Afghanistan. By the time the Soviets began to withdraw their troops in 1988, about 1-1/2 million Afghans had died.

An estimated 5 million Afghans lost their homes when the Soviets and the Afghan government bombed their villages. More than 3 million fled to refugee camps in Pakistan.

Throughout the struggle, the mujahideen were greatly outnumbered in air power, artillery, and tanks. However, their guerrilla tactics—hiding in the mountains and moving by night—confused their enemy. In the end, the Soviet and government troops controlled only main highways and urban centers.

When the Soviet occupation ended in 1989, most Afghans began to plan the rebuilding of their country's damaged economy. However, conflict between the mujahideen and the government continued.

Continued violence

In April 1992, the mujahideen overthrew the government. Several factions (small groups) within the mujahideen agreed to set up a transitional government. Burhanuddin Rabbani became president with the help of a northern warlord, Abdul Rashid Dostam. But fighting continued. Gulbuddin Hikmatyar, a factional leader who had fought the Communists, laid siege to Kabul. Thousands of civilians died in rocket and artillery attacks.

In 1994, Dostam switched sides to support Hikmatyar against President Rabbani. Rabbani's term as president was due to end in June 1994, but Afghanistan's Supreme Court

---

FACT BOX

COUNTRY

Official name: Da Afghanistan Dowlat (in Pashto) or Dowlati Afghanistan (in Dari), both meaning State of Afghanistan
Capital: Kabul
Terrain: Mostly rugged mountains; plains in north and southwest
Area: 251,773 sq. mi. (652,090 km²)

Climate: Arid to semiarid; cold winters and hot summers
Main rivers: Helmand, Farah, Arghandab
Highest elevation: Nowshak, 24,557 ft. (7,485 m)
Lowest elevation: In Sistan Basin, 1,640 ft. (500 m) above sea level

AFGHANISTAN

GOVERNMENT

Form of government: Transitional
Head of state: Transitional president
Head of government: Transitional president
Administrative areas: 32 provinces

Legislature: Nonfunctioning as of June 1993
Court system: Nonfunctioning as of March 1995, although there are local Sharīa (Islamic law) courts throughout the country
Armed forces: N/A

PEOPLE

Estimated 2002 population: 24,977,000
Population growth: 3.54%
Population density: 99 persons per sq. mi. (38 per km²)
Population distribution: 80% rural, 20% urban
Life expectancy in years:
 Male: 47
 Female: 46
Doctors per 1,000 people: 0.1
Percentage of age-appropriate population enrolled in the following educational levels:
 Primary: N/A
 Secondary: N/A
 Further: N/A

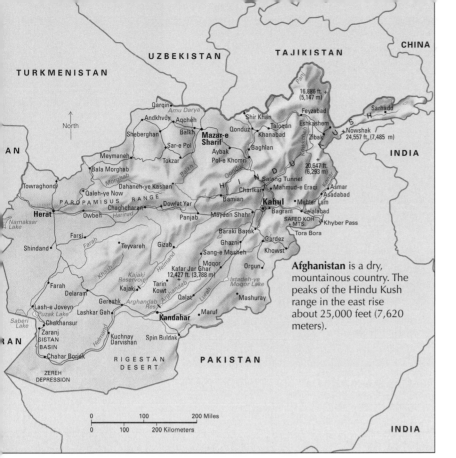

Afghanistan is a dry, mountainous country. The peaks of the Hindu Kush range in the east rise about 25,000 feet (7,620 meters).

extended his term. Hikmatyar's siege of Kabul continued.

In March 1995, a military force of Islamic youths, known as the Taliban (seekers of truth), pushed Hikmatyar's forces away from the city and ended the siege.

The Taliban captured Kabul in September 1996 and claimed power as the new national government. They set up a new Council of

Ministers to rule the country. In 1997, Taliban authorities changed the official name of the country to the Islamic State of Afghanistan. But only three countries recognized the Taliban as a legal government—Pakistan, Saudi Arabia, and the United Arab Emirates.

In 1998, the United States accused the Taliban of harboring the Saudi millionaire Osama bin Laden, who was wanted in connection with terrorist attacks against two U.S. embassies in Africa. The United States launched missile strikes against suspected terrorist training camps in Afghanistan. A Taliban spokesman acknowledged that bin Laden was in Afghanistan under Taliban protection. In 1999, the United Nations imposed trade sanctions against Afghanistan for refusing to surrender bin Laden.

In 2001, the United States accused bin Laden and his terrorist organization of carrying out attacks that year against the World Trade Center in New York City and the Pentagon Building near Washington, D.C. The attacks killed thousands of people from many different countries. The United States demanded that the Taliban hand over bin Laden and shut down terrorist training camps in Afghanistan. The Taliban refused to do so, and the United States and its allies launched a military campaign against the Taliban. The campaign included massive air strikes in support of Afghan rebels who opposed the Taliban. This support enabled the rebels to drive the Taliban from power later in 2001.

Afterward, the United Nations helped the leaders of Afghanistan's main factions organize a temporary government. They also developed a plan for creating a new constitution and a permanent, more democratic goverment. In June 2002, a *loya jirga* (grand council of Afghan leaders) met in Kabul. The loya jirga created a transitional goverment to rule Afghanistan for up to two years. Hamid Karzai, head of the Popalzai, an important clan of the dominant Pashtun ethnic group, was chosen as the country's transitional president. Meanwhile, warlords and tribal groups in Afghanistan continued to compete for territory and power. In January 2004, another loya jirga adopted a permanent constitution for Afghanistan.

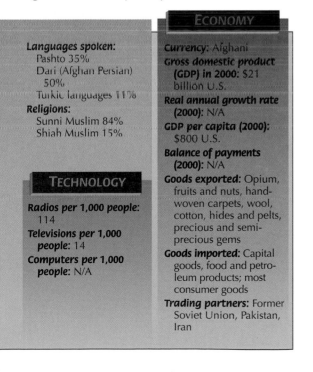

Languages spoken:
Pashto 35%
Dari (Afghan Persian) 50%
Turkic languages 11%

Religions:
Sunni Muslim 84%
Shiah Muslim 15%

TECHNOLOGY

Radios per 1,000 people: 114

Televisions per 1,000 people: 14

Computers per 1,000 people: N/A

ECONOMY

Currency: Afghani

Gross domestic product (GDP) in 2000: $21 billion U.S.

Real annual growth rate (2000): N/A

GDP per capita (2000): $800 U.S.

Balance of payments (2000): N/A

Goods exported: Opium, fruits and nuts, hand-woven carpets, wool, cotton, hides and pelts, precious and semi-precious gems

Goods imported: Capital goods, food and petroleum products; most consumer goods

Trading partners: Former Soviet Union, Pakistan, Iran

People

About 20 different ethnic groups, most with their own language and culture, call Afghanistan their home. They are united only by their devotion to Islam. Most Afghans are a blend of many early peoples who came to the country through migration or invasion. Many feel greater devotion and loyalty to their ethnic group than to their country.

More than a fourth of Afghanistan's people have left the country since the Soviet invasion began in 1979. These people fled to Pakistan and Iran, where they now live in refugee camps. Most of the remaining people of Afghanistan live in rural areas.

A Kirghiz shepherd boy guards a flock of sheep and goats in a mountain valley. This small, semi-nomadic ethnic group roams the remote northeast.

The Pashtuns

The Pashtuns are the largest ethnic group in Afghanistan. They make up about one-half of the total population. Most Pashtuns live in eastern Afghanistan, in the mountainous areas near the Pakistan border. They speak Pashto, a language related to Persian and one of the two official languages of Afghanistan.

The Pashtuns are divided into two major groups, the Durranis and the Ghilzais. Each group has it own tribes and subtribes. In all, there are about 40 Pashtun tribes. Each tribe is led by a chief called a *khan*.

Because of their strong warrior tradition, the Pashtuns have a reputation for bravery in battle. During the 1800's and early 1900's, Pashtuns fought and won a series of wars with the British.

Today, many Pashtuns are farmers. They raise crops of wheat and other grains, fruits, nuts, and sugar beets. Others are nomadic herders, living in tents made of goat hair and tending their horses, sheep, goats, cattle, and camels.

Although Pashtuns are Sunni Muslims, their traditional tribal code of honor, rather than Islamic law, governs their daily life. This tribal code, known as *Pashtunwali*, teaches that personal honor is a Pashtun's most prized possession and must always be defended.

The Tajiks

The Tajiks are the second largest ethnic group in Afghanistan, making up about 25 per cent of the population. Like the Pashtuns, the Tajiks are Sunni Muslims. They live in central and northeastern Afghanistan. Their language is Dari, the country's other official language, which comes from *Farsi* (Persian).

The Tajiks do not live in tribal groups. Some are farmers and herders. Many live in the cities, where they work as craft workers, merchants, or administrators.

Other ethnic groups

The Uzbeks and the Turkomans are Turkic-speaking people who live in north and northwestern Afghanistan. Many Uzbeks are farmers, and some are skilled craft workers widely known for their embroidered silk coats called chapan. The Turkomans, on the other hand, still live in tribal groups.

Other ethnic communities include the Baluchis, the Chahar Aimaks, and the Brahui. A group called the Hazaras live in the south-central mountain ranges and are said to be descended from the Mongols. Along with the Kizilbash, a smaller group, the Hazaras are Shiah Muslims.

A rug merchant in Herat relaxes with his stock. Herat is one of the oldest trading centers in Asia. It lies on a plain along the caravan route between Iran and India.

This rural tribesman, like most Afghan men, wears the traditional turban, which may be tied in a certain way to indicate an ethnic group.

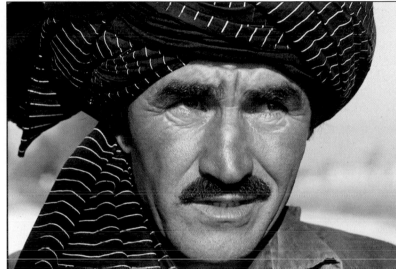

Inhabitants of the city of Mazar-e Sharif gather in front of the Blue Mosque. Inside this blue-tiled mosque is the tomb of Ali, son-in-law of the prophet Muhammad. Built in the 1500's, it is an important holy site for Shiah Muslims and other Muslims. Shiah Muslims make up a small minority of the population. Most Afghans are Sunni Muslims.

High in the mountain valleys of the Hindu Kush in eastern Afghanistan live the Nuristanis. They have fair complexions and light-colored eyes. According to legend, the Nuristanis are descended from the Greek warriors who marched into Afghanistan under Alexander the Great in 330 B.C. Until the Nuristanis converted to Islam, they were known as *Kafirs* (infidels). After their conversion in the 19th century, they were given the name of Nuristanis, which means "people of the light."

Land and Economy

Afghanistan is a rugged, arid, mountainous country with dramatic scenery. The country also has many rivers, river basins, lakes, and desert areas.

Landscape and climate

Afghanistan can be divided into three land regions: (1) the Northern Plains, (2) the Central Highlands, and (3) the Southwestern Lowlands.

The Northern Plains extend across northern Afghanistan. They consist of mountain plateaus and rolling hills.

Although the soil in the region is fertile, the land can be cultivated only in river valleys and mountain areas, where water is available. Afghan farmers have built large irrigation systems along the Harirud, Helmand, Qonduz, and other rivers to provide water for their crops.

Seminomadic people also live in the Northern Plains. They wander on its vast grasslands with their flocks of sheep and goats.

Summers in the Northern Plains are hot and dry, with average temperatures of about 90° F. (32° C). Winters are cold and dry, with average temperatures of about 38° F. (3° C).

The Central Highlands consist of the Hindu Kush mountain range and its branches. This region covers about two-thirds of Afghanistan. Most Afghans live in the high, narrow valleys of the Hindu Kush.

Winters in the Central Highlands are cold, with average temperatures of about 25° F. (−4° C) in January. Summers are mild, with average temperatures of 75° F. (24° C).

The Southwestern Lowlands are mainly desert or semidesert. The Helmand River crosses the region, flowing from the Hindu Kush to the Sistan Basin on the Iranian border. Barley, corn, fruits, and wheat are grown in the Helmand Valley.

Temperatures in the Southwestern Lowlands average about 35° F. (2° C) in Janu-

Corn dries on the roof of a mud hut in the Panj River Valley.

Cave dwellings are carved into high cliffs that overlook the fields of the fertile Bamian valley.

Carpet weaving is part of a large handicraft industry. Rugs from Afghanistan are known for having rich, deep colors such as red and navy.

Farming and raising livestock is how most Afghans make their living, *map below*. The people who live off the land make their homes in the high mountain valleys and on the broad, rolling grasslands that cover much of the country.

Painted Afghan trucks, *above*, carry goods through crowded streets as well as through mountain passes.

ary and about 85° F. (29° C) in July. The Sistan Basin suffers from a crop-destroying summer wind called the "wind of 120 days."

The economy

Even though only about 12 per cent of Afghanistan's land is suitable for farming, about 85 per cent of its people work the land for a living. To water their fields, Afghan farmers depend on river irrigation systems and underground springs and streams called *qanats*.

Wheat is Afghanistan's chief crop. Other crops include barley, corn, cotton, fruits, nuts, rice, sugar beets, and vegetables. The chief livestock products are dairy items, mutton, wool, animal hides, and the skins of karakul sheep.

Afghanistan's rich mineral resources, including iron ore, are still undeveloped. Since natural gas was discovered in the northern Sheberghan area during the 1960's, it has become the fastest-growing part of the country's economy. Most of the natural gas is exported to the former Soviet republics by pipeline.

The civil war between the government and the resistance fighters severely damaged Afghanistan's economy. Because so many Afghans fled the country, much farmland has been left uncultivated. In addition, irrigation systems have been neglected or damaged by the fighting.

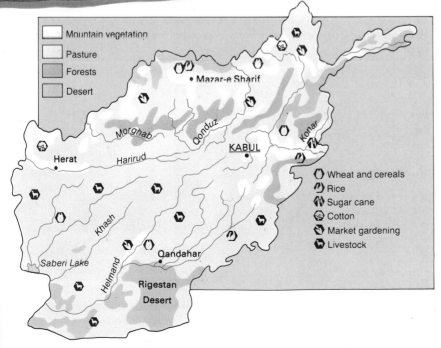

	Mountain vegetation
	Pasture
	Forests
	Desert

Mazar-e Sharif

Morghab
Qonduz
Konar
KABUL
Herat
Harirud

Khash

Saberi Lake
Helmand
Qandahar

Rigestan
Desert

- Wheat and cereals
- Rice
- Sugar cane
- Cotton
- Market gardening
- Livestock

The Khyber Pass

The Khyber Pass is a 33-mile (53-kilometer) passage through the Hindu Kush mountain range. It connects the northern frontier of Pakistan with Afghanistan. At its narrowest point, the pass is only 50 feet (15 meters) wide. On the north side of the Khyber Pass rise the towering, snow-covered mountains of the Hindu Kush. The name *kush*, which means *death*, may have been given to this range because of its dangerous passes.

The Khyber Pass is one of the most famous mountain passes in the world. It is the best land route between India and Pakistan and has had a long and often violent history. Conquering armies have used the Khyber as an entry point for their invasions. It has also been a major trade route for centuries.

Invading armies

The history of the Khyber Pass as a strategic gateway dates from 326 B.C., when Alexander the Great and his army marched through the Khyber to reach the plains of India. From there, he sailed down the Indus River and led his army across the desert of Gedrosia.

In the A.D. 100's, Persian, Mongol, and Tatar armies forced their way through the Khyber, bringing Islam to India. Centuries later, India became part of the British Empire, and British troops defended the Khyber Pass.

Caravans from China

For hundreds of years, great camel caravans traveled through the Khyber Pass, bringing goods to trade. These ancient merchants and traders brought luxurious silks and fine porcelain objects from China to the Middle East. Often, they stopped at Herat, the great oasis in western Afghanistan.

The traders traveled in caravans as a protection against the hazards of travel. Even so, they were often robbed by local tribesmen when traveling through the Khyber Pass.

A Pashtun tribesman is ready for battle, whether defending his personal honor or serving as a resistance fighter.

Watchtowers on the hills of the Khyber Pass are a reminder of the days when caravans were ambushed by bandits in the narrow pass.

The Khyber Pass today

Today, two highways thread their way through the Khyber Pass—one for motor traffic, and one for the traditional caravans. A railway line also travels to the head of the pass. Recently, the Khyber has been used to transport refugees from the Afghan civil war into Pakistan.

Villages lie on each side of the Khyber Pass. The people of the Khyber region are mainly Pashtuns. They live in both Afghanistan and Pakistan.

The Pashtuns are a warlike people who claim to be descended from the lost tribes of ancient Israel. They are known for their traditional gunmaking skills.

The Khyber Pass is one of the most important passes between Afghanistan and Pakistan. It is known as the gateway to India. Ancient Persians and Greeks, Tatars, and Moguls passed through the Khyber to reach India.

A crowded bus travels through the Khyber Pass over a highway that links Kabul in Afghanistan with Peshawar in Pakistan. Another highway is reserved for caravans.

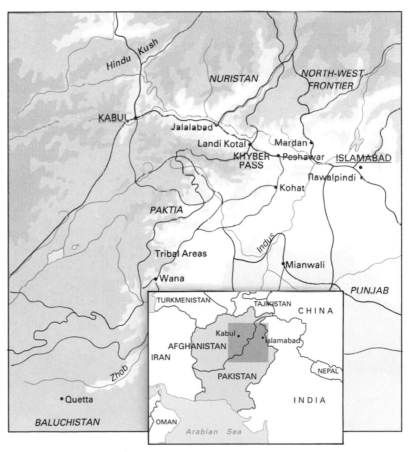

Albania

Albania is a small, mountainous nation on the Balkan Peninsula and one of the least developed countries in Europe. It became a Communist country in 1944. Until the breakup of complete control of the Communist Party in 1990, Albania was one of the most politically isolated countries in the world.

Early history

In ancient times, much of the territory that is now Albania was settled by the Illyrians. In 167 B.C., the Romans conquered the Illyrians and spread their civilization throughout the region. In A.D. 395, when the Roman Empire was divided, much of Albania became part of the East Roman (Byzantine) Empire. Between the 300's and the 1000's, Albania was invaded by Goths, Bulgarians, Slavs, and Normans. In the 1300's, much of Albania became part of the Serbian Empire.

In 1468, the Ottomans conquered Albania, and it remained part of the Ottoman Empire for more than 400 years. In 1913, after Albania gained independence during the First Balkan War, European powers set the country's boundaries and made it a self-governing principality.

During World War I (1914–1918), the Austro-Hungarians, Italians, Serbs, and French all occupied Albania. In 1925, Ahmed Beg Zogu seized power, formed a republic, and became the country's first president. Three years later, Zogu declared himself King Zog I and ruled as a dictator until 1939.

Shortly before World War II (1939–1945), Italy invaded Albania, and it became part of the Italian Empire. After Italy surrendered to the Allies in 1943, the Germans occupied Albania until they were driven out the following year.

The rise of Communism

During World War II, Albania found a new national hero in Enver Hoxha, leader of the National Liberation Front (NLF). The NLF, a Communist organization, was one of the Albanian resistance movements that fought against the Italians and the Germans. In 1944, the Germans were driven from Albania, and Hoxha set up a Communist government and began ruling as first secretary of the Communist Party. He ruled Albania for more than 40 years, until his death in 1985.

Ramiz Alia succeeded Hoxha as first secretary of Albania's Communist Party. His government introduced some social and economic reforms. However, Albanians felt that the reforms did not go far enough. Their protests in 1990 to force the Communists from power led the Communists to allow new political parties to form.

FACT BOX

COUNTRY

Official name: Republika e Shqiperise (Republic of Albania)
Capital: Tiranë
Terrain: Mostly mountains and hills; small plains along coast
Area: 11,100 sq. mi. (28,748 km²)
Climate: Mild temperate; cool, cloudy, wet winters; hot, clear, dry summers; interior is cooler and wetter

Main rivers: Bunë, Drin, Mat, Shkumbin, Vjosë
Highest elevation: Mount Korab, 9,068 ft. (2,764 m)
Lowest elevation: Adriatic Sea, sea level

ALBANIA

GOVERNMENT

Form of government: Emerging democracy
Head of state: President
Head of government: Prime minister
Administrative areas: 36 rrethe (districts) and 1 bashki (municipality)

Legislature: Kuvendi Popullor (People's Assembly) with 155 members serving four-year terms
Court system: Supreme Court
Armed forces: N/A

PEOPLE

Estimated 2002 population: 3,152,000
Population growth: 0.26%
Population density: 284 persons per sq. mi. (110 per km²)
Population distribution: 54% rural, 46% urban
Life expectancy in years: Male: 69 Female: 75
Doctors per 1,000 people: 1.3
Percentage of age-appropriate population enrolled in the following educational levels: Primary: 107* Secondary: 38 Further: 11

Once a hard-line Communist nation that followed a rigid policy of self-isolation, Albania encountered political problems in the early 1990's as popular opposition groups forced the collapse of the Communist government. The nation is situated on the west side of the Balkan Peninsula in southeastern Europe. It is a mountainous country, and the North Albanian Alps rise about 8,800 feet (2,680 meters) on its northern border. The coastal plains along the Adriatic Sea are the only large areas of flatland.

This Orthodox church in Apollonia stood abandoned during the years religious practice was forbidden by Albania's Communist government. Apollonia was an important city of Illyria, an ancient kingdom which at one time covered much of what is now Albania.

Languages spoken:
Albanian
Greek

Religions:
Muslim 70%
Albanian Orthodox 20%
Roman Catholic 10%

Enrollment ratios compare the number of students enrolled to the population which, by age, should be enrolled. A ratio higher than 100 indicates that students older or younger than the typical age range are also enrolled.

TECHNOLOGY

Radios per 1,000 people: 243

Televisions per 1,000 people: 123

Computers per 1,000 people: 6.4

ECONOMY

Currency: Lek

Gross national income (GNI) in 2000: $3.8 billion U.S.

Real annual growth rate (1999–2000): 7.8%

GNI per capita (2000): $1,120 U.S.

Balance of payments (2000): -$156 million U.S.

Goods exported: Textiles and footwear; asphalt, metals and metallic ores, crude oil; vegetables, fruits, tobacco

Goods imported: Machinery and equipment, foodstuffs, textiles, chemicals

Trading partners: Italy, Greece, Germany, Turkey

In the multiparty elections of March 1991, the Communists won a majority, but protests continued, and by June the Communist prime minister and his cabinet were forced to resign. A temporary government was formed, and new elections were held in March 1992. The Democratic Party, the leading opposition group, won a majority of seats in the National Assembly. The assembly elected Sali Berisha president.

In late 1996, the collapse of fraudulent nationwide pyramid schemes triggered civil unrest that turned to armed rebellion in 1997. Thousands of Albanians fled to Greece and Italy. In April, the UN sent an international force to Albania to oversee relief efforts and to help restore order. The elections held in June and July brought the Socialist Party into power, and the UN left in August. In 1998, a new constitution was adopted.

Land and Economy

Albania is bordered on the west by the Adriatic Sea, on the north and the northeast by Serbia and Montenegro, on the east by Macedonia, and on the southeast and the south by Greece. About 70 per cent of the land is mountainous.

In the northern part of the country, the North Albanian Alps gradually give way to thick forests of oak, elm, and conifers in the central uplands. The central uplands flatten out to the west and form the Adriatic coastal plain. The mountains of the south extend down to the Albanian Riviera, where their sheer cliffs plunge into the Adriatic Sea.

Albania's coastal region has a Mediterranean climate, with warm, dry summers and mild, wet winters. Rain falls mostly in the winter, but the distribution is uneven, with the northern mountains receiving the most rain.

Standard of living

Living standards are extremely low for the people of this mountainous country. About 60 per cent of Albania's people work on farms and the remainder work in factories, plants, and other industrial facilities. All workers are expected to put in an 8-hour day, 6 days a week. Wages are controlled by the government, and incomes are small, but the Albanians pay no income tax and prices of food and other consumer items are strictly regulated by the government. Health care, social services, and education are free.

Very few Albanians own such modern conveniences as a television set. Before 1991, people were forbidden by law to own an automobile. Their diet consists mainly of bread, cheese, milk, and vegetables.

In 1967, the Communist government outlawed all religious groups and seized their property. Before the ban went into effect, about 70 per cent of the Albanians were Muslims, about 20 per cent belonged to the Eastern Orthodox Church, and about 10 per cent were Roman Catholics. In 1990, a new law permitted the public practice of religion, and places of worship began to reopen.

In modern Albania, the small clans have united into two distinct groups–the Ghegs and the Tosks. Most of the Ghegs live north of the Shkumbin River and speak a different

Pedestrians crowd the sidewalks and streets of Tiranë, Albania's capital and largest city. Most Albanians use buses, bicycles, and trains to get around because few people can afford the luxury of owning an automobile.

The unspoiled woodlands and sandy beaches, *right,* that line the shore of the Adriatic Sea make Albania's west coast an area of great scenic beauty. Pine forests have been planted along the coast to prevent erosion.

Albanian dialect than the Tosks, who live south of the river.

Agriculture and industry

Although the Communist government encouraged the development of industry, Albania remains a primarily agricultural country. The most important farming regions are located on the Adriatic coastal plain. The valleys in the interior of the country, particularly Korcë in the southeast region, are also used for agriculture.

Albania's chief crops are corn, grapes, olives, potatoes, sugar beets, and wheat.

Farmers also raise livestock, including cattle, sheep, goats, pigs, and chickens. Under the Communist government, all agriculture in Albania was organized into state or collective farms. The government tried to increase agricultural production by introducing modern equipment and chemical fertilizers. In 1991, the new government took steps toward breaking up the socialist agricultural system and establishing private ownership of the land. Today, much farmland is privately owned.

Albania still has only a few industrial plants. Many small businesses are now privately owned. But the government still owns many larger businesses, especially mines and factories. The chief manufactured products include cement, fertilizers, food products, and textiles. Many of these light industries are centered in Tiranë, Albania's capital and largest city.

Albania is rich in mineral deposits, and mining is the leading industrial activity. Albania is an important producer and exporter of chromite, and *lignite* (brown coal) is mined in central and southern Albania. Albania's mines also produce copper and nickel. An extensive reforesting program has been successful in replanting forests that had been cleared, and the country's forests are another important resource.

Young people pause along a path in the northern Albanian countryside to chat with the village elders, *far left*. Since 1945, Albania's education system has improved, and illiteracy has been greatly reduced.

A small town in the central uplands of Albania nestles in the mountain slopes. Albania is a land of towns and villages. Only 11 Albanian cities have populations of more than 20,000.

Algeria

Traditionally, Algeria was part of the Maghreb—the North African lands that also included Morocco, Tunisia, and part of Libya. The name *Maghreb,* an Arabic word meaning *the place of the sunset—the west,* reflects Algeria's Arab history.

People have lived in what is now Algeria for at least 40,000 years. About 3000 B.C., nomadic Berbers migrated into the region—probably from Europe or Asia. During the 1100's B.C., the Phoenicians sailed from the eastern Mediterranean and established trading posts on the Algerian coast.

About 200 B.C., the Romans helped a Berber chieftain named Massinissa form a kingdom called Numidia in northern Algeria, where he ruled as king. The land was part of the Roman Empire from 46 B.C. until the Vandals, a barbarian tribe from northern Europe, took control of the country in the A.D. 400's. Later, Byzantines ruled the area.

During the A.D. 600's, Arabs invaded the Maghreb. The Arabs brought their religion, Islam, to the region. In time, the Berbers became *Muslims* (followers of Islam), and the Arabic culture and language spread throughout the region.

Spanish Christians captured coastal towns in Algeria during the early 1500's, but in 1518, a Turkish sea captain named Barbarossa took control of Algiers and drove the Spaniards out of most of Algeria. Barbarossa then joined the areas under his control with the Ottoman Empire, an Islamic empire based in Turkey.

Algeria remained part of the Ottoman Empire until the early 1800's. During that period, Algerian pirates called *corsairs* provided Algeria with its main source of income by attacking and looting ships in the Mediterranean Sea.

In 1830, France gained control of northern Algeria. European settlers, given French citizenship and large sections of Algerian land, soon controlled Algeria's economy and government. Many Algerians rebelled against the French, but in 1847, the French defeated the rebel forces under Abd al-Qadir, a Muslim religious leader. By 1914, France controlled all of Algeria.

As part of France, Algeria fought on the side of the Allies during World War I (1914–1918). During World War II (1939–1945), Algeria itself became a battleground. In 1940, France surrendered to the invading German forces of Adolf Hitler, and cooperative French officials set up a government under German control in Vichy, France. The Vichy government ruled Algeria until 1942, when Allied forces invaded Algeria and Morocco.

After the war, control of Algeria was returned to France. When France refused to give Algerians a greater voice in their government, many Algerians began to demand independence.

On Nov. 1, 1954, a revolution was launched by the Algerian Front de Libération Nationale (FLN), or National Liberation Front. A long and bloody war followed. The FLN ambushed, assassinated, and bombed French and other European settlers. The French, in turn, destroyed farms, forced millions of Algerians into concentration camps, and tortured rebel leaders. On July 3, 1962, after more than 250,000 French and Algerians had died in the fighting, France finally granted Algeria its independence.

Most of the European settlers left Algeria during or soon after the revolution. A rebel leader, Ahmed Ben Bella, became Algeria's first president. Ben Bella declared Algeria a socialist state.

In 1965, Ben Bella was overthrown by Houari Boumedienne, an army commander. Boumedienne launched a program of rapid economic development, using the money from oil and natural gas production to build fertilizer plants, steel mills, and factories.

Boumedienne died in 1978, and Chadli Bendjedid was elected president the following year. Bendjedid slowed industrial development and devoted more money to producing farm and consumer goods.

Until 1989, the FLN was the only legal political party. The first multiparty elections were held in 1991 and won by the main opposition party, the Islamic Salvation Front (FIS). A military-dominated High State Committee seized power. Political violence began. In 1999, the armed branch of the FIS ended its fight against the government.

Algeria Today

The North African nation of Algeria is the second largest country on the continent—only Sudan is larger. Algiers, the nation's capital and largest city, lies on the Mediterranean coast. South of the narrow coastal region, on the other side of the Atlas Mountains, lies the vast desert land of the Sahara.

Algeria belonged to France for about 130 years. After a bloody eight-year revolution, Algeria became a democratic republic. Algerians 19 years old or older could vote in national and local elections.

Until 1991, the voters elected a president who was in charge of national defense and served as commander in chief of the armed forces. The president appointed a prime minister to run the daily affairs of the government. The prime minister, in turn, appointed a cabinet called the Council of Ministers to supervise various government departments.

The people also elected a national legislature called the Popular National Assembly. After the main opposition party, the Islamic Salvation Front (FIS), won 1991 elections, the government dissolved the National Assembly. It was replaced by the High State Committee, which has five members, most of them from the military. The committee is advised by a 60-member Consultative Council. The courts banned FIS. In June 1992, Muhammad Boudiaf, the head of the High State Committee, was assassinated.

When the country first gained independence, Algerians formed a socialist government. In 1965, Houari Boumedienne initiated a program of rapid economic development, chiefly financed with income from the government-owned petroleum and natural gas industries.

An Algerian Constitution, adopted in 1976, proclaimed the Front de Libération Nationale (FLN), or National Liberation Front, as the country's only political party. The FLN was committed to socialism. But the Constitution was revised in 1989 to allow other parties to run candidates.

Chadli Bendjedid served as Algeria's president from 1979 until 1992. He resigned after the military seized power to prevent a parliamentary election victory by FIS. Since the takeover, civil strife and terrorism have claimed tens of thousands of lives.

Since winning independence from France in 1962, large numbers of poor rural Algerians have moved to the cities looking for factory work, but many have been unable to find jobs. This enormous increase in population, along with the shortage of jobs and housing, has led to the development of large slums in many cities.

Many Algerians have also called for a stricter observance of Islamic teachings.

FACT BOX

COUNTRY

Official name: Al Jumhuriyah al Jaza'iriyah ad Dimuqratiyah ash Shabiyah (Democratic and Popular Republic of Algeria)
Capital: Algiers
Terrain: Mostly high plateau and desert; some mountains; narrow, discontinuous coastal plain
Area: 919,595 sq. mi. (2,381,740 km²)

Climate: Arid to semiarid; mild, wet winters with hot, dry summers along coast; drier with cold winters and hot summers on high plateau
Main river: Chelif
Highest elevation: Tahat, 9,573 ft. (2,918 m)
Lowest elevation: Chott Melrhir, 102 ft. (31 m) below sea level

GOVERNMENT

Form of government: Republic
Head of state: President
Head of government: Prime minister
Administrative areas: 48 wilayas (provinces)

Legislature: Parliament consisting of the Al-Majlis Ech-Chaabi Al-Watani (National People's Assembly) with 380 members serving four-year terms and the Council of Nations with 144 members serving six-year terms
Court system: Cour Supreme (Supreme Court)
Armed forces: 122,000 troops

PEOPLE

Estimated 2002 population: 32,813,000
Population growth: 1.74%
Population density: 36 persons per sq. mi. (14 per km²)
Population distribution: 51% urban, 49% rural
Life expectancy in years:
Male: 69
Female: 72
Doctors per 1,000 people: 1.0
Percentage of age-appropriate population enrolled in the following educational levels:
Primary: 109*
Secondary: 66
Further: 15

ALGERIA

Islam, the religion of almost all Algerians, governs much of daily life. Under the nation's Constitution, Islam is the country's official religion, and it is strongly supported by the Algerian government. For example, the government pays for the maintenance of *mosques* and the training of mosque officials.

Although Algeria has spent a great deal of money in its efforts to improve and expand its educational system, only about 45 per cent of all Algerians aged 15 or older can read and write. More than 90 per cent of the nation's children attend elementary school. The University of Algiers, with about 17,000 students, is the country's largest university.

A street vendor sells French *baguettes* (long, crusty loaves of bread) in the dusty square of an Algerian town. Algeria, once a French colony, retains such French influences, in spite of the government's efforts to remove them. In 1970, a "cultural revolution" was launched to help Algerians recover their national identity.

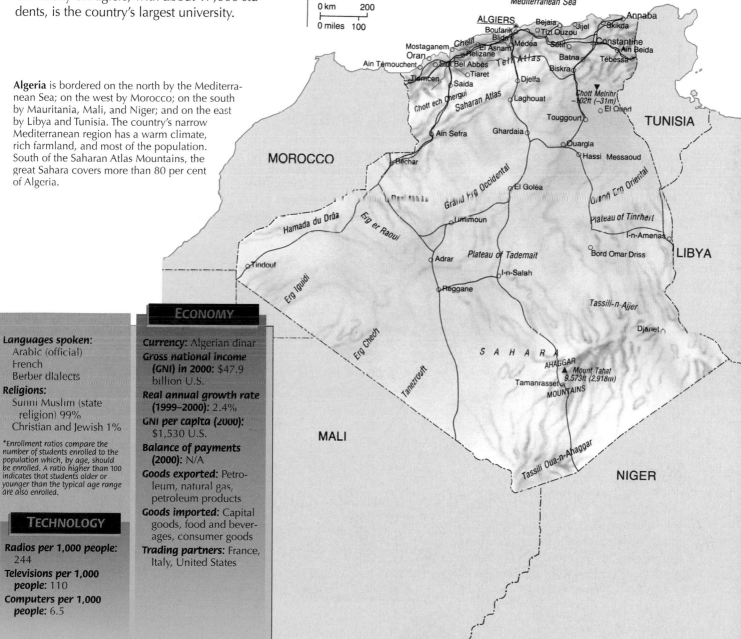

Algeria is bordered on the north by the Mediterranean Sea; on the west by Morocco; on the south by Mauritania, Mali, and Niger; and on the east by Libya and Tunisia. The country's narrow Mediterranean region has a warm climate, rich farmland, and most of the population. South of the Saharan Atlas Mountains, the great Sahara covers more than 80 per cent of Algeria.

Languages spoken:
Arabic (official)
French
Berber dialects

Religions:
Sunni Muslim (state religion) 99%
Christian and Jewish 1%

Enrollment ratios compare the number of students enrolled to the population which, by age, should be enrolled. A ratio higher than 100 indicates that students older or younger than the typical age range are also enrolled.

TECHNOLOGY

Radios per 1,000 people: 244

Televisions per 1,000 people: 110

Computers per 1,000 people: 6.5

ECONOMY

Currency: Algerian dinar

Gross national income (GNI) in 2000: $47.9 billion U.S.

Real annual growth rate (1999–2000): 2.4%

GNI per capita (2000): $1,530 U.S.

Balance of payments (2000): N/A

Goods exported: Petroleum, natural gas, petroleum products

Goods imported: Capital goods, food and beverages, consumer goods

Trading partners: France, Italy, United States

Land and People

The northern coastal area of Algeria, called the Tell, stretches along the Mediterranean Sea. This region has the mild temperatures and moderate rainfall typical of a Mediterranean climate. The Tell extends only about 80 to 200 miles (130 to 320 kilometers) south of the coast, but more than 90 per cent of the Algerian people live in this narrow strip. The Tell is Algeria's heartland. The word *tell* means *hill* in Arabic, and the region is aptly named for its gently rolling hills and coastal plains. Much of Algeria's best farmland lies in the western and central Tell. Rugged mountains make up the eastern Tell, and the Tell Atlas Mountains rise along the region's southern edge.

South of this range lie the High Plateaus, which are cooler and drier than the Tell at about 1,300 to 4,300 feet (400 to 1,300 meters) above sea level. The plateaus are home to about 7 per cent of the Algerian people.

The High Plateaus end with the Saharan Atlas Mountains. To the south lies the barren, sun-baked Sahara, the largest desert on earth. Fewer than 3 per cent of the Algerian people live in this desolate region, which covers more than 80 per cent of the country's land.

The vast Sahara actually has a variety of landscapes. Sand dunes cover much of the northern Sahara. Two huge seas of sand, called *ergs,* dominate this area: the Grand Erg Occidental (Great Western Erg) and the Grand Erg Oriental (Great Eastern Erg). Other parts of the Sahara include vast stretches of bare rock, boulders, and gravelly stone.

In southeast Algeria, the Ahaggar Mountains tower up to 9,573 feet (2,918 meters). Northeast of the Ahaggar, in a highland area called Tassili-n-Ajjer, needlelike rocks point to the sky, and huge, petrified sand formations rise like castles from the desert floor. To the west of the Ahaggar, an almost lifeless pebble desert stretches to the Mali border.

Daytime temperatures in the Sahara can soar above 120° F. (49° C). During the summer, a hot, dusty wind called the *sirocco* blows north across the desert and blasts the High Plateaus. The sirocco reaches as far as the Tell about 20 days of the year.

The Tell's pleasant climate and fertile farmland have drawn most of Algeria's

people to this area. More than 1-1/2 million people live in Algiers alone. Although many rural Algerians have moved to the cities seeking work, only about 45 per cent of the population lives in urban areas.

Most Algerians are of mixed Arab and Berber descent. Berbers settled the region at least 5,000 years ago, and Arabs invaded during the A.D. 600's. Over the centuries, so many Arabs and Berbers intermarried that today it is difficult to separate the groups by ancestry or appearance.

Instead, people are identified as Arab or Berber largely by their way of life—by the language they speak and the customs they follow. About 20 per cent of Algeria's people speak Berber languages and follow Berber customs, so they are considered Berbers.

When the Arabs invaded Algeria, they brought their religion, Islam, with them. About 99 per cent of Algerians today are Muslims. The teachings of Islam govern family relationships and many other aspects of daily life.

Following Algerian Islamic tradition, men

A massive rock formation looms above the barren landscape near the Ahaggar Mountains in southeast Algeria. The Ahaggar, together with the highland region Tassili-n-Ajjer, help make the Saharan region of Algeria a land of great scenic diversity.

Heavily veiled women, with all but their eyes hidden by voluminous, white garments called *haiks,* walk through the streets of Beni Isguen, a small town in the north central Algerian desert. Many urban women in Algeria do not veil their faces.

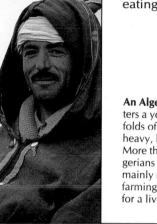

and women have lived vastly different lives. For example, women usually wear veils in public because it is considered improper for a woman's face to be seen by a man who is not related to her. As Algeria wrestles with Western ideas, some younger and more educated women resist such practices. Some city people follow other Western customs as well, wearing Western-style clothing and eating Western foods, for example.

An Algerian farmer shelters a young goat in the folds of his *burnoose*—a heavy, hooded cloak. More than half of all Algerians live in rural areas, mainly raising livestock or farming small plots of land for a living.

A shallow stream, *left,* provides a valuable and scarce resource in Algeria—water. In the desert, dry streambeds called *wadis* fill with water for a short time after the infrequent rains.

Nomadic herders live in tents made of animal skins or mats thrown over a framework of wooden poles. This kind of shelter allows them to move easily in search of water and grazing land for their animals. Less than 3 per cent of the Algerian people live in the Sahara, and many of them have abandoned their nomadic life styles to settle in oases.

Economy

After Algeria won its independence in 1962, many French and other European settlers fled the country. These were the people who had been running Algeria's most modern farms and factories. Algerians then formed a socialist government—one that owns or controls the means of producing goods, such as the farms and factories.

Since 1962, the government has tried to follow a three-stage economic program by: (1) developing industry, especially the petroleum industry, but also manufacturing and construction; (2) using the money from industry to develop modern methods of agriculture; and (3) developing industries that produce consumer goods.

By following this program, the government hoped to meet the needs of the people while creating a modern economy. Algeria is now a leader among the world's developing nations.

Mining

Algeria's huge deposits of petroleum and natural gas have been a major factor in its development. The northeastern part of the Sahara in Algeria has especially rich oil fields. Natural gas, petroleum, and petroleum products account for about 90 per cent of the total value of Algeria's exports.

Algeria belongs to the Organization of Petroleum Exporting Countries (OPEC), an association of countries whose economies depend heavily on oil exports.

Although it employs only about 2 per cent of the nation's workers, mining accounts for about 30 per cent of Algeria's economic production. In addition to natural gas and petroleum, minerals mined in Algeria include iron ore, lead, mercury, phosphate rock, and zinc.

Service, manufacturing, and construction

Service industries account for a slightly larger portion of Algeria's economic production—34 per cent. Yet they employ about 35 per cent of the nation's workers—many more people than does mining. Service workers include people with jobs in banks, government agencies, hospitals, insurance companies, and schools. Most service industries are privately owned.

Manufacturing and construction account for about 25 per cent of Algeria's economic production and employ about 30 per cent of its workers. The nation's chief manufactured products include construction materials, iron and steel, liquid natural gas, refined petroleum products, and textiles.

While most small factories are privately owned, the government has poured money into building factories and controls key manufacturing industries. Almost all factories are located in the Mediterranean coastal area in such cities as Algiers, Annaba, Arzew, Constantine, and Skikda. However, there are still not enough manufacturing jobs, and many Algerians must seek work in France and other foreign countries.

Agriculture

Agriculture accounts for only 6 per cent of Algeria's economic production, but about 30 per cent of its workers are farmers. Most farmers own small plots that produce only enough to feed their own families. Some farmers work on large government farms.

Camels wait patiently to be loaded with bricks of salt and bundles of grain, *top*. Camel caravans still carry goods and people across the great Sahara, though today more modern methods of transportation, such as jeeps and planes, are also used.

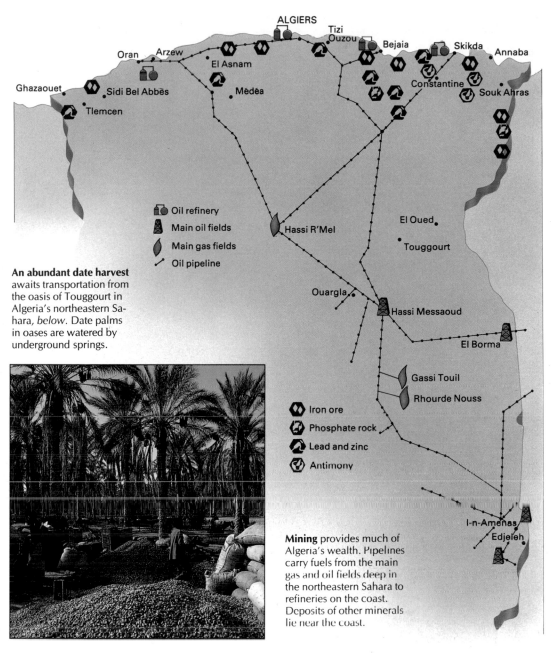

Oil refinery
Main oil fields
Main gas fields
Oil pipeline

An abundant date harvest awaits transportation from the oasis of Touggourt in Algeria's northeastern Sahara, *below*. Date palms in oases are watered by underground springs.

Iron ore
Phosphate rock
Lead and zinc
Antimony

Mining provides much of Algeria's wealth. Pipelines carry fuels from the main gas and oil fields deep in the northeastern Sahara to refineries on the coast. Deposits of other minerals lie near the coast.

Oil workers rest from their labors in the shade of a tanker truck. The production and refining of petroleum and natural gas are the mainstay of the nation's economy.

However, the country imports more than a third of its food.

The western and central Tell have the nation's best farmland. Grains, especially wheat and barley, are Algeria's chief crops. Farmers also produce citrus fruits, dates, grapes, olives, and potatoes. Many people in the High Plateaus herd cattle, sheep, and goats, providing dairy products and meat.

Transportation and communication

Most of Algeria's 50,000 miles (80,000 kilometers) of roads and about 2,500 miles (4,000 kilometers) of railroad track lie north of the Sahara. Camel caravans still wind across the desert, transporting goods and people as they have done for centuries. But today, planes, jeeps, and trucks are also used.

The government controls the country's four daily newspapers and operates all radio and television stations. The few Algerians who own radios—and the even fewer who own TV sets—live mainly in urban areas. In rural areas, one radio serves many listeners, and few people ever see television.

American Samoa

A territory of the United States, American Samoa lies south of the equator, about 2,300 miles (3,700 kilometers) southwest of Hawaii. The seven islands that make up American Samoa have a total area of 76 square miles (197 square kilometers). Six of the territory's seven islands are divided among three groups—Tutuila and Aunuu; Ofu, Olosega, and Tau; and Rose. These islands are in the Samoan chain. The seventh, Swains Island, lies 200 miles (310 kilometers) north. Tutuila, the largest and most important island, lies at the western end of American Samoa. Pago Pago (pronounced PAHNG oh PAHNG oh), American Samoa's capital and only urban center, is on Tutuila. Pago Pago has one of the best and most beautiful harbors in the South Pacific.

Rose and Swains islands are coral islands, while the others are the remains of extinct volcanoes. American Samoa has a wet, tropical climate. Only a third of the territory's land can be cultivated. Most of the land is mountainous, with some fertile soil in the valleys. The islands have few natural resources.

People

Almost all the territory's 65,446 people are Polynesian people whose ancestors have occupied Samoa for at least 2,000 years. Their main language is Samoan, a Polynesian dialect, and many people speak English. Most American Samoans practice some sort of Christianity.

Most people live in villages, and their lives center around their families. Each family group is headed by a chief who represents the family in the village council, controls its property, and takes care of the sick or aged.

Economy

In 1961, when the United States began an economic development program in American Samoa, many people left their villages to take jobs in industries around Pago Pago. As part of the economic development program, thatch-roofed houses were replaced by hurricane-proof concrete buildings, new schools were built, and teaching by television was introduced.

American Samoa's leading industry is tuna canning. Fish products make up more than 96 per cent of all exports. The U.S. government has provided large amounts of money to help American Samoa develop a prosperous economy. A jet airport and a luxury hotel were built in the 1960's, and tourism is increasing.

History and government

European explorers first reached Samoa in 1722, but there was little outside interest in the islands until the first mission was established in 1830. During the mid-1800's, two royal families ruled different parts of Samoa and fought over who would be king. Germany, the United Kingdom, and the United States supported rival groups.

In 1872, the Samoans agreed to let the United States use Pago Pago Bay as a naval coaling station, and the United States was later given trading rights in the islands. In 1899, Germany and the United States signed a treaty dividing the islands between them.

Samoan children, *below,* wear traditional as well as Western clothing. They attend new schools built with U.S. funds, and many are taught by television. Children from ages 6 to 18 must attend school.

A parade float in Pago Pago depicts a mermaid holding an American flag. American Samoa's people are *nationals,* but not citizens, of the United States. They may freely enter the United States at any time.

28

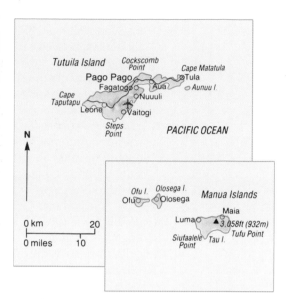

American Samoa lies in western Polynesia, about 2,300 miles (3,700 kilometers) southwest of Hawaii. The territory consists of seven islands, which have a total land area of 76 square miles (197 square kilometers).

Fishing boats, *top left,* in Pago Pago harbor bring in their catch. Fish products make up more than 96 per cent of all exports, and tuna canning is American Samoa's leading industry. The United States and Japan are the chief consumers of tuna.

Pago Pago, the capital and only urban center on American Samoa, has one of the best—and most beautiful—harbors in the South Pacific.

The U.S. Navy administered the U.S. islands until 1951, when they were transferred to the Department of the Interior. Afterward, the secretary of the interior appointed the governor of American Samoa.

In the early 1970's, the United States proposed that the territory elect its own governor, but the Samoans voted against the proposal three times. Many believed that the change would weaken their ties to the United States. American Samoans finally approved the proposal in 1976 and elected a governor in 1977. Governors serve four-year terms. The territory has a legislature with an 18-member Senate and a 20-member House of Representatives.

The U.S. Congress classifies American Samoa as an *unorganized and unincorporated territory.* Unincorporated territories are not eligible to become states and have fewer rights than incorporated territories. American Samoans elect a delegate to the United States House of Representatives. The delegate may vote in House committees, but not in House votes.

Andorra

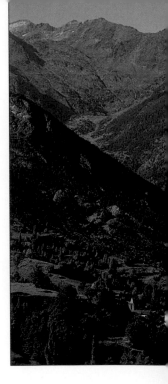

Andorra is one of the smallest countries in the world, situated high in the Pyrenees Mountains between France and Spain. Although it is one of the smallest nations in the world, Andorra's unusual political history and interesting geography make it a fascinating country.

In the past, the steep, rocky mountains that surround Andorra made transportation and communication almost impossible. As a result, Andorra was cut off from the rest of the world for hundreds of years.

Visitors come to Andorra to enjoy the country's picturesque landscape, with old churches nestled in steep, rocky mountainsides. Tourism is the country's largest source of income, and Andorra's capital, Andorra la Vella, has become a leading tourist center.

High in the Pyrenees, Andorra welcomes visitors to ski its mountain slopes, visit its ancient buildings, and shop for bargains in Swiss watches, French wines, and other products at discount stores where import *duties* (charges) are low.

Early history

A Spanish ruler, the Count of Urgel, was the first known ruler of Andorra. He controlled the region in the A.D. 800's, until he gave it to the diocese of Urgel. In the 1000's, the bishop of Urgel asked a Spanish noble, the Lord of Caboet, to defend the region.

Later, a French noble, the Count of Foix, inherited the lord's duties through marriages. Soon, the French count and the bishop of Urgel were fighting over control of Andorra.

They ended their differences by signing the Treaty of Lerida in 1278. The treaty made them joint rulers and remains in effect to this day.

Andorra is a parliamentary co-principality. Until 1993, the president of France and the bishop of Urgel, Spain, acted as co-princes of Andorra. In 1993, the citizens of Andorra adopted their first constitution. The constitution made elected officials responsible for governing Andorra, and the role of the princes became largely ceremonial.

FACT BOX

ANDORRA

COUNTRY

Official name: Principat d'Andorra (Principality of Andorra)
Capital: Andorra la Vella
Terrain: Rugged mountains dissected by narrow valleys
Area: 181 sq. mi. (468 km²)

Climate: Temperate; snowy, cold winters and warm, dry summers
Main rivers: Valira del Norte, Valira del Orient, Madriu
Highest elevation: Coma Pedrosa, 9,665 ft. (2,946 m)
Lowest elevation: Riu Runer 2,756 ft. (840 m)

GOVERNMENT

Form of government: Parliamentary democracy
Head of state: Two co-princes, the president of France and bishop of Seo de Urgel, Spain, who are represented locally by their representatives
Head of government: Executive council president
Administrative areas: 7 parroquies (parishes)

Legislature: Consell General de las Valls (General Council of the Valleys) with 28 members serving four-year terms
Court system: Tribunal de Batlles (Tribunal of Judges); Tribunal de Corts (Tribunal of the Courts); Tribunal Superior de Justicia d'Andorra (Supreme Court of Justice of Andorra); lower courts
Armed forces: France and Spain are responsible for Andorra's defense

PEOPLE

Estimated 2002 population: 69,000
Population growth: 1.22%
Population density: 394 persons per sq. mi. (152 per km²)
Population distribution: 95% urban, 5% rural
Life expectancy in years: Male: 81 Female: 87
Doctors per 1,000 people: N/A
Percentage of age-appropriate population enrolled in the following educational levels: Primary: N/A Secondary: N/A Further: N/A

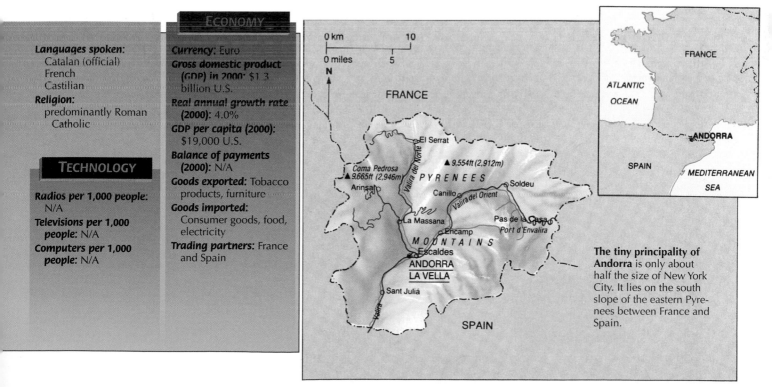

The wildlife of the Pyrenees enjoy one of the last areas of Europe that is free from human activity. The mountains form an effective barrier between people and nature, allowing many species to thrive.

1. Pyrenean ibex (goat)
2. Brown bear
3. Griffon vulture
4. Imperial eagle
5. Ptarmigan
6. Snow finch
7. Pyrenean desman
8. Alpine salamander
9. Turk's-cap lily
10. Pyrenean squill
11. Crocus
12. Pyrenean snakeshead
13. Scotch pine
14. Mountain pine

Way of life

Andorra's mountainous landscape limits agriculture. Only a few Andorrans farm, raising crops such as buckwheat, corn, oats, rye, and tobacco. Most of the mountain slopes are used for grazing sheep and cattle.

The opening of roads to France and Spain in the 1970's, as well as the growth of tourism in the 1950's, changed some of the old ways that had been a part of Andorran life for hundreds of years. Many farmers and shepherds became shopkeepers and hotel owners, for example.

Despite the changes, life for most Andorrans still centers around the family, and political issues are still decided by family clans. Many Andorrans still live in big farmhouses with stone walls and rough slate roofs. Almost all of them are Roman Catholics, and their faith greatly influences their everyday lives.

Languages spoken:
Catalan (official)
French
Castilian

Religion:
predominantly Roman Catholic

TECHNOLOGY

Radios per 1,000 people: N/A

Televisions per 1,000 people: N/A

Computers per 1,000 people: N/A

ECONOMY

Currency: Euro

Gross domestic product (GDP) in 2000: $1.3 billion U.S.

Real annual growth rate (2000): 4.0%

GDP per capita (2000): $19,000 U.S.

Balance of payments (2000): N/A

Goods exported: Tobacco products, furniture

Goods imported: Consumer goods, food, electricity

Trading partners: France and Spain

The tiny principality of **Andorra** is only about half the size of New York City. It lies on the south slope of the eastern Pyrenees between France and Spain.

Angola

The southwest African nation of Angola became independent in November 1975. Until that time, parts had been ruled by Portugal almost continuously since the early 1500's. From the 1960's to the early 1990's, the Angolans were plagued by violent revolution and civil war.

Early history

Angola's history started long before the Portuguese arrived on its shores. As early as 50,000 B.C., people are known to have lived in what is now Angola. Bantu-speaking groups settled there about 2,000 years ago. The Portuguese came in the early 1500's, and by the early 1600's they were taking great numbers of the local people as slaves for their colony in Brazil.

During the 1800's, the slave trade declined, and the Portuguese began to plant corn, sugar cane, and tobacco in Angola. In the late 1920's, after the Portuguese dictator António de Oliveira Salazar came to power, Portugal started to improve the region's economy, and thousands of Portuguese moved to Angola to start businesses.

Independence and civil war

During the 1950's, many Angolans began to demand freedom from Portuguese rule, and in 1956, they organized the Popular Movement

A group of Angolans gather around a roadside trader at a rural crossroads. Most of Angola's roads, like this one, are unpaved. The majority of the people are black Africans living in rural areas. Farming and herding are their main occupations, but most raise only enough food for their own use. Mining and manufacturing are becoming more important, but the country's economy suffered greatly during the civil war.

for the Liberation of Angola (MPLA). In Luanda in 1961, MPLA members began a revolt that spread quickly throughout the country and soon developed into a bloody guerrilla war. A Portuguese army, together with a large number of Angolans, put down the uprising, but the MPLA rebels set up bases in neighboring countries.

Other rebel groups began to spring up, and in 1962, northern rebels organized the Front for the Liberation of Angola (FNLA). Four years later, southern rebels formed the

---

FACT BOX

COUNTRY

Official name: Republica de Angola (Republic of Angola)
Capital: Luanda
Terrain: Narrow coastal plain rises abruptly to vast interior plateau
Area: 481,354 sq. mi. (1,246,700 km²)

Climate: Semiarid in south and along coast to Luanda; north has cool, dry season (May to October) and hot, rainy season (November to April)
Main rivers: Cuanza, Cunene, Cuango
Highest elevation: Morro de Moco, 8,596 ft. (2,620 m)
Lowest elevation: Atlantic Ocean, sea level

GOVERNMENT

Form of government: Transitional government, nominally a multiparty democracy with a strong presidential system
Head of state: President
Head of government: President
Administrative areas: 18 provincias (provinces)

Legislature: Assembleia Nacional (National Assembly) with 220 members serving four-year terms
Court system: Tribunal da Relacao (Supreme Court)
Armed forces: 112,500 troops

PEOPLE

Estimated 2002 population: 13,684,000
Population growth: 2.15%
Population density: 28 persons per sq. mi. (11 per km²)
Population distribution: 68% rural, 32% urban
Life expectancy in years: Male: 38 Female: 40
Doctors per 1,000 people: 0.1%
Percentage of age-appropriate population enrolled in the following educational levels: Primary: 91 Secondary: 16 Further: 1

ANGOLA

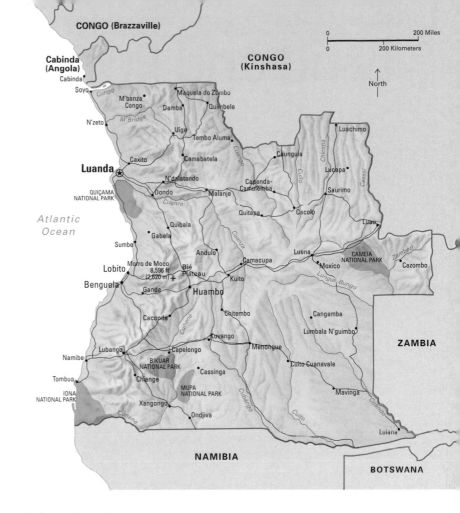

National Union for the Total Independence of Angola (UNITA).

Then in 1975, Portuguese military officers who had overthrown the Portuguese government decided to give Angola its independence. At first, the Angolans agreed to set up a government with representatives from all three rebel groups, but each group wanted to head the government and a civil war began.

The FNLA and UNITA united against the MPLA, who received considerable aid from the Communist countries of Cuba and the Soviet Union. When the MPLA finally won

Angola lies on the southwest coast of Africa. Cabinda, in the northwest, is part of Angola, even though it is separated from the rest of the country by the Congo River and a narrow strip of Congo (Kinshasa).

the war in April 1976, it formed a *Marxist* government—that is, one based on the ideas of the German thinker Karl Marx, who developed the philosophy of Communism.

Angola's new government faced major problems. UNITA, aided by South Africa, continued to wage guerrilla war against it. Meanwhile, Cuban troops helped the government fight the UNITA rebels.

Then in late 1988, South Africa stopped aiding the UNITA rebels, and all Cuban troops were withdrawn by mid-1991. In June 1989, the government and UNITA announced a cease fire.

In 1991, the MPLA legalized all political parties. In multiparty elections held in 1992, the leader of the MPLA became president. But UNITA protested that the elections were fraudulent, and civil war erupted once again. In 1994, the warring parties signed a peace treaty. The United Nations peacekeeping force helped maintain the peace through the mid-1990's. However, the cease-fire has been broken many times. In 1998 and 1999, violence increased and the peace agreement broke down. A more recent cease-fire ended the war in 2002.

Languages spoken:
Portuguese (official)
Bantu
other African languages
Religions:
Indigenous beliefs 47%
Roman Catholic 38%
Protestant 15%

TECHNOLOGY

Radios per 1,000 people:
74

Televisions per 1,000 people: 19

Computers per 1,000 people: 1.1

ECONOMY

Currency: Kwanza
Gross national income (GNI) in 2000: $3.8 billion U.S.
Real annual growth rate (1999–2000): 2.1%
GNI per capita (2000): $290 U.S.
Balance of payments (2000): -$4 million U.S.
Goods exported:
Mostly: crude oil
Also: diamonds, refined petroleum products, gas, coffee
Goods imported: Machinery and electrical equipment, vehicles and spare parts; medicines, food, textiles, military goods
Trading partners: United States, Portugal, South Africa

Land and People

Angola forms part of the large inland plateau of southern Africa. The land gradually rises from the interior to the west, where it drops sharply to a narrow plain on the Atlantic coast.

Little vegetation grows on the coastal plain, but hilly grasslands cover most of the rest of the country. A rocky desert spans the south, while tropical forests cover the north.

Many rivers cross Angola. A few serve as waterways into the interior. Some, like the Cuango, flow north into the Congo River system. Others, like the Cuanza, flow west directly into the Atlantic Ocean.

Angola has 928 miles (1,493 kilometers) of coastline along the Atlantic. Railroads connect Angolan towns on the coast with the interior, providing an important link to the sea for neighboring Zambia and Congo (Kinshasa). Luanda, the capital and largest city of Angola, is a major African seaport. Fishing is also an important economic activity along the coast.

However, the economy of Angola is based largely on agriculture. About 60 per cent of Angola's people live in rural areas and farm or herd for a living, often raising just enough food for their families. Their main food crops are bananas, cassava, corn, and sugar cane. Some grow coffee for export.

Mining is becoming increasingly important, however. Angola's land is rich in some mineral resources, especially diamonds, iron ore, and petroleum. Most of the petroleum comes from Cabinda, the small Angolan district that lies to the northwest, separated from the rest of the nation by the Congo River and part of Congo (Kinshasa).

Manufacturing is increasing in importance too. Angolan factory workers produce cement, chemicals, processed foods, and textiles. Foundries and sawmills have been built in Luanda.

Before Angola became independent, more than 400,000 Europeans and *mestizos* (people with both black African and European ancestors) lived in Angola. Most fled the country after 1975, during the civil war between the government and rebel troops. Most of those who stayed live in Angola's urban areas and run small businesses or hold other jobs that require technical and management skills.

At a diamond mine, tons of rock must be mined and crushed to produce just one small stone. Diamonds are among the valuable mineral resources found in Angola. Angola also has vast deposits of iron ore and petroleum.

Fishery workers prepare their catch for market by drying it in the hot Angolan sun. Fishing is an important industry along Angola's coastline.

A young Angolan woman, *right,* displays her finery—an elaborate beaded cap and a wealth of necklaces. Today, almost all the people of Angola are black Africans. Most Europeans fled the country during its civil war.

A rural settlement sprawls over an Angolan hillside among the grasslands and scattered trees of the inland plateau, *right.* About 75 per cent of Angola's people live in rural areas and work as farmers and herders.

Dockside cranes tower over the Atlantic coast at Lobito, one of Angola's seaports. The city lies at the end of a railroad that has carried goods to and from neighboring Congo (Kinshasa) as well as the interior of Angola. But Angola's civil war severely disrupted the railroad's operations.

Before 1975, Europeans and mestizos held most such jobs, and when they left, the country experienced a shortage of executives, professionals, and technicians. Today, however, training programs started by the government have enabled blacks to take over these jobs.

Almost all the people of Angola are black Africans. They belong to several different ethnic groups—the largest are the Ovimbundu, the Mbundu, the Kongo, and the Luanda-Chokwe.

Long ago, the Kongo people had a great kingdom that included part of Angola. Their capital, Mbanza, lay near what is now the northern Angolan town of Damba. The Kongo kingdom was weakened and eventually destroyed by the Portuguese slave trade.

Most of Angola's black Africans, including the Kongo, speak languages that belong to the Bantu language group, while Europeans, mestizos, and educated blacks speak Portuguese, the official language. Only about 40 per cent of the population can read and write in any language.

After independence was won in 1975, civil war broke out between the government party, the Popular Movement for the Liberation of Angola (MPLA), and the National Union for the Total Independence of Angola (UNITA). MPLA was Angola's only legal political party until 1991, when other parties were legalized. In 1992, MPLA won a multiparty election. UNITA claimed fraud, and civil war erupted again. Both sides prevented the delivery of food to cities occupied by their enemies, and many people died of starvation. On Nov. 20, 1994, both sides signed a peace pact promising to end the war and rebuild the nation. The war ended in 2002.

Antarctica

Over 2,000 years before Antarctica was discovered, ancient Greek philosophers believed that a continent covered the southern end of the earth. Finally this nearly barren land was sighted in 1820. During the mid-1800's, navigators sailed along its icy coast and learned that it was large enough to be called a continent. In the early 1900's, inland exploration began, and in 1911 the Norwegian explorer Roald Amundsen reached the continent's best-known location, the South Pole.

Antarctica is larger in area than either Europe or Australia, but it would be the world's smallest continent if it did not have its icecap. This icy layer, which averages approximately 7,100 feet (2,200 meters) thick, increases Antarctica's surface area by connecting the central land mass with a string of volcanic peaks that form the Antarctic Peninsula, an extension of the Andes Mountains of South America. If the icecap were to melt, these peaks would become separate islands. The icecap also makes Antarctica the highest continent in terms of average elevation.

The stormy waters of the Atlantic, Indian, and Pacific oceans isolate Antarctica from the other continents. Ships must steer around massive icebergs and break through huge ice sheets to reach the continent. On land, gigantic glaciers move slowly downhill toward the sea. Antarctica is the coldest, iciest region on earth.

Temperatures in Antarctica rarely rise above 32° F. (0° C). The world's lowest temperature, −128.6° F. (−89.2° C), was recorded at Vostok Station in Antarctica on July 21, 1983. Strong, bitter winds also chill the air. Only a few small plants and insects can survive in Antarctica's dry interior. Its coastal waters, however, are rich in wildlife, and penguins, seals, and flying birds live or nest on the peninsula and offshore islands.

Antarctica is the site of two south poles. The south geographic pole, commonly referred to as the South Pole, is the point where all lines of longitude meet. It lies near the center of the continent. The south magnetic pole is the point indicated by compass needles. This location moves by as much as 5 to 10 miles (8 to 10 kilometers) in a year. In the 1980's, it was off the coast of Wilkes Land.

Today, scientists from many countries maintain year-round research stations in Antarctica. Activities on the continent encourage international coopoeration and the sharing of scientific knowledge. Several countries have claimed parts of the continent in the hope of controlling mineral resources found there, but the United States and many other nations refuse to recognize these claims.

Environment

The Antarctic icecap, a thick layer of ice and snow that buries most of Antarctica, is formed by layers of snow that were pressed together over millions of years. High mountain peaks and a few bare rocky areas are the only visible land on the icecap. Underneath the ice, however, Antarctica has mountains, lowlands, and valleys—much like the landforms of other continents. The icecap's thickest parts lie over deep basins that dip far below sea level.

The Antarctic icecap forms the largest body of fresh water or ice in the world. With a volume of 7-1/4 million cubic miles (30 million cubic kilometers), it represents about 70 per cent of the world's fresh water. If the icecap melted, the earth's oceans would rise and flood coastal cities around the world.

The Transantarctic Mountains cross the entire continent. Several ranges make up the Transantarctic chain. Some peaks rise more than 14,000 feet (4,300 meters). Two large gulfs cut into the continent at opposite ends of the mountains, smaller bays indent the coastline, and channels separate offshore islands from the mainland.

Broad, flat sheets of the icecap called *ice shelves* float in several of Antarctica's bays and channels. The largest one is the Ross Ice Shelf, which measures about 2,300 feet (700 meters) thick at its inner edge. In summer, the outer edges of these ice shelves break away and form immense, flat icebergs. Some of these icebergs have measured as much as 5,000 square miles (13,000 square kilometers) in area.

The Transantarctic Mountains divide Antarctica into two natural land regions—East Antarctica and West Antarctica.

East Antarctica, more than half the continent, faces the Atlantic and Indian oceans. This region consists of rocks that are more than 570 million years old. Mountains, valleys, and glaciers line the coast.

The central part of East Antarctica is a plateau about 10,000 feet (3,000 meters) above sea level. The South Pole lies on the plateau, at the center of the continent. This pole, also known as the *south geographic pole,* is the earth's southernmost point, where all lines of longitude meet. East Antarctica also has the *south magnetic pole,* the southern point indicated by compass needles.

Antarctica lies beneath a layer of ice and snow that measures up to 15,700 feet (4,800 meters) at its thickest points. The Transantarctic Mountains divide the continent into two regions: East Antarctica and West Antarctica. The South Pole lies near the center on an icy, windswept plateau. The southern parts of the Atlantic, Indian, and Pacific oceans meet at Antarctica to form a body of water often called the Antarctic Ocean or Southern Ocean.

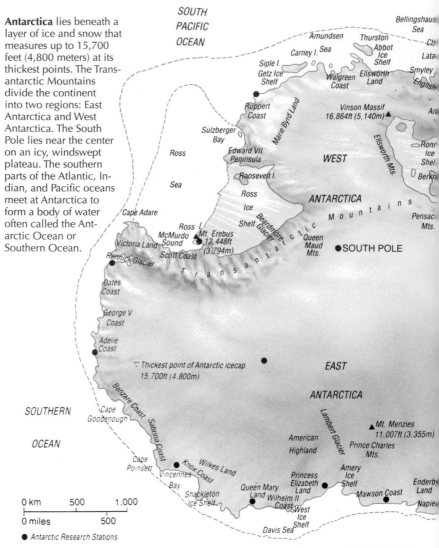

Antarctica's coast, *right,* has a milder, moister climate than the inland plateau. Coastal precipitation averages 24 inches (61 centimeters) per year. The plateau, which is sometimes called a "polar desert," has one of the driest climates on earth. It receives no rain and hardly any new snow each year.

West Antarctica, which borders the Pacific Ocean, contains little of the old rock of East Antarctica. West Antarctica developed later as part of the Ring of Fire, a string of volcanoes that encircles the Pacific Ocean. The region includes several mountain ranges and volcanoes. Vinson Massif, the highest point in Antarctica at 16,864 feet (5,140 meters), stands in the Ellsworth Mountains. Mount Erebus, Antarctica's most active volcano, towers 12,448 feet (3,794 meters) above Ross Island.

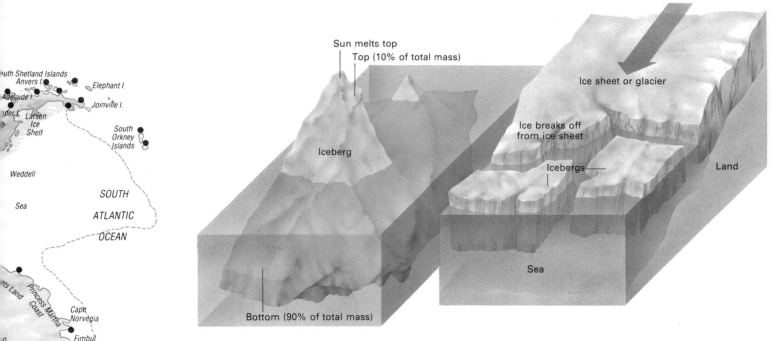

Sun melts top
Top (10% of total mass)

Iceberg

Bottom (90% of total mass)

Ice sheet or glacier

Ice breaks off from ice sheet

Icebergs

Land

Sea

The top of an iceberg is melted by the sun and wind. The bottom, hidden underwater, melts much more slowly and becomes extremely dangerous to ships. Antarctic icebergs form in summer when the outer edges of broad, flat sheets called *ice shelves* break away. Other icebergs form when a chunk of ice breaks off the lower end of a coastal glacier.

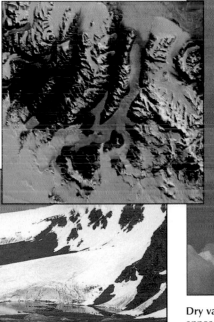

Dry valleys, or ice-free areas, *above left,* appear where Antarctica's glaciers have retreated and wind prevents snow from collecting. This satellite photograph shows a rocky, ice-free area in Victoria Land.

Towering icebergs drift away from the great icecap. Explorers have written vivid descriptions of the color and beauty of icebergs, and compared them to towers, spires, pyramids, cathedrals, and palaces. Icebergs 10 miles (16 kilometers) long are common in the Antarctic.

Wildlife

Many millions of years ago, Antarctica was an ice-free continent. Scientists have found fossils of trees, dinosaurs, and small mammals that once lived there. Today, only a few small plants and insects can survive in Antarctica's dry interior. Most land animals live at the edges of the continent. The continent's largest land animal is a wingless *midge,* a type of fly no more than 1/2 inch (12 millimeters) long. To avoid freezing to death, some lice, mites, and ticks cling to mosses, the fur of seals, or the feathers of birds.

Few plants grow in Antarctica's forbidding, ice-covered land and harsh climate. Mosses, the most common Antarctic plants, cling to rocky areas, mostly on the coasts. Only two flowering plants grow in Antarctica, both on the northern part of the Antarctic Peninsula. One is a grass that forms dense mats on sunny slopes, while the other, an herb, grows in short, cushionlike bunches.

Life in the ocean

The Antarctic Ocean has abundant wildlife. The most common ocean animal is the *krill,* a small, shrimplike creature that feeds on tiny floating organisms. Many other Antarctic animals depend on krill for food. Many Antarctic animals also eat *squid*—a soft, boneless sea animal. In addition, about 100 kinds of fish live in the ocean, including Antarctic cod, icefish, and plunderfish.

Several kinds of whales migrate to Antarctica for the summer. The blue whale—the largest animal that has ever lived—is one of these. This rare mammal feeds on krill and grows up to 100 feet (30 meters) long. Humpback whales and killer whales are among the other kinds of whales that spend summers in Antarctica.

Various kinds of seals also live in Antarctica, spending most of their lives in the water, where they swim, dive, and catch food. Most of them nest on the coasts, but the Antarctic fur seal nests on nearby islands. The southern elephant seal, the largest seal in the world, also lives in the Antarctic region. These seals have large noses and tough skin, and the males may reach a length of 21 feet (6.4 meters).

Curious crabeater seals cluster around a diver under a hole in the ice. While many kinds of seals are slow and clumsy on land or ice, the crabeater seal can move at a speed of about 15 miles (24 kilometers) per hour—almost as fast as a person can run.

Fossils, such as these of ferns from the Triassic Era, *below,* show that Antarctica was once an ice-free continent with more types of green plants than the mosses common today. Mosses cling to rocky areas, mostly on the coasts.

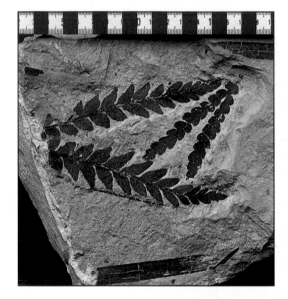

A Weddell seal nuzzles her pup. Seals have few enemies besides people and killer whales. To escape enemies, Weddell seals of the Antarctic can dive as deep as 2,360 feet (719 meters) and stay underwater as long as 43 minutes.

Birdlife

Four kinds of penguins, the well-known flightless birds, breed on the continent. On land, these birds waddle awkwardly, but in water they are swift, skillful swimmers that feed on fish and other food they find in the ocean.

Adélie penguins, the most common kind, build nests of pebbles on the coasts. Other inhabitants of the mainland are the quieter emperor penguins. After the female emperor lays an egg on the ice, the male rests the egg on his feet to warm it. Chinstrap and gentoo penguins nest on the Antarctic Peninsula and on islands. Others, including kings, macaronis, and rockhoppers, nest only on islands north of Antarctica.

More than 40 kinds of flying birds spend the summer in Antarctica. Birds that nest on land but spend most of their time diving for food include albatrosses, prions, and a large group of sea birds known as petrels. Other birds, such as cormorants and gulls, return to land more frequently. Some steal food from the nests of other birds.

Emperor penguins, *above,* are the world's largest penguins, growing to about 4 feet (1.2 meters) tall. Young emperors huddle under the body of an adult bird to keep warm.

The Antarctic food chain nourishes a great variety of wildlife. Tiny floating organisms known as *plankton* (1) support *krill* (2), a small, shrimplike creature that is the most common animal of the Antarctic Ocean. Swarms of krill form huge red masses in coastal waters during the day and glow bluish-green at night. Krill is rich in protein and a key source of food for many varieties of fish (3), birds (4), and larger creatures such as fin whales (5). Fish, in turn, provide food for penguins (6) and several species of seal (7). Leopard seals (8) hunt other seals as well as penguins. Killer whales (9) also hunt seals, penguins, and smaller whales.

Problems and Challenges

Scientists believe that Antarctica originally belonged to a land mass that included Africa, Australia, India, and South America. However, about 140 million years ago, the land began to break apart. The parts gradually drifted to their present locations, and Antarctica became a separate continent. Evidence for this theory of continental drift comes from studying mountain systems, fossils, and magnetism in ancient rocks.

Antarctica has a variety of mineral resources. Geologists have found small copper deposits in the Antarctic Peninsula. East Antarctica has traces of chromium, gold, iron, lead, manganese, molybdenum, and zinc. Coal beds lie within the Transantarctic Mountains, and—perhaps most important—scientific drilling and coring operations have revealed the possibility of petroleum reserves.

Several countries have claimed parts of the continent in the hope of controlling mineral resources found there. However, most of Antarctica's mineral deposits are too small to be mined efficiently. Icebergs, rough waves, and strong winds hamper drilling operations at sea. In addition, many scientists fear that large-scale mining would harm Antarctica's environment.

During the International Geophysical Year (July 1, 1957, to Dec. 31, 1958), 12 countries established more than 50 scientific stations on Antarctica and nearby islands. Seven of those countries have claimed parts of Antarctica, but the other five countries do not recognize Antarctic claims.

In 1959, officials of the 12 countries signed the Antarctic Treaty. The treaty, which took effect in 1961, allows people to use Antarctica for peaceful purposes only, such as exploration and scientific research, and requires scientists to share any knowledge that results from their studies. The treaty forbids military forces to enter Antarctica, except to assist scientific expeditions, and outlaws the use of nuclear weapons and the disposal of radioactive wastes in Antarctica.

Since the Antarctic Treaty took effect, several other countries have signed the document and set up scientific programs in Antarctica. Members have also added laws that protect Antarctic plants and animals.

Some Antarctic studies concern all the continents. For example, researchers hope to find ways to use the icecap as a source of fresh water, such as by towing large icebergs to desert areas. Significant research also deals with *ozone,* a form of oxygen. A layer of ozone surrounding the earth protects all living things from certain harmful rays of the

PANTHALASSA

A scientist takes magnetic readings near an Antarctic base, *below.* Researchers there have studied such topics as earthquakes, gravity, magnetism, oceans, and solar activity. Others have measured the icecap's thickness.

sun. In the mid-1980's, scientists discovered a "hole" in the ozone layer above Antarctica.

Antarctica has long been the subject of debate between those determined to preserve the continent's fragile environment and those who support the development of its resources. In October 1991, Antarctic Treaty members signed an agreement setting a 50-year moratorium on all mining activities and oil exploration on Antarctica. The agreement, which extends the terms of the 1959 treaty and will enter into effect once ratified by all members, also establishes new regulations for wildlife conservation, water pollution, and waste disposal on the continent.

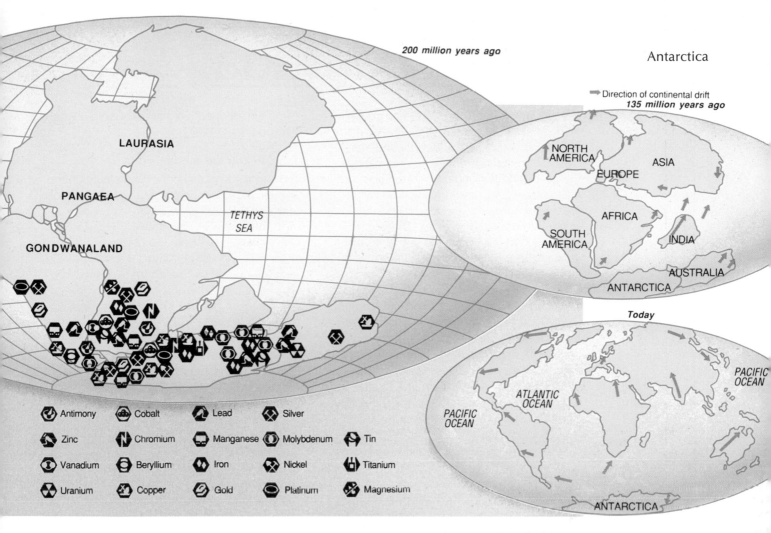

200 million years ago

LAURASIA

PANGAEA

TETHYS SEA

GONDWANALAND

➡ Direction of continental drift
135 million years ago

NORTH AMERICA
EUROPE
ASIA
AFRICA
SOUTH AMERICA
INDIA
AUSTRALIA
ANTARCTICA

Today

PACIFIC OCEAN
ATLANTIC OCEAN
PACIFIC OCEAN
ANTARCTICA

⊘ Antimony	⊘ Cobalt	⊘ Lead	⬡ Silver
⬡ Zinc	⬡ Chromium	⬡ Manganese	⬡ Molybdenum	⬡ Tin
⬡ Vanadium	⬡ Beryllium	⬡ Iron	⬡ Nickel	⬡ Titanium
⬡ Uranium	⬡ Copper	⬡ Gold	⬡ Platinum	⬡ Magnesium

McMurdo Station, the U.S. research base on Ross Island, *left,* has Antarctica's largest community. About 1,000 scientists, pilots, and other specialists live there each summer. Fewer than 200 people stay at the station for the winter, which lasts from May through August.

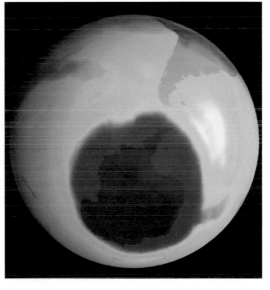

The "hole" in the earth's ozone layer over Antarctica shows up in this satellite image. The ozone layer protects living things from certain harmful rays of the sun.

The theory of continental drift says that all the continents once formed part of an enormous land mass called Pangaea. About 200 million years ago, Pangaea began to break up into two large land masses called Gondwanaland and Laurasia. Later, Gondwanaland separated into Africa, Antarctica, Australia, India, and South America. Laurasia broke up to form Europe and North America. Mineral deposits in southern Africa and the Andes region cause geologists to think that major mineral resources may also lie beneath the ice of Antarctica. So far, however, the mineral deposits discovered have been small.

43

Antigua and Barbuda

Antigua and Barbuda is an island country lying at the northern end of the Lesser Antilles, just east of St. Christopher and Nevis. The nation consists of three islands: Antigua, Barbuda, and Redonda. Most islanders are descendants of black African slaves, while people of European and mixed ancestry form a small minority.

Antigua and Barbuda has a total population of about 66,500. About 98 percent of the people live on Antigua and 2 percent on Barbuda.

When Christopher Columbus discovered Antigua in 1493, the island was inhabited by Carib Indians. The Spaniards killed many of the Caribs and forced others to work in the mines of Hispaniola. British settlers established a colony on Antigua in 1632, and later they also colonized Barbuda and Redonda. All three islands became known as the colony of Antigua.

The British settlers established sugar-cane plantations and brought black African slaves to work on them. After slavery was abolished in 1833, most of the British people began leaving the islands, but the United Kingdom kept control of the colony.

In 1967, Antigua became part of the West Indies Associated States and gained control of its internal affairs. On Nov. 1, 1981, it became the independent nation of Antigua and Barbuda.

Tourism and the economy

Tourism is the main economic activity on the islands, and the tourist industry employs most of the people. About 175,000 vacationers visit Antigua and Barbuda every year, in addition to passengers from the numerous cruise ships that stop on the islands. Most of the resorts are owned by foreign hotel chains, which means that profits from tourism generally are taken out of the country. Even so, Antigua and Barbuda is one of the more developed nations of the Third World.

Sugar and cotton production are also important to the economy. However, the government has encouraged farmers to grow a greater variety of crops, which would help reduce the nation's need to import food.

Environment

The islands of Antigua and Barbuda are volcanic in origin, but erosion by wind and rain has worn down the volcanoes, and the islands are now mostly flat. Beautiful white sandy beaches line the coasts.

Antigua also has a number of bays and inlets. St. John's, situated on the northwest coast of the island, is the capital and largest

The magnificent English Harbour at St. John's, Antigua, *top right,* was formerly a British naval dockyard. Today, it is a popular port of call for cruise ships and yachts. Tourism is the backbone of the economy of Antigua and Barbuda, but the government also encourages the development of small industries.

Tourists watch as an Antiguan cook prepares freshly caught lobsters, *center.* The teeming underwater life of its lagoons and coral reefs makes Antigua and Barbuda a paradise for divers and snorkelers.

FACT BOX

COUNTRY

Official name: Antigua and Barbuda
Capital: St. John's
Terrain: Mostly low-lying limestone and coral islands, with some higher volcanic areas
Area: 171 sq. mi. (442 km²)

Climate: Tropical marine; little seasonal temperature variation
Highest elevation: Boggy Peak, 1,319 ft. (402 m)
Lowest elevation: Caribbean Sea, sea level

ANTIGUA AND BARBUDA

GOVERNMENT

Form of government: Constitutional monarchy
Head of state: British monarch, represented by governor general
Head of government: Prime minister
Administrative areas: 6 parishes and 2 dependencies

Legislature: Parliament consisting of the Senate with 17 members and the House of Representatives with 17 members serving five-year terms
Court system: Eastern Caribbean Supreme Court
Armed forces: 150 troops

PEOPLE

Estimated 2002 population: 69,000
Population growth: 0.73%
Population density: 388 per sq. mi. (150 per km²)
Population distribution: N/A
Life expectancy in years:
Male: 69
Female: 73
Doctors per 1,000 people: N/A
Percentage of age-appropriate population enrolled in the following educational levels:
Primary: N/A
Secondary: N/A
Further: N/A

Antigua and Barbuda

city—and a famous port of call for cruise ships.

Barbuda, less developed than Antigua, is mainly a nature preserve. Unlike many islands in the West Indies, Barbuda still has abundant animal life. The island provides a haven for many species of birds, lizards, and turtles. Barbuda also has a large colony of rare frigate birds, and turtles lay their eggs on the beaches. Many kinds of fish swim in the lagoons, which lie within protective coral reefs.

The island of Barbuda lies north of Antigua and covers 62 square miles (161 square kilometers). Much of the land is a nature preserve, where birds, turtles, and lizards thrive.

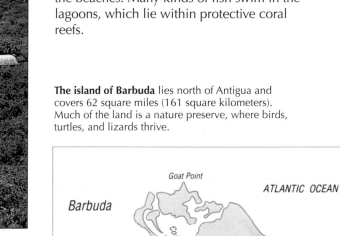

Antigua is the largest of the three islands that make up the Caribbean nation of Antigua and Barbuda. This island country lies about 430 miles (692 kilometers) north of Venezuela and covers 108 square miles (280 square kilometers). About 98 per cent of the people live on Antigua, and the remaining 2 per cent live on Barbuda. Redonda, the third island in the group, is an uninhabited rocky islet.

Argentina

Argentina is a huge, sprawling land that occupies most of the southern part of the South American continent. It is the second largest country in South America in area and in population; only Brazil is larger.

Argentina's landscape ranges from lofty mountains and arid deserts to vast plains and dense forests. Argentina is a country of many contrasts—not only in its geography, but also in its people and their way of life.

From the rolling, grass-covered plains of the north to the wild and windswept plateaus of the south, Argentina has a rugged, natural beauty all its own. The craggy, snow-covered Andes Mountains rise up along its western border with Chile, while the South Atlantic Ocean forms its eastern shoreline.

Parts of Argentina are parched with drought most of the year. But along the Brazilian border, the thundering waters of mile-wide Iguaçu Falls plunge 237 feet (72 meters) in one of the most spectacular sights on the South American continent.

Most Argentines are of Spanish or Italian ancestry. Indians—the original inhabitants of what is now Argentina—make up only a small part of the country's population. Today, Argentina has only about 50,000 Indians of unmixed ancestry. Most of them live in isolated areas, such as the Andes, the Gran Chaco, and Patagonia.

Like the land around them, the Argentines are hardy, rugged people. On the huge ranches of the Pampa, *gauchos* (cowboys) herd cattle in the proud tradition of their ancestors. In Buenos Aires, the elegant Colón Theater—one of the world's finest opera houses—draws large, enthusiastic audiences. Argentine families enjoy seaside vacations along the white, sandy beaches of the country's Atlantic coast.

Argentina Today

Argentina has enjoyed greater social and economic development than many other South American countries. Argentina has a large middle class, and about 94 per cent of all Argentines 15 years of age and older can read and write.

Argentina's political development, however, has not fared nearly as well. Throughout its history, the country has suffered through unstable governments, harsh military dictatorships, and political terrorism. Since 1930, military dictatorships have often ruled the country, and parts of the Constitution were suspended in 1976 when the military overthrew President Isabel Perón's government.

Isabel Perón was the third wife of Juan Perón, who had served as Argentina's president between 1946 and 1955 and again from October 1973 until his death in July 1974. Isabel Perón became president when he died.

Argentina's problems began to increase after Isabel Perón took office. The inflation rate soared. Political extremists engaged in terrorist attacks. In 1976, military leaders arrested Perón, dissolved the Congress, and took control of the government.

Military rule

The reign of terror that followed Perón's removal from office became known as the "dirty war." To the military, it was an attempt to rid the country of leftist opposition and political terrorism. But to the people of Argentina, it was a dark period of violence.

In their effort to crush their opponents, the military not only restricted civil rights but also imprisoned, tortured, and killed thousands of people.

In 1982, a war with the United Kingdom over control of the Falkland Islands further damaged the Argentine economy and led to serious political unrest. The following year, Raúl Alfonsín was elected president, and the new civilian government took office in December 1983. Alfonsín promised an investigation into the actions of previous governments. Three former presidents and several other officials were convicted and sentenced to prison for their involvement in murders and torture.

In 1989, Carlos Saúl Menem, leader of the Peronist Party, was elected president. He granted pardons to some of the people convicted in the mid-1980's for their involvement in murders and torture.

Problems continue

Menem was reelected in 1995. During his second term, the government borrowed heavily, and its debts increased. Domestic interest rates rose, many companies closed, and many workers lost their jobs. By the late

---

FACT BOX

COUNTRY

Official name: Republica Argentina (Argentine Republic)
Capital: Buenos Aires
Terrain: Rich plains of the Pampas in northern half, flat to rolling plateau of Patagonia in south, rugged Andes along western border
Area: 1,073,519 sq. mi. (2,780,400 km²)

Climate: Mostly temperate; arid in southeast; subantarctic in southwest
Main rivers: Paraná, Uruguay, Negro, Salado, Colorado, Bermejo
Highest elevation: Cerro Aconcagua, 22,831 ft. (6,959 m)
Lowest elevation: Salinas Chicas, located on Peninsula Valdes, 131 ft. (40 m) below sea level

GOVERNMENT

Form of government: Republic
Head of state: President
Head of government: President
Administrative areas: 23 provincias (provinces), 1 distrito federal (federal district)

Legislature: Congreso Nacional (National Congress) consisting of the Senate with 72 members serving six-year terms and the Chamber of Deputies with 257 members serving four-year terms
Court system: Corte Suprema (Supreme Court)
Armed forces: 70,500 troops

PEOPLE

Estimated 2002 population: 37,919,000
Population growth: 1.16%
Population density: 35 persons per sq. mi. (13 per km²)
Population distribution: 90% urban, 10% rural
Life expectancy in years:
Male: 72
Female: 79
Doctors per 1,000 people: 2.7
Percentage of age-appropriate population enrolled in the following educational levels:
Primary: 120*
Secondary: 89
Further: 47

Soldiers guarding Argentina's presidential residence in Buenos Aires wear a traditional ceremonial uniform in the style of the 1800's.

1990's, Argentina was in a recession. In addition, its exports and foreign investment declined. The fixed peso-dollar exchange rate meant foreign investors and buyers could get more for the same price in other countries.

Fernando de la Rua was elected president in 1999. In 2000, his government increased taxes and made massive spending cuts. In late 2001, many people feared that the government would reduce the value of the peso, so they rushed to banks to withdraw money and convert their pesos to dollars. In

Argentina is the second largest country in South America in area and population. The name Argentina comes from *argentum,* the Latin word for silver. The Spanish conquistadors who arrived in the 1500's believed that Argentina had large deposits of silver and gold.

ECONOMY

Languages spoken:
  Spanish (official)
  English
  Italian
  German
  French

Religions:
  Roman Catholic 92%
  Protestant 2%
  Jewish 2%

Enrollment ratios compare the number of students enrolled to the population which, by age, should be enrolled. A ratio higher than 100 indicates that students older or younger than the typical age range are also enrolled.

Currency: Peso

Gross national income (GNI) in 2000: $276.2 billion U.S.

Real annual growth rate (1999–2000): -0.5%

GNI per capita (2000): $7,460 U.S.

Balance of payments (2000): -$8,870 million U.S.

Goods exported: Edible oils, fuels and energy, cereals, feed, motor vehicles

Goods imported: Machinery and equipment, motor vehicles, chemicals, metal manufactures, plastics

Trading partners: European Union, Brazil, United States

TECHNOLOGY

Radios per 1,000 people: 681

Televisions per 1,000 people: 293

Computers per 1,000 people: 51.3

response, the government limited the amount people could withdraw each month from their accounts. Violent protests broke out. Soon, the president and his cabinet resigned.

An unsettled period followed, during which three other leaders served as president, holding office for only hours or days. In 2002, Argentina's Congress chose Eduardo Duhalde as president. His government suspended payments on Argentina's foreign debt and ended the one-to-one link between the dollar and the peso. The peso's value then fell sharply, and prices began to rise. Poor and middle-class Argentines continued to hold protests. Until late 2002, the government continued to limit bank withdrawls in an effort to keep money from flowing out of the country.

Environment

Argentina is the eighth largest country in the world. It shares the southern part of the South American continent with Chile, its neighbor to the west. Bolivia, Brazil, Paraguay, and Uruguay also border Argentina. Because Argentina covers such a vast expanse of land, its climate and geography range from hot and humid plains in the north to a bare, wind-swept plateau in the south. The country's four main land regions are Northern Argentina, the Pampa, the Andine, and Patagonia.

Northern Argentina

Northern Argentina is a huge lowland plain that lies east of the Andes Mountains and north of the Córdoba Mountains. The Paraná River divides Northern Argentina into two parts—the Gran Chaco, or Chaco, and Mesopotamia.

Few people live in the Chaco. Much of the region is covered by forests, and harvesting the quebracho tree is the main economic activity. The quebracho yields tannin, a chemical used in the leather industry, and the very hard wood of the quebracho tree is used to make telephone poles and railroad ties.

The Chaco has drought conditions most of the year, but heavy rains fall during the summer, causing riverbeds to overflow. Farmers plant corn, cotton, wheat, and other crops in the watered land after the summer floods.

Like its ancient Middle Eastern namesake, Mesopotamia lies between two rivers. Argentina's Mesopotamia—also known as *Entre Ríos* (Between Rivers)—lies between the Paraná and the Uruguay. Mesopotamia is a region of fertile, grass-covered plains where citrus fruits, corn, flax, rice, and tea flourish in the hot, humid climate. The holly tree grows wild in Mesopotamia, and its dried leaves are used to make the tea known as *maté*—Argentina's national beverage.

The Pampa

The Pampa is a fertile plain that fans out around Buenos Aires, extending south and west all the way to the Andean foothills and making up about one-fifth of Argentina's total area. This vast, seemingly endless plain boasts some of the world's richest soil. Fields of alfalfa, corn, and wheat cover much of the land. In the drier western Pampa, huge herds of cattle graze on large *estancias* (ranches).

A small settlement on the banks of the Chubut River, *right,* stands out against the barren landscape of Patagonia. Although Patagonia covers about one-fourth of Argentina, less than 3 per cent of the people live there.

A spectacular wall of ice on the Perito Moreno glacier on Lake Argentino sparkles in the sunlight. Perito Moreno is located in the magnificent Glacier National Park in the southern Argentine Andes.

Grassy plains, *above,* extend as far as the eye can see on a large ranch in Northern Argentina's Mesopotamia region. Ranchers graze cattle, sheep, and horses on Mesopotamia's vast pastureland, one of the leading wool-producing regions in Argentina.

Argentina's climate is as varied as its geography. The tropical north has high temperatures, with plentiful rainfall in the northeast, while most of Patagonia receives less than 10 inches (25 centimeters) of rain a year.

0-1,640 feet (0-500 meters)
1,640-6,562 feet (500-2,000 meters)
Over 6,562 feet (over 2,000 meters)

More than two-thirds of Argentina's people live in the Pampa. In addition to Buenos Aires, with a population of about 10 million in its metropolitan area, several other large cities stand in or near the Pampa.

The Andine and Patagonia

The Andine, the mountainous western region of Argentina, is made up of two subregions—the Andes and the Piedmont. The Andes, which separate Argentina from Chile, include Aconcagua, the highest mountain in

the Western Hemisphere at 22,831 feet (6,959 meters).

In the northern part of the Argentine Andes, an area of plateaus called the Puna provides grazing land. The south consists mainly of snow covered peaks and sparkling lakes. East of the Andes lies the Piedmont, a region of low mountains and desert valleys. Mountain streams provide water for irrigation, making the Piedmont suitable for growing such crops as alfalfa, corn, cotton, and sugar cane.

Patagonia is a dry, windswept plateau in southern Argentina. Few people live there. Sheep-raising is the chief occupation. In the northern part of the region, farmers raise some fruits in river valleys. The islands of Tierra del Fuego lie off the southern tip of South America.

51

People

About 250,000 Indians may have lived on the land that is now Argentina when the first Europeans arrived in the 1500's, but, 300 years later, the Indian population had greatly declined. During the Spanish occupation, many Indians were killed by the Europeans, and many others died from diseases brought by the settlers. Some intermarried with the Europeans and produced a mestizo population.

Today, Argentina has a small Indian population compared with other South American countries—only about 50,000 Indians of unmixed ancestry live there. Most of the Indians have settled in isolated areas, such as the Andes, the Gran Chaco, and Patagonia.

About 85 per cent of Argentina's people are of European ancestry, and mestizos make up most of the remaining 15 per cent of the population. European immigration has had an important effect on the growth of Argentina's population.

During the mid-1800's, only about a million people lived in the area known as the United Provinces of the Río de la Plata, which included much of the region that is now Argentina, except Patagonia. The United Provinces of La Plata had declared its independence from Spain in 1816, and named itself Argentina in 1860.

To encourage settlement of the country's vast interior, the leaders of the new republic developed an immigration policy that attracted Europeans wishing to build a new life in a new land. As a result, over the next several decades, huge waves of immigrants increased the population dramatically. By 1914, Argentina's population had reached nearly 8 million.

Most of the immigrants between 1860 and 1930 came from Italy and Spain, but Argentina also attracted settlers from such countries as Austria, France, Germany, Great Britain, Portugal, Russia, and Switzerland. After 1930, many immigrants came from Eastern Europe—especially Poland—and from the Middle East.

Because such a large percentage of the Argentine population is of European ancestry, many people speak a second European language in addition to Spanish, the official language. Also, many Argentines read one of the foreign-language newspapers published daily in Buenos Aires.

Most European immigrants settled in the cities, where greater job and educational opportunities enabled the newcomers to enter the middle class. Today, middle-class people in Argentina—a group that is larger than the

The Andes form a backdrop for one of the world's southernmost settlements—Ushuaia, on the island of Tierra del Fuego. Although only about 11,000 people live in Ushuaia, the growing popularity of trips to Antarctica has made the island a tourist center.

Buenos Aires' Colón Theater, *below,* presents fine opera, ballet, and concerts to large, enthusiastic audiences made up of Argentina's affluent upper-class and middle-class people.

middle class of most Latin-American countries—enjoy a comfortable life and adequate diet.

Argentines are noted for their love of meat, especially beef. Barbecues are a favorite event, and Argentines especially enjoy *asado con cuero,* in which beef is roasted in its hide over an open fire. *Pucheros* (stews of chicken or other meat with vegetables) and *empanadas* (pastries stuffed with meat or seafood, eggs, vegetables, and fruit) are also popular.

Argentines also enjoy many religious festivals throughout the year. About 90 per cent of the people are Roman Catholics, and their colorful processions and fireworks celebrate important church holidays.

During the *carnival,* a festival held before Lent, Argentines dance in the streets. In addition to religious festivals, their merrymaking includes wine and beer festivals and corn and wheat festivals. Festivals of folklore and music are also frequent events in many parts of the country.

A street vendor in the city of La Plata barbecues beef and sausages for his customers. The Argentine diet emphasizes meat, especially beef, and some Argentines eat beef at every meal.

Soccer fans wave the Argentine flag at a World Cup match in Río de la Plata stadium. Soccer is Argentina's most popular team sport, and soccer games draw thousands of fans. Another favorite sport is *pato,* in which players on horseback try to toss a six-handled ball into a high basket.

53

Gauchos

Out on the Argentine frontier, where the prairies of the Pampa stretch out as far as the eye can see, large herds of cattle graze peacefully under the bright afternoon sun. Suddenly, the sound of hooves breaks the silence, and a lone figure on horseback appears in the distance.

Sitting high in the saddle, the rider wears the colorful woolen poncho that has become his trademark, and he carries a *bola*—a long cord with stone balls tied at the end. Holding the horse's reins with one hand, he twirls the bola over his head with the other. The twirling bola makes a whooshing sound as he rides deep into the herd. The gaucho throws the bola so that it winds around and entangles the animal at which it is aimed.

He is a freedom-loving, rough-and-tumble *gaucho*—one of the South American cowboys made famous through story, song, and literature. Today, the gauchos work mainly as extra hands on Argentina's *estancias* (cattle ranches), but in the 1800's, the gauchos roamed the Pampa, living a wild and independent life that has come to symbolize the essence of freedom.

For 200 years, the gaucho way of life has captured the Argentine imagination. The spirit of the gaucho lives on, not only in folk tales, but also in the works of Argentina's greatest writers. The poet José Hernández wrote about the gauchos in his epic *Martín Fierro:* "Dead, the gaucho still survives—in the literature he inspired . . . and in the blood of every Argentine."

The gaucho also influenced other Argentine arts. The country's first important painter, Prilidiano Pueyrredón, created popular gaucho scenes during the 1800's. During the early 1900's, the classical composer Alberto Ginastera drew upon gaucho songs and dances in his works.

The first gauchos

While Hernández' poem *Martín Fierro* portrays the gauchos as heroes, describing their lonely life on the plains and their battles with Indians and with a government that did not understand them, history tells a somewhat different story. The forerunners of the gauchos—mestizos who roamed the plains during the 1600's—were thought of as trou-

Performing in a rodeo, a gaucho, *above,* displays the horsemanship for which the gauchos have been famous since the 1800's. In the past, gauchos lived off the land and spent most of their money on silver spurs, silver belts, and dazzling ornaments for their horses.

A gaucho in Buenos Aires shows off the traditional costume of these fiercely independent cowboys. A brightly colored poncho is worn over a cloth jacket, with a silver belt and *facón* (knife) at the waist. A wide-brimmed, cowhide hat completes the outfit.

blemakers and horse thieves. Often desperately poor, they wandered the frontier on horseback, spending most of their time in the saddle and sleeping under the stars.

In those days, thousands of semiwild cattle that had escaped the Spanish settlements grazed on the Pampa. These cattle provided fresh meat for the gauchos, and water from the rivers was readily available. The abundance of food and drink allowed the gauchos to live freely on the wild frontier, following no law but their own. Because they were skilled horsemen and familiar with the countryside, they were very successful in avoiding the authorities.

The gauchos caught wild cattle and sold their hides in illegal trade on the Brazilian frontier. At night, they gathered around roaring fires for *asados* (barbecues of fresh beef). While drinking *maté* (tea) from a gourd, they swapped stories of their adventures and sang haunting melodies to the strum of a guitar.

Modern gauchos

The gaucho way of life came to an end in the late 1800's with the development of refrigerator ships. The ability to export meat made cattle-raising a big business, and a growing number of cattle ranches began to appear on the frontier. Finally, what was once a vast wilderness became the fenced-off property of wealthy *estancieros* (farmers).

Today, the descendants of the original gauchos display their legendary rope-throwing skills and horsemanship at rodeos. With each performance, they celebrate the proud, independent tradition born long ago on the Argentine frontier, and the gaucho spirit remains alive.

A spirit of rugged independence is seen on this gaucho's face. The origins of the word *gaucho* are unknown, but some people trace it to the Arawakan Indian word *cachu,* meaning *comrade.*

In time-honored fashion, a modern-day gaucho uses a *bola* to catch a fleeing calf. When thrown, the bola coils around an animal's legs, bringing it to the ground.

Buenos Aires

Buenos Aires, the capital and by far the largest city in Argentina, is also the nation's chief port and industrial center. The city lies along the southern shore of a wide, funnel-shaped bay called the *Río de la Plata* (Silver River).

Buenos Aires is one of the largest metropolitan areas in the world, and about 33 per cent of Argentina's people live there. The city itself covers 77 square miles (200 square kilometers), and the metropolitan area spreads over 1,421 square miles (3,680 square kilometers).

Despite its enormous size and huge population, Buenos Aires has an air of spaciousness and tranquillity. Only a few skyscrapers dot the skyline, while numerous parks and plazas line the city's broad avenues. The world's widest street, the Avenida 9 de Julio, runs through the central business district. The Avenida 9 de Julio is 425 feet (130 meters) wide and divided into three smaller streets by grassy strips.

The people of Buenos Aires proudly call themselves *porteños* (port dwellers). About 75 per cent of the porteños are of Spanish or Italian ancestry, and other groups are descended from English, French, German, Lebanese, Polish, Russian, Jewish, and Syrian immigrants. Many of these immigrants were part of the huge wave of European immigration during the late 1850's.

Plaza de Mayo

The elegant Plaza de Mayo lies in the heart of Buenos Aires. Originally known as the Plaza de Armas, this site was chosen by Juan de Garay in 1580 for the first *cabildo* (town hall) of the new settlement of Buenos Aires. Spanish settlers had first established a settlement where Buenos Aires now stands in 1536, but abandoned it only five years later because of Indian attacks. Juan de Garay and his fellow settlers reestablished the city and called it *Buenos Aires* (fair winds).

Today, the Plaza de Mayo is lined with restaurants, movie theaters, boutiques, bookstores, art galleries, and the city's finest hotels. At its east end stands the *Casa Rosada* (Pink House), which houses the office of the president of Argentina. To the west lies the Congress Building, which has its own square, known as the Plaza de Congreso. This square features a famous sculpture by Auguste

Rodin, *The Thinker,* as well as the *zero kilometer stone,* from which all distances in Argentina are measured.

The barrios

Most of the northwestern, western, and southern sections of Buenos Aires consist of residential neighborhoods called *barrios,* each with its own churches, schools, and markets. Among the city's most colorful barrios is La Boca, known for its brightly painted houses and Italian restaurants.

Home to Buenos Aires' large Italian community, La Boca is also the birthplace of the *tango,* the first Latin-American dance to become internationally popular. In addition, La Boca boasts one of Argentina's most famous soccer clubs, the Bocauniors.

The extreme differences between the rich and the poor in Buenos Aires are evident from one barrio to another. Many wealthy families live in mansions in the northern barrios or in elegant homes near the center of

In the quiet of the early morning, a cafe owner in Buenos Aires prepares to open for business. *Porteños,* as the citizens of Buenos Aires are called, enjoy chatting with friends in the many cafes that line the city's streets and boulevards.

These brightly painted houses, *right,* are typical of the *barrio* (residential neighborhood) of La Boca. Every Sunday, local artists gather to display their work along Caminito Lane in La Boca.

the city. In other barrios, thousands of poor families live in makeshift wooden shacks.

In the late 1800's and early 1900's, Buenos Aires was the cultural capital of Latin America and one of the most beautiful and modern cities in the Western Hemisphere. Today, however, the city faces many problems caused by the massive migration of rural people into its metropolitan area. Buenos Aires' industries have been unable to employ all the newcomers, and many of these people live in terrible poverty.

The Plaza de Mayo stands at the heart of Buenos Aires. The square was once called the Plaza de Armas, according to a Spanish tradition dictating that all towns be built around a square so named. Porteños renamed the square *Plaza de Mayo*, after the month in which they gained independence from Spain.

Buenos Aires—the gateway to Argentina— was named by early Spanish sailors for the patron saint of fair winds, Nuestra Señora Santa María del Buen Aire. *Buenos Aires* is Spanish for *fair winds*. Major landmarks include the Plaza de Mayo (1), the Congress Building (2), the elegant Colón Theater (3), and the historic Cabildo, or town hall (4). Among the city's other points of interest are Almirante Brown Park (5), the Zoo and Botanical Gardens (6), Teatro Nacional Cervantes (7), and La Plata stadium (8).

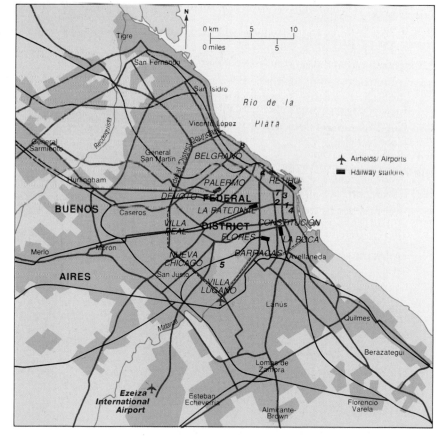

Economy

Fertile farmland, Argentina's most important natural resource, is the basis of the country's economy. Agriculture and livestock production have traditionally supplied the nation with 70 to 95 per cent of its export earnings. Cattle and sheep are raised for their meat and hides, and many Argentine factories process farm products. In addition, many of the nation's service industries, such as transportation and banking, depend heavily on agriculture.

Livestock production

Argentina is one of the world's most important producers of cattle and sheep, with about 4 per cent of the world's cattle and about 3 per cent of the world's sheep. After the Spanish explorer Pedro de Mendoza introduced cattle into Argentina in 1536, the animals were allowed to run wild, and they multiplied quickly on the lush grasses of the Pampa.

The development of refrigerator ships in the late 1800's helped turn these vast, wild herds of cattle into a profitable industry. With refrigeration, Argentina's cattle ranchers could ship meat to Europe and other markets without spoilage.

As the meat industry developed, foreign-owned meat-packing plants became more interested in the quality of the livestock they purchased, rather than just the weight of the animal. As a result, livestock producers in Argentina introduced higher-quality breeds into their stock and began using selective cross-breeding techniques. Today, agriculture employs 13 per cent of the country's workers, and the industry—including livestock and crop production—accounts for about 6 per cent of Argentina's *gross domestic product* (GDP).

Agriculture

Wheat is Argentina's leading crop. Huge fields of hard red winter wheat stretch across the fertile plain of the Pampa. Barley, corn, and rice are also major crops. In addition, Argentina is one of the world's largest producers of flax, which is mainly exported in the form of linseed oil. Other important crops include cotton, potatoes, sugar cane, sorghum, sunflower seeds, and tea.

Fruit growing has developed rapidly in Argentina since the 1940's, particularly in the province of Mendoza, the center for the nation's vineyards. Apples, bananas, grapefruits, lemons, limes, oranges, and peaches are important crops.

Argentina's farms vary greatly in size. The owners of the huge, sprawling estates that cover much of the Pampa rent land to tenant farmers, and hire workers to tend livestock and help with planting and harvesting. In the north, many people own small farms, raising only enough to feed themselves. These farmers use horse-drawn equipment or rent machinery to help them work the land, while the large estates own modern equipment.

Service industries and manufacturing

Service industries employ over 50 per cent of the country's workers. Manufacturing accounts for 22 per cent of Argentina's GDP and employs 14 per cent of all workers. Ar-

A busy lead-refining plant in the town of Comodoro Rivadavia reflects the increased economic activity in Patagonia. Oil and natural gas fields in Patagonia and the Piedmont supply much of Argentina's energy.

Wheat, Argentina's leading crop, *right,* is harvested in Mesopotamia, also known as Entre Ríos. Argentina produces about 80 per cent of all wheat grown in Latin America.

gentine factories include meat-packing plants and other food-processing facilities; leather-making factories; and plants that manufacture electrical equipment, printed materials, and textiles.

About two-thirds of the nation's factories are located in Buenos Aires and its suburbs. Factories in Córdoba manufacture automobiles, railroad cars, and tractors. The city is also a leading manufacturer of textiles and of glass and leather products. Rosario, a major inland seaport, has oil refineries as well as metal- and chemical-producing plants.

A gaucho and his herd present a classic image of the wild frontier, but most gauchos today work as ranch hands. Cattle raising and crop production have been the basis of Argentina's economy since the 1800's.

Inflation soared during the 1980's, when U.S. dollars, *above,* were often used in place of the almost worthless Argentine currency. A 1991 economic plan made the *austral,* Argentina's unit of currency, freely convertible with the U.S. dollar. While agriculture, *right,* remains the foundation of the nation's economy, manufacturing and mining now provide many jobs. In the late 1980's, Argentina's foreign debt, *far right,* ranked among the highest of all Latin-American nations.

Farmland
Grazing land
Forest
Semi-desert and desert (unproductive)

Salta
Santa Fe
Mendoza
Rosario
BUENOS AIRES
Bahía Blanca
Comodoro Rivadavia
San Sebastián

Wheat
Corn
Sugar cane
Grapes
Orchards
Citrus fruit
Cotton
Cattle
Sheep
Oil
Gas
Coal
Lead/zinc
Silver

Colombia $13 bn
Venezuela $39 bn
Mexico $93 bn
Brazil $115 bn
Peru $13 bn
Debtor nations in South America (US$ billions; 1986)
Above $5 bn (exact figures)
$2.5 bn – $5 bn
$1 bn – $2.5 bn
Bolivia
Paraguay
Uruguay $29 bn
Chile $18 bn
Argentina $48.4 bn

History

When the Spanish explorer Juan Díaz de Solís landed on the shores of the Río de la Plata in 1516, he became the first European to reach what is now Argentina. Between 1527 and 1529, Sebastian Cabot also explored Argentina and founded the fort of Sancti Spiritus, the first Spanish settlement in the Río de la Plata Basin.

Sancti Spiritus was destroyed by an Indian attack in 1529, but in 1536, Pedro de Mendoza established another settlement on the Río de la Plata where Buenos Aires now stands. Starvation and Indian raids killed many settlers, and the settlement was abandoned after five years.

Meanwhile, Spanish colonists living in what is now Peru crossed the Andes using the old Inca routes. They founded Santiago del Estero, Tucumán, and other towns in the northwest. In 1580, Juan de Garay founded a new settlement at Buenos Aires.

The Spaniards ruled what is now Argentina for 300 years, but they largely ignored the colony after they discovered it did not have huge deposits of gold and silver. Spanish rulers encouraged settlement in the area only to protect it from Portuguese expansion.

The Viceroyalty of La Plata

In 1776, the Spaniards created one large colony out of its territories in southeastern South America. The colony was called the Viceroyalty of La Plata. It consisted of what are now Argentina, Paraguay, Uruguay, and part of Bolivia, Brazil, and Chile. Buenos Aires became the capital.

In 1806 and 1807, British troops tried to seize Buenos Aires, but the residents fought them off without help from Spain. This victory led the people of Buenos Aires to believe that they could fight off Spanish troops in a battle for independence.

In 1810, Buenos Aires set up an independent government to administer the Viceroyalty of La Plata. However, the provinces outside Argentina opposed the movement and eventually broke away.

Huge crowds gather in the Plaza de Mayo in Buenos Aires, *above,* in support of Juan Perón. Perón won the support of Argentina's working classes by giving them higher wages, more paid holidays, and other benefits.

A.D. 1480   The Inca conquer the northwestern region of what is now Argentina.
1516   The first Spanish expedition arrives at the Rio de la Plata.
1527–1529   Sebastian Cabot explores the Rio de la Plata.
1536   The Spaniards found a short-lived settlement on the shores of the Rio de la Plata.
1580   Juan de Garay establishes permanent settlement of Buenos Aires.
1776   Viceroyalty of the Río de la Plata is created.
1806 and 1807   British troops invade Buenos Aires.
1810   Buenos Aires forms an independent government.
1816   Argentine provinces declare their independence from Spain.
1829–1852   Manuel de Rosas rules the United Provinces of the Río de la Plata as dictator.
1853   All the Argentine provinces except Buenos Aires agree to adopt a federal Constitution.
1860   The country takes the name of Argentina.
1862   Buenos Aires joins Argentina.
1877   First export of refrigerated meat from Argentina.
1881   Patagonia becomes part of Argentina.
1912   The Sáenz Peña Law reforms national elections.
1929   The Great Depression begins.
1930   Army officers overthrow the elected government.
1943   Juan Perón begins his rise to power.
1946   Perón is elected president. His second wife, Eva, serves as his chief assistant until her death in 1952.
1955   A military revolt overthrows the Perón dictatorship. Perón flees the country.
1973   Perón returns from exile and is elected president.
1974   Perón dies, and his third wife, Isabel, becomes president.
1976   Military leaders remove Isabel Perón from office.
1982   Argentina loses a war with Great Britain over control of the Falkland Islands.
1983   Civilian rule is restored following free elections.
1985–1986   Senior military officers are convicted of terrorism, including murders and torture, and are sentenced to prison.
Late 1990's   Country is in a recession.
2000–2002   Government increases taxes, makes massive spending cuts.

José de San Martín (1778–1850) is Argentina's greatest hero.

Juan Perón (1895–1974), *far left,* was president of Argentina from 1946 to 1955, and again from 1973 to 1974.

Jorge Luis Borges (1899–1986), *left,* was an Argentine man of letters who won international acclaim for his writings.

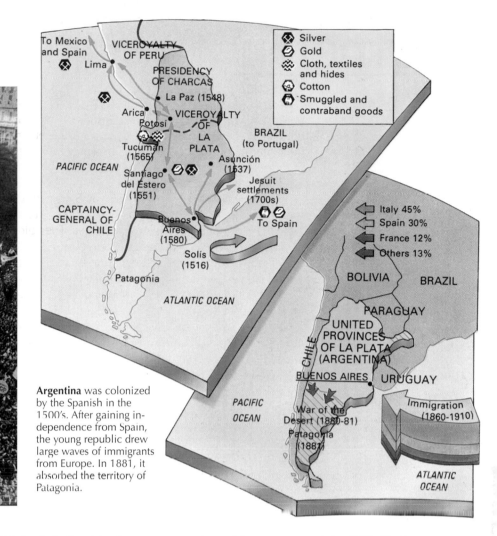

Argentina was colonized by the Spanish in the 1500's. After gaining independence from Spain, the young republic drew large waves of immigrants from Europe. In 1881, it absorbed the territory of Patagonia.

The *Peronistas*, followers of Juan Perón's policies, regained power with the election of Carlos Saúl Menem in 1989. Menem introduced several emergency measures to help pull the country out of an economic crisis, including price controls and devaluation of Argentina's currency.

Beginning in 1812, José de San Martín, an Argentine general, led the fight against Spanish rule. In 1816, representatives of the Argentine provinces formally declared their independence at the Congress of Tucumán. The new country took the name of the United Provinces of the Río de la Plata.

Two new Constitutions

In 1852, delegates from all provinces except Buenos Aires drew up a Constitution that set up a strong national government. In 1860, the country took the name of Argentina, and in 1862, Buenos Aires agreed to the union and became the nation's capital. In 1881, Argentina annexed the territory of Patagonia.

The people of Argentina enjoyed nearly 70 years of political stability. Argentina was hit hard by the Great Depression, a worldwide economic slump that began in 1929. Military leaders took over the government, and Colonel Juan Perón was elected president in 1946. In 1955, the army and navy revolted, and Perón fled the country.

During the late 1960's and early 1970's, a succession of military and civilian governments ruled Argentina. The country's eco-

nomic problems worsened. In 1973, Perón returned from exile to be president again.

Perón's third wife, Isabel, was elected vice president and became president when Perón died in 1974. In 1976, the military seized power and launched a period of violent repression. Thousands were imprisoned without trial, tortured, and killed. In 1982, Argentina seized the British-controlled Falkland Islands. Britain won an ensuing 74-day war.

Unrest forced the military to relinquish power. In 1983, Raúl Alfonsín was elected president. In 1989, amid worsening inflation, Carlos Saúl Menem was elected leader. Menem introduced an emergency economic program, and the rate of inflation dropped. Menem pardoned some of those found guilty of involvement in murders and torture.

In 1994, a new Constitution took effect. Under the Constitution, a president may serve two four-year terms instead of one six-year term. Problems the country had in 2001, however, resulted in a period in which three leaders held the office of president for only a matter of hours or days before Eduardo Duhalde of the Justicialist Party became leader in January 2002.

Armenia

Armenia, once a republic of the now-defunct Soviet Union, is an independent country and a member of the Commonwealth of Independent States (CIS). Armenia was under the strict control of the Soviet central government until 1990, when the republic called for greater control of its own affairs. In the midst of political upheaval in the Soviet Union in August 1991, Armenia declared its independence. When the Soviet Union was dissolved in December 1991, Armenia joined the newly established CIS.

Earthquakes occur frequently in the geologically active region. A violent quake devastated western Armenia in 1988, killing about 25,000 people and causing severe property damage. The force of the earthquake virtually destroyed the town of Spitak, which lay at its epicenter.

About two-thirds of the value of Armenia's economic production comes from manufacturing, including chemicals, electronic products, machinery, processed food, synthetic rubber, and textiles. Armenia is also a leading distiller of cognac. Armenian farmers produce such fruit crops as almonds, figs, and pomegranates on terraced hillsides, while barley, corn, and wheat thrive on the lower plains.

The small, ancient land of Armenia has

Armenia lies on the Armenian Plateau, a rugged highland. The average altitude of Armenia is 5,000 ft. (1,500 m).

seen periods of great power and prosperity, but there have also been times in which its people suffered greatly under foreign rule. From earliest times, the Armenian people have had to fight hard to preserve their ethnic culture.

King Tigran II, who came to power in 95 B.C., built an independent Armenian empire that stretched from the Caspian Sea to the

FACT BOX

COUNTRY

Official name: Hayastani Hanrapetut'yun (Republic of Armenia)
Capital: Yerevan
Terrain: Armenian Highland with mountains; little forestland; fast flowing rivers; good soil in Aras River valley
Area: 11,506 sq. mi. (29,800 km²)

Climate: Highland continental, hot summers, cold winters
Main river: Razdan, a tributary of the Aras
Highest elevation: Mt. Aragats, 13,419 ft. (4,090 m)
Lowest elevation: Debet River, 1,312 ft. (400 m)

GOVERNMENT

Form of government: Republic
Head of state: President
Head of government: Prime minister
Administrative areas: 10 marzer (provinces), 1 city

Legislature: Azgayin Zhoghov (National Assembly) with 131 members serving four-year terms
Court system: Supreme Court, Constitutional Court
Armed forces: 53,400 troops

PEOPLE

Estimated 2002 population: 3,543,000
Population growth: -0.28%
Population density: 308 persons per sq. mi. (119 per km²)
Population distribution: 67% urban, 33% rural
Life expectancy in years:
Male: 62
Female: 71
Doctors per 1,000 people: 3.2
Percentage of age-appropriate population enrolled in the following educational levels:
Primary: 87
Secondary: 90
Further: 12

Mediterranean Sea. The Romans defeated Tigran in 55 B.C. and made Armenia part of the Roman Empire.

The Arabs conquered the region in the A.D. 600's, followed by the Seljuks in the mid-1000's. In 1375, the Armenian kingdom fell to Mameluke invaders, and by 1514, the Ottomans had gained control of Armenia. The Persians took over eastern Armenia in 1639 and ruled the region until 1828, when Russia annexed it. Western Armenia remained under Ottoman control.

During World War I (1914–1918), Armenia became a battleground between the Ottoman Empire and Russia. The Ottomans deported countless Armenians to what is now Syria to keep them from aiding Russia. About 1 million Armenians died from lack of water and starvation or were killed by Ottoman soldiers or Arabs and Kurds. Those who survived fled to Russian Armenia, where an independent Armenian republic was established in 1918.

When conflicts resurfaced between the Armenian republic and the Ottoman Empire, the Armenians reluctantly turned to Soviet Russia for protection. In December 1920, eastern Armenia became a Soviet republic, while the Ottomans kept the rest of Armenia. In 1922, Soviet Armenia became part of the Soviet Union.

The Jermuk Waterfall spills down the rocky mountainside in a spectacular sight in the Armenian highlands. Thousands of people from neighboring regions come to the Jermuk Spa to enjoy the pure mountain air and picturesque scenery.

Most of the people are Armenians, but small numbers of Azerbaijanis, Kurds, and Russians also live in Armenia. In the late 1980's and early 1990's, disputes arose over the status of Nagorno-Karabakh—a district in neighboring Azerbaijan where the majority of the population was Armenian. The disputes led to fighting between Armenians and Azerbaijanis. By the end of 1993, Armenia controlled the district and occupied about 20 per cent of Azerbaijan. In May 1994, the two countries agreed to a cease-fire.

In 1996, Armenia's presidential election was protested because many believed it had been marred by fraud. Within a couple years, the president resigned and the prime minister was elected as the new president. In October 1999, gunmen entered the parliament building and assassinated Armenia's prime minister and several other officials. The gunmen were caught, and replacements were appointed for the slain officials.

Languages spoken:
Armenian 96%
Russian 2%
Religion:
Armenian Orthodox 94%

TECHNOLOGY

Radios per 1,000 people: 225
Televisions per 1,000 people: 244
Computers per 1,000 people: 7.1

ECONOMY

Currency: Dram
Gross national income (GNI) in 2000: $2.0 billion U.S.
Real annual growth rate (1999–2000): 6.0%
GNI per capita (2000): $520 U.S.
Balance of payments (2000): -$278 million U.S.
Goods exported: Diamonds, scrap metal, machinery and equipment, cognac, copper ore
Goods imported: Natural gas, petroleum, tobacco products, foodstuffs, diamonds
Trading partners: Belgium, Iran, Russia, United States, the United Kingdom

Australia

The name *Australia* comes from the Latin word *australis,* meaning *southern.* And because it lies entirely within the southern hemisphere, Australia is often referred to as ''down under.'' Australia is the only country that is also a continent. In area, it ranks as the sixth largest country and smallest continent.

Australia is a dry, thinly populated land. Only a few coastal areas receive enough rainfall to support a large population. Most of Australia's people live in the southeastern coastal region, which includes the country's two largest cities—Sydney and Melbourne. Australia's vast interior is mostly desert or dry grassland and has few settlements. The country as a whole has an average of only 6 persons per square mile (2 per square kilometer).

Australia is famous for its vast open spaces, bright sunshine, enormous numbers of sheep and cattle, and unusual wildlife. Kangaroos, koalas, platypuses, and wombats are only a few of the many exotic animals that live there.

Along the northeast coast of the continent lies the Great Barrier Reef, the largest group of coral reefs in the world. This unique area supports an unmatched variety and quantity of coral polyps.

The first Australians, a dark-skinned people known today as *Aborigines,* had lived in Australia for at least 40,000 years before the first white settlers arrived. Since then, the number of whites has steadily increased and the number of Aborigines has declined. Today, the vast majority of Australians are white.

Australia is one of the world's developed countries, with bustling cities, modern factories, and highly productive farms and mines. Its economy is increasingly diversified, with a healthy service industry and a gradual shift of the value of exports from mining to manufacturing. The income from the nation's exports has given most of Australia's people a high standard of living.

Great Britain settled Australia as a prison colony in the late 1700's, and most Australian people are of British ancestry. These immigrants brought many British customs with them. For example, tea is Australia's favorite hot drink, and people drive on the left side of the road in Australia as they do in Britain. In addition, English—with many British terms—is the official language. Nevertheless, just as the people of Australia have given the language a distinctive slant with their own terms and pronunciation, so have they developed a way of life all their own.

Australia Today

Australia has a population of nearly 20 million. Approximately 80 per cent of the people live in the southeastern quarter of the country, with most of the remaining population living along the northeast and extreme southwest coasts. Canberra, the national capital and the largest inland city, lies about 80 miles (130 kilometers) from the ocean. More than 80 per cent of Australia's people live in cities and towns, making it one of the world's most urbanized countries. About 70 per cent of the population live in cities of more than 100,000 people. Only about 15 per cent of Australia's people live in rural areas.

The Commonwealth of Australia is a federation of six states—New South Wales, Queensland, South Australia, Tasmania, Victoria, and Western Australia. Each state has its own government. Australia's Constitution gives certain powers to the federal government and leaves all others to the states. Australia also has two mainland territories—the Australian Capital Territory and the Northern Territory—that do not have the status of statehood.

In Australia's *parliamentary* system of government, the national government is controlled by the political party or combination of parties with a majority of seats in the lower house of parliament. The leader of the majority heads the government as prime minister.

The prime minister appoints members of parliament to serve as *ministers,* the heads of government departments. The prime minister and department heads form the Cabinet, which establishes major government policies.

Australia is a constitutional monarchy like the United Kingdom. The British monarch is also Australia's monarch and head of state. However, the monarch serves mainly as a symbol of the historical ties between the two countries and has little or no power in the Australian government. Australia is a member of the Commonwealth of Nations, with many other former British colonies. In the late 1990's, Australia considered becoming a republic, but the idea was ultimately voted down.

Australia is one of the world's rich, developed countries. Most developed countries have become rich through the export of manufactured goods, but Australia's wealth has come chiefly from farming and mining.

Like many other developed countries, Australia faces the problems of continuing inflation and unemployment as well as a growing international debt. The country's hopes for economic growth are closely tied to the growth of its mining industry.

Uranium is Australia's most valuable undeveloped mineral resource. However, Australians who oppose nuclear power because

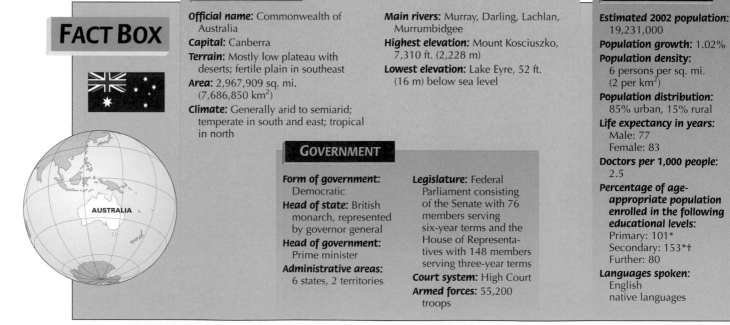

FACT BOX

COUNTRY

Official name: Commonwealth of Australia
Capital: Canberra
Terrain: Mostly low plateau with deserts; fertile plain in southeast
Area: 2,967,909 sq. mi. (7,686,850 km²)
Climate: Generally arid to semiarid; temperate in south and east; tropical in north

Main rivers: Murray, Darling, Lachlan, Murrumbidgee
Highest elevation: Mount Kosciuszko, 7,310 ft. (2,228 m)
Lowest elevation: Lake Eyre, 52 ft. (16 m) below sea level

GOVERNMENT

Form of government: Democratic
Head of state: British monarch, represented by governor general
Head of government: Prime minister
Administrative areas: 6 states, 2 territories

Legislature: Federal Parliament consisting of the Senate with 76 members serving six-year terms and the House of Representatives with 148 members serving three-year terms
Court system: High Court
Armed forces: 55,200 troops

PEOPLE

Estimated 2002 population: 19,231,000
Population growth: 1.02%
Population density: 6 persons per sq. mi. (2 per km²)
Population distribution: 85% urban, 15% rural
Life expectancy in years: Male: 77 Female: 83
Doctors per 1,000 people: 2.5
Percentage of age-appropriate population enrolled in the following educational levels: Primary: 101* Secondary: 153*† Further: 80
Languages spoken: English native languages

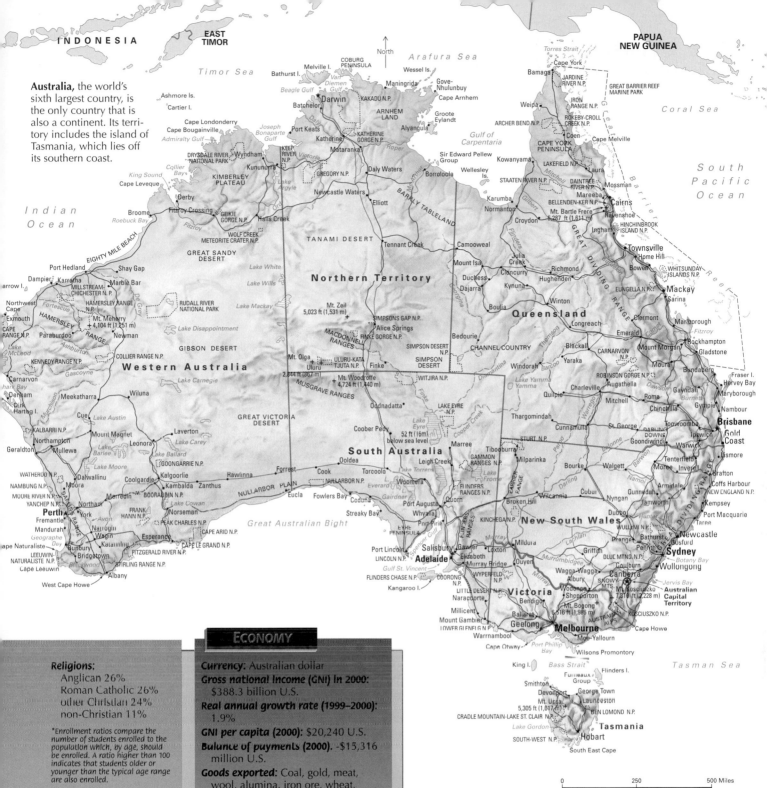

Australia, the world's sixth largest country, is the only country that is also a continent. Its territory includes the island of Tasmania, which lies off its southern coast.

ECONOMY

Currency: Australian dollar

Gross national income (GNI) in 2000: $388.3 billion U.S.

Real annual growth rate (1999–2000): 1.9%

GNI per capita (2000): $20,240 U.S.

Balance of payments (2000): -$15,316 million U.S.

Goods exported: Coal, gold, meat, wool, alumina, iron ore, wheat, machinery and transport equipment

Goods imported: Machinery and transport equipment, computers and office machines, telecommunication equipment and parts; crude oil and petroleum products

Trading partners: European Union, Japan, United States, Association of Southeast Asian Nations

TECHNOLOGY

Radios per 1,000 people: 1,908

Televisions per 1,000 people: 738

Computers per 1,000 people: 464.6

of its potential hazards also oppose plans to mine and export uranium. In addition, some of the richest uranium deposits lie in the traditional tribal lands of the Aborigines, and Aboriginal groups are trying to obtain legal control over their tribal lands, including the uranium-mining areas.

Environment

The northern third of the Australian continent lies in the tropics and is warm or hot the year around. The rest of the country lies south of the tropics and has warm summers and mild or cool winters. Rainfall is seasonal in most of Australia.

Wet and dry seasons

During the wet season, heavy downpours and violent storms cause floods in many parts of Australia. However, the droughts that plague the nation are usually a far more serious problem. Nearly every section of Australia has a drought during the annual dry season. These droughts can cause severe water shortages that require strict conservation measures. In addition, destructive bush fires are more common during droughts.

Australia's rivers are one of its most vital resources. They provide the towns and cities with drinking water, and supply farmers with much-needed water for irrigation. However, most of Australia's rivers are dry at least part of the year, so dams and reservoirs on all the largest rivers store water for use during the dry season.

Land regions

Australia can be divided into three major land regions. The easternmost region is the Eastern Highlands—sometimes known as the *Great Dividing Range* because these mountains divide the flow of rivers in the region. The Eastern Highlands include the highest elevations in Australia. A low plain bordered by sandy beaches and rocky cliffs stretches along the Pacific coast. More rain falls on this coastal plain than anywhere else in the country.

The highlands consist mainly of high plateaus broken in many places by gorges, hills, and low mountain ranges. Grass or forests cover some plateaus in the Eastern Highlands, but many plateaus have fertile soils and are used as cropland. The southeastern section of the plain, from Brisbane to Melbourne, is by far the most heavily populated part of Australia. The Australian Alps, with their Snowy Mountains, lie in the southern part of this region. The Murray River, Australia's longest permanently flowing river, starts in the Snowy Mountains.

The Pinnacles in the Western Plateau's desert region are spines of rock carved out by wind and water. Three major deserts cover the center of the Western Plateau. Australia's fourth desert is in the Central Lowlands.

Uluru, *right,* is a popular tourist attraction in central Australia. The walls of the many caves in the sandstone rock are covered with paintings made long ago by Aboriginal artists.

The Flinders Range of southern Australia, *above,* extends north from Spencer Gulf, an arm of the Indian Ocean that cuts into the land near Adelaide. Wind and water have eroded the reddish rocks of the range, giving them sharp outlines.

Australia's land regions consist of the Western Plateau, which covers much of the continent and contains three deserts; the Central Lowlands, which have the lowest elevations in Australia; and the Eastern Highlands, which run down the Pacific coast.

Arnh
Lan

Kimberley
Plateau

Great Sandy
Desert

MacDor
Rang

Hamersley Range

Ulu

WESTERN
PLATEAU

Musg
Rang

Darling Range

Great
Victoria Dese

Nullarbor Plai

Grea
Australi
Bight

Tropical conditions prevail in the northern third of Australia. During the rainy season, the damp climate and extreme heat can produce an uncomfortable level of humidity.

Salt crystals, *below,* cover the bed of the dry Lake Eyre in southern Australia. Most of Australia's natural lakes are dry for months or years at a time. *Playas,* dry beds of salt or clay that fill with water only after heavy rains, are common in South Australia and Western Australia.

The Central Lowlands, Australia's second major region, is a generally flat area with infrequent rainfall, except along the north and south coasts and near the Eastern Highlands. Farmers in the southern part of the Lowlands grow wheat, but most of the region is too dry or too hot for crops. However, the coarse grass or shrubs that cover much of the land make it suitable for grazing livestock. The two largest towns in the region have fewer than 30,000 people each.

The Western Plateau, Australia's third major region, covers the western two-thirds of Australia. A vast, dry, treeless plateau extends about 400 miles (640 kilometers) along the region's southern edge, while deserts stretch across the central part. Most of the desert area consists of swirling sands that often drift into giant dunes. Where the deserts give way to land covered by grass and shrubs, the land can be used to graze livestock. The extreme north and southwest have the region's heaviest rainfall, and most of its cropland. Adelaide and Perth are the region's two largest cities.

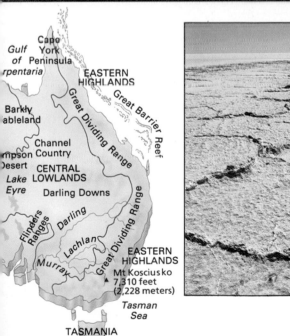

Wildlife

At one time, all the world's continents were part of one huge land mass. The region that is now Australia became separated from this land mass about 200 million years ago, and as a result, the animal life of Australia developed differently from that of other continents. For example, *marsupials*—animals with pouches—are Australia's most unusual and famous creatures.

Unique animal life

Most mammals give birth to relatively well developed offspring, but Australia's marsupials give birth to tiny, poorly developed offspring. The marsupial newborn undergoes most of its development while attached to one of its mother's nipples in a pouch called the *marsupium.* Kangaroos, koalas, wallabies, and wombats are marsupials. Australia has about 150 species of marsupials, all of which have pouches.

The platypus and the echidna, found only in Australia, are the only mammals in the world that hatch their young from eggs. Platypuses live in long burrows that they dig in the banks of streams. Except for females with their young, each platypus lives in its own burrow. Platypuses can walk on land as well as swim, and they use their bills to scoop their food from the bottom of streams.

Australia also has about 700 species of native birds. They include the world's only black swans and about 60 kinds of cockatoos, parakeets, and other parrots. The emu, a large, flightless bird, has long legs for running and stands 5-1/2 feet (1.7 meters) high. The kookaburra, one of Australia's best-known birds, nests in tree holes and has a call that sounds like a loud laugh.

Plant life

Two kinds of native plants dominate Australia's landscape. Varieties of acacias and eucalyptuses are the most common shrubs in dry areas and the most common trees in moist areas. Acacias, which Australians call *wattles,* bear their seeds in pods. Australia has about 700 species of acacias, many with brightly colored flowers.

Impressive jumpers, kangaroos can reach a top speed of about 40 miles (65 kilometers) per hour. Each jump covers an average distance of about 13 feet (4 meters).

A female koala and her young rest in a forked tree. The koala, a native of Australia's eastern forests, was near extinction in the 1920's. Today, as a protected species, this charming creature has been making a slow comeback.

Two species of crocodile, *right,* live in the coastal regions of tropical north and east Australia. The saltwater crocodile can be ferocious, while the smaller freshwater species is considered harmless.

Kangaroos are the symbol of Australia to people throughout the world. The kangaroo family includes about 50 species. They range in size from the huge red and gray kangaroos, which stand about 6 feet (1.8 meters) tall, to tiny creatures smaller than a domestic cat.

Eucalyptuses, or *eucalypts,* as the Australians call them, are the most widespread plants in the country. Most species have narrow, leathery leaves that contain a fragrant oil. Scrubby eucalyptuses cover large areas of Australia's hot, dry interior. Eucalyptus trees, known as *gum trees* or *gums,* are the tallest trees in the country and among the tallest in the world. Some types of eucalyptus may grow to a height of 330 feet (100 meters). At one time, the eucalyptus grew only in Australia and on a few islands to the north. But these trees have been planted in California, Hawaii, and in many other warm areas.

Australia has thousands of wildflowers. Many are desert species whose seeds lie buried in the ground until heavy rain brings them to life. These plants can make deserts look like gardens right after a desert rain. The waratah, a tall shrub found only in Australia, grows under trees in open forests and bears large, bright-red flowers. Its name comes from an Aboriginal word meaning *seen-from-afar*.

To a great extent, Australia's wildlife has suffered at the hands of the European settlers, who have greatly changed the environment since they arrived in the 1700's. Many wildlife species became extinct in the 1800's, and many others have been lost since then. Today, at least 40 Australian animals are endangered. Many others are protected.

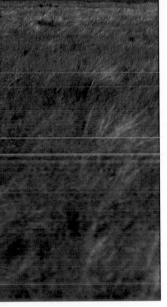

Emus cannot fly, but their long legs can carry them to speeds of nearly 30 miles (50 kilometers) per hour. They are found everywhere in the country except the rain forests.

Galah parrots are pink and gray cockatoos that live in many inland areas of Australia. Many people keep these parrots as pets. Galahs eat the seeds of grasses and other plants.

The Aborigines

Aborigines are Australians whose ancestors were the first people to live in Australia. The name comes from the Latin phrase *ab origine,* meaning *from the beginning.* Most scientists believe the ancestors of today's Aborigines arrived in Australia at least 40,000 years ago from Southeast Asia. By the time the Europeans arrived, in 1788, 500 tribes of Aborigines had developed, each with its own language.

Traditional culture

The Aborigines traditionally lived by hunting and gathering food. They did not settle in one place but roamed over limited areas of the countryside, and they made weapons, tools, and utensils from local resources. For men, the most important weapons were spears, which they used in fighting, hunting, and fishing. Women gathered vegetables and small animals.

Australia's first people lived close to nature. They knew the habits of all the creatures and plants around them. In addition, all adult Aborigines knew where they could find water within their territory. Little girls went out gathering food with their mothers and other women. Boys began to practice throwing toy spears quite early.

The size of a tribe depended partly on the amount of food and water in its territory. A tribe had no political chief or formal government, but older, respected men generally made important tribal decisions and directed the ceremonies. Each tribe consisted of various subgroups. Based on their ties to a common ancestor, these family groups owned certain lands and conducted ceremonial rituals.

Religion linked the Aborigines to the land and nature through ancestral beings who, according to Aboriginal beliefs, had created the world long ago in a time called the *Dreaming,* or *Dreamtime.* These beings never died, but merged with nature to live in sacred beliefs and rituals. Aborigines could renew their ties with the Dreaming through their rituals.

Cool, dark caves inside Ayers Rock, or *Uluru,* have sheltered Aborigines for thousands of years. The land where Ayers Rock stands was returned to its traditional Aborigine owners in 1985.

Young Aborigines are born with light-brown or blond hair that gradually darkens during childhood.

Spears were the Aborigines' most important weapons, and they were used for fighting, hunting, and fishing. A tool called a spearthrower increased the spear's speed and force. The men also used boomerangs for hunting.

Aborigine camps, *right,* often lie close to sacred sites, such as Ayers Rock, or *Uluru,* in the Northern Territory. This territory pioneered establishing Aborigine settlements with improved living conditions and granting land rights to Aborigines.

Ceremonies called *corroborees* consist of songs and dances that are performed for amusement and relaxation rather than for religious reasons. The ancient dances are passed on to the children unchanged.

1700's to today

At first, many Aborigines supposed that the European newcomers, with their pale skins, were the spirits of their own dead relatives. But the Aborigines' image of Europeans soon changed to that of evil spirits. The Europeans killed many Aborigines or forced them from their homes. Other Aborigines died from diseases, such as smallpox and measles, brought by the newcomers.

Today, Australia has only about 206,000 Aborigines—about 1 per cent of the country's population. Some Aborigines live partly as their ancestors did, with their own customs, beliefs, and language. Many others lost most or all of their traditions but were excluded from mainstream society.

In general, the Aborigines lag far behind white Australians in both education and income. In addition, most lack decent housing and proper health care.

Only since the 1930's has the Australian government worked to include the Aborigines more closely in the country's economic and political life.

In 1967, the Constitution was changed so that Aborigines were allowed to vote and receive social service benefits. Today, many Aborigines are striving to regain ownership of their traditional lands. Large areas in the Northern Territory and in the state of South Australia have been returned to the Aborigines.

The Outback

Australians call the countryside the *bush*. The term *outback* refers specifically to the interior of the country, which consists mainly of open countryside, including vast expanses of grazing land. Only about 13 per cent of Australia's people live in these rural areas. Many live extremely isolated lives on cattle or sheep ranches, called *stations*. The largest stations cover more than 1,000 square miles (2,600 square kilometers) and may be 100 miles (160 kilometers) or more from the nearest town.

The outback has few paved roads, so travel by automobile is difficult or impossible. Floods sometimes close roads for weeks at a time. Most wealthy farm families own a light airplane, which they use for trips to town. Other families may get to town only a few times a year, making it difficult to maintain supplies of food and other necessities.

Many children in remote areas of the outback receive elementary and secondary education at home by means of correspondence schools and schools of the air. Each state operates a correspondence school, and the Northern Territory operates two such schools. Students of correspondence schools receive and turn in their assignments by mail. In schools of the air, teachers stationed at broadcasting centers in various parts of the country talk with students by means of two-way radio.

The largest settlements in rural Australia are the widely scattered towns that developed to support Australia's mining industry. For example, Kalgoorlie, a town in Western Australia, is the center of Australia's major gold and nickel fields. The town lies in an arid region about 375 miles (600 kilometers) east of Perth. Water must be pumped from about 350 miles (560 kilometers) away, and the town must supply most of its own needs.

All rural areas in Australia are subject to such disasters as droughts, floods, and bushfires. Because they share the threat of frequent catastrophe, rural Australians tend to develop strong ties with one another. Many communities have their own traditional fairs, festivals, and sports competitions.

Outback animal life is varied and includes native species such as kangaroos, wallabies, and emus, and introduced species, such as

Musgrave Ranges, an Aboriginal reserve in the heart of the Australian continent, is typical of much of the outback landscape. Its natural vegetation is sparse grassland with scrubby trees and bushes.

A wind pump, *top right,* draws water from the Great Artesian Basin in central Australia. This vast underground rock formation extends across much of eastern Australia. The water it provides is often too salty for people to drink, but is suitable for livestock.

The rodeo, *lower right,* allows farmhands in the outback to put aside their daily chores and show off their riding and roping skills. Riders compete in events such as bareback bronc riding, calf roping, and steer wrestling.

rabbits. The size of agricultural stations makes it prohibitive to fence off crops from the wildlife, and some of these animals have caused extensive damage to crop and grazing lands. Wild rabbits, in particular, have been destructive. In recent years, rabbits have been the target of a drive to wipe them out with a deliberately introduced disease, myxomatosis.

The standard of living in rural Australia is as high as it is in the cities, or even higher. Most farm families own their farms and live in comfortable wood or brick houses with electric power. A growing number have air conditioning. Economic difficulties, however, are growing as a result of a drop in demand and prices for many farm products, especially wheat.

Persons per square

mile	kilometer
More than 15	more than 6
5 to 15	2 to 6
2 to 5	1 to 2
Less than 2	less than 1

● Capital city

● Cities with population more than 1 million

● Cities with population more than 500,000

⬤ Major Aboriginal settlements

The population distribu-tion of Australia is uneven. Most people live in the big cities along the southern and eastern coasts of the continent. The southwest corner of Australia also has a siz-able population, but the dry center of the country has few settlements. The Aboriginal people live in small groups, mainly in rural areas.

Farmers on horseback check on their beef cattle in a remote part of the out-back.

The flying doctor service brings medical care to iso-lated communities. Before the days of radiotele-phones and airplanes, these communities had no medical care at all.

Agriculture

Much of Australia's wealth comes from the farmland that covers about 65 per cent of the nation. However, most of this land is dry grazing land. Crops are grown on only about 5 per cent of the farmland, but farmers use modern agricultural methods that make the cropland highly productive.

Farms on the east coast of Queensland grow bananas, pineapples, sugar cane, and other crops that need a wet, tropical climate. Wine grapes and oranges grow in some parts of the country, and apples and pears grow in all the states. Cattle and calves, wheat, and wool are Australia's leading farm products and are also the country's chief agricultural exports. Australia ranks as the world's largest wool producer and exporter.

Sheep, cattle, and wheat

Sheep and cattle are raised in all Australian states, though some states raise far more than others. New South Wales and Western Australia together raise more than half of the country's sheep and produce about half of its wool. Most farmers also raise cattle and grow wheat.

New South Wales and Queensland raise more than half of Australia's beef cattle. The mild Australian winters allow beef cattle to graze throughout the year. Australian farmers can therefore produce beef at lower costs than farmers in most of Europe and the United States, where cattle must be housed and hand-fed in winter.

Australia's wheat production grew rapidly during the 1980's. Today, Australia is the world's fifth largest wheat exporter. Western Australia devotes the most land to wheat cultivation, but New South Wales produces the most wheat. Australian white wheats are world renowned for their resistance to disease.

Modern farm methods

At one time, farmers believed that their production depended entirely on how much land they used. Today, farmers know that they can greatly increase production without increasing the area they cultivate. For example, by adding small quantities of certain

Growing wheat and raising sheep are often combined on the farms of New South Wales. Raising sheep is the main type of farming in almost every part of this state. Fruits, cotton, and rice are also grown here.

Wine grapes, *above,* are produced in the Barossa Valley of South Australia as well as in New South Wales and Victoria. These regions produce especially fine wines.

A field of sugar cane on the east coast of Queensland, *below,* thrives under the hot, tropical sun. Sugar cane is Queensland's chief crop.

A flock of Merino sheep await a shearing on an Australian sheep station, *center.*

Agriculture

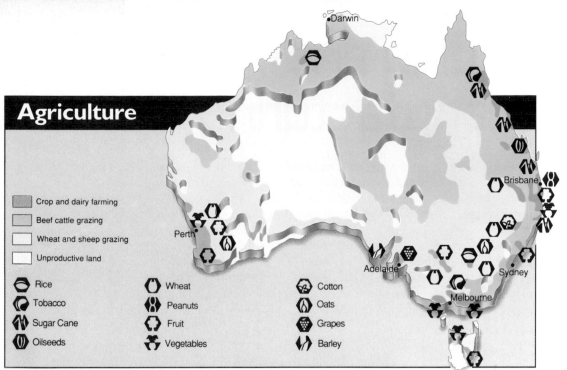

Legend:

- Crop and dairy farming
- Beef cattle grazing
- Wheat and sheep grazing
- Unproductive land

- Rice
- Tobacco
- Sugar Cane
- Oilseeds
- Wheat
- Peanuts
- Fruit
- Vegetables
- Cotton
- Oats
- Grapes
- Barley

Darwin • Brisbane • Perth • Adelaide • Melbourne • Sydney

Most of Australia's cropland is concentrated along the country's southwest, southeast, and east coasts, the only areas that get enough rainfall for growing crops. The drier inland areas can support only sheep and cattle grazing and wheat growing.

Workers bring in the tomato harvest in the Northern Territory, *left.* Most of the crop farming in the Northern Territory takes place in the northern and south-central regions.

Wheat production is heavily concentrated in New South Wales and Western Australia. The crop is grown in areas where there is medium rainfall and moderate temperatures. Australia sells large quantities of wheat to China, Japan, and other Asian countries.

elements to the land, scientists have transformed areas of poor land, such as the Ninety Mile Desert in South Australia, into good grazing land. Research workers have also devoted a great deal of effort to developing new, improved varieties of rice, sugar, and wheat.

Because the amount of Australia's rainfall is low and unpredictable, the full development of Australia's agricultural resources also depends on irrigation. Irrigation gives farmers control over the water supply and allows them to grow fruits and vegetables in areas where it would not otherwise be possible. Irrigation also enables farmers to obtain higher crop yields.

Mining and Manufacturing

Mining has long been a cornerstone of economic development in Australia. However, manufacturing has also come to play an important part. In the mid-1980's, mining accounted for 30 per cent of the nation's total exports, compared with about 25 per cent for manufacturing. While mining employs only 2 per cent of Australia's labor force, manufacturing employs 16 per cent. Mining also accounts for only 7 per cent of Australia's *gross domestic product (GDP)*—the total value of goods and services produced within the country in one year. Manufacturing accounts for 19 per cent of the GDP.

Mineral wealth

Australia has become one of the world's major mining countries, ranking first in the production of bauxite, diamonds, and lead. The nation is also a leading producer of coal, copper, gold, iron ore, manganese, nickel, silver, tin, titanium, tungsten, zinc, and zircon. Nearly all the world's high-quality opals are mined in Australia.

The continent's energy-producing resources are among the richest in the world. Australia has enough coal and natural gas to meet all its energy needs. It has large reserves of brown and black coal, which are used to produce Australia's electricity. Black coal is exported in large quantities. Also, Australia's oil wells produce enough crude oil to meet almost all of the nation's needs.

However, many of Australia's mineral deposits lie in the country's dry areas, far from major settlements. Such deposits are extremely expensive to mine. Roads and railroads to the mining sites must be constructed, and towns must be built for the miners and their families. The costs of mining development in Australia are so high that the mining industry depends heavily on support from foreign investors.

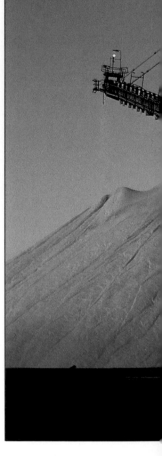

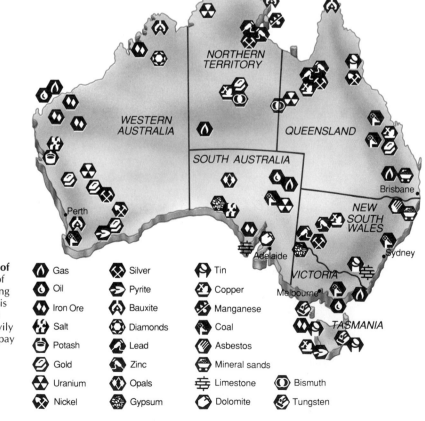

Australia's abundance of deposits makes it one of the world's major mining countries. The country is almost self-sufficient in minerals but relies heavily on foreign investors to pay the costs of mining.

Gas	Silver	Tin
Oil	Pyrite	Copper
Iron Ore	Bauxite	Manganese
Salt	Diamonds	Coal
Potash	Lead	Asbestos
Gold	Zinc	Mineral sands
Uranium	Opals	Limestone
Nickel	Gypsum	Dolomite
		Bismuth
		Tungsten

A mountain of salt piles up at Port Hedland in Western Australia. The country produces from 5 to 6 million short tons (4.5 to 5.4 million metric tons) of salt per year. Australia exports more than 80 per cent of its salt production, mainly to Japan.

Opals only show their real beauty after polishing, *lower far right.* These valuable gems are mined in South Australia, *right.* The country produces 95 per cent of the world's opals.

Two men pan for gold, *right,* in the Hill End district of New South Wales. During the 1850's, the rich gold fields of New South Wales and Victoria attracted adventurers from all over the world who hoped to make quick fortunes.

Highly mechanized coal mines are a common sight in New South Wales. The major markets for coal produced in the state are local power stations, the iron and steel industry, and export trade to such countries as Japan, South Korea, and Taiwan.

Manufacturing power

After World War II (1939-1945), the Australian government determined that its industry should become self-sufficient, and that at least one brand of automobile must be made entirely in Australia—including the engine and parts. Australia today produces most of its own metals, such as iron and steel, for local industrial use.

But unlike most other developed countries, Australia still imports more manufactured goods than it exports. Australian factories produce most of the nation's *consumer goods,* such as processed foods and household articles. But many *producer goods,* such as factory machinery and construction equipment, must be imported. Iron and steel are the chief exceptions.

Most of Australia's factories specialize in assembly work and light manufacturing, and many plants process farm products or minerals for export. Automobiles, chemicals, household appliances, metals, paper, processed foods, and textiles are among Australia's leading products. New South Wales and Victoria are the chief manufacturing states, with most factories located in and around Sydney and Melbourne.

Sydney and Melbourne

The two largest cities in Australia are Sydney and Melbourne. Sydney has about 3 million people, and Melbourne, about 2-2/3 million. Both are state capitals and the major commercial, industrial, and cultural centers of their states. Each city was laid out near the mouth of a river and close to a good ocean harbor. The rivers provided drinking water and the harbors enabled the settlements to develop into centers of trade and immigration.

Today, both Sydney and Melbourne have problems common to big cities everywhere. Poor inner-city areas have high rates of unemployment and crime. Air pollution and rush-hour traffic jams plague the city's residents.

Sydney

The oldest city in Australia, Sydney is the capital of the state of New South Wales. The city and its suburbs cover about 4,700 square miles (12,000 square kilometers) on the country's southeastern coast. The British founded Sydney as a prison colony in 1788.

The city's mild climate enables the people of Sydney, called *Sydneysiders,* to enjoy the outdoors during most of the year. Sydney's vast harbor makes the area famous for water sports, such as sailing. Most Sydneysiders have British ancestors, but many other Europeans and smaller numbers of Asians have settled in the city since the mid-1900's. Sydney also has a few thousand Aborigines. Most Sydney families own a house and garden in one of the suburbs. Sydney has almost no slums, but some of the Aborigines live in substandard housing.

High-rise buildings dominate the skyline of Sydney's central business district. Sydney Harbor, one of the world's major ports, is also Australia's most important port for shipping farm products. The city has about 12,000 manufacturing plants, which employ a total of over a million workers. Leading factory products include chemical and paper goods, food products, and machinery equipment. Sydney also serves as the banking and business center of New South Wales.

Sydney's famous Opera House, completed in 1973, includes facilities for concerts, op-

Sydney Harbor is one of the world's major ports. Its white shell-like Opera House and the Sydney Harbor Bridge are landmarks recognized around the world. The bridge links the city center with suburbs on the north shore of the harbor.

era, and theater. Many architects consider it one of the finest buildings constructed during the 1900's.

Melbourne

Melbourne lies on Port Phillip Bay on Australia's southeastern coast. John Batman, an Australian farmer, founded Melbourne in 1835. He came from the nearby island of Tasmania, seeking land for sheep farms. He bought 600,000 acres (240,000 hectares) from the Aborigines and paid them with blankets, tomahawks, and other goods. Today, the city and its suburbs cover more than 2,300 square miles (5,960 square kilometers).

Bondi Beach, *below,* a beautiful stretch of sand close to the center of bustling downtown Sydney, provides a peaceful refuge for many Sydneysiders.

Melbourne has only about 2,700 people who are descended from the Aborigines. Almost one-fourth of Melbourne's population was born outside Australia. About one-third of all immigrants came from Great Britain and Ireland. Other immigrants include those from Italy, Greece, and Yugoslavia. Australia's small Asian community consists mostly of descendants of Chinese immigrants who arrived during the gold rush of the 1800's. Each ethnic group has introduced its own type of food, entertainment, and clothing, making Melbourne a truly cosmopolitan city.

More than 10,000 factories in Melbourne employ a total of about 400,000 workers. The city's chief manufactured products include automobiles, chemicals, food products, machinery, and textiles. Wholesale and retail trading and important financial institutions make Melbourne a major commercial center.

Old meets new in Melbourne, Australia's second largest city, *left.* Christmas celebrations under the summer skies remind visitors that the country lies in the Southern Hemisphere.

Sydney and its suburbs cover about 4,700 square miles (12,000 square kilometers). Downtown Sydney stands on the south side of Sydney Harbor. East of the downtown area lies a series of parks, including the Royal Botanic Gardens. The parliament house for New South Wales is also in this area. Suburbs spread out in every direction from the city. Two large recreation areas—Royal National Park and Ku-Ring-Gai Chase—lie within 25 miles (40 kilometers) of downtown Sydney.

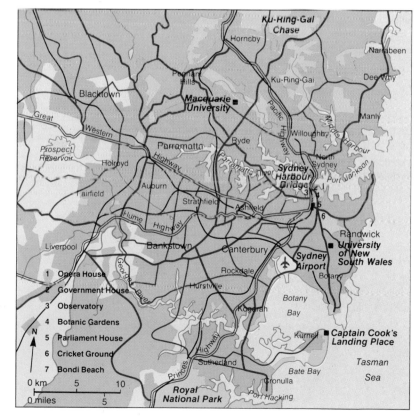

1 Opera House
2 Government House
3 Observatory
4 Botanic Gardens
5 Parliament House
6 Cricket Ground
7 Bondi Beach

History

Australia's first settlers, the ancestors of today's Aborigines, probably reached the continent at least 40,000 years ago. The Europeans discovered Australia much later. They first entered the area during the 1500's, when Portuguese and Spanish explorers landed in New Guinea. These explorers and their successors were searching for a mysterious land they believed lay south of Asia. They called the continent *Terra Australis Incognita,* Latin for *Unknown Southern Land.*

In 1606, a Dutch navigator named Willem Jansz briefly visited what he thought was the coast of New Guinea. Actually, it was the coast of extreme northeastern Australia. Jansz thus became the first European known to sight the continent and land in Australia. Between 1616 and 1636, other Dutch navigators explored Australia's west, southwest, and northwest coasts.

In 1642 and 1643, Abel Janszoon Tasman, a Dutch sea captain, sailed around the continent and briefly visited a land mass that he thought was part of the continent. Actually, it was an island, later named *Tasmania* in his honor. Finally, in 1770, James Cook of the British Royal Navy became the first European to see and explore Australia's fertile east coast. He claimed the region for Great Britain and named it *New South Wales.*

Settlement and exploration

Before the Revolutionary War in America (1775–1783), Britain shipped many convicts to its American colonies to relieve overcrowding in British jails. After the United States won its independence, Britain had to find a new place to send convicts. In 1786, the British decided to start a prison colony in New South Wales. Captain Arthur Phillip was appointed to establish the colony and serve as its governor. He sailed from England in May 1787 with 11 ships carrying 730 convicts, about 200 British soldiers, about 30 soldiers' wives, and a few children.

Phillip's ships reached Botany Bay, on Australia's east coast, in January 1788. He settled his group near a large harbor north of

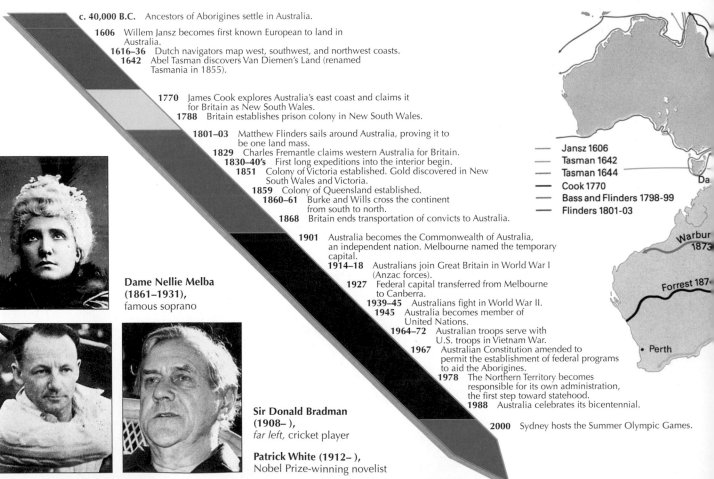

c. 40,000 B.C. Ancestors of Aborigines settle in Australia.

1606 Willem Jansz becomes first known European to land in Australia.

1616–36 Dutch navigators map west, southwest, and northwest coasts.

1642 Abel Tasman discovers Van Diemen's Land (renamed Tasmania in 1855).

1770 James Cook explores Australia's east coast and claims it for Britain as New South Wales.

1788 Britain establishes prison colony in New South Wales.

1801–03 Matthew Flinders sails around Australia, proving it to be one land mass.

1829 Charles Fremantle claims western Australia for Britain.

1830–40's First long expeditions into the interior begin.

1851 Colony of Victoria established. Gold discovered in New South Wales and Victoria.

1859 Colony of Queensland established.

1860–61 Burke and Wills cross the continent from south to north.

1868 Britain ends transportation of convicts to Australia.

1901 Australia becomes the Commonwealth of Australia, an independent nation. Melbourne named the temporary capital.

1914–18 Australians join Great Britain in World War I (Anzac forces).

1927 Federal capital transferred from Melbourne to Canberra.

1939–45 Australians fight in World War II.

1945 Australia becomes member of United Nations.

1964–72 Australian troops serve with U.S. troops in Vietnam War.

1967 Australian Constitution amended to permit the establishment of federal programs to aid the Aborigines.

1978 The Northern Territory becomes responsible for its own administration, the first step toward statehood.

1988 Australia celebrates its bicentennial.

2000 Sydney hosts the Summer Olympic Games.

Dame Nellie Melba (1861–1931), famous soprano

Sir Donald Bradman (1908–), *far left,* cricket player

Patrick White (1912–), Nobel Prize-winning novelist

— Jansz 1606
— Tasman 1642
— Tasman 1644
— Cook 1770
— Bass and Flinders 1798-99
— Flinders 1801-03

Da

Warbur 1873

Forrest 187

• Perth

The Australian *bicentennial,* or 200th anniversary, was celebrated in 1988, *top*. In 1788, British ships reached New South Wales, and the passengers established the first white settlement in Australia.

Botany Bay and thus founded the first white settlement in Australia. This was the beginning of the city of Sydney.

When New South Wales was first settled, no one knew whether Australia consisted of one huge land mass or of two or more large islands. From 1801 to 1803, Matthew Flinders sailed around the continent. He proved the mainland to be one vast land mass.

In 1829, a British sea captain named Charles Fremantle landed on Australia's southwest coast and claimed the entire western part of the continent for Britain. Later that year, a group of about 70 English settlers officially established the colony of Western Australia and founded its capital, Perth. In 1860 and 1861, Robert O'Hara Burke and William Wills became the first white people to cross the continent from south to north.

Becoming a nation

After the explorers came the sheep farmers and the prospectors. The farmers established rich grazing lands and became some of the largest landholders in Australia. With the discovery of Australian gold in the 1850's, the continent's population grew from about 400,000 to more than 1.1 million. In 1868, Britain ended its practice of sending convicts to Australia. As the number of free settlers in Australia grew, so did the colonists' demands for self-government. By the 1890's, all the Australian colonies had been granted self-government.

However, a growing number of Australians believed that the colonies would be better off as a single nation with a unified government. In 1897 and 1898, a federal convention drew up a Constitution for Australia. The people approved it in balloting during 1898 and 1899, and Britain approved it in 1900. On Jan. 1, 1901, the six colonies became the states of a new nation—the Commonwealth of Australia.

— Blaxland 1813
— Hume and Hovell 1824
— Sturt 1829-30
— Mitchell 1835
— Eyre 1840-41
— Leichhardt 1844-45
— Burke and Wills 1860-61
— Stuart 1861-62
— Warburton 1873
— Forrest 1874

Gulf of Carpentaria

Leichhardt 1844-45
Burke and Wills 1860-61
ice
orings
Eyre 1840-41
Mitchell 1835
Sturt 1829-30
aide
Brisbane
Blaxland 1813
Sydney
Botany Bay
Hume and Hovell 1824
Melbourne

Australia, *left,* had its coastline first explored by the Dutch. In 1770, James Cook claimed Australia's east coast for Britain. Later, bold adventurers tried to cross the continent's interior.

Australian and New Zealand troops, *above,* called *Anzacs,* won a reputation for outstanding bravery during World War I. About 59,000 Australians were killed during the war.

Regions and States

Australia has six states and two territories. Canberra, the national capital of Australia, is in the Australian Capital Territory (A.C.T.) in southeast Australia. Planners estimate that only about a third of the A.C.T. is ever likely to be developed, but Canberra is the nation's leading example of large-scale city planning. The economy is dependent on the activities of the national government, which employs about two-thirds of the city's workers.

The Northern Territory occupies almost a sixth of the Australian continent. Although it was granted self-government in 1978, the Northern Territory has not yet been granted state status. The territory is known for its magnificent landscape and its mineral wealth. Nearly half the territory's people live in Darwin, and almost one-fourth of its people are Aborigines.

Queensland, in the northeastern corner of the Australian continent, is the second largest state in Australia. About 40 per cent of the people live in the Brisbane area, and most of the remainder live in the larger cities and towns along the eastern coast.

South Queensland produces large quantities of wheat and other grains, and Queensland leads Australia in the production of beef cattle. Queensland also has productive copper, lead, and zinc mines.

New South Wales, south of Queensland, is the oldest state in Australia and has the largest population. It is also the richest and one of the most developed Australian states.

Most people in New South Wales live in the three main cities—Sydney, Newcastle, and Wollongong. The state has more than 10,000 factories, which manufacture goods such as chemicals, fertilizers, machinery, and raw and processed steel and copper.

Victoria, in the southeastern corner of the Australian continent, is the smallest and most densely populated of the mainland states. Victoria is a highly industrialized, highly urbanized area, and most of its people work in manufacturing and commerce. Melbourne, Victoria's capital, is one of the 50 largest cities in the world. The majority of the state's population and industry are concentrated

Queensland lies within the tropics and subtropics. Some plateau and mountain areas receive a high rainfall and support lush forests.

there. Rich crop- and dairy-farming lands lie in the southeast, while the southwest has extensive grazing lands. In the north, these two areas merge into wheat-farming plains.

Tasmania, the island state of Australia, is the smallest state and is also one of the most beautiful. Many Australians enjoy vacations in Tasmania. Swift rivers rise in the mountains of the central region, and the coastline has many scenic capes and bays. Tasmania's lakes and rivers supply electricity for industry. Most of Australia's petroleum and much of its natural gas come from huge offshore deposits in the Bass Strait, the rough waters that separate Tasmania from the mainland.

South Australia is the third largest state in Australia. It occupies a central position on the southern coast and covers one-eighth of the country. Adelaide, where two-thirds of

Tasmania, *left,* has a variety of scenery and historic relics that attract many tourists.

Perth, *left,* the capital and cultural center of Western Australia, has a high standard of living, a splendid climate, and excellent sporting facilities. Fremantle, just to the south, is the port of Perth.

The Olgas are a group of 30 gigantic, dome-shaped rocks west of Ayers Rock, called *Uluru* by the Aborigines, in the Northern Territory. Many people consider these colorful rocks to be even more spectacular than Uluru.

the state's people live, is an important industrial and cultural center. Although South Australia is the driest state in the country, it produces much of Australia's barley, wheat, wine, and salt, and its iron-ore deposits are a major source of raw materials for the nation's iron and steel industries. Manufacturing industries account for about two thirds of South Australia's economy.

Western Australia, the largest of the six Australian states, occupies the western third of the country but has only about 8 per cent of the people. Large areas of desert and semidesert cover its inland regions. About 70 per cent of the people of Western Australia live in the Perth region, the only large urban area in Western Australia. More than three-quarters of the gold mined in Australia is produced in Western Australia, but iron ore is the state's most important mineral.

People

The great majority of the Australian people belong to the middle class. Most Australians also have similar educational backgrounds and hold similar values and attitudes. The ways of life throughout the country are therefore remarkably uniform. Even the differences between life in the cities and life in rural areas are relatively minor.

Ancestry

Most Australians are European immigrants or descendants of European immigrants. Aborigines make up only about 1 per cent of the population. Traditionally, Australia has relied heavily on immigrants to build up its labor force. Through the years, millions of immigrants have been attracted to Australia by the promise of high-paying jobs.

Australia has admitted about 4-3/4 million immigrants since World War II (1939–1945). Approximately half of the newcomers came from the United Kingdom. Most of the others came from mainland Europe, especially Italy, Greece, Germany, and the Netherlands. Since the 1970's, however, the number of immigrants from New Zealand and Southeast Asia has increased rapidly.

Way of life

About 70 per cent of all Australians live in cities of more than 100,000 people. Most city dwellers live in *suburbs,* the residential areas that extend outward from the central business district. Most families live in single-story houses, each with its own yard and garden. Australian cities have few apartment buildings.

English is Australia's official language. Australian English includes many British terms but differs from British English in certain ways. British settlers had to develop a vocabulary to describe the many unfamiliar animals and plants in their new environment, and, in some cases, they borrowed words from the Aborigines. For example, *kangaroo* and *koala* are Aborigine words. Pioneer settlers in the Australian interior also invented a large, colorful vocabulary. Ranches became known as *stations,* wild horses as *brumbies,* and bucking broncos as *buckjumpers.* Understanding Australia's most famous song,

The Aborigines were the first Australians. Today, some Aborigines live in tribal settlements and preserve traditional ways of life. Many Aborigines lag far behind white Australians in both education and income.

Cricket, an English game played with a bat and ball, is a favorite summer sport in Australia. The Australian national cricket team regularly plays against teams from other countries.

Surf lifesavers stand ready to demonstrate the use of a surf reel as a rescue method at one of Australia's popular *surf carnivals*. Australia was the first country in the world to develop a surf lifesaving movement, which consists of trained voluntary lifesavers who patrol ocean beaches each weekend to make them safe for swimmers. Surf carnivals are colorful and spectacular competitions held by surf lifesaving clubs to promote the public's interest in the lifesaving movement.

"Waltzing Matilda," requires translation of many local terms: a *matilda* is a blanket roll, to *waltz matilda* means "to tramp the roads," a *swagman* is a tramp, and so on.

Each Australian state and the Northern Territory has its own laws concerning education. The federal government regulates education in the rest of the country—that is, the Capital Territory and certain areas, mainly islands, not otherwise assigned to states or territories.

Australian children attend elementary schools for six to eight years, in some cases including a year of kindergarten, depending on the state or territory. Australian secondary schools offer five or six years of education. However, about one-third of the students leave school when they reach the age requirement, and may complete only three or four years of secondary education. Most students who graduate from secondary school go on to a university or college.

The Australian Constitution forbids a state religion and guarantees religious freedom. The great majority of Australians are Christians, but many do not attend church regularly. Roman Catholics make up more than one-quarter of the population.

Outdoor sports are extremely popular in Australia. Many people enjoy skin diving, surfing, swimming, and boating, as well as golf and tennis. Team sports are a national pastime. Australians begin to play team sports in elementary school, and many continue to enjoy them throughout life. The best players may work their way up through local and state competitions and even win a position on one of the national teams. Australia's professional sports teams have large and enthusiastic followings.

A variety of cuisines is available in Australia, *below*. Greek, Italian, and various other European styles of cooking have become increasingly popular as the number of immigrants from those countries has increased. Many Australians have also developed a taste for Chinese, Indonesian, and Vietnamese foods.

The Great Barrier Reef

Along the northeast coast of Australia lies the Great Barrier Reef, the largest group of coral reefs in the world. This chain consists of more than 2,500 reefs and many small islands, and extends for about 1,250 miles (2,010 kilometers). In some sections, it lies more than 100 miles (160 kilometers) from the Australian coast. Other parts lie only about 10 miles (16 kilometers) out.

A special ecosystem

A coral reef is a limestone formation that lies under the sea or just above the surface. The coral that forms the Great Barrier Reef is made up of hardened skeletons of dead water animals called *polyps*. Billions of living coral polyps are attached to the reef. They range in diameter from much less than 1 inch (2.5 centimeters) to 12 inches (30 centimeters). The polyps are extremely colorful, as are the many sea animals that live in the Great Barrier Reef. Together, they create a beautiful sea garden.

The Great Barrier Reef supports about 400 species of polyps, about 1,500 species of fish, and several kinds of birds. Crabs, giant clams, and sea turtles also live on the reef. The warm waters around the reefs and the beauty of the coral formations attract swimmers, skin divers, and tourists from all around the world.

Protecting the reef

The reef region has long been used as a source of food and raw materials. For example, such sea animals as scallops, prawns, and fish are abundant there. The Great Barrier Reef, or parts of it, were explored and used by Aboriginal fishermen and hunters many thousands of years ago. Since the arrival of Europeans in 1788, the reef has supported business ventures. The prospect of finding oil in the region has attracted petroleum companies that want to drill in the area. During the late 1960's, however, public concern grew about damage to the reef from these and other sources.

In 1970, government commissions were established to investigate the risks of oil drilling in Great Barrier Reef waters. Following the investigation, the Australian government made most of the reef a national park. The Great Barrier Reef Park Authority, an Australian government agency, works to protect

An aerial view of the Great Barrier Reef shows the extreme clarity of the warm tropical water. Visitors can get a close-up view of the reefs with scuba and snorkeling equipment, glass-bottomed boats, and underwater observatories.

About 1,500 species of fish find shelter in the hard coral of the Great Barrier Reef, *far right*. Coral reefs harbor more species of fish than any other marine environment. Other animals that live on the reefs include crabs, giant clams, and sea turtles.

A scuba diver, *below,* is attracted to the warm waters and beautiful fan coral formations of the Great Barrier Reef. These corals have strong, flexible skeletons that branch to form a lacy network.

Fringing reefs, *below,* are submerged platforms of living coral animals that extend from the shore into the sea. They surround small tropical islands, such as this one in the Capricorn Group off the Queensland coast.

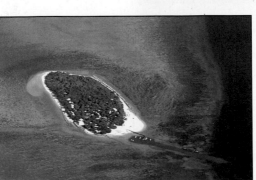

The colorful sea slug, *left,* belongs to the *nudibranch* (sea snails) family. Frilly outgrowths from the body, called *cerata,* are thought to be respiratory organs.

the reef from damage. The government has made it illegal to collect any of the coral, and mining is no longer allowed within the park. In addition, oil drilling is prohibited in the Great Barrier Reef region.

Since the 1960's, the reefs have faced an additional threat—the crown-of-thorns starfish. These starfish feed on living polyps, leaving the skeletons behind. Large numbers of these starfish—sometimes millions of them—can suddenly appear, feed in large groups, and then disappear, having killed up to 95 per cent of the corals on any one reef. Between 1982 and 1984, scientists estimated that about 16 per cent of the Great Barrier Reef was infested. In 1985, they estimated about 2 per cent was infested. Marine scientists are not sure if the outbreaks are natural events or the result of human activity, such as overfishing the natural enemies of the starfish. In the late 1980's, about 50 scientists began an intensive research program on the starfish to determine the cause of the outbreaks.

Austria

Austria is a small, landlocked country in central Europe. It shares boundaries with Switzerland and Liechtenstein to the west, Germany, the Czech Republic, and Slovakia to the north, Hungary to the east, and Slovenia and Italy to the south.

Austria's scenic beauty attracts millions of visitors each year. Skiers enjoy the Austrian Alps and a host of other winter sports. In addition to the majestic snow-capped Alps and their foothills, which stretch across the western, southern, and central parts of the country, Austria has many crystal-clear lakes, and thick forests cover much of the land. Many of Austria's picturesque villages nestle in the broad, green valleys.

People also come to Austria to enjoy the many impressive sights and sounds of one of the great cultural centers of Europe. Austria has made outstanding contributions in the fields of architecture, literature, painting, and, above all, music. Joseph Haydn, Wolfgang Amadeus Mozart, Johann Strauss, and Johann Strauss, Jr., are among the great composers Austria has produced, and the country's musical tradition continues today, as thousands flock to its concerts, operas, and music festivals.

Vienna, Austria's capital and largest city, is also the country's leading cultural, economic, and political center. About 20 per cent of Austria's people live in Vienna. The city's historical section contains many art galleries, churches, theaters, and other beautiful buildings. Many people gather at the sidewalk cafes to enjoy the view and sample some of the delicious pastries and coffee with whipped cream for which Vienna is famous.

Although Vienna lost much of its political importance after World War I (1914-1918), its many landmarks, including the Schönbrunn Palace, recall Austria's former position as one of the most powerful countries in Europe. Austria was the center of a huge empire ruled by the royal Habsburg family from the 1200's until the empire collapsed in 1918. Austria then became a republic, and a long period of economic difficulty and political unrest followed.

By the early 1950's, however, industry had increased, and Austria's economy began to recover. The country also achieved political stability. Today, as a neutral nation, Austria often serves as a meeting place where representatives of different countries gather to exchange ideas. For example, Vienna hosted meetings of the Strategic Arms Limitations Talks (SALT) between the United States and what is now the former Soviet Union. In addition, the Austrian capital is home to several United Nations agencies. In a nationwide election held in June 1994, Austrians voted to join the European Union (EU). The country became an EU member on Jan. 1, 1995.

Austria Today

Austria is a federal republic. Its national government, which was formed after World War II, is based on the democratic Constitution adopted in 1920.

The president, Austria's head of state, is elected by the people to a six-year term. The president's duties are largely ceremonial and include appointing ambassadors and acting as commander in chief of the armed forces.

The chancellor, or prime minister, and Cabinet run the Austrian government. The president appoints the chancellor, who is usually the leader of the political party with the most seats in the *Nationalrat* (National Council).

The chancellor selects the Cabinet members to head government departments. Government policies formed by the chancellor and the Cabinet must be approved by Parliament.

Austria's Parliament is made up of two houses: the Nationalrat, the lower house, and the *Bundesrat* (Federal Council), the upper house. The 183 members of the Nationalrat are elected by the people, and the 64 members of the Bundesrat are elected by the country's nine *Landtags* (provincial legislatures).

The land

Austria's six main land regions are the Granite Plateau, the Eastern Forelands, the Alpine Forelands, the Northern Limestone Alps, the Central Alps, and the Southern Limestone Alps. Austria's alpine regions have a beautiful scenic landscape of rolling hills, forested mountain slopes, and rugged peaks, dotted with large glaciers and sparkling lakes. The Granite Plateau in northern Austria is a region of hills and mountains that consist mostly of granite. Dense forests cover part of this area.

Most of Austria's land is too mountainous for raising crops. The country's chief agricultural area—a lowland called the Vienna Basin—is located in the northern part of the Eastern Forelands. Vienna, Austria's capital and largest city, stands in this region.

The people

Most Austrians live in the Eastern Forelands and in the area just south of the Danube River. More than 60 per cent of the people live in urban areas, such as the major cities of Vienna, Graz, Innsbruck, Linz, and Salzburg.

The people of Austria enjoy good food. A Viennese dish called *Wiener schnitzel*

FACT BOX

COUNTRY

Official name: Republik Oesterreich (Republic of Austria)
Capital: Vienna
Terrain: In the west and south, mostly mountains (Alps); along the eastern and northern margins, mostly flat or gently sloping
Area: 32,378 sq. mi. (83,858 km²)

Climate: Temperate; continental, cloudy; cold winters with frequent rain in lowlands and snow in mountains; cool summers with occasional showers
Main rivers: Danube, Drava, Inn, Enns, Mur
Highest elevation: Grossglockner, 12,457 ft. (3,797 m)
Lowest elevation: Neusiedler See, 377 ft. (115 m)

GOVERNMENT

Form of government: Federal republic
Head of state: President
Head of government: Chancellor
Administrative areas: 9 bundeslaender (states)
Legislature: Bundesversammlung (Federal Assembly) consisting of Bundesrat (Federal Council) with 64 members serving four- or six-year terms and the Nationalrat (National Council) with 183 members serving four-year terms

Court system: Oberster Gerichtshof (Supreme Judicial Court); Verwaltungsgerichtshof (Administrative Court); Verfassungsgerichtshof (Constitutional Court)
Armed forces: 40,500 troops

PEOPLE

Estimated 2002 population: 8,255,000
Population growth: 0.25%
Population density: 255 persons per sq. mi. (98 per km²)
Population distribution: 65% urban, 35% rural
Life expectancy in years:
Male: 75
Female: 81
Doctors per 1,000 people: 3.0
Percentage of age-appropriate population enrolled in the following educational levels:
Primary: 100
Secondary: 96
Further: 50
Language spoken: German

The Republic of Austria, *map above,* is divided into nine provinces: Burgenland, Carinthia, Lower Austria, Salzburg, Styria, Tyrol, Upper Austria, Vienna, and Vorarlberg. About 75 per cent of the country is covered by mountains, and much of the remainder consists of rolling hills and broad valleys. Most of Austria's people live in the eastern part of the country just south of the Danube River.

(breaded veal cutlet) has become a favorite in many countries, and the delicious cakes and pastries created by Austrian bakers are world renowned. Austrians also love the outdoors, and they enjoy a variety of outdoor sports throughout the year in the country's many forests, lakes, and mountains.

Religions:
 Roman Catholic 78%
 Protestant 5%
 Muslim and other 17%

TECHNOLOGY

Radios per 1,000 people: 753

Televisions per 1,000 people: 536

Computers per 1,000 people: 276.5

ECONOMY

Currency: Euro

Gross national income (GNI) in 2000: $204.5 billion U.S.

Real annual growth rate (1999–2000): 3.0%

GNI per capita (2000): $25,220 U.S.

Balance of payments (2000): -$5,205 million U.S.

Goods exported: Machinery and equipment, paper and paperboard, metal goods, chemicals, iron and steel; textiles, foodstuffs

Goods imported: Machinery and equipment, chemicals, metal goods, oil and oil products; foodstuffs

Trading partners: European Union, United States, Hungary, Switzerland

Austria's Parliament Building, *above,* in Vienna, was completed in 1883. The building was designed in the classical Greek style, with rows of impressive stone columns. A 13-foot (4-meter) statue of Athena, the Greek goddess of warfare and wisdom, stands in front of the Parliament Building. The clock tower atop Vienna's City Hall, or *Rathaus,* rises in the background.

History

Celtic tribes moved into central and eastern Austria around 400 B.C. By 15 B.C., the Romans controlled the country south of the Danube. After the Roman Empire collapsed in A.D. 476, many different peoples invaded Austria.

Finally, in 955, Austria came under the rule of Otto I, the king of Germany. In 962, the pope crowned Otto emperor of what later became known as the Holy Roman Empire. German emperors ruled the Holy Roman Empire until it ended in 1806.

The Habsburg Empire

The Babenberg family controlled northeastern Austria from 976 until 1246, when the last Babenberg duke died without an heir and the king of Bohemia seized the region. In 1273, a member of the Swiss Habsburg family became Holy Roman Emperor Rudolf I. Rudolf claimed the Babenberg lands and defeated the Bohemian king at the Battle of Marchfeld in 1278.

The Habsburgs lost the Holy Roman crown in the 1300's, but a Habsburg was once again elected emperor in 1438. From then on, the Habsburgs held the title almost continuously.

In the 1400's and 1500's, the Habsburg emperors acquired new lands, including Bohemia and Hungary, but their authority was shaken by the Protestant Reformation in the 1500's and the Thirty Years' War of 1618 to 1648. During these centuries, Austria emerged as the chief state in the empire. The Ottoman Turks tried to drive Austria from Hungary and made two unsuccessful attacks on Vienna, but they were defeated in the late 1600's.

In 1740, Empress Maria Theresa also fought to maintain her possessions. When the fighting ended in 1748, Maria Theresa lost Silesia to Prussia.

In 1806, after suffering several defeats in the Napoleonic Wars of the late 1700's and early 1800's, Emperor Francis II was forced to dissolve the Holy Roman Empire.

During the 1800's, revolutions broke out across Europe. Austria's minister of foreign affairs, Prince Klemens von Metternich,

Empress Maria Theresa of Austria, *right,* was one of Europe's most powerful rulers during the second half of the 1700's.

400 B.C. Celtic tribes occupy Austria.
15 B.C. The Romans control Austria south of the Danube River.
A.D. 100's Invasions by tribes from the north weaken Roman control.
976 The Babenberg family controls northeastern Austria.
1156 Vienna becomes capital.

1278 Rudolf I, a Habsburg, begins to acquire the Babenberg lands for his family.

1438-1806 The Habsburgs hold the title of Holy Roman emperor almost continuously.
1453 The Duchy of Austria becomes the Archduchy of Austria.

1683 Austria defeats the Turks at Vienna.

1740 Maria Theresa inherits her father's lands and the War of the Austrian Succession begins.
1740-1748 Maria Theresa loses Silesia to Prussia in the War of the Austrian Succession.
1806 Holy Roman Empire is dissolved.
1814-1815 At the end of the Napoleonic Wars, the Congress of Vienna returns to Austria most of the land it had lost during the wars.
1848 Revolutionaries in Vienna demand the establishment of a constitutional government.
1867 Austria-Hungary is established.
1914-1918 Austria-Hungary is defeated in World War I.
1920 Austria adopts a democratic Constitution.
1938 Adolf Hitler unites Austria with Germany.
1939-1945 The Allies defeat Germany in World War II.
1945-1955 The Allies occupy Austria.
1955 Austria agrees to be permanently neutral in international military affairs.
1987 The Socialist Party forms a new coalition with the People's Party.
1995 Austria joins the European Union.

Prince Klemens von Metternich, *left,* (1773-1859)

Johann Strauss, Jr., *far left,* (1825-1899)

Emperor Francis Joseph, *left,* (1830-1916)

94

tried to suppress all revolutionary movements in the Austrian Empire, but in 1848, revolutionaries demanded the establishment of a constitutional government and Metternich fled.

Although the Austrian army had put down all revolts by 1851, the empire weakened in the years that followed. Austria lost its land in Italy to Italian and French forces, and Prussia replaced Austria as the leader of the German states in Europe. In 1867, Austrian Emperor Francis Joseph was forced to give equal status to his Hungarian holdings and create the Dual Monarchy of Austria-Hungary.

World wars

In the late 1800's and early 1900's, Slavs in Austria-Hungary demanded the right to govern themselves. Then, in 1914, Gavrilo Princip, a member of the Slavic nationalist movement in Serbia, killed Archduke Francis Ferdinand, the heir to the Austro-Hungarian throne. In response, Austria-Hungary declared war on Serbia, thus starting World War I. Germany and other countries joined Austria-Hungary in fighting the Allies—Britain, France, Russia, and, eventually, the United States.

In 1918, Austria-Hungary was defeated. The last Habsburg emperor was overthrown and the empire was split into several countries. Austria became a republic. It adopted a democratic Constitution in 1920, but conflicting political parties struggled for supremacy. In 1934, members of the Austrian Nazi Party killed Chancellor Engelbert Dollfuss, and in 1938, German troops seized Austria. Adolf Hitler united Austria and Germany and led both countries into World War II in 1939.

After Germany was defeated in 1945, Austria was occupied by the Allies, and a government based on Austria's 1920 Constitution was established. In 1955, the Allies ended their occupation with the understanding that Austria would remain permanently neutral in international military affairs.

Since the 1950's, Austria's economy has grown steadily, and the country has been politically stable. As a neutral nation, Austria has been the site of many international diplomatic meetings.

The defeat of the Turks at Vienna in 1683 is depicted in the painting above. An army led by Austria's Duke of Lorraine conquered a Turkish army of more than 200,000 men. Austria's success was seen as a victory of Christianity over Islam.

The Habsburg empire grew from lands acquired in the late 1200's by Rudolf I, *map below*. By 1526, the Habsburg family had taken control of large parts of Bohemia and Hungary. Over the next four centuries, the borders and dominant areas within the empire shifted. At the end of World War I, the empire ended and the republic of Austria was born.

Original Habsburg territory 1525
Habsburg acquisitions 1526
Austrian empire 1815-59
Austria 1919

PRUSSIA
RUSSIAN EMPIRE
POLAND
SAXONY
SILESIA
BOHEMIA
GALICIA
BAVARIA
MORAVIA
Dnestr
VORARLBERG
Vienna
BUCOVINA
AUSTRIA
Budapest
TYROL
CARINTHIA
HUNGARY
LOMBARDY
CARNIOLA
TRANSYLVANIA
VENICE
CROATIA
SLAVONIA
BANAT
PARMA
ISTRIA
WALLACHIA
MODENA
DALMATIA
BOSNIA
SERBIA
Danube
TUSCANY
BULGARIA
CORSICA
PAPAL STATES
OTTOMAN EMPIRE

South and West Provinces

1 Vorarlberg
2 Tyrol
3 Salzburg
4 Carinthia

Several high ranges of the Alps, separated by beautiful river valleys, cross southern and western Austria. The southern and western provinces consist of Vorarlberg, Tyrol, Salzburg, and Corinthia. Innsbruck and Salzburg are the chief cities.

Vorarlberg

Vorarlberg is a small province in the western corner of Austria. Vorarlberg's ancient capital, Bregenz, is a charming town on the eastern shore of Lake Constance. Summer festivals held on the lake attract many visitors each year.

Much of the land in Vorarlberg is too mountainous for raising crops, but dairy animals graze in the high areas and yield large quantities of milk and cheese. Skilled craftworkers in the region produce fine embroidery, and other goods include watches, clocks, metals, chemicals, and pharmaceuticals. Tourism is also a leading industry in the province, and sports centers draw visitors to the province the year around.

The people of Vorarlberg, who speak a German dialect known as *Alamannic,* have formed close relationships with the Alamannic-speaking populations of the Allgäu region of Bavaria in southwestern Germany, the Lake Constance area of eastern Switzerland, and Liechtenstein. As a result, the province has established close economic ties with these regions, and many people from Vorarlberg commute across international borders every day to work in Liechtenstein or St. Gallen, Switzerland.

Tyrol

After World War I, the region of Tyrol was divided into two parts: Northern Tyrol, which was given to Austria, and Southern Tyrol, which was given to Italy. Austrian Tyrol, or Northern Tyrol, lies in the mountainous western part of the country.

One of the most popular holiday areas in Europe, Tyrol offers superb facilities for summer and winter sports. The Alps cover most of the province, and Grossglockner, the highest mountain in Austria, rises

Hohensalzburg Castle, *above,* overlooks the old section of the city of Salzburg. The castle, which is more than 900 years old, was rebuilt in the 1500's.

12,457 feet (3,797 meters) in this region. The wide, fertile Inn River Valley extends over the northern part of Tyrol.

Innsbruck, the capital city of the province, lies in the Alps north of Brenner Pass. This Alpine pass links northern Europe with the Mediterranean countries. Innsbruck's many beautiful buildings include the Hofkirche, a church that contains the tomb of Maximilian I, the Holy Roman emperor from 1493 to 1519.

Innsbruck, *above,* the old provincial capital of Tyrol, retains many of its medieval buildings, narrow streets, and tall houses. It is home to a university and several industries.

The province is Austria's favorite holiday destination, and tourism is Tyrol's main economic activity. Other industries in the region produce leather, processed foods, stained glass, and textiles.

Salzburg and Carinthia

The province of Salzburg lies in the valley of the Salzach River. The region produces salt (for which it is named), as well as leather, paper, textiles, and timber. Agricultural activities in the area include dairy farming and horse breeding.

Salzburg is also the cultural heart of central Austria. Its capital city, also named Salzburg, is the birthplace of Wolfgang Amadeus Mozart, one of the world's greatest composers. Annual music and theater festivals draw people from all over the world to this beautiful city on the Salzach River. Salzburg's many magnificent buildings include Hohensalzburg Castle, set high on a hill overlooking the historical section of the city, and the Residenz, once the palace of Salzburg's prince bishops, in the heart of the city. Other important buildings include Salzburg's baroque cathedral, built between 1614 and 1628, and Mozart's birthplace. Carinthia lies in south-central Austria in a sheltered basin surrounded by mountains. The region is known as the country's "sun terrace" because of its comparatively warm climate. Forests cover more than half of the province.

Carinthia's warm summers attract numerous visitors to its resort areas, including beautiful Lake Wörther. Another popular attraction is the splendid Schloss Hochosterwitz, a castle perched on a cliff near St. Veit.

Tourism plays a major part in the local economy, but agriculture, dairy farming, forestry, mining, and paper production are also important industries. The small town of Ferlach is famous for its manufacture of high-quality hunting rifles.

The church of St. Maria Wörth, *left,* lies on the Wörther See, the largest of the Alpine lakes of Corinthia.

North and East Provinces

1 Upper Austria
2 Lower Austria
3 Vienna
4 Burgenland
5 Styria

The Wachau Valley, *right,* stretching along the Danube between Melk and Krems in Lower Austria, is widely considered to be the most beautiful part of the Danube. The Bohemian Forest lies to the northwest, and the Dunkelsteiner Forest to the southeast. The region contains quaint old towns surrounded by vineyards and overlooked by historic castles.

The Danube River flows across a varied area of hills, mountains, and valleys in northeastern Austria. The north and east provinces include Upper Austria, Lower Austria, Vienna, Burgenland, and Styria. The chief cities are Vienna, Graz, and Linz.

Upper Austria

Upper Austria, a province in northern Austria, is spanned by the Danube River. Linz, its capital, is Austria's third largest city, and it is the country's most important heavy industrial center. Manufactured items include ball bearings, engineering products, steel, and vehicles.

The province also contains many natural resources. Upper Austria's farmland yields cereals, fruit, potatoes, and sugar beets, while the Alpine foothills support livestock production, and large forests cover the higher elevations. The ancient salt mines in the lake district of Salzkammergut are still productive, and the Danube and Enns rivers generate power for large hydroelectric stations.

Upper Austria's natural beauty also contributes to the economy. Tourists flock to the province's Alpine region, and many people visit the area's spas and health resorts.

Lower Austria and Vienna

Lower Austria, the country's largest province, lies in the northeastern corner of Austria, and completely surrounds the small province of Vienna. Vienna is Austria's capital and largest city as well as its smallest province in area. The two provinces were separated in 1922, but Vienna is still the focal point of both. It is Austria's chief industrial city and a leading European cultural center.

The main towns in Lower Austria include St. Pölten (its capital), Wiener Neustadt, and Baden. The province has one of the most varied landscapes in Austria, ranging from high mountains and wooded hills to fertile valleys and grasslands. Due to efficient agricultural methods, the available farmland yields sugar

beets, wheat, and wine grapes. Farmers also raise livestock.

Heavy industry in the region south of the fertile Vienna Basin includes chemical plants, iron and steel works, and textile- and food-processing industries. A number of large hydroelectric power stations lie along the Danube, which runs through the middle of the province. Tourism is also an important industry in Lower Austria, and resorts in the province's eastern Alpine region attract many visitors.

Burgenland

Burgenland, the most easterly of Austria's provinces, is composed of lands that shifted between Austria to Hungary from the 1400's to 1647, when Hungary took control. Austria acquired the territory from Hungary in 1921, when four regions were united to form Burgenland. However, one of the regions was soon returned to Hungary.

The province's landscape includes Alpine foothills as well as the fringes of the Upper Hungarian Lowlands, a popular vacation area. The picturesque castles and

The Benedictine Abbey of Melk, *above,* stands high above the banks of the Danube River in Lower Austria. Built between 1702 and 1738, the abbey occupies the former site of an ancient castle.

Iron miners have worked in the Erzberg, near Eisenerz in Styria, since the Middle Ages. The Erzberg has one of the largest iron ore deposits in Europe.

Wilhering Abbey, *right,* has an ornate interior with superb frescoes that date from the 1700's. The abbey, which stands near Linz on the banks of the Danube, was founded in 1146.

fortresses that line Neusiedler Lake, the lowest point in Austria, also attract many visitors.

Much of the province lies in the Vienna Basin, whose fertile soil helps make Burgenland the country's chief agricultural area. Farmers in the area grow corn, fruit, grapes, sugar beets, and vegetables. Even the industries in the province — sugar refining and canning — reflect its agricultural importance.

Styria

Styria, in the southeast, is Austria's second largest province. The area has a variety of landscapes and climates, ranging from the chilly Alpine regions of the north and central parts of the province to the warm, sunny plains of the south and west. Graz, which lies on the Mur River, is the capital of Styria and Austria's second largest city. The city contains many historic buildings, including the Charles Francis University, which dates from 1586, and a cathedral built in the 1400's.

Grapes, corn, and wheat are grown in Styria's fertile Alpine foothills, and dairy animals graze on the higher Alpine pastures. The timber industry flourishes in the thickly forested mountainous regions. Iron ore deposits mined from the Erzberg (Ore Mountain) near Eisenerz provide raw materials for the area's iron and steel works. Styria's rivers are harnessed as a source of hydroelectric power.

Economy

Austria's economy was brought to a standstill as a result of World War II. After the war, with aid from the United States and other Western nations, the Austrian government bought up certain key industries, including coal and metal mining, electric power production, iron and steel production, and oil drilling and refining. Since the early 1950's, Austria has become increasingly industrialized, and its economy has grown steadily. Today, Austria is a prosperous country with little unemployment.

Austria's leading manufacturing activities are the production of metals, such as iron and steel, and metal products, including automobiles and other motor vehicles. Other major manufactured products include chemical products, electrical equipment, processed foods and beverages, and textiles and clothing. In addition, many smaller factories and workshops produce fine handicrafts, such as glassware, jewelry, needlework, porcelain objects, and woodcarvings.

Service industries

Service industries also make an important contribution to the economy, providing about 60 per cent of the total value of Austria's annual economic production, and employing about 60 per cent of the country's workers. Wholesale and retail trade form the most important service industry in terms of value of production. Other leading service industries include communications, finance, government, transportation, and utilities.

Tourism is also important to Austria's economy, and the nation is one of Europe's most popular vacation spots. Sports centers in the Alps attract many winter vacationers, particularly skiers, and the lake resorts in central Austria are popular in the summer. In addition, many people come to Austria to enjoy the museums and concert halls of Vienna, as well as the summer music festivals held throughout the country.

Agriculture and natural resources

By the 1970's, the development of manufacturing and service industries resulted in

The Danube River, *left,* shown here flowing through Linz, is a major shipping route for trade between Austria and nearby countries. Passenger vessels also travel on the Danube. Most of Austria's large factories are located in the valleys of the Danube and other rivers.

Most farms in Austria are small, and all are privately owned, *left*. Some farmers—unable to earn enough from agricultural production—make extra money by opening their houses to tourists during the summer.

Wine grapes are cultivated in the warmer eastern provinces of Lower Austria, Burgenland, and Styria, *right*. More than half of Austria's grapes are grown along the Danube Valley northwest of Vienna on steep, terraced vineyards.

Skiers from many countries flock to Innsbruck, Kitzbühel, and other superb ski areas in the Austrian Alps, *left*. Austria's booming tourist industry adds more than $1 billion a year to the country's income.

a sharp decrease in the number of people employed in agriculture. Nevertheless, Austrian farmers today supply more than 75 per cent of the nation's food. Although only about 20 per cent of the land is suitable for farming, modern machinery and farming methods have greatly increased production.

While the heart of Austria's cropland is the Vienna Basin, farms are found in every province. Dairy farming and livestock are the main sources of farm income, producing all the eggs, meat, and milk needed by the people. Austria's farmers also grow all of the country's potatoes and sugar beets

and most of its barley, oats, rye, and wheat. Other farm crops grown in Austria include apples, corn, grapes, hay, hops, and vegetables. Farm animals graze in mountainous areas, where the ground is too rugged and the climate too cold for crops.

Although Austria is rich in mineral resources, many deposits are low-grade or too small to be profitably mined. The coal mines in Styria, for example, mainly yield a low-grade coal called *lignite*. As a result, Austria must import high-quality coal, as well as petroleum and natural gas.

On the other hand, Austria is one of the world's leading producers of magnesite and graphite. In addition, Austria's forests, which cover about 40 per cent of the country, provide plentiful timber, paper, and other products. Swift-flowing rivers, perhaps the country's most important natural resource, provide energy for the hydroelectric power stations that produce most of the nation's electricity.

A Musical Nation

Austria's strong musical tradition dates back more than 200 years. Many great composers, such as Joseph Haydn, Wolfgang Amadeus Mozart, and Franz Schubert were born in Austria, and during the 1700's and 1800's, Vienna in particular became an important center for the German-speaking music world. Ludwig van Beethoven, Johannes Brahms, Haydn, Mozart, Schubert, and Johann Strauss all lived in Vienna.

Plaques and memorials throughout the country testify to Austria's glorious musical past. In Vienna, where Haydn spent the last years of his life, visitors can see the Haydn Museum. Haydn developed the symphony and helped make it one of the most important forms of musical composition. Haydn and Mozart, who is also honored in Vienna, were the leading composers of the classical period of music, from the mid-1700's to the early 1800's. The rooms in Vienna where Mozart composed one of his operas, *The Marriage of Figaro* (1786), are open to the public, and Mozart's birthplace in Salzburg also attracts music enthusiasts from all over the world.

Of course, Austria's composers are best remembered through their enchanting music, and the pleasure of relaxing at a Viennese sidewalk cafe is often enhanced by the accompanying strains of a Strauss waltz. The beautiful songs of Schubert, Gustav Mahler, and other great Austrian composers are regularly broadcast over Austrian radio.

The tradition in the 1900's

Austria's Arnold Schoenberg became one of the most revolutionary composers of the early 1900's. He developed a new system of composition called the *twelve-tone technique* and influenced many other composers, including fellow-Austrians Alban Berg and Anton Webern.

Today, the country continues to make important musical contributions. The Vienna Boys' Choir, Vienna Philharmonic Orchestra, Vienna State Opera, and Vienna Symphony Orchestra have won international fame, and Austria has many fine

The **Vienna State Opera House,** *right,* is internationally renowned for its impressive staging of operas and ballets.

Dancers at the Concordia Ball, *above,* twirl to the strains of a romantic Strauss waltz. The ball is a major event in Viennese high society.

music schools, such as the Academy of Music in Vienna, which draws students from all over the world. The Vienna State Opera House presents operas to packed houses almost every evening for 10 months of the year, and enthusiastic crowds throng Austria's many music festivals, which are held nearly all year-round.

Music festivals

Every year in May and June, Vienna hosts the Vienna Festival, a celebration of music, art, and theater. However, the emphasis is on music, and the city's concert halls are filled with the sounds of Austria's favorite composers. Opera is also highlighted at the festival in superb performances at the State Opera House and the Volksoper.

Festivals in Salzburg take place throughout the year. At the annual summer

Street musicians add a colorful note in many Austrian cities. Traveling gypsy musicians and struggling young music students entertain passers-by with everything from folk songs to classical music.

Salzburg Festival, a great musical and theatrical event, performances featuring works by Mozart are presented in the converted stables and riding school of the Archbishops of Salzburg. Another festival house was carved into the face of a mountain behind the stables. Other festivals include Mozart Week, which is held in January, and the Easter Music Festival, held during Easter week.

Music festivals also take place in other cities and towns throughout Austria. At the summer festival in Bregenz, concerts are performed on a floating stage on Lake Constance; a festival in Linz honors the works of Anton Bruckner, an Austrian composer of the middle and late 1800's who once lived in that city; and Innsbruck stages the Tyrolean Summer Festival. Classical music offerings are presented in Innsbruck's concert halls, while brass bands, folk music, and dances can often be enjoyed outdoors.

The simple table and chair at which Mozart worked are displayed at the Mozarteum, a music academy in Salzburg *below.* Mozart composed his opera *The Magic Flute* in 1791, the year he died in poverty in Vienna.

Salzburg's Getreidegasse, *right,* the street where Mozart was born, attracts many visitors.

Vienna

Vienna, Austria's capital city, lies in the northeastern part of the country on the south bank of the Danube River. The city's location at the intersection of a number of trade routes helped its growth. The Habsburgs made Vienna their capital in 1273, and the city's economic and political importance grew rapidly thereafter. Vienna was badly damaged during World War II, but the Viennese rebuilt almost all of the city's landmarks, and the city regained much of its former spirit and wealth.

A modern city

Today, Vienna is Austria's chief industrial city. Its industries manufacture chemicals, clothing, leatherware, medicine, and radio and television products. The city also hosts several international agencies, including a United Nations (UN) center that serves as a conference site and provides office space for some UN agencies.

Vienna is also considered one of the leading cultural centers in Europe. During the 1700's and 1800's, the city was a renowned center of literature, music, and science. A number of famous composers, scientists, and writers made their home in the city, among them Ludwig van Beethoven, Sigmund Freud, and Hugo von Hofmannsthal.

Today, tourists come from around the world to enjoy the city's cultural attractions. Vienna has one of the greatest collections of art treasures in Europe, showcased in such museums and art galleries as the Albertina and the Museum of Art History. Viennese opera houses, such as the State Opera House, and major theaters, such as the Burgtheater, all have worldwide reputations. The city's orchestras, including the Vienna Symphony Orchestra and the Vienna Philharmonic, have also won international fame. Throughout the summer, the city offers ballet and opera performances, concerts, and musical festivals.

Architectural landmarks

Vienna has also preserved most of its architectural treasures. Many of the city's historic buildings and landmarks as well as its most fashionable shopping districts are in the old "Inner City" section in central Vienna.

St. Stephen's Cathedral, with its high church tower, stands at the heart of the Inner City. Several blocks west is the Hofburg, a palace that combines the modern with the medieval. The royal apartments of the Hofburg, occupied by Austria's rulers for more than 600 years, are now the official residence of the president of Austria. Other buildings in the Hofburg include the Imperial Library, several museums, and the Spanish Riding School where the famous Lipizzan horses are trained. Nearby are two of Vienna's most beautiful parks—the Burggarten and the Volksgarten, which is well known for its roses.

A band of streets called the Ringstrassen encircles the Inner City. Some of Vienna's most impressive public buildings line these streets, including the Museum of Art History, the City Hall, the Opera House, the

Lipizzan horses learn to perform graceful jumping and dancing feats at the Spanish Riding School in the Hofburg. These beautiful show horses have been trained at the Viennese school for more than 400 years.

The south tower of St. Stephen's Cathedral is one of the highest church towers in the world at 446 feet (136 meters). Visitors can climb 312 steps to a chamber at the top of the tower and enjoy a magnificent view of Vienna's cobbled streets, churches, and palaces.

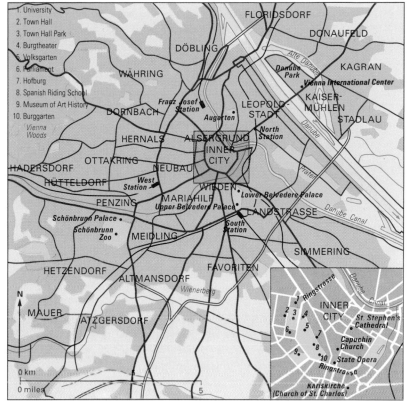

Map legend:
1. University
2. Town Hall
3. Town Hall Park
4. Burgtheater
5. Volksgarten
6. Parliament
7. Hofburg
8. Spanish Riding School
9. Museum of Art History
10. Burggarten

Vienna, *above,* covers about 160 square miles (415 square kilometers). Many of the city's most famous landmarks stand in its central section—the Inner City. The Schönbrunn Palace, with its gardens and zoo, and the Vienna Woods lie near the outskirts of the city.

Cakes and pastries tempt customers in a Konditorei, or Viennese pastry shop. Many people enjoy gathering at sidewalk cafes in the Inner City to drink coffee, eat cake, and watch the world go by.

Parliament Building, and the Stock Exchange. These buildings date from the second half of the 1800's.

Several important buildings, such as the Karlskirche (Church of St. Charles) and the Belvedere Palace, lie outside the Ringstrassen in the older suburban districts of the city. These structures rank among the finest existing examples of *baroque* architecture, a highly decorative style of the 1600's and 1700's.

The Schönbrunn Palace, another splendid baroque building, stands at the southwestern edge of the city. The Schönbrunn Zoo, in the palace grounds was built in 1752 and ranks as the world's oldest zoo. A long park called the Prater lies north of the Danube. In the Prater is an amusement park with a famous Ferris wheel. Instead of seats for two people, the rim of the Ferris has large enclosed cabins, each of which can carry dozens of people. The Vienna Woods line the western edge of the city.

Azerbaijan

In 1991, Azerbaijan declared itself an independent country and a member of the Commonwealth of Independent States (CIS). Azerbaijan was formerly a republic of the now-defunct Soviet Union.

Azerbaijan was under the strict control of the Soviet central government until the late 1980's, when popular opposition groups demanded greater control of the republic's own affairs. In the midst of political upheaval in the Soviet government following an attempted coup in August 1991, Azerbaijan declared its independence.

Farmers in Azerbaijan grow such crops as corn, cotton, fruits, rice, tea, tobacco, vegetables, and walnuts. In the north, Azerbaijani herders graze their livestock on the pastures of the mighty Caucasus Mountains. The waters of the Caspian Sea provide large catches of carp and sturgeon, which are processed into caviar and canned products.

However, Azerbaijan's chief source of wealth is the oil that comes from rich deposits on the Apsheron Peninsula. Baku, the capital of Azerbaijan, is now one of the world's major oil-producing regions. Other mineral resources include iron and aluminum ores and cobalt.

In addition to its oil deposits, Baku is also known for its beautiful historic buildings.

Azerbaijan lies on the western shore of the Caspian Sea. The lowlands of the River Kur and its tributary, the Aras, cover most of the republic.

Often called *the pearl of the Caspian Sea,* the city boasts a well-preserved ancient town known as the Citadel, where many architectural masterpieces from the Middle Ages have been carefully preserved. Along a maze of narrow streets and blind alleys can be found the majestic tower of Kyz Kalasy (the Maiden's Tower), the Synyk Kala minaret, and the palace of the Shirvan Shahs.

FACT BOX

COUNTRY

Official name: Azarbaycan Respublikasi (Azerbaijani Republic)
Capital: Baku
Terrain: Large, flat Kur-Araz Ovaligi (Kura-Araks Lowland), much of it below sea level, with Great Caucasus Mountains to the north, Qarabag Yaylasi (Karabakh Upland) in west; Baku lies on Abseron Yasaqligi (Apsheron Peninsula) that juts into Caspian Sea

Area: 33,436 sq. mi. (86,600 km²)
Climate: Dry, semiarid steppe
Main rivers: Aras, Kur
Highest elevation: Mt. Bazardyuzyu, 14,652 ft. (4,466 m)
Lowest elevation: Caspian Sea, 92 ft. (28 m) below sea level

GOVERNMENT

Form of government: Republic
Head of state: President
Head of government: Prime minister
Administrative areas: 59 rayonlar (rayons), 11 saharlar (cities), 1 muxtar respublika (autonomous republic)

Legislature: Milli Mejlis (National Assembly) with 125 members serving five-year terms
Court system: Supreme Court
Armed forces: 69,900 troops

PEOPLE

Estimated 2002 population: 7,854,000
Population growth: 0.27%
Population density: 235 persons per sq. mi. (91 per km²)
Population distribution: 52% urban, 48% rural
Life expectancy in years: Male: 59 Female: 68
Doctors per 1,000 people: 3.6
Percentage of age-appropriate population enrolled in the following educational levels: Primary: 103* Secondary: 84 Further: 22

Azerbaijan's location between the Caucasus Mountains and the Caspian Sea has made it a strategically important area since ancient times. Over the years, Mongols, Persians, and Turks took control of Azerbaijan. Then, in the late 1820's, after a successful war with Persia, Russia made Azerbaijan part of its empire. In 1920, Communists gained power in Azerbaijan and established a Soviet republic. In 1922, Azerbaijan joined with Soviet Armenia and Georgia to form the Transcaucasian Federation. This federation was one of the four republics that formed the Soviet Union later that year.

In 1923, the mainly Armenian district of Nagorno-Karabakh became an autonomous region within Azerbaijan. The region of Nakhichevan was incorporated into Azerbaijan in 1924.

The Azerbaijani people, who make up about 80 per cent of the population, are of mainly Turkish ancestry and follow the religion of Islam. Most Azerbaijanis wish to be united with their ethnic kin in Iran.

When Nagorno-Karabakh voted to secede from Azerbaijan in 1988, the long-standing hostility between the Muslim Azerbaijanis and their Christian Armenian neighbors erupted into bloody violence. Political turmoil continued in 1993, as former

Azerbaijan's capital city of Baku, which lies 40 feet (12 meters) below sea level on the Caspian Sea, is the center of a great oil industry.

Languages spoken:
 Azeri 89%
 Russian 3%
 Armenian 2%

Religions:
 Muslim 93%
 Russian Orthodox 3%
 Armenian Orthodox 2%

Enrollment ratios compare the number of students enrolled to the population which, by age, should be enrolled. A ratio higher than 100 indicates that students older or younger than the typical age range are also enrolled.

TECHNOLOGY

Radios per 1,000 people: 22

Televisions per 1,000 people: 259

Computers per 1,000 people: N/A

ECONOMY

Currency: Manat

Gross national income (GNI) in 2000: $4.9 billion U.S.

Real annual growth rate (1999-2000): 11.1%

GNI per capita (2000): $600 U.S.

Balance of payments (2000): -$150 million U.S.

Goods exported:
 Mostly: oil and gas
 Also: machinery, cotton, foodstuffs

Goods imported: Machinery and equipment, foodstuffs, metals, chemicals

Trading partners: Turkey, Russia, Georgia, Ukraine

Communist Heydar Aliyev was appointed parliament chairman after elected president Abulfaz Elcibey was forced from office by a military revolt.

In May 1994, Aliyev signed a truce with Armenia even though it left Armenia in control of 20 per cent of Azerbaijan. In October, special police mounted an abortive coup against Aliyev.

The Azores and Madeiras

In addition to its mainland territory, the nation of Portugal also includes two island groups in the Atlantic Ocean, the Azores and the Madeiras. The Azores lie about 800 miles (1,300 kilometers) off the west coast of Portugal. The Madeiras are situated about 350 miles (560 kilometers) off the northwest coast of Morocco. Both are *autonomous* (self-governing) regions of Portugal.

The Azores

The Azores are actually the peaks of a huge undersea volcanic mountain range that extends down the Mid-Atlantic Ridge from Iceland almost to Antarctica. The islands consist of three groups spread across about 390 miles (630 kilometers) of ocean. About 249,500 people live in the Azores.

Navigator Gonzalo Cabral claimed the Azores for Portugal in 1431. At the time, the islands were uninhabited, but Portuguese from the mainland soon began to settle on the islands. They were later joined by Flemish, Breton, and Spanish immigrants. The islands were never a colony; they were always considered part of Portugal.

The Azores played an important role in World War II (1939–1945). Because of the islands' strategic location, Great Britain used them as a naval base in their fight against Nazi submarines. Although Portugal remained neutral, an ancient treaty allowed Britain to use the islands in time of war. Today, the United States keeps military installations there.

Hot springs, geysers, and huge craters are reminders of the Azores' volcanic beginnings, and the forces of nature can still be felt during the islands' occasional earthquakes. In some areas, lush green vegetation extends right down to the sea, creating a vast blanket of exotic flowers. The climate is cool and humid throughout the year, typical of the North Atlantic region.

Farmers grow bananas, corn, pineapples, potatoes, tobacco, vegetables, wheat, and wine grapes, and cattle graze on stretches of grassland. Fishing crews catch tuna. Manufacturing on the islands is quite modest in scale, but the production of pottery, leather goods, and other handicrafts is increasing to meet the demands of the growing tourist industry.

Volcanic formations, framed by the shimmering blue waters of the Atlantic, form a dramatic background as fishing crews work in Madeira's coastal waters. Black scabbard—fish caught at a depth of 6,600 feet (2,000 meters)—is a local delicacy.

For a farmer and his son, *below,* horseback is still the best way to get around the steep hills of the Azores.

The Lagoa do Fogo and the Lagoa das Sete Cidades, two adjoining lakes, fill the crater of an extinct volcano on the island of São Miguel in the Azores.

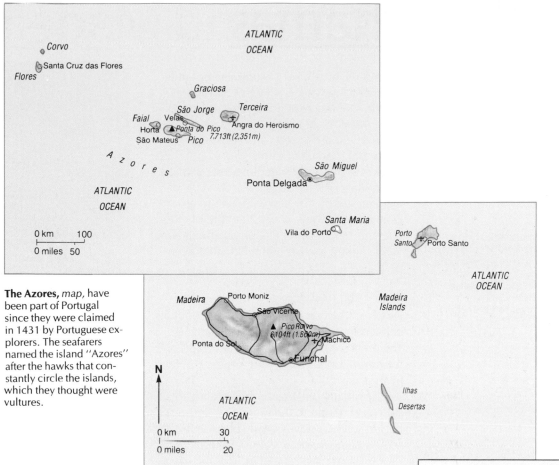

The Azores, *map,* have been part of Portugal since they were claimed in 1431 by Portuguese explorers. The seafarers named the island "Azores" after the hawks that constantly circle the islands, which they thought were vultures.

Portuguese explorers sailed to the Madeiras in 1419. The Islands are best known for their fine Madeira wines. Wine-making is the principal industry.

The Madeira Islands

The ancient Romans named these beautiful islands *Purpuriarae* (Purple Islands). The Portuguese, who arrived in 1419, gave them their present name, which means *wood,* because of the extensive forests they found there. These are the Madeiras—born of volcanic lava, home of the world-famous Madeira wine, and, some say, a breathtaking glimpse of paradise.

The Madeiras consist of the main island of Madeira, its smaller neighbor Porto Santo, and two uninhabited groups of islets, the Desertas and the Selvagens. The islands cover a total area of 308 square miles (797 square kilometers). Like the Azores, the Madeiras are the peaks of undersea volcanic mountain ranges.

The island of Madeira is the largest and most important island in the chain. Madeira rises to its highest point at Pico Ruivo, which has an elevation of 6,104 feet (1,860 meters). Deep valleys cut through its mountainous landscape, and steep cliffs rise sharply out of the sea on the northeast side. The island's settlements and farms are built on terraces, which are covered with exotic flowers and trees.

After the Portuguese arrived in 1419, Madeira became a regular port of call for seafarers. Ships from all over Europe, the Far East, and the New World stopped there, and many left specimens of exotic plants. The island's warm, sunny climate and rich volcanic soil soon turned Madeira into a garden of subtropical fruits, vegetables, and flowers.

Most of the Madeiras' population, which numbers about 258,000, make their living in agriculture or tourism. Chief crops include bananas, corn, oranges, pomegranates, sugar cane, and wine grapes. Because rain falls only in winter, water for the crops is stored and distributed by stone aqueducts called *levadas.*

Madeira has long been one of Portugal's most popular tourist stops. Funchal, the capital of the Madeiras as well as the largest city and chief seaport, is the islands' center for tourism. Many people, including children, work in the islands' cottage industries, making embroidery, lace, and willow wicker baskets.

The Bahamas

In 1492, Christopher Columbus first landed in America at what is now San Salvador Island in the Bahamas. Today, this independent nation consists of nearly 700 islands and about 2,300 rocky islets and reefs near the coasts of Florida and Cuba.

Most of the islands are limestone with only a thin layer of infertile, stony soil. Many of them are partly covered with pine forests. People live on only about 20 of the islands, but their beauty and mild climate bring about 1-1/4 million tourists to the Bahamas every year.

A cruise ship, *right,* approaches the palm-fringed beaches of Nassau, capital and largest city of the Bahamas. The Bahamas welcome about 1-1/4 million tourists each year.

People and history

People of African descent make up about 80 per cent of the population of the Bahamas. The other 20 per cent are mainly whites or *mulattoes* (people of mixed African and European ancestry).

Many black Bahamians are descendants of Africans brought to the islands by British settlers to work as slaves. Many of these British settlers came from the United States after the Revolutionary War ended in 1783.

The British began settlements in the Bahamas as far back as the 1600's. The islands had been claimed for Spain in 1492, but the Spaniards never settled the islands. Instead, they enslaved the Lucayo Indians who lived there and took many of them to work in gold mines on nearby islands.

Spain began to attack the British settlements in the late 1600's. Pirates, who used the coves and islets as bases for their raids, also attacked the settlements. The Bahamas became a British colony in 1717, and Spain gave up its claim to the islands in 1783.

In the mid-1800's, the Bahamas prospered from shipping and trade. During the U.S. Civil War, the Bahamas were used as a base for ships breaking the Union blockade of Southern ports. After the war, the Bahamian economy declined, but prosperity returned about 100 years later, when large numbers of tourists began visiting the islands.

FACT BOX

COUNTRY

Official name: Commonwealth of the Bahamas
Capital: Nassau
Terrain: Long, flat coral formations with some low rounded hills
Area: 5,382 sq. mi. (13,940 km²)
Climate: Tropical marine; moderated by warm waters of Gulf Stream
Highest elevation: Mount Alvernia on Cat Island, 207 ft. (63 m)
Lowest elevation: Atlantic Ocean, sea level

GOVERNMENT

Form of government: Constitutional parliamentary democracy
Head of state: British monarch, represented by governor general
Head of government: Prime minister
Administrative areas: 21 districts
Legislature: Parliament consisting of the Senate with 16 members serving five-year terms and the House of Assembly with 40 members serving five-year terms
Court system: Supreme Court; Court of Appeal; magistrate's courts
Armed forces: 860 troops

PEOPLE

Estimated 2002 population: 317,000
Population growth: 1.01%
Population density: 59 persons per sq. mi. (23 per km²)
Population distribution: 84% urban, 16% rural
Life expectancy in years: Male: 66 Female: 73
Doctors per 1,000 people: N/A
Percentage of age-appropriate population enrolled in the following educational levels: Primary: N/A Secondary: N/A Further: N/A

BAHAMAS

The Bahamas consists of a chain of about 3,000 coral islands and reefs that stretches for more than 500 miles (800 kilometers). Only about 20 of the islands are inhabited. About 75 per cent of the Bahamians live on either New Providence or Grand Bahama. Most of the islands are long, narrow strips of lime-stone. At one time a haven for pirates, they are now a subtropical paradise for tourists.

In 1964, the United Kingdom granted the Bahamas internal self-government, and in 1967 the Progressive Liberal Party, made up largely of Bahamians of African descent, won control of the government. For the first time, the black majority was in power. The government then worked for full independence, which was achieved on July 10, 1973.

Government and economy

The monarch of the United Kingdom, represented by a governor general, is the official head of state of the Commonwealth of the Bahamas. Voters elect the members of the House of Assembly, one house of the legislature. The head of the party that wins the most Assembly seats becomes prime minister. Members of the second house of the legislature, the Senate, are appointed.

Tourism is the leading economic activity of the Bahamas. Many Bahamians work in hotels or other tourist-related businesses. Less than 2 per cent of the people farm the land. Farmers grow bananas, citrus fruits, cucumbers, pineapples, and tomatoes. Fishermen catch crawfish and other seafood for domestic consumption and for export.

Food processing ranks as a major industry. Foreign corporations run businesses in the Bahamas, and the country has branches of many foreign banks.

Languages spoken:
English
Creole (among Haitian immigrants)

Religions:
Baptist 32%
Anglican 20%
Roman Catholic 19%
Methodist 6%
Church of God 6%
other Protestant 12%

TECHNOLOGY

Radios per 1,000 people: N/A

Televisions per 1,000 people: N/A

Computers per 1,000 people: N/A

ECONOMY

Currency: Bahamian dollar

Gross national income (GNI) in 2000: $4.533 million U.S.

Real annual growth rate (1999–2000): 4.5%

GNI per capita (2000): $14,960 U.S.

Balance of payments (2000): N/A

Goods exported: Pharmaceuticals, cement, rum, crawfish, refined petroleum products

Goods imported: Foodstuffs, manufactured goods, crude oil, vehicles, electronics

Trading partners: United States, Italy, Japan, Switzerland, the United Kingdom

Bahrain

Bahrain is an island country in the Persian Gulf made up of more than 30 islands, including the largest, which is also named Bahrain. Although surrounded by water, the islands have a dry desert climate.

For hundreds of years, Bahrain was a center of trade and communications in the Persian Gulf region. Dilmun, a prosperous trading civilization, occupied the islands about 4,000 years ago. In the 1700's, al Khalifah Arabs from Saudi Arabia took control of Bahrain and have ruled it ever since, though the country was a protectorate of the United Kingdom from 1861 to 1971.

Bahrain was an underdeveloped nation until 1932, when petroleum was discovered on the island of Bahrain. The country now enjoys one of the highest standards of living in the Persian Gulf area. It has one of the highest literacy rates in the region, and education is free. The government also provides free medical care.

In 2001, Bahraini voters approved a national charter to reform their country's government. The reforms, which went into effect in 2002, changed Bahrain from an *emirate*, ruled by an *emir* with absolute power, to a constitutional monarchy, with a king and a two-house legislature. The people elect the members of one house in the parliament, and the king appoints the members of the other house. The country had a national assembly elected by the people, but it was disbanded by the emir, Sheik Isa Khalifah, in 1975. In the mid-1990's, widespread demands for the restoration of parliament led to violent antigovernment riots and bombings.

About 80 per cent of Bahrain's people are Arabs. Large groups of Indians, Iranians, and Pakistanis also live in the country. Almost all the people are Muslims, and Islam is the national religion. Arabic is the official language, though Farsi—the language of Iran—and English are also spoken. Many Bahrainis, especially younger people, wear clothes reflecting Western influence, but others still wear traditional Arab dress.

Most of Bahrain's people live in towns in the northern part of the island of Bahrain. The majority live in houses or apartments, but some villagers build thatched huts. Fresh-water springs provide ample drinking water on the northern coast of Bahrain, and farmers also use this water to irrigate their land.

Northern Bahrain receives most of the little rain that falls—about 3 inches (8 centimeters) a year, mainly during the winter. Summers are hot and humid. Bahrain has one of the best electric service systems in the Middle East, so refrigerators and air conditioners are common in this desert land.

The electricity, free medical care, and other services Bahrainis enjoy are due mainly to oil profits. Bahrain actually has only a

FACT BOX

COUNTRY

Official name: Dawlat al Bahrayn (State of Bahrain)
Capital: Manama
Terrain: Mostly low desert plain rising gently to low central escarpment
Area: 239 sq. mi. (620 km²)

Climate: Arid; mild, pleasant winters; very hot, humid summers
Highest elevation: Jabal ad Dukhan, 443 ft. (135 m)
Lowest elevation: Persian Gulf, sea level

GOVERNMENT

Form of government: Constitutional monarchy
Head of state: King
Head of government: Prime minister
Administrative areas: 12 manatiq (municipalities)
Legislature: The Cabinet assumed legislative powers in 1975 when the National Assembly was dissolved; bicameral legislature created by National Action Charter in 2000; approved by referendum in 2001
Court system: High Civil Appeals Court
Armed forces: 11,000 troops

PEOPLE

Estimated 2002 population: 636,000
Population growth: 1.78%
Population density: 2,373 persons per sq. mi. (916 per km²)
Population distribution: 88% urban, 12% rural
Life expectancy in years:
Male: 71
Female: 76
Doctors per 1,000 people: N/A
Percentage of age-appropriate population enrolled in the following educational levels:
Primary: N/A
Secondary: N/A
Further: N/A

BAHRAIN

small supply of petroleum, but its oil refinery, on the island of Sitrah, is one of the world's largest and most modern. The Sitrah refinery processes all of Bahrain's crude petroleum, as well as much of the oil that comes from Saudi Arabia via pipeline.

While Bahrain's economy depends largely on the petroleum industry, the government has taken steps to broaden the economy. It has established programs designed to develop commerce, construction, fishing, manufacturing, and transportation. Also, Bahrain today ranks as a major banking and financial center for the Persian Gulf region. Modern warehouse and port facilities help make it a major trading center as well.

Ship repairing is also an important industry in Bahrain. Factories produce aluminum and aluminum products, ammonia, iron, liquid natural gas, methanol, and petroleum products. Farmers grow dates, tomatoes, and other fruits and vegetables on irrigated land, and also raise cattle and poultry. Fish and shrimp are caught in the country's coastal waters.

Manama, Bahrain's capital city, lights up for a religious festival. Bahrain, a major banking and financial center for the Persian Gulf area, also serves as the Middle East headquarters of many international companies.

Languages spoken:
Arabic
English
Farsi
Urdu

Religions:
Shiah Muslim 70%
Sunni Muslim 30%

TECHNOLOGY

Radios per 1,000 people: N/A

Televisions per 1,000 people: N/A

Computers per 1,000 people: N/A

ECONOMY

Currency: Bahraini dinar

Gross domestic product (GDP) in 2001: $8.4 billion U.S.

Real annual growth rate (2001): 4%

GDP per capita (2001): $13,000 U.S.

Balance of payments (2001): N/A

Goods exported:
Mostly: petroleum and petroleum products
Also: aluminum

Goods imported: Nonoil, crude oil

Trading partners: Saudi Arabia, India, Japan, United States, the United Kingdom

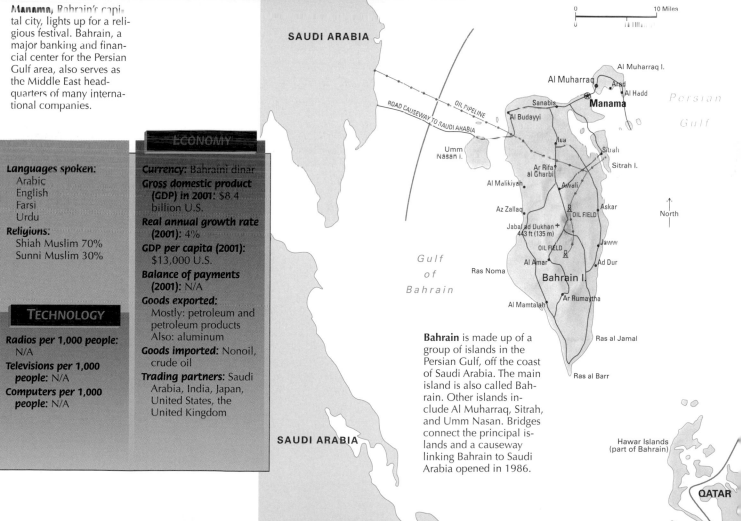

Bahrain is made up of a group of islands in the Persian Gulf, off the coast of Saudi Arabia. The main island is also called Bahrain. Other islands include Al Muharraq, Sitrah, and Umm Nasan. Bridges connect the principal islands and a causeway linking Bahrain to Saudi Arabia opened in 1986.

Bangladesh

Bangladesh, an independent nation since 1971, is almost completely surrounded on three sides by the northeast part of India. Myanmar touches Bangladesh's southwest coast, and its south coast opens to the Bay of Bengal, which is the northern part of the Indian Ocean.

Rivers and rich soil

Bangladesh has some of the richest, most fertile soil in the world. Most of the country consists of an *alluvial plain,* which is land formed from soil left by rivers.

Three major rivers—the Brahmaputra, the Ganges, and the Meghna—flow through Bangladesh and into the Bay of Bengal. Another of the country's rivers, the Padma, is a branch of the Ganges. The Padma River begins where the Ganges meets the Jamuna River. It then flows 78 miles (126 kilometers) to join the Meghna River at Chandpur.

During the rainy season, the rivers of Bangladesh overflow and deposit sediment along their banks. The built-up soil deposits form the Ganges Delta.

Rice, the country's main source of food, and *jute,* a plant whose fibers are made into string or woven into cloth, thrive in the wet delta region. They are two of the country's most important crops. Bangladesh, in fact, is one of the world's leading rice producers.

The rivers that provide Bangladesh's rich soil begin high in the Himalaya. However, the clearing of forests on the mountains causes much of the region's soil to wash down the slopes. As a result, sediment builds up in the riverbeds. When the snow melts in the mountains and the monsoon rains arrive, the rivers cannot contain the extra water. The rivers then overflow and flood the surrounding countryside.

The struggle for independence

Bangladesh was formerly part of Pakistan, which was established in 1947 when India became independent. Because of the fighting between India's Hindus and Muslims under British rule, Indian and British leaders decided to divide India into two countries. India became the Hindu nation, and Pakistan became the Muslim nation.

Pakistan was further divided into West Pakistan, on India's northwest border, and

East Pakistan, on India's northeast border. Unfortunately, the two areas had little in common except their religion.

Through the years, East Pakistanis became dissatisfied with the government of Pakistan. In 1971, fighting broke out. That same year, East Pakistan declared its independence from West Pakistan and became the nation of Bangladesh.

Early beginnings

The country that is now often called *the poorest of the poor* was once a busy and successful commercial center.

Bangladesh is part of the region known as Bengal, which also includes the Indian state of West Bengal. In the 1500's, European traders following the traditional Indian Ocean routes came to Bengal. There they found a rich land dotted with many small commercial centers. At the heart of these centers was a busy handloom weaving industry that produced high-quality textiles.

The Europeans were also interested in Bengal's many rivers. Because they led deep into the country's interior, the rivers were ideal for transporting goods.

By the early 1700's, the Mogul Empire, which ruled Bengal at the time, had grown steadily weaker. Soon, the British East India Company became the most powerful force in Bengal.

The British then decided to move their center of operations to Calcutta in West Bengal. This move proved to be a fateful turn of events for the region as commercial interests and investment money moved steadily westward.

At the same time, the Industrial Revolution in Europe brought mechanization to Britain's own textile industry. Textile exports from Bengal were discouraged, and British-made goods flooded the region.

Bengal's craft industries were completely ruined and its trade and commerce collapsed. As a result, the region became a purely agricultural society during the 1800's, with few opportunities for development.

Bangladesh Today

Bangladesh is a poor, underdeveloped country. Throughout its short history, it has seen more than its share of civil war, natural disaster, and poverty. The civil war that brought Bangladesh into being, left the nation with serious economic, social, and political problems. Because Bangladesh cannot grow or import enough food for its huge population, many Bangladeshis go hungry. Cyclones, tornadoes, tidal waves, and floods occur almost every year. These disasters cause much death and destruction.

Strong beliefs and hardships

The short and troubled history of Bangladesh has its beginnings when the country was still known as East Pakistan. In 1970, a cyclone and tidal wave struck East Pakistan, killing about 266,000 people. Many of the survivors believed that the West Pakistan government held back on relief shipments. Tensions between East and West Pakistan grew.

In a December 1970 election to select a new assembly, the Awami League, a political party led by East Pakistan's Sheik Mujibur Rahman, won a majority of the seats. The Awami League strongly supported increased self-government for East Pakistan.

When the president of Pakistan postponed the first meeting of the assembly in March

1971, East Pakistan protested. West Pakistan troops were brought in to put down the protest and Sheik Mujibur Rahman (known as Sheik Mujib) was imprisoned in West Pakistan. On March 26, 1971, Bangladesh declared itself an independent nation.

The civil war that followed lasted until December 16. With the help of Indian troops, Bangladesh defeated West Pakistan, but the effects of the civil war were devastating to the new nation. Even as the government set up programs to rebuild the country, floods and food shortages brought more troubles.

Bangladesh is still a long way from solving its problems. Many political, economic, and social issues must be dealt with before life can become better for its people.

Economy

Although the country's warm, humid climate and fertile soil are ideal for farming, crop yields are low. Most Bangladeshi farms cover only about 3-1/2 acres (1.4 hectares), and the farmers use outdated tools and methods.

Jute is the chief export crop of Bangladesh. However, the development of petroleum-based synthetics in the 1960's has reduced worldwide demand for the fiber.

Because the country has few natural resources, its chances for industrial develop-

---

FACT BOX

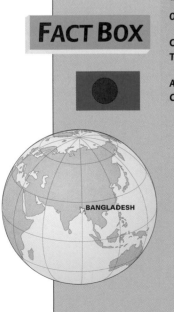

COUNTRY

Official name: People's Republic of Bangladesh
Capital: Dhaka
Terrain: Mostly flat alluvial plain; hilly in southeast
Area: 55,599 sq. mi. (144,000 km²)
Climate: Tropical; cool, dry winter (October to March); hot, humid summer (March to June); cool, rainy monsoon (June to October)

Main rivers: Brahmaputra, Ganges, Meghna, Jamuna
Highest elevation: Keokradong, 4,034 ft. (1,230 m)
Lowest elevation: Indian Ocean, sea level

GOVERNMENT

Form of government: Republic
Head of state: President
Head of government: Prime minister
Administrative areas: 5 divisions

Legislature: Jatiya Sangsad (National Parliament) with 330 members serving five-year terms
Court system: Supreme Court
Armed forces: 137,000 troops

PEOPLE

Estimated 2002 population: 133,557,000
Population growth: 1.59%
Population density: 2,402 persons per sq. mi. (927 per km²)
Population distribution: 80% rural, 20% urban
Life expectancy in years:
Male: 61
Female: 61
Doctors per 1,000 people: 0.2
Percentage of age-appropriate population enrolled in the following educational levels:
Primary: 122*
Secondary: 47
Further: 5

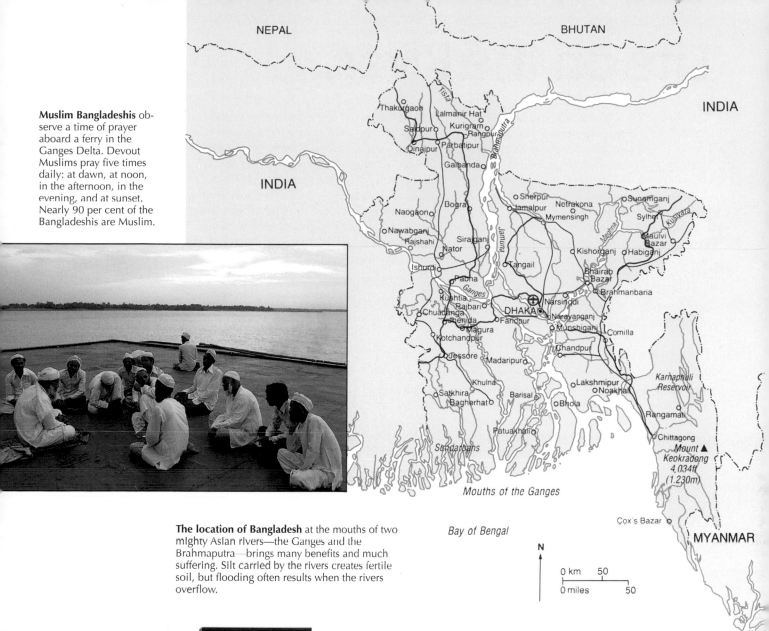

Muslim Bangladeshis observe a time of prayer aboard a ferry in the Ganges Delta. Devout Muslims pray five times daily: at dawn, at noon, in the afternoon, in the evening, and at sunset. Nearly 90 per cent of the Bangladeshis are Muslim.

NEPAL
BHUTAN
INDIA
INDIA

Thakurgaon
Lalmanir Hat
Saidpur
Kurigram
Rangpur
Dinajpur
Parbatipur
Gaibanda
Sherpur
Jamalpur
Netrakona
Sunamganj
Bogra
Mymensingh
Sylhet
Naogaon
Siraiganj
Kishorganj
Maulvi Bazar
Nawabganj
Nator
Habiganj
Rajshahi
Tangail
Ishurdi
Pabna
Bhairab Bazar
Kushtia
Ganges
Narsingdi
Brahmanbaria
Rajbari
DHAKA
Chuadanga
Faridpur
Narayanganj
Jhenida
Magura
Munshiganj
Comilla
Kotchandpur
Chandpur
Jessore
Madaripur
Khulna
Lakshmipur
Noakhali
Karnaphuli Reservoir
Satkhira
Barisal
Rangamati
Bagherhat
Bhola
Sundarbans
Patuakhali
Chittagong
Mouths of the Ganges
Mount Keokradong 4,034ft (1,230m)
MYANMAR
Cox's Bazar

The location of Bangladesh at the mouths of two mighty Asian rivers—the Ganges and the Brahmaputra—brings many benefits and much suffering. Silt carried by the rivers creates fertile soil, but flooding often results when the rivers overflow.

Bay of Bengal

N

0 km   50
0 miles   50

Languages spoken:
Bangla (official)
English

Religions:
Muslim 88%
Hindu 11%

Enrollment ratios compare the number of students enrolled to the population which, by age, should be enrolled. A ratio higher than 100 indicates that students older or younger than the typical age range are also enrolled.

TECHNOLOGY

Radios per 1,000 people: 49

Televisions per 1,000 people: 7

Computers per 1,000 people: 1.5

ECONOMY

Currency: Taka

Gross national income (GNI) in 2000: $47.9 billion U.S.

Real annual growth rate (1999–2000): 5.9%

GNI per capita (2000): $370 U.S.

Balance of payments (2000): $2 million U.S.

Goods exported: Garments, jute and jute goods, leather, frozen fish and seafood

Goods imported: Machinery and equipment, chemicals, iron and steel, textiles, raw cotton, food, crude oil and petroleum products, cement

Trading partners: United States, Germany, India, the United Kingdom, China, Japan

ment are limited. Bangladesh also lacks equipment and skilled labor, so industry is confined to the processing of jute and tea. Natural gas deposits supply part of the country's energy requirements and support a small petrochemical industry.

Bangladesh ranks as one of the poorest nations of the world. Its economic future depends on its ability to solve the growing problem of overpopulation.

Life on the River

Bangladesh is a country of rivers and streams. Countless waterways flow across the flat river plain that makes up most of the land. Three major Asian rivers—the Brahmaputra, the Ganges, and the Meghna—unite in Bangladesh to form the great Ganges Delta at the Bay of Bengal.

Bangladesh depends on the rivers for its very existence. Most of the country, which lies only about 50 feet (15 meters) above sea level, would be permanently flooded if the river system did not carry away the water from the monsoon rains and the melting Himalayan snows.

A life-giving force

For the people of Bangladesh, the rivers are both a life-giving force and an instrument of destruction. The soil deposited along their fertile banks creates some of the richest farmland in the world, but when the rivers overflow, the flooding brings death and disaster.

Life in Bangladesh revolves around the rivers. Villagers watch the changing flow of the waters and build their houses on whatever high ground is available. Before the floods arrive, farmers try to guess which areas will be affected, how deep the floods will be, and how long the flooding will last.

The names given to the rivers reflect the importance of these waterways in the lives of the people. *Khlamati,* for example, means *fulfiller of desires*. *Kirtinasha* means *destroyer of achievements*. River themes are common in the tales of the *alapanis* (storytellers), who entertain their audiences with a variety of ancient tales.

Major rivers

Bangladesh's major rivers include the Ganges, the Brahmaputra, the Jamuna, and the Meghna.

The 160-mile-long (258-kilometer-long) Ganges River extends from the western border with India to its confluence with the Jamuna River.

The Brahmaputra *(son of Brahma)* River flows down from India, and where it meets the Tista River, it forms the Jamuna River. No permanent settlements exist along the banks of the Jamuna River. Its violent floods, which do not allow the soil to mature, create a landscape of *chars* (seasonal islands).

The Meghna River flows from the northeast part of Bangladesh to where it meets the Ganges in south-central Bangladesh.

Houses are built on stilts as protection against rising floodwaters, *right*. Annual monsoon flooding causes great loss of human life, as well as damage to property and communication systems. The government has developed major flood-control projects.

The jute harvest, *above*, provides many Bangladeshis with their only source of income. Jute, a fiber used in making burlap, sacks, mats, rope, and carpet backing, is the chief export of Bangladesh. It grows in the wet delta region.

Fishing boats set off down a river. The nation's waterways contain large supplies of fish, which is an important food source. However, a traditional disrespect for fishermen has slowed the development of a fishing industry.

A map of Bangladesh shows areas likely to be damaged by flooding and areas where floods pose a lesser threat. Few regions are free from risk.

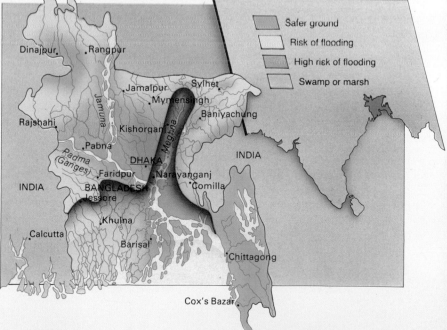

Safer ground

Risk of flooding

High risk of flooding

Swamp or marsh

Dinajpur

Rangpur

Jamalpur

Sylhet

Mymensingh

Baniyachung

Rajshahi

Kishorganj

Jamuna

Pabna

Meghna

Padma
(Ganges)

DHAKA

INDIA

Faridpur

Narayanganj

INDIA

Comilla

BANGLADESH

Jessore

Khulna

Calcutta

Barisal

Chittagong

Cox's Bazar

People

The ancestors of present-day Bangladeshis probably came from Myanmar, Tibet, and northern India thousands of years ago. More than 95 per cent of the population are *Bengalis,* a short, dark-skinned people. Their national language is Bengali, which has a rich cultural heritage in literature, music, and poetry.

Tribal groups form the second largest ethnic group in Bangladesh. The four largest tribes are the Chakmas, the Marmas, the Mros, and the Tipperas. They live primarily in the Chittagong Hills of southeastern Bangladesh. The culture of the tribal groups differs greatly from that of other Bangladeshis. They follow the Buddhist religion and speak Tibeto-Burman languages.

Another ethnic group, the Biharis, includes the Urdu-speaking, non-Bengali Muslim refugees from Bihar and other parts of northern India. The Biharis were once the upper class of Bengali society. Many held jobs on the railroads and in heavy industry.

The Biharis did not want East Pakistan to separate from West Pakistan in 1971 because they felt financially threatened by the separation. After Bangladesh became independent, hundreds of thousands of Biharis returned to West Pakistan. Those who remain live in their own small communities. They are often persecuted for their loyalty to West Pakistan.

Religion

Bangladeshis take great pride in their Bengali heritage. Their national language, Bengali, is particularly important to them, and the religion of Islam provides an important foundation for their daily life.

Islam came to Bengal long after it was established in Pakistan. The Muslims conquered Pakistan in A.D. 711. Islam did not reach the Bengalis until 500 years later, when Turkish Muslims extended their control into the eastern region of Bengal. Before that, Hindu or Buddhist dynasties had ruled Bengal.

Today, many strict Muslims do not accept Bangladeshis as true Muslims. They believe that Bangladeshis owe their faith to conversion rather than natural inheritance. This belief is one of the major reasons for the long-standing disagreement between East and West Pakistan.

Villagers honor the river in a ceremony along the banks of the Kali River. The rivers of Bangladesh provide fish for food and for export. Rivers are also the country's chief transportation routes.

A Muslim wedding party, *below,* leaves the ceremony by bus. Men in Muslim families have far more freedom than women. Muslim women have few activities outside the home and many cover their heads with veils in the presence of strangers.

Population growth

Bangladesh is one of the world's most densely populated countries and one of the countries in the world with the highest population. In the year 2000, the population of Bangladesh was around 130 million. Bangladesh does not have the resources to feed and educate its huge population. Many Bangladeshis do not have enough to eat, and about 75 per cent of the people over 15 years old cannot read and write.

Because of the rapid population growth, poverty and overcrowding are serious problems in both urban and rural areas. Rural villagers live in one- or two-room huts made of bamboo. In urban slums, shelters are built of cardboard, scraps of wood, or sticks.

The fertile soil of Bangladesh yields two—and often three—harvests a year, but even these large harvests cannot feed all the people in Bangladesh. Land that could grow crops is now used for living space. The rapid population growth has kept most Bangladeshis poor. Many people have moved from rural villages to urban areas in an effort to improve their lives, but few jobs are available.

Waterways take the place of roads in Bangladesh, where countless rivers and streams flow through the country. Large passenger and cargo ships provide transportation between the cities. Smaller boats operate between villages.

Way of life

Bangladesh ranks as one of the poorest nations in the world. But in spite of their poverty and hardships, Bangladeshis are a friendly and good-natured people. The men enjoy gathering in cafes and marketplaces to trade goods as well as gossip while women visit each other's homes. Villagers are often entertained by storytellers, and they also enjoy singing and listening to folk ballads. Craft workers carry on the tradition of embroidery, weaving, pottery, and other decorative arts.

A Country at Risk

Bangladesh is both a beneficiary and a victim of its climate and geography. The country receives a great deal of rainfall, brought mostly by the monsoon between mid-May and October. The far northeast region gets the most rain—as much as 250 inches (635 centimeters) a year.

Too much rainfall during the monsoon season causes large-scale flooding while too little rainfall brings drought. Cyclones, which sweep into the country from the Bay of Bengal, are also a constant threat. Between 1947 and 1988, 13 severe cyclones hit Bangladesh. These storms usually strike at the end of the monsoon season and may also be accompanied by tidal waves.

These natural disasters are a sad fact of life in Bangladesh. Floods, cyclones, and tidal waves have had an important effect on the history of the country. It was, in fact, a cyclone that helped bring the nation of Bangladesh into being.

In November 1970, a cyclone rose in the Bay of Bengal and a tidal wave swept over the countryside of what was then East Pakistan. It killed about 266,000 people and destroyed many villages.

The victims of the disaster felt that the government of Pakistan delayed rescue operations and held back relief supplies. Their bitter feelings helped trigger the civil war that led to the independence of Bangladesh.

After the war, the new government set up many programs to help rebuild the country, and a huge international relief effort was coordinated by the United Nations. In mid-1974, just as the programs were beginning to make progress, disaster struck again. The worst floods in decades swept through Bangladesh. By September, food shortages brought famine, and tens of thousands of people died.

Weather-related problems continued throughout the 1970's and 1980's. A devastating cyclone struck the coastal areas in May 1985. The storm began to develop on May 22 in the Bay of Bengal and swept onto the coast in the early hours of May 24. The cyclone's winds hit the coast at more than 80 miles (130 kilometers) per hour and created tidal waves 13 feet (4 meters) high.

Many Bangladeshis were unprepared for this particular cyclone. The bamboo and jute dwellings in which the villagers took shelter

The monsoon rains that bring many benefits to Bangladesh can also result in major flooding, crop destruction, and food shortages.

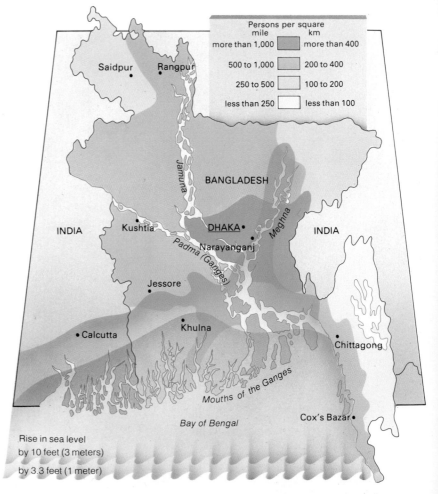

Persons per square	
mile	km
more than 1,000	more than 400
500 to 1,000	200 to 400
250 to 500	100 to 200
less than 250	less than 100

Saidpur
Rangpur

Jamuna

BANGLADESH

INDIA

Kushtia

DHAKA

Meghna

INDIA

Padma (Ganges)

Narayanganj

Jessore

Khulna

Calcutta

Chittagong

Mouths of the Ganges

Bay of Bengal

Cox's Bazar

Rise in sea level
by 10 feet (3 meters)
by 3.3 feet (1 meter)

Bangladeshis swarm across a new canal. Water-control projects are designed to reduce the effects of floodwaters on farmland and other property. With so many mouths to feed, protecting the food supply is the government's most important task.

were no match for the storm's tremendous strength. Thousands of people were swept away by floods and tidal waves.

The 1985 cyclone killed 11,000 people, damaged more than 94,000 houses, and killed about 135,000 head of livestock. But it was not to be the end of weather troubles for Bangladesh. The summer of 1988 brought the worst floods in the nation's history.

Caused by heavy runoff of monsoon rains in the Himalaya, the floods killed about 1,600 people and an additional 500 died from diseases resulting from the floods. The damage to land and property was far worse than the 1985 disaster. In some districts, the entire population was left homeless.

About 10 million acres (4 million hectares) of crops were completely destroyed, and an additional 7.4 million acres (3 million hectares) were partly destroyed. Also, many railroad bridges and tracks, roads, schools, and other buildings were completely or partly destroyed.

Only three months later, a killer cyclone struck southeastern Bangladesh. About 600 people were killed, and more than 100 ships sank or ran aground as 10- to 15-foot (3- to 4.6-meter) waves hit the coastal areas.

It is clear that Bangladesh will always suffer from weather-related problems. There are no precautions against tidal waves and cyclones, but if people get some advance warning, they can take shelter in safe public buildings.

On average, a catastrophe that destroys 10 per cent or more of the nation's food supply is likely to occur every two or three years. This makes it even more difficult for Bangladesh to provide for its people.

Some scientists believe that global warming, or the *greenhouse effect,* will significantly raise ocean levels over the next few decades. The map shows areas of Bangladesh that would be permanently flooded if sea levels rose by 3.3 feet (1 meter) or by 10 feet (3 meters). Permanently flooded areas would mean even less space for the people to live and grow food—a disaster for this overpopulated country. Some scientists also predict that global warming will change rainfall patterns and bring more cyclones.

Cyclones usually strike at the end of the monsoon season. Contaminated floodwaters bring even more problems. Disease spreads quickly, and food supplies are destroyed. Floods also isolate villages from rescue operations.

Barbados

Of all the islands in the West Indies, Barbados is the most British in character. Like London itself, the capital city of Bridgetown has a Trafalgar Square, as well as a Nelson's Column even older than its better-known counterpart across the sea. The distinct British flavor of Barbados, along with its beautiful landscape, gives the island a unique and special charm.

Most of Barbados is flat, with a high, rugged region lying in the middle of the northeast coast. The land descends from this region to a lowland plateau that stretches to the coast all around the island. Fine sandy beaches extend along the west and southwest coasts.

Little of the island's original vegetation remains, and most of Barbados' land is covered by vast fields of sugar cane. But at Turner's Hall Woods and Welchman Hall Gully, in the interior of the island, small patches of the tropical rain forest that once covered Barbados still survive. Many vine-covered trees, including locust, mastic, Spanish oak, and kapok, tower over the land, and the rain forest provides shelter for such introduced animals as wild green monkeys, hares, mongooses, and colorful tropical birds.

Passengers keep cool in an open-sided bus in Bridgetown, the capital of Barbados. Many of the graceful buildings in this busy port date from the time the British ruled the island.

History

British settlers arrived in Barbados in 1625, and the first permanent British settlement was established in 1627. In 1639, the landowners of Barbados elected a House of Assembly. The new colony prospered, and many British families settled on the island in the 1700's and 1800's.

In 1958, Barbados joined the West Indies Federation, a union of British islands in the West Indies. But the federation broke up in 1962, when Jamaica and Trinidad and Tobago became independent.

Barbados itself became an independent nation in 1966. Over the next 10 years, the Democratic Labor Party (DLP) held the majority of the seats in the House of Assembly, but in 1976, the Labor Party won a majority of seats. It was not until 1986 that parliamentary elections returned the DLP to power. In 1994 and 1999, Owen Arthur of the Labor Party was elected prime minister.

A Barbadian farmer inspects his sugar-cane crop as Caribbean waves break on a reef in the background. More than half the nation's farmland is used to grow sugar. Processing plants on the island produce refined sugar, molasses, and rum from the sugar cane.

FACT BOX

COUNTRY

Official name: Barbados
Capital: Bridgetown
Terrain: Relatively flat; rises gently to central highland region
Area: 166 sq. mi. (430 km²)
Climate: Tropical; rainy season (June to October)

Main river: Constitution
Highest elevation: Mount Hillaby, 1,115 ft. (340 m)
Lowest elevation: Atlantic Ocean, sea level

GOVERNMENT

Form of government: Parliamentary democracy
Head of state: British monarch, represented by the governor general
Head of government: Prime minister
Administrative areas: 11 parishes

Legislature: Parliament consisting of the Senate with 21 members and the House of Assembly with 28 members serving five-year terms
Court system: Supreme Court of Judicature
Armed forces: 610 troops

PEOPLE

Estimated 2002 population: 272,000
Population growth: 0.55%
Population density: 1,639 persons per sq. mi. (633 per km²)
Population distribution: 62% rural, 38% urban
Life expectancy in years: Male: 71 Female: 76
Doctors per 1,000 people: N/A
Percentage of age-appropriate population enrolled in the following educational levels: Primary: N/A Secondary: N/A Further: N/A

Barbados, *above right,* lies about 250 miles (402 kilometers) northeast of Venezuela. It is the easternmost island in the West Indies. Profits from tourism and foreign investment—along with its hard-working people and the advantages of membership in the British Commonwealth of Nations—have helped develop Barbados's economy.

Language spoken:
English
Religions:
Protestant 67% (Anglican 40%, Pentecostal 8%, Methodist 7%, other 12%)
Roman Catholic 4%
none 17%

TECHNOLOGY

Radios per 1,000 people: N/A

Televisions per 1,000 people: N/A

Computers per 1,000 people: N/A

ECONOMY

Currency: Barbadian dollar

Gross national income (GNI) in 2000: $2,469 million U.S.

Real annual growth rate (2000): -2%

GNI per capita (2000): $9,250 U.S.

Balance of payments (2000): N/A

Goods exported: Sugar and molasses, rum, other foods and beverages, chemicals, electrical components, clothing

Goods imported: Consumer goods, machinery, foodstuffs, construction materials, chemicals, fuel

Trading partners: United States, United Kingdom, Trinidad and Tobago

People and economy

Barbados is one of the most densely populated islands in the world. About 80 per cent of the people are descended from slaves brought to the island from Africa between 1636 and 1833, when slavery was abolished there. More than 15 per cent of the people are of mixed African and British ancestry. About 4 per cent are of European—chiefly British—descent.

Barbados's economy is based on manufacturing and processing, tourism, and agriculture. Sugar cane, introduced to the island about 1640, is the country's chief agricultural product. In May, at the peak of the sugar-harvesting season, most of the island's farmers work on the sugar plantations. The islanders also raise carrots, corn, sweet potatoes, and yams.

Belarus

Belarus (formerly Byelorussia) is an independent country and a member of the Commonwealth of Independent States (C.I.S.), which was formed in late 1991. The country was formerly a republic of the now-defunct Soviet Union.

Belarus was under the strict control of the Soviet central government until the early 1990's. In the midst of political upheaval in the Soviet government following an attempted coup in August 1991, Belarus declared its independence. In December 1991, Belarus was one of the three former Soviet republics, including Russia and Ukraine, to establish the C.I.S. The country's economy neared collapse in 1994. In April 1994, the government announced an agreement to merge the economy with Russia's. Many opposed economic union, and in October the union was postponed. The parliament outlawed use of the Russian ruble for domestic transactions.

The dense hardwood forests that cover almost a quarter of Belarus make lumbering an important industry. Timber, used in the manufacture of furniture, is floated to market down the Dnieper, Western Dvina, and Nyoman rivers.

The wet summers and sandy soils of Belarus are ideal for growing potatoes—for use as animal feed as well as for human consumption. Other crops include barley, flax, oats, rye, and wheat.

Factories in the chief manufacturing centers of Minsk, Homyel, Mahilyow, Vitsyebsk, Hrodna, and Brest produce automobiles, glass, textiles, bicycles, farm machinery, and building materials.

The land that is now Belarus was first settled by East Slavic tribes in the 400's. In the 800's, the region came under the influence of the Kievan state, and during the 1100's, it was subdivided into several Kievan principalities. In the early 1300's, Belarus became part of the grand duchy of Lithuania, which merged with Poland in 1569.

Following the union of Lithuania and Poland, Belarus participated in the Polish Renaissance culture of the 1500's and 1600's. During this period, about 25 per cent of its people became Roman Catholics. In the late 1700's, when Austria, Prussia, and Russia divided Poland up among themselves, Belarus became part of the Russian Empire.

During World War I (1914-1918) and the Soviet-Polish War (1919-1920), Belarus suffered great devastation. Communists formed the Byelorussian Republic in 1919, and in 1922, it joined the Union of Soviet Socialist Republics (U.S.S.R.). The Treaty of Riga had

FACT BOX

COUNTRY

Official name: Respublika Byelarus' (Republic of Belarus)
Capital: Minsk
Terrain: Generally flat and contains much marshland
Area: 80,155 sq. mi. (207,600 km²)
Climate: Cold winters, cool and moist summers; transitional between continental and maritime

Main rivers: Dnieper, Nyoman, Western Dvina
Highest elevation: Dzerzhinskaya Gora, 1,135 ft. (346 m)
Lowest elevation: Nyoman River, 295 ft. (90 m)

GOVERNMENT

Form of government: Republic
Head of state: President
Head of government: Prime minister
Administrative areas: 6 voblastsi, 1 harady (municipality)

Legislature: Natsionalnoye Sobranie (Parliament) consisting of the Soviet Respubliki (Council of the Republic) with 64 members serving four-year terms and the Palata Pretsaviteley (Chamber of Representatives) with 110 seats
Court system: Supreme Court, Constitutional Court
Armed forces: 80,900 troops

PEOPLE

Estimated 2002 population: 10,175,000
Population growth: -0.17%
Population density: 127 persons per sq. mi. (49 per km²)
Population distribution: 70% urban, 30% rural
Life expectancy in years:
Male: 62
Female: 75
Doctors per 1,000 people: 4.4
Percentage of age-appropriate population enrolled in the following educational levels:
Primary: 98
Secondary: 93
Further: 44

Bison roam in the ancient Belovezha Forest, a nature preserve covering 210,000 acres (85,000 hectares) in the Brest region of Belarus.

awarded the western part of the republic to Poland in 1921, but the area was returned to the Soviets in 1939.

Because it lay along the direct route between Berlin and Moscow, Belarus suffered tremendous losses during World War II (1939-1945) as the German Army advanced along the Western Front. During the Nazi occupation, 1.5 million Belarusians were permanently moved east of the Volga River, and a large section of the Jewish population fled abroad. More than three-quarters of the republic's towns and cities were destroyed.

After World War II, Belarus rebuilt and restored its urban areas. By the late 1970's, it was one of the leading Soviet republics in urban and industrial growth.

An explosion at the Chernobyl nuclear power plant in Ukraine in 1986 had a major impact on Belarus. The winds caused about 70 per cent of the radioactive fallout to land on Belarus. The radiation contaminated the republic's food and water supplies and caused many health problems.

Languages spoken:
Byelorussian
Russian

Religions:
Eastern Orthodox 80%, other (including Roman Catholic, Protestant, Jewish, and Muslim) 20%

TECHNOLOGY

Radios per 1,000 people: 299

Televisions per 1,000 people: 342

Computers per 1,000 people: N/A

ECONOMY

Currency: Belarusian ruble

Gross national income (GNI) in 2000: $28.7 billion U.S.

Real annual growth rate (1999-2000): 5.8%

GNI per capita (2000): $2,870 U.S.

Balance of payments (2000): -$162 million U.S.

Goods exported: Machinery and equipment, chemicals, metals, textiles, foodstuffs

Goods imported: Mineral products, machinery and equipment, metals, chemicals, foodstuffs

Trading partners: Russia, Ukraine, Poland, Germany

Belarus, also known as *White Russia,* is a land of hills and marshes surrounded by Poland in the west, Lithuania and Latvia in the north, Russia in the east, and Ukraine in the south.

Belgium

Belgium, a small country in northwestern Europe, borders France, the Netherlands, and Germany. A narrow strip of the North Sea separates Belgium from Great Britain. Its geographical position helped Belgium become an important European industrial and trade center, but its location has also made it a battleground for warring nations. Belgium suffered great destruction during World War I (1914-1918) and World War II (1939-1945).

With about 844 persons per square mile (326 per square kilometer), Belgium is one of the most densely populated countries in the world. Most of the people are divided into two major groups, the Flemings and the Walloons. The Flemings live in northern Belgium—Flanders—and speak Dutch; the Walloons live in southern Belgium—Wallonia—and speak French. Both Flemings and Walloons live in Brussels, the nation's capital. Dutch and French are both official languages of the country, but the differences in language and other cultural traditions have long caused friction between the two groups.

Despite its small size, Belgium has a varied landscape. Dunes and beaches line its northern coast, while forest-covered hills extend across much of the southeastern part of the country. The central region, which has Belgium's best soil, is also the site of many of the nation's largest cities, including Brussels and Liège. Several large rivers serve as transportation routes. The country has no large natural lakes, but engineers have created several lakes in the south by damming the rivers.

Belgium has a rich architectural and artistic heritage. Stately buildings and churches erected hundreds of years ago still stand in many towns and cities, and museums are filled with works by such outstanding Flemish artists as Jan van Eyck, Pieter Bruegel the Elder, and Peter Paul Rubens. In literature, too, Belgium has made contributions—both in French and Dutch. The Flemish writer Maurice Maeterlinck won the Nobel Prize for literature in 1911 for his plays, including *The Blue Bird,* written in French. The Flemish poet and novelist Hugo Claus is generally considered the leading Belgian writer in Dutch since the mid-1900's.

Since World War II, Belgium has played a leading role in European economics and politics. It is a member of Benelux—the economic union of Belgium, the Netherlands, and Luxembourg—and is the headquarters for the European Union and the North Atlantic Treaty Organization (NATO). The futuristic sculpture called Atomium, symbol of the 1958 Belgian World's Fair, also represented Belgium's new position in the 1900's.

Belgium Today

Until it gained its independence from the Netherlands in 1830, Belgium was governed by many different foreign rulers, including the Romans, the Franks, the Spanish, the Austrians, the French, and the Dutch. The Belgians revolted against Dutch rule in August 1830 and declared their independence on October 4. In 1831, Belgium adopted a Constitution and chose Prince Leopold of Saxe-Coburg as its king. Leopold was the uncle of Queen Victoria of the United Kingdom.

Belgium is a constitutional monarchy, but the king has little real power. Executive power lies in the hands of the prime minister and the members of a cabinet called the Council of Ministers, which consists of equal numbers of Dutch-speaking and French-speaking members. The prime minister holds office as long as the support of Belgium's two-house parliament lasts.

Political and cultural regions

On the local level, Belgium is divided into 10 provinces, each of which is headed by a governor and a council. Belgium is also divided into three cultural communities—those of the Flemings, Germans, and Walloons—and three economic regions—Flanders, Wallonia, and Brussels.

FACT BOX

COUNTRY

Official name: Royaume de Belgique/Koninkrijk Belgie (Kingdom of Belgium)
Capital: Brussels
Terrain: Flat coastal plains in northwest, central rolling hills, rugged mountains of Ardennes Forest in southeast
Area: 11,780 sq. mi. (30,510 km²)

Climate: Temperate; mild winters, cool summers; rainy, humid, cloudy
Main rivers: Schelde, Sambre, Meuse (or Maas)
Highest elevation: Signal de Botrange, 2,277 ft. (694 m)
Lowest elevation: North Sea, sea level

GOVERNMENT

Form of government: Federal parliamentary democracy
Head of state: Monarch
Head of government: Prime minister
Administrative areas: 10 provinces
Legislature: Parliament consisting of a Senaat, in Dutch, or Senat, in French (both meaning Senate) with 71 members serving four-year terms and a Kamer van Volksvertegenwoordigers,
in Dutch, or Chambre des Representants, in French (both meaning Chamber of Deputies) with 150 members serving four-year terms
Court system: Hof van Cassatie, in Dutch, or Cour de Cassation, in French (both meaning Supreme Court)
Armed forces: 41,750 troops

PEOPLE

Estimated 2002 population: 10,165,000
Population growth: 0.18%
Population density: 863 persons per sq. mi. (333 per km²)
Population distribution: 97% urban, 3% rural
Life expectancy in years:
Male: 75
Female: 82
Doctors per 1,000 people: 3.8
Percentage of age-appropriate population enrolled in the following educational levels:
Primary: 103*
Secondary: 146*†
Further: 57

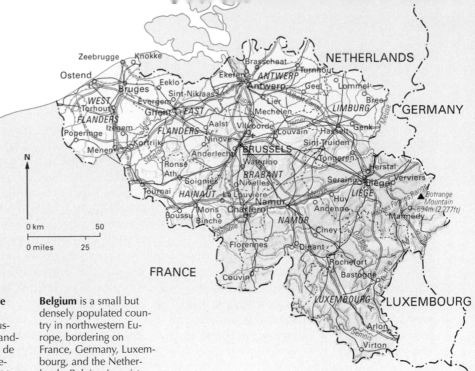

The imposing Palais de Justice, or law courts building, is one of Brussels' most important landmarks. The broad Rue de la Régence, in the foreground, runs northeast toward the Palais de Roi, the residence of Belgium's monarch.

Belgium is a small but densely populated country in northwestern Europe, bordering on France, Germany, Luxembourg, and the Netherlands. Belgium's moist, moderate climate benefits the country's farmland.

Efforts by the Flemings and Walloons to preserve their separate cultural identities have sometimes bordered on civil war. Their conflict not only divides the country culturally, but politically and economically as well. In an effort to seek a solution to the division between the language communities, the Belgian government granted both groups limited self-rule in 1980.

Languages spoken:
Dutch 58%
French 32%
German 10%

Religions:
Roman Catholic 75%
Protestant or other 25%

*Enrollment ratios compare the number of students enrolled to the population which, by age, should be enrolled. A ratio higher than 100 indicates that students older or younger than the typical age range are also enrolled.

†Includes training for the unemployed.

TECHNOLOGY

Radios per 1,000 people: 793

Televisions per 1,000 people: 541

Computers per 1,000 people: 344.5

ECONOMY

Currency: Euro

Gross national income (GNI) in 2000: $251.6 billion U.S.

Real annual growth rate (1999–2000): 4.0%

GNI per capita (2000): $24,540 U.S.

Balance of payments (1998): $11,844 million

Goods exported: Machinery and equipment, chemicals, diamonds, metals and metal products

Goods imported: Machinery and equipment, chemicals, metals and metal products

Trading partners: Germany, France, Netherlands

Land regions

Belgium's landscape varies greatly for so small a country. Belgium's four main land regions are the Coastal and Interior Lowlands, the Kempenland, the Central Low Plateaus, and the Ardennes.

The Coastal and Interior Lowlands extend across most of northern Belgium. Sandy beaches line the North Sea coast, while sea walls and drainage canals protect the nearby lowlands from flooding. The fertile inland region provides good farmland.

The Kempenland, also called the *Campine*, is a mining and industrial area in northeastern Belgium. Many of the birch forests that grew there until the early 1900's have been cleared and replanted with fast-growing evergreens for timber harvest.

The Central Low Plateaus in central Belgium have the country's richest soil. This region is also the site of many of the nation's largest cities.

The Ardennes region, which covers southeastern Belgium, consists mainly of forested hills separated by winding rivers. Many deer and wild boars roam these forests.

Torrential rain led to severe floods in Belgium in January 1995.

Flemings and Walloons

A visitor traveling through Belgium could hardly fail to notice that people in the northern part of the country speak Dutch, while those in the south speak French. The Dutch-speaking Flemings, who live in the northern region of Flanders, make up about 55 per cent of the Belgian population. The French-speaking Walloons, who live in the southern region of Wallonia, make up about 30 per cent of the population. Although the capital city of Brussels is located in Flanders, both languages are spoken there. The language difference has been a source of political and economic conflict between the two regions for more than 150 years.

Roots of the conflict

The conflict began in 1830, when Belgium achieved independence and French was recognized as the new nation's only official language. The Flemings were poorly represented in the Belgian government, and many Dutch speakers protested the domination of Belgium by French speakers. The Walloons also dominated the nation economically. Between 1830 and 1870, heavy industry developed rapidly in Wallonia, and it became one of Belgium's major economic centers.

In the late 1800's, the Flemings won recognition of Dutch as the nation's second official language. However, conflict between the Flemings and the Walloons continued into the 1900's as each group sought to advance its own economic and cultural interests.

Tensions between the two groups increased during the 1960's. The Flemings held mass demonstrations to demand political equality and cultural independence. And in the 1970's, energy crises caused a decline in industrial Wallonia's wealth, and high unemployment followed. As a result, the economic and political balance shifted to the Flemings.

The situation today

In 1971, Parliament revised the Constitution to divide the nation into three cultural communities: Dutch speakers, French speakers, and German speakers. About 1 per cent of Belgians speak German, and live near the German border. Each community was given its own cultural council, which must approve all legislation dealing with language, education, or other cultural matters. The revised Constitution also set up three economic regions in Belgium: Flanders, Wallonia, and Brussels. Finally, in 1980, the Belgian government granted limited self-rule to Flanders and Wallonia.

Today, the Belgian government and most businesses use both French and Dutch. In Flanders, schools teach in Dutch. And language-based political parties have an important influence on Belgian politics.

Many problems remain, however, especially in the realm of economics. The conflict between the Flemings and the Walloons hinders the cooperation needed to deal with Belgium's high rate of unemployment and low rate of economic growth.

Mass demonstrations held in the 1960's signified the tensions between the Flemings and the Walloons.

Signs in Dutch and French in Brussels indicate the nation's bilingual status.

In Belgium, one of the most densely populated countries of the world, about 95 per cent of the people live in cities and towns. A jagged east-west line across the country's map, *below,* indicates its division into French-speaking Wallonia in the south and Dutch-speaking Flanders in the north. The small German-speaking community in the east maintains its own cultural identity.

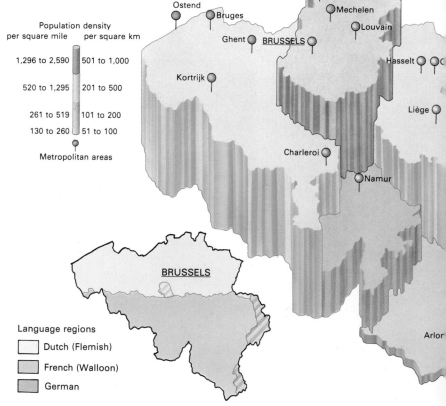

Population density

per square mile	per square km
1,296 to 2,590	501 to 1,000
520 to 1,295	201 to 500
261 to 519	101 to 200
130 to 260	51 to 100

Metropolitan areas

Language regions
- Dutch (Flemish)
- French (Walloon)
- German

The Mons region of French-speaking Wallonia, *left,* reflects the decay of a declining industrial area. Since the 1960's, Wallonia has lost its commercial dominance over Flanders.

Antwerp's Grote Markt flourishes in the new-found prosperity of Flanders. During the 1500's, Antwerp's harbor helped the city become one of the richest trading centers in the world. Today, the harbor at Antwerp is still among the world's largest, and the city also benefits from the petrochemical plants established in Flanders.

Medieval Cities of Flanders

Until 1830, Flanders was a political unit that included areas that are now part of France and the Netherlands as well as the northern half of Belgium. During the Middle Ages, Flanders was one of Europe's most important economic centers, largely as a result of its cloth-making industry. The area's position at the crossroads of trading routes to the south and east also contributed to its development. The wealth of the merchant class that settled in Ghent, Bruges, Antwerp, and Ostend is still reflected in these cities.

Ghent

Ghent, which lies at the fork of the Schelde and Leie rivers, has been the capital of Flanders since the 1100's. By the 1400's, the city was one of the most important trading towns in the Hanseatic League and the center of the Flanders cloth trade.

For many years afterward, however, Ghent's economy was destroyed by revolutions and war. The cloth industry eventually revitalized the city's economy in the 1800's. Ghent is connected to the North Sea by a ship canal built in 1886, and the city now ranks as Belgium's second largest seaport.

Ghent's historic buildings, particularly the guildhalls that line its squares, testify to its former position as a great commercial city. Ghent was also a renowned art center, and numerous paintings, including many by famous Flemish artists, hang in its churches and museums.

The city's medieval buildings, along with some 200 bridges spanning its waterways, make a timeless setting. The fortified castle of 's Gravensteen, which overlooks Ghent, presents an excellent view of the city's old section.

Bruges

From 1240 to 1426, Bruges was one of the most important cities in Europe. As a member of the Hanseatic League, Bruges rivaled the great trading empire of Venice. Ships carrying cloth, silks, gold, salt, and spices sailed directly into the port at Bruges via an inlet that connected the city with the North Sea. Much of the wealth of the city, however, came from the wool trade, which Bruges essentially monopolized.

The city's importance decreased as the Hanseatic League declined and the inlet dried up. Bruges finally experienced an economic revival in the 1900's, due to the construction of the Bruges maritime canal and the expansion of the port of Zeebrugge.

Today, although Bruges is an important lacemaking center, tourism has replaced trade as the city's major economic activity. Thousands of visitors come to Bruges to see the magnificent buildings dating back to the Middle Ages and their beautiful carvings and paintings. Such buildings include the Market Hall, built in the 1200's, and the city's Gothic town hall, built in the 1300's. The many bridges that cross the network of canals gave the city its name—*Bruges* means *bridges*.

Waterways, *above,* **link the historic lacemaking town of Mechelen** with other communities of northern Belgium.

Ostend, *right,* is a popular seaside resort as well as one of Belgium's major seaports. A fortified town in the 1500's, Ostend became a fashionable resort in the late 1800's.

The view of Bruges from above shows why many people consider it to be the most beautiful city in Belgium. Filled with historic buildings and threaded by picturesque canals, Bruges has preserved much of its medieval past.

Ghent, *below,* was once the medieval capital of Flanders and an important art center. The city's St. Bavon Cathedral contains the famous Ghent Altarpiece, painted by Flemish artist Jan van Eyck in the 1400's.

Antwerp's lively "Bird Market," *left,* deals in many varieties of animals as well as birds. It provides a colorful contrast to the city's many artistic and architectural treasures. Antwerp has been an important commercial and cultural center for centuries.

Brussels

Brussels, Belgium's capital, ranks as the nation's fifth largest city but Brussels and its suburbs, with a population of about 1 million people, make up the country's largest metropolitan area. While both Dutch and French are used for education and public communication in metropolitan Brussels, French is the everyday language of most of the people. The city is called *Brussel* in Dutch and *Bruxelles* in French.

History of the city

Historians do not know when Brussels was founded. By the A.D. 900's, the city had become an important stopping point on trade routes linking western Germany and northern France. By the 1200's, Brussels itself was an important center of trade and industry, and famous for its fine tapestries and other textile products.

For centuries thereafter, Brussels was part of empires controlled by foreign rulers, including the Burgundians, Spaniards, Austrians, French, and Dutch. The city became the capital of Belgium when the country gained independence in 1830. German troops occupied Brussels during World War I (1914-1918) and again during World War II (1939-1945), but the city suffered little physical damage in these wars.

Sometimes called the "capital of Europe," Brussels today is a center of international economic and political activity. The European Union (EU) and the North Atlantic Treaty Organization (NATO) are based in or near the city. Many of Brussels' residents work for the government or for EU agencies.

With its large office buildings, cafes, hotels, shops, and network of wide expressways, Brussels appears to be a very modern city. However, many reminders of its past are found in the city's old section.

The lower city

The oldest section of the city, called the *lower city,* lies in the center of Brussels. At its heart stands the Grand' Place, the main square of Brussels. This marketplace is bordered by elaborately decorated buildings constructed during the late 1600's to house merchant and craft guilds.

The Grand' Place, *above*, is at its most colorful on Sunday mornings when the square is transformed into a bird and flower market. The buildings lining the square were constructed in the late 1600's to house merchant guilds.

These buildings were erected after French cannon fire destroyed most of the square in 1695. Only Brussels' town hall, the Hôtel de Ville—dating from the 1400's—survived the destruction. Atop the building's graceful spire, a statue of Saint Michael, the city's patron saint, faces the square.

Brussels' best-loved landmark, the *Manneken-Pis,* can be found on a street near the Grand' Place. Known as the "Oldest Citizen of Brussels," this bronze statue of a small, naked boy symbolizes the city's spirit of cheerful independence.

The upper city

The *upper city,* which lies east of the lower city, contains many important buildings erected during the 1800's and early 1900's, including the royal palace and the Parliament building, as well as elegant residential neighborhoods. Near the royal palace stands the Palais de Justice, which houses Belgium's highest court. This massive building can be seen from many parts of Brussels.

The Cité Berlaymont, *right,* is the headquarters of the European Commission, which administers the European Union (EU). Many other international agencies, including NATO and Benelux, also meet in Brussels.

Beautiful lace has been one of the most famous products of Belgium since the 1500's, when Italy and Belgium were the chief centers of early lace-making. A plaque at the left marks the residence of the famous French author Victor Hugo, who lived in Brussels during his exile from France.

The Cathedral of Saint Michael, north of the Palais de Justice, is renowned for its stained-glass windows, dating from the early 1500's. The church, which stands on the site of an earlier chapel, was itself begun in 1226.

Art and education

Many people come to Brussels to see the magnificent art collections in its museums. The Museum of Fine Arts features works by Belgian artists of the 1400's through 1800's, while the Museum of Modern Art houses more recent works. Other cultural attractions include the Museum of Natural History, the Albert I Library, and the Théâtre de la Monnaie, which offers performances of operas and ballets.

The Free University of Brussels is actually two institutions. Consistent with the city's official bilingual status, the university has one division for French-speaking students and another for those who speak Dutch.

Brussels, *right,* lies between French-speaking Wallonia and Dutch-speaking Flanders. Its oldest section, the lower city, includes the Grand' Place and town hall. To the east lies the upper city, which includes the royal palace, the Parliament building, and other government buildings. Modern neighborhoods and suburbs surround the upper and lower cities.

The ornate buildings on the Grand' Place, *left,* provide an impressive setting for a sidewalk cafe. Many people in Brussels enjoy getting together for coffee, beer, or a wine called Porto in the numerous cafes that line the city's streets.

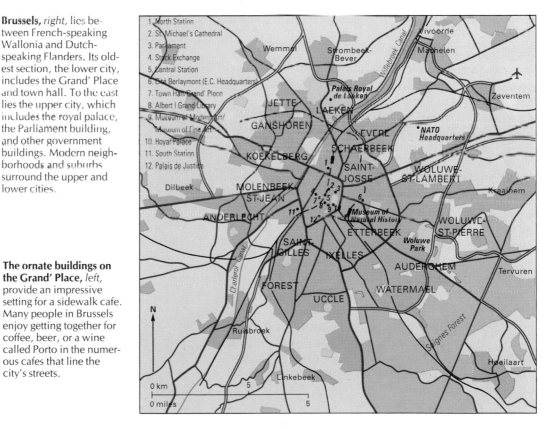

1. North Station
2. St Michael's Cathedral
3. Parliament
4. Stock Exchange
5. Central Station
6. Cité Berlaymont (E.C. Headquarters)
7. Town Hall/Grand' Place
8. Albert I Grand Library
9. Museum of Modern Art/Museum of Fine Art
10. Royal Palace
11. South Station
12. Palais de Justice

Economy

Belgium has one of the most highly developed economies in the world. The government owns and manages parts of the nation's transportation system, but the economy is based mainly on free enterprise.

In recent years, Belgium's economy has undergone considerable restructuring. Traditional industries, such as coal mining, have declined. In addition, important industries that were once concentrated in Wallonia, such as the production of steel, have moved to Flanders.

Economy in Wallonia and Flanders

The province of Hainaut in Wallonia is the country's oldest industrial region. Coal mines along the Sambre River once helped make southern Belgium a prosperous area, but since 1958, many mines have closed down due to high production costs and the exhaustion of the coal deposits.

Steel industries located in Wallonia declined during the worldwide steel crisis of the 1970's and were not modernized thereafter. These plants used coal rather than more-efficient petroleum.

At the same time, much of the farmland in Flanders was transformed into modern industrial areas. The Belgian steel industry, which had been concentrated near the coal mines in Wallonia, moved to Flanders. The industry now uses imported petroleum—instead of coal—to power the steel-making process, so the new steel plants are located near the North Sea. The ports of Antwerp, Ghent, and Zeebrugge have all benefited from the expansion of industry in Flanders.

In the 1970's, the Belgian government established Flanders and Wallonia as relatively independent economic regions. However, Belgium's future economic development depends on the government's success in achieving economic equality for the inhabitants of both areas. Improved cooperation between the Flemings and Walloons is also necessary to reduce Belgium's high rate of unemployment, keep inflation down, and further stimulate the economy's growth.

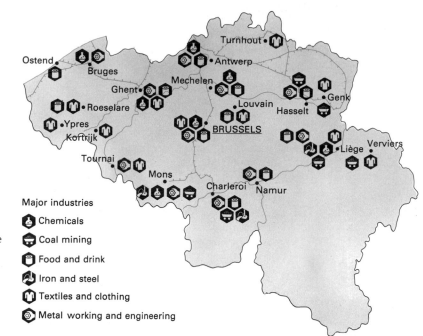

Many of Belgium's key industries, *right,* rely heavily on foreign trade, due to limited natural resources and a small internal market. Since the heart of the steel industry shifted from Wallonia to the Flanders region, huge petrochemical plants have developed around the seaport of Antwerp.

Major industries

🜄 Chemicals

⬡ Coal mining

🥫 Food and drink

⚒ Iron and steel

Ⓜ Textiles and clothing

◎ Metal working and engineering

Barges crowd Antwerp's busy port, *above,* which ranks as one of Europe's largest. Located near the mouth of the Schelde River, Antwerp has a varied industry, which includes brewing, diamond-cutting and trading, petro-chemicals, and sugar refining.

Highly productive Belgian farms average about 27 acres (11 hectares) in size. Most farms are run by families, many of whom rent the land. Modern farm machinery has replaced the horses which used to pull plows and other farm implements until the 1960's.

A carpet factory, *above right,* in Mouscron, western Belgium, produces one of the country's chief textile products. Belgium's long-established textile industry also exports synthetic fibers, lace, and linen.

Industry and agriculture

Steel production is the country's most important manufacturing industry. Belgium is among the world's leading nations in *per capita* (per person) steel production.

The chemical industry manufactures basic chemicals as well as pharmaceutical products and plastics. Belgium's textile products include its world-famous lace and linen. Food processing, including the manufacture of Belgian chocolates, also ranks as an important industry. And there are more than 100 breweries in Belgium, many located in monasteries.

Antwerp is Belgium's main seaport and the economic center of Flanders. In addition to its vast trade, the city has many industries, including sugar refining, lace-making, brewing, and shipbuilding. Antwerp is also a major diamond center. More than half of the world diamond trade is carried on in Antwerp, and the city is also the world's largest diamond-cutting center.

Belgium depends heavily on foreign trade because the country has very few natural resources. The nation's main trading partners are other members of the European Community, but it also does business with Sweden, Switzerland, the United States, and Japan.

Machines and other engineering goods make up the largest share of Belgium's foreign trade. The country also imports cotton, grains, and petroleum. Other major exports include chemicals, processed foods, glass products, steel, and textiles.

Farmers make up less than 5 per cent of the Belgian work force, but they produce more than 80 per cent of the country's food needs. Dairy farming and livestock production account for more than 65 per cent of Belgium's farm income. The nation's agricultural land is used to grow barley, flax, hops, potatoes, sugar beets, and wheat. Belgium also produces large quantities of flowers, fruits, and vegetables.

Belize

Belize is a tiny country in Central America. It lies close to Honduras on the southeast coast of the Yucatán Peninsula, south of Mexico and east of Guatemala.

Until 1973, Belize was called British Honduras. The United Kingdom ruled the country from the mid-1800's until 1981, when Belize became an independent nation. However, British troops remained until 1993 because Guatemala claimed part of Belize. Guatemala gave up this claim in 1991.

As a former British colony, Belize is now part of the Commonwealth of Nations. It is a constitutional monarchy with the British monarch as its head. The government is a parliamentary democracy.

Belize's legislature consists of a House of Representatives and a Senate. The people elect the members of the House, and the leader of the majority party becomes the prime minister. With the help of 10 Cabinet ministers, the prime minister runs the government. A governor general represents the British monarch.

The land and economy

Most of coastal Belize is warm, swampy lowland. Inland, the north is flat, but the land in the south rises to the low peaks of the Maya Mountains. The country is covered by many

Belize City, *right,* is the largest city in Belize and has about a fourth of the nation's population. The city, which lies at the mouth of the Belize River, has been a major shipping center for hardwoods for 300 years.

FACT BOX

COUNTRY

Official name: Belize
Capital: Belmopan
Terrain: Flat, swampy coastal plain; low mountains in south
Area: 8,865 sq. mi. (22,960 km²)

Climate: Tropical; very hot and humid; rainy season (May to February)
Main river: Belize
Highest elevation: Victoria Peak, 3,680 ft. (1,122 m)
Lowest elevation: Caribbean Sea, sea level

GOVERNMENT

Form of government: Parliamentary democracy
Head of state: British monarch, represented by governor general
Head of government: Prime minister
Administrative areas: 6 districts

Legislature: National Assembly consisting of the Senate with 8 members serving five-year terms and the House of Representatives with 29 members serving five-year terms
Court system: Supreme Court
Armed forces: 1,050 troops

PEOPLE

Estimated 2002 population: 251,000
Population growth: 2.75%
Population density: 29 persons per sq. mi. (11 per km²)
Population distribution: 50% rural, 50% urban
Life expectancy in years: Male: 70 Female: 74
Doctors per 1,000 people: N/A
Percentage of age-appropriate population enrolled in the following educational levels: Primary: N/A Secondary: N/A Further: N/A

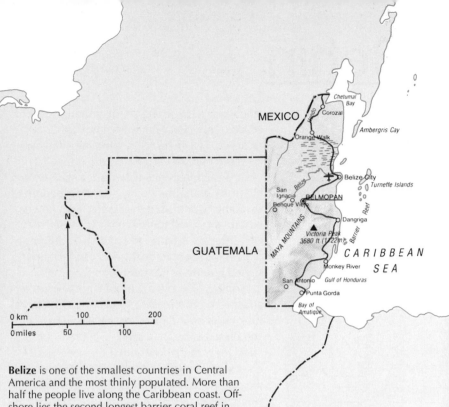

Mayan ruins, *above,* reveal part of the history of Belize. The Mayas spread south from Mexico and thrived in this area.

Belize is one of the smallest countries in Central America and the most thinly populated. More than half the people live along the Caribbean coast. Offshore lies the second longest barrier coral reef in the world. The Belize River cuts across the country.

forests, though large areas have been cut for lumber. Pine and such hardwoods as mahogany and cedrela are important forest products.

Belize is a developing country, and its economy is based on agriculture. The country's chief crop is sugar cane, which is grown on large plantations. Farmers also raise bananas, corn, grapefruit, and oranges.

Belize's industries are small. They include sugar refining and food processing—processed sugar is the country's chief export. Some small industries process wood; others produce clothing, cement, and bricks.

Belize's location on the Caribbean Sea helps contribute to its economy. The sea provides conch, fish, lobsters, and shrimp. Belizeans are also building resort hotels and other facilities to attract tourists.

The people

The ancient Mayas spread into what is now Belize from the northern part of the Yucatán Peninsula. Some Belizeans still speak Mayan Indian languages today.

However, about half the people of Belize are descended at least in part from black Africans, who worked as slaves on the Caribbean islands. About one-fifth are descended from Maya or Carib Indians, who lived on the Caribbean islands before Europeans arrived. *Mestizos,* who have European and Indian ancestry, also make up about one-fifth of the population. The rest of the people are of European, East Indian, Chinese, or Lebanese descent.

Most Belizeans are poor. About half the people live in urban areas, and half live in rural areas. Unemployment is high in the cities, and farm production is low in the rural areas.

Languages spoken:
English (official)
Spanish
Mayan
Garifuna (Carib)
Creole

Religions:
Roman Catholic 62%
Protestant 30%
none 2%

TECHNOLOGY

Radios per 1,000 people:
N/A

Televisions per 1,000 people: N/A

Computers per 1,000 people: N/A

ECONOMY

Currency: Belizean dollar

Gross national income (GNI) in 2000: $746 million U.S.

Real annual growth rate (1999–2000): 10.2%

GNI per capita (2000): $3,110 U.S.

Balance of payments (2000): N/A

Goods exported: Sugar, bananas, citrus fruits, clothing, fish products, molasses, wood

Goods imported: Machinery and transportation equipment, manufactured goods, food, fuels, chemicals, pharmaceuticals

Trading partners: United States, United Kingdom, Mexico, European Union

Benin

The long, narrow west African country of Benin, known as Dahomey until 1975, stretches 415 miles (688 kilometers) inland from the Gulf of Guinea. More than 400 years ago, Europeans established slave-trading posts along the coast, and the kingdom of Dahomey controlled the region with power based largely on the slave trade.

During the 1800's, the palm oil trade replaced the slave trade, and in 1851 France signed a trade agreement with the king of Dahomey. However, when Dahomey soldiers attacked French trading posts in 1892, France took over the area and, in 1904, made it a French territory. The French built roads and railroads that made Benin a crossroads for coastal road traffic and provided an outlet to the sea for inland territories. Self-government was granted to Dahomey in 1958, and in 1960 it became a fully independent nation.

The government has undergone frequent changes since independence, however. In 1972, a military group overthrew a civilian government, and a military government led by army officer Mathieu Kerekou took control of the nation's most important businesses. Three years later, the government changed the nation's name from Dahomey to Benin.

The production of wool is a traditional livelihood in Benin. A Bariba man of northern Benin, *above,* lifts a skein of wool yarn from a dyeing vat.

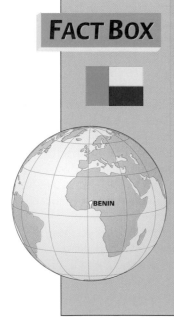

The horned headdress that adorns this young woman may reflect her spiritual beliefs. Many of Benin's people practice *animism,* the belief that all things in nature have spirits.

FACT BOX

COUNTRY

Official name: Republique du Benin (Republic of Benin)
Capital: Porto-Novo (official), Cotonou (seat of government)
Terrain: Mostly flat to undulating plain; some hills and low mountains
Area: 43,483 sq. mi. (112,620 km²)

Climate: Tropical; hot, humid in south; semiarid in north
Main rivers: Ouémé, Okpara
Highest elevation: Mont Sokbaro, 2,159 ft. (658 m)
Lowest elevation: Atlantic Ocean, sea level

GOVERNMENT

Form of government: Republic
Head of state: President
Head of government: President
Administrative areas: 6 provinces, also known as departments

Legislature: Assemblee Nationale (National Assembly) with 83 members serving four-year terms
Court system: Cour Constitutionnelle (Constitutional Court), Cour Supreme (Supreme Court), High Court of Justice
Armed forces: 4,800 troops

PEOPLE

Estimated 2002 population: 6,422,000
Population growth: 3.03%
Population density: 148 persons per sq. mi. (57 per km²)
Population distribution: 62% rural, 38% urban
Life expectancy in years: Male: 49 Female: 51
Doctors per 1,000 people: 0.1
Percentage of age-appropriate population enrolled in the following educational levels: Primary: 78 Secondary: 18 Further: 3

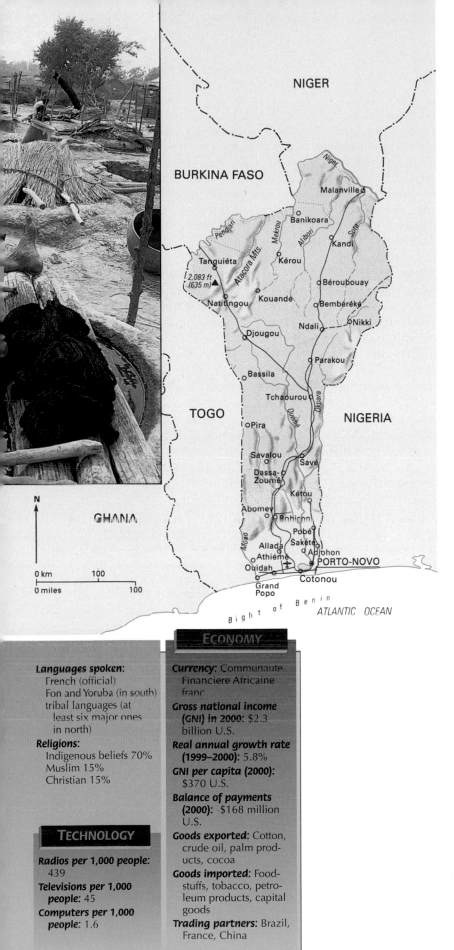

Benin

Benin is a long, narrow west African country, extending 415 mi. (668 km) inland from the coast. Porto-Novo is the capital city, but most government activity occurs in Cotonou.

In 1990, Kerekou's government was dissolved, all political parties were legalized, and a temporary government was set up. Kerekou remained president, but Nicephore Soglo became prime minister and leader of Benin. The temporary government served until early 1991, when Soglo was elected president and a new legislature was chosen. Benin's new government ended nearly all governmental control of businesses. In 1996, Kerekou was elected again as president.

Benin is mainly an agricultural country, and palm trees remain the nation's chief source of wealth. Palm oil and kernels are its leading exports. The few industrial plants in the country include palm oil refineries and cotton mills in southern Benin.

Farmers in Benin grow beans, corn, cassava, millet, rice, sorghum, and yams, and raise such livestock as cattle, goats, pigs, and sheep. Almost 50 per cent of Benin's people farm the land or raise livestock.

Most of the people of Benin are black Africans, but they belong to some 60 ethnic groups. The largest group, which makes up about 60 per cent of the population, consists of the closely related Fons and Adjas. They live in southern Benin along with the Yorubas, who make up about 10 per cent of the population. The Baribas, who also make up about 10 per cent, are the largest group in the north.

In the far northwestern Atacora Mountains, the people live in round mud houses with thatched roofs, while those who live in the lagoon areas that lie north of the coast build bamboo huts perched on stakes to protect them from the water. Some of Benin's people, particularly in the cities, live in houses made of concrete.

The women of Benin wear brightly colored dresses, and many of the men wear the agbade—an outfit of trousers, a full-length robe, and a short jacket. However, many people, particularly in southern Benin, wear Western-style clothing.

ECONOMY

Languages spoken:
French (official)
Fon and Yoruba (in south)
tribal languages (at least six major ones in north)

Religions:
Indigenous beliefs 70%
Muslim 15%
Christian 15%

TECHNOLOGY

Radios per 1,000 people: 439

Televisions per 1,000 people: 45

Computers per 1,000 people: 1.6

Currency: Communaute Financiere Africaine franc

Gross national income (GNI) in 2000: $2.3 billion U.S.

Real annual growth rate (1999–2000): 5.8%

GNI per capita (2000): $370 U.S.

Balance of payments (2000): -$168 million U.S.

Goods exported: Cotton, crude oil, palm products, cocoa

Goods imported: Foodstuffs, tobacco, petroleum products, capital goods

Trading partners: Brazil, France, China

Bermuda

It is not surprising that Bermuda is a popular resort area. This string of coral islands and islets is blessed with a mild climate, beautiful beaches, swaying palm trees, and colorful flowers. Every year, thousands of tourists and honeymooners visit Bermuda.

Bermuda actually consists of more than 300 islands and tiny islets, about 670 miles (1,080 kilometers) southeast of New York City in the North Atlantic Ocean. The islands are the northernmost coral islands in the world, lying midway between Nova Scotia and the West Indies.

Only about 20 of the islands are inhabited. The four largest islands—Bermuda, St. George's, St. David's, and Somerset—extend in a chain about 22 miles (35 kilometers) long. These islands and several smaller ones are linked by bridges.

Bermuda's total land area is about 21 square miles (54 square kilometers). The island of Bermuda takes up about two-thirds of that area.

Bermuda has hills and ridges that rise up out of the sea as high as 250 feet (76 meters). Scenic beaches line the coasts, and caves are found throughout the islands.

Bermuda is noted for its dangerously narrow, winding roads. Only small automobiles are permitted, and the top speed limit is 20 miles (32 kilometers) per hour.

Bermuda's climate is mild, and rainfall is fairly plentiful. Rainfall is important because Bermuda has few underground sources of fresh water. Rain water is collected on rooftops and stored in tanks under buildings. To help keep the water supply pure, roofs are kept clean and whitewashed. Like the southeast coast of North America, Bermuda is sometimes struck by hurricanes in the fall months.

About 63,000 people live on the 20 inhabited islands. People of African descent make up about 60 per cent of the population; people of European descent make up about 40 per cent.

Tourism is the major source of income on the islands. Bermuda also attracts businesses from other countries by giving them tax breaks. For that reason, about 5,000 foreign companies operate in Bermuda, including many insurance and investment firms. There is little land that can be farmed, so Bermuda imports about 80 per cent of its food.

Government

Bermuda is a self-governing British dependency. The British monarch appoints the governor of Bermuda, who is assisted by an 8-member council.

Bermuda's parliament, established in 1620, is the world's oldest British overseas parlia-

Rocks jutting out of the water in the bay near St. George show the rugged beauty of Bermuda.

Shining beaches attract about 600,000 tourists to Bermuda every year.

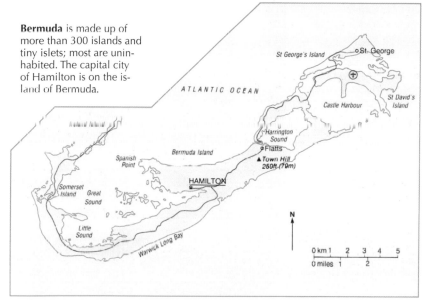

Bermuda is made up of more than 300 islands and tiny islets; most are uninhabited. The capital city of Hamilton is on the island of Bermuda.

Fishing in Bermuda is chiefly a tourist sport, but a few Bermudians make their living by commercial fishing. In this photograph, members of a fishing crew clean their catch.

ment. It is made up of an 11-member appointed Senate and a 40-member elected House of Assembly.

Bermuda's government, like its economy, is largely controlled by the European minority. During the late 1960's and the 1970's, many people of African descent protested against this control. Violence erupted, and the governor of Bermuda was killed. The political power of people of African descent has increased somewhat since that time.

History

The islands were named for Juan de Bermúdez, a Spaniard who discovered them in the 1500's. In 1609, a ship carrying colonists to Virginia was destroyed in a violent storm, and the passengers took refuge in Bermuda. All except two sailed away the next year. Those two people became Bermuda's first permanent settlers.

In 1684, the British government took control of the islands. The English settlers kept African slaves as domestic servants and boat builders. During the 1800's, Bermuda carried on a thriving trade with the West Indies and North America. The salvage of shipwrecks, blockade running, and smuggling are all part of Bermuda's history. It has also been the site of U.S. military bases. Today the North Atlantic Treaty Organization (NATO) provides for Bermuda's defense.

Bhutan

Bhutan is a small mountain kingdom that lies in the eastern Himalaya between India and Tibet. It is a *hereditary* (inherited) monarchy headed by a powerful king. Bhutan was isolated from the rest of the world until 1959, when China claimed part of the country.

Bhutan's early history is uncertain. The country's original settlers, the Bhutia Tephoo, were conquered by Tibetan invaders in the A.D. 800's. In the 1600's, a Tibetan *lama* (Buddhist monk) took control of the country's religious and political affairs. In 1907, Ugyen Wangchuk became Bhutan's first king.

Over the past 200 years, both India and the United Kingdom have taken control of Bhutan's affairs. During the 1700's and 1800's, the United Kingdom controlled Bhutan's foreign relations. In 1910, the British Indian government took over but left Bhutan in control of its own internal affairs. In 1949, India agreed to help Bhutan develop its economy. Bhutan strengthened its ties to India in 1959 and began to modernize its economic, educational, and health care systems.

Bhutia fathers often carry their young children on their backs. The dress of the Bhutias, who make up more than half the population of Bhutan, reveals their Tibetan ancestry.

Landscape and economy

Bhutan has three major land regions. Along the Indian border lies a region of plains and river valleys with a hot, humid climate where bananas, citrus fruits, and rice are grown.

FACT BOX

COUNTRY

Official name: Kingdom of Bhutan
Capital: Thimphu
Terrain: Mostly mountainous with some fertile valleys and savanna
Area: 18,147 sq. mi. (47,000 km²)
Climate: Tropical in southern plains; cool winters and hot summers in central valleys; severe winters and cool summers in Himalaya

Main rivers: Wong Chu, Sankosh, Tongsa, Bumtang, Manas, Kuru
Highest elevation: Kula Kangri, 24,783 ft. (7,554 m)
Lowest elevation: Drangme Chhu, 318 ft. (97 m)

GOVERNMENT

Form of government: Monarchy
Head of state: Monarch
Head of government: Foreign minister
Administrative areas: 18 dzongkhag (districts)

Legislature: Tshogdu (National Assembly) with 150 members serving three-year terms
Court system: Supreme Court of Appeal, High Court
Armed forces: N/A

PEOPLE

Estimated 2002 population: 2,238,000
Population growth: 2.19%
Population density: 123 persons per sq. mi. (48 per km²)
Population distribution: 85% rural, 15% urban
Life expectancy in years: Male: 54 Female: 53
Doctors per 1,000 people: N/A
Percentage of age-appropriate population enrolled in the following educational levels: Primary: N/A Secondary: N/A Further: N/A

BHUTAN

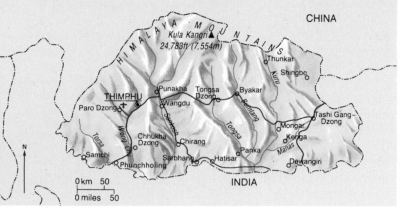

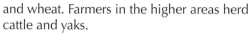

Bhutan

The independent state of Bhutan depends on its huge neighbor to the south, India, to handle its foreign affairs and its defense. In the last three decades, India has also helped Bhutan improve its industries and train its workers.

Taktsang Monastery, *left,* clings to the side of a sheer cliff in the Himalayan region. It can be reached only by a steep, narrow path. The monastery is known as the "Tiger's Nest" because of Bhutanese legends about the site.

The mid-Himalayan region is covered with forests of ash, oak, poplar, and willow trees. The climate in this region is moderate.

In the northernmost region of Bhutan, the mountains of the Himalaya rise over 24,000 feet (7,320 meters). In addition to its towering peaks, this region includes freezing lakes and huge glaciers. The climate is very cold.

Most of Bhutan is unsuitable for farming, with very little flat land, steep valleys, and poor soil. Even so, Bhutan's farmers manage to grow enough food for themselves. Their chief crops are barley, fruit, rice, vegetables,

and wheat. Farmers in the higher areas herd cattle and yaks.

The Indian government has helped the Bhutanese to modernize their economy by establishing orchards and stock-breeding farms and building hydroelectric power stations. India has also helped Bhutan build roads and train its farmers and workers.

Way of life

More than half of the Bhutanese people are descendants of Tibetan settlers. They speak Dzongkha, a Tibetan dialect, which is also the country's official language. They practice Lamaism, also known as Tibetan Buddhism.

About a fourth of the Bhutanese people are Nepalese. They speak Nepali and practice Hinduism. In the early 1990's, friction between the Nepali-speaking people of Southern Bhutan and the ruling north Bhutanese led to tens of thousands of southern Bhutanese fleeing to refugee camps in Nepal, Assam, and West Bengal.

Languages spoken:
Dzongkha (official)
Tibetan dialects
Nepalese dialects
Religions:
Lamaistic Buddhist 75%
Indian- and Nepalese influenced Hinduism 25%

TECHNOLOGY

Radios per 1,000 people: N/A
Televisions per 1,000 people: N/A
Computers per 1,000 people: N/A

ECONOMY

Currency: Ngultrum
Gross national income (GNI) in 2000: $479 million U.S.
Real annual growth rate (1999–2000): 7.0%
GNI per capita (2000): $590 U.S.
Balance of payments (2000): N/A
Goods exported: Cardamom, gypsum, timber, handicrafts, cement, fruit, electricity, precious stones, spices
Goods imported: Fuel and lubricants, grain, machinery and parts, vehicles, fabrics, rice
Trading partners: India, Bangladesh, Japan

A Buddhist festival honors the Indian teacher Padmasambhava, who is said to have introduced Buddhism into Tibet in the A.D. 700's. From there, Buddhism spread into Bhutan, where Padmasambhava became known as Guru Rimpoche. Padmasambhava is almost as highly esteemed as Buddha himself.

Bolivia

Wrapped in woolen ponchos and shawls for protection against the chilly mountain dampness, three Indian women are ready to begin their daily chores. Their colorful garments stand out boldly against the desolate landscape of Bolivia's Altiplano. A high plateau that lies between two craggy ranges of the Andes Mountains, the Altiplano is home to about 40 per cent of the country's population. Many inhabitants of this region live in La Paz, the capital and largest city. *Campesinos*—the poor Indian farmers who make up Bolivia's largest social class—live in the countryside.

The campesinos wear the traditional clothing of their ancestors. The women dress in full, sweeping skirts that almost touch the ground, and many wear derby hats. The men wear striped ponchos. The campesino customs and way of life are also deeply rooted in the past. In many parts of Bolivia, the Indians live much as their ancestors did before the Spaniards conquered them in the 1530's.

Early civilizations

American Indians lived in the region that is now Bolivia as long as 10,000 years ago. About A.D. 100, the Tiahuanaco Indians developed a major civilization near Lake Titicaca. They built gigantic monuments and carved statues out of stone. The Tiahuanaco civilization declined during the 1200's, and by the late 1300's, a warlike tribe called the Aymara Indians controlled the area. The Aymara were conquered by the Inca during the 1400's, and the region became part of the great Inca empire. In the 1530's, the Spanish conquistadors defeated the Inca.

Spanish colonial rule brought years of misery and suffering to the Bolivian Indians. Forced to work on the *haciendas* (large ranches) and in the silver mines, many died from mistreatment and from diseases brought by the Spaniards. The Indians frequently revolted against Spanish tyranny, but they were quickly and brutally crushed. The most famous rebellion was organized in 1781 by Tupac Amaru II, who would have been the official heir to the Inca throne.

Bolívar and liberation

In 1824, the great Venezuelan general Simón Bolívar sent Antonio José de Sucre to free Bolivia from Spanish rule. Sucre's forces defeated the Spaniards in 1825, and Bolivia declared its independence. Sucre became the country's first president.

Unfortunately for Bolivia, the tyranny of the Spaniards was replaced by chaos and violence during the years following independence. Many of Bolivia's leaders showed far more concern for their own political power and wealth than for the needs of the people.

In addition, Bolivia lost more than half of its territory in disputes with neighboring countries. In the Great War of the Pacific (1879–1883), Chile seized Bolivia's nitrate-rich land along the Pacific Ocean. Bolivia has been completely landlocked ever since.

In the late 1800's, the world price of silver increased greatly, and large deposits of tin were discovered in Bolivia. The export of these minerals became highly important to Bolivia's economy. Political parties representing the interests of the mine owners grew more and more powerful. They controlled Bolivia until the 1930's and helped the country achieve greater political stability. Bolivia's presidents during this time devoted much effort to promoting mining and the building of railroads.

Between 1936 and 1952, Bolivia had 10 presidents, most of them military leaders whose governments violated the civil rights of the people. The nation's frequent wars and revolutions hampered its economic growth, and today Bolivia has one of the lowest standards of living in the Western Hemisphere. Modern-day Bolivians, descendants of the mighty Inca, can barely eke out a living in their remote mountain world.

Bolivia Today

Although most of Bolivia's people are poor, the land itself is rich in natural resources. The country's mineral deposits, pastureland, timber, and fertile soil have great economic potential, but the nation's political problems have held back its industrial growth, and Bolivia's natural resources remain underdeveloped.

Since gaining independence from Spain in 1825, the country has had 16 constitutions. Bolivia has also experienced scores of successful and unsuccessful attempts to overthrow its government. Until the 1950's, Bolivia's people had little political freedom and almost no possibility of social advancement.

Revolution and reform

When the world price of silver shot up in the late 1800's, profits from Bolivia's silver mines helped boost the economy. During the same period, large deposits of tin were discovered. Political parties representing the mine owners came to power and managed to maintain political stability until the Chaco War broke out in 1932.

The Chaco War erupted between Bolivia and Paraguay over ownership of the Gran Chaco, a lowland plain bordering both countries. Bolivia lost the war in 1935, and Paraguay won the Gran Chaco. Tremendous

political disorder followed this defeat. During this period, tin miners formed unions and went out on strike for better wages and working conditions.

In 1952, the *Movimiento Nacionalista Revolucionario* (National Revolutionary Movement), a political party supported by the tin miners, overthrew the military government then in power. Victor Paz Estenssoro, an economist and party leader, became president. The new government nationalized the tin mines and introduced land reforms, breaking up the vast estates of the landowners and dividing them among poor Indian farmers. But perhaps most important, all adult Bolivians gained the right to vote, marking the first time the Indian population was included in the political system.

Return to military government

The period of reform came to an end when military dictators regained control of the government. From 1964 to 1982, one violent coup succeeded another. The dictators prohibited any opposition to their policies and imprisoned or killed their enemies. In 1967, Ché Guevara, a revolutionary famous for his activities in Cuba, tried to organize a revolt against military rule, but he was captured and executed.

Members of Bolivia's labor unions carry brightly colored banners through La Paz on National Day, held every year in August.

FACT BOX

COUNTRY

Official name: Republica de Bolivia (Republic of Bolivia)
Capital: Sucre (legal capital and seat of judiciary), La Paz (seat of government)
Terrain: Rugged Andes Mountains with a highland plateau (Altiplano), hills, lowland plains of the Amazon Basin

Area: 424,164 sq. mi. (1,098,580 km²)
Climate: Varies with altitude; humid and tropical to cold and semiarid
Main rivers: Grande, Mamore, Beni
Highest elevation: Nevado Sajama, 21,463 ft. (6,542 m)
Lowest elevation: Rio Paraguay, 295 ft. (90 m)

GOVERNMENT

Form of government: Republic
Head of state: President
Head of government: President
Administrative areas: 9 departamentos (departments)

Legislature: Congreso Nacional (National Congress) consisting of Camara de Senadores (Chamber of Senators) with 27 members serving five-year terms and Camara de Diputados (Chamber of Deputies) with 130 members serving five-year terms
Court system: Corte Suprema (Supreme Court)
Armed forces: 32,500 troops

PEOPLE

Estimated 2002 population: 8,691,000
Population growth: 1.83%
Population density: 20 persons per sq. mi. (8 per km²)
Population distribution: 62% urban, 38% rural
Life expectancy in years:
 Male: 62
 Female: 67
Doctors per 1,000 people: 1.3
Percentage of age-appropriate population enrolled in the following educational levels:
 Primary: N/A
 Secondary: N/A
 Further: 24

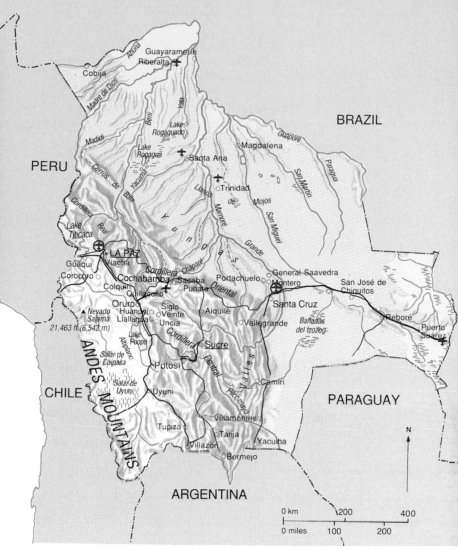

La Paz, *above,* **the highest capital city in the world,** lies in a valley in the Altiplano region. Modern high-rise buildings dominate the central business district of the city, while the huts of the poor sprawl along the valley's slopes.

Bolivia lies south of the equator near the center of South America. Despite its wealth of natural resources, Bolivia's economic progress has been hampered by political instability and a poor transportation system.

Languages spoken:
  Spanish (official)
  Quechua (official)
  Aymara (official)
Religion:
  Roman Catholic 95%
  Protestant

TECHNOLOGY

Radios per 1,000 people:
  676
Televisions per 1,000 people: 119
Computers per 1,000 people: 16.8

ECONOMY

Currency: Boliviano
Gross national income (GNI) in 2000: $8.2 billion U.S.
Real annual growth rate (1999–2000): 2.4%
GNI per capita (2000): $990 U.S.
Balance of payments (2000): -$464 million U.S.
Goods exported: Soy beans, natural gas, zinc, gold, wood
Goods imported: Capital goods, raw materials and semi-manufactures, chemicals, petroleum, food
Trading partners: United States, Japan, United Kingdom

In 1980, Bolivia held an election for a civilian government, but military leaders once again seized power before the elected government could take office. Then, in 1982, the military relaxed its grip and allowed a return to civilian government. The Congress elected in 1980 chose Siles Zuazo as president. He had been president 22 years earlier and had been elected by the people in 1980.

In the 1985, 1989, 1993, and 1997 presidential elections, no candidate got a majority of the popular vote. Therefore, Congress chose the president following each election. Bolivia's economy continued to suffer inflation, while floods and droughts created food shortages.

Bosnia-Herzegovina

The republic of Bosnia-Herzegovina lies in the Balkan Peninsula in southeastern Europe. It was formerly one of the six federal republics of Yugoslavia. In 1991, the Yugoslav federation began to break apart, and in 1992 Bosnia-Herzegovina became an independent republic.

Geographically, Bosnia-Herzegovina is made up of two regions. Bosnia, the northern part, is a mountainous land covered with thick forests, while Herzegovina, the southern part, consists mainly of rolling hills and flat farmland.

Bosnia-Herzegovina remains primarily a rural country with few cities and towns. Its chief industries produce electrical appliances and textiles.

Before war broke out in 1992, Bosnia-Herzegovina was a culturally diverse region, blending Islamic, Christian, Central European, and Mediterranean traditions. The languages spoken are Bosnian, Croatian, and Serbian.

The region that is now Bosnia-Herzegovina was settled by Illyrian tribes more than 2,000 years ago. It became part of a Roman province in about 11 B.C. After A.D. 395, control of the area shifted among Byzantine, Croatian, Hungarian, and Serbian rulers until the Ottomans took over in the late 1400's.

Between the 800's and the 1000's, Bosnia belonged to the medieval Croatian kingdom, while Herzegovina was incorporated into the Serbian kingdoms. Hungary conquered Bosnia in the early 1100's. The first Bosnian state emerged in the late 1110's.

Bosnia-Herzegovina was part of the Ottoman Empire from the mid-1400's until Austria-Hungary gained control in 1878. In 1914, a Serbian patriot from Bosnia assassinated the heir to the throne of Austria-Hungary in the city of Sarajevo. The assassination touched off World War I (1914-1918). After the war ended, Bosnia-Herzegovina became part of the Kingdom of the Serbs, Croats, and Slovenes, later renamed Yugoslavia.

In 1946, Bosnia-Herzegovina became one of the six republics of the Federal People's Republic of Yugoslavia. In March 1992, a majority of Bosnian Muslims and ethnic Croats in Bosnia-Herzegovina voted for independence from Yugoslavia in a referendum that was boycotted by the Serbs.

Fighting broke out between the Serbs, who claimed part of the republic, and the Muslims and Croats. The Serbs, who wished to "cleanse" the region of all non-Serbs, soon gained control of more than two-thirds of Bosnia-Herzegovina. Much of the fighting centered around the capital city of Sarajevo.

FACT BOX

COUNTRY

Official name: Bosna I Hercegovina (Bosnia and Herzegovina)
Capital: Sarajevo
Terrain: Mountains and valleys
Area: 19,741 sq. mi. (51,129 km²)
Climate: Hot summers and cold winters; areas of high elevation have short, cool summers and long, severe winters; mild, rainy winters along coast

Main rivers: Bosna, Drina, Neretva, Sava, Una
Highest elevation: Maglic, 7,828 ft. (2,386 m)
Lowest elevation: Adriatic Sea, sea level

GOVERNMENT

Form of government: Emerging democracy
Head of state: Chairman of the presidency
Head of government: Vacant
Administrative areas: 2 first-order administrative divisions and a self-governing administrative unit

Legislature: Skupstina (Parliamentary Assembly) consisting of the Vijece Opcina (National House of Representatives) with 42 members serving two-year terms and the Vijece Gradanstvo (House of Peoples) with 15 members serving two-year terms
Court system: Constitutional Court
Armed forces: N/A

PEOPLE

Estimated 2002 population: 3,890,000
Population growth: 3.1%
Population density: 197 persons per sq. mi. (75 per km²)
Population distribution: 60% rural, 40% urban
Life expectancy in years: Male: 70 Female: 75
Doctors per 1,000 people: 1.4
Percentage of age-appropriate population enrolled in the following educational levels: Primary: N/A Secondary: N/A Further: N/A

In June 1994, a United Nations (UN) commission investigating war crimes in Bosnia-Herzegovina accused Bosnian Serbs of a campaign of genocide against Bosnian Croats and Muslims.

In July 1994, the Bosnian Serbs rejected an international peace plan which called for the partitioning of Bosnia. The plan, which was accepted by the Croats and Bosnians, would have given the Bosnian Serbs 49 per cent of the territory and 51 per cent to the Muslim-Croat federation.

In November 1994, a Bosnian army offensive drove Serbs off land they held in northwest Bosnia-Herzegovina. In retaliation, the Serbs attacked Bihac, a Muslim stronghold. In 1995, the presidents of Bosnia-Herzegovina, Croatia, and Serbia agreed on a peace plan. Under the plan, Bosnia-Herzegovina would keep its borders but split into two substates, one dominated by Bosnian Serbs and one by the Muslim-Croat federation. In 1996, Muslim, Croat, and Serb forces withdrew from the zones of separation established by the peace agreement. The exchange of territory was marked by violence on all sides.

By early 2001, multiethnic and reformist parties assembled a coalition to rule the country. Soon afterward, the Bosnian Croats announced plans to create their own state within Bosnia.

Set amid the rolling hills of southern Herzegovina, the village of Počitelj, *above,* has preserved the traditional elements of Turkish architecture—low wooden houses topped with roofs made of red tile.

Languages spoken:
Bosnian
Croatian
Serbian
Religions:
Muslim 40%
Orthodox 31%
Roman Catholic 15%
Protestant 4%

TECHNOLOGY

Radios per 1,000 people:
243
Televisions per 1,000 people: 111
Computers per 1,000 people: N/A

ECONOMY

Currency: Convertible marka
Gross national income (GNI) in 2000: $4.9 billion U.S.
Real annual growth rate (1999–2000). 5.9%
GNI per capita (2000): $1,230 U.S.
Balance of payments (2000): N/A
Goods exported: N/A
Goods imported: N/A
Trading partners: N/A

Formerly a federal republic of Yugoslavia, Bosnia-Herzegovina became an independent republic in 1992.

Botswana

Botswana lies far from the sea in the center of southern Africa. More than 100 years ago, after the local people asked for British protection from white South African settlers, it was governed by the United Kingdom and called the Bechuanaland Protectorate. After repeatedly refusing South Africa's requests to turn the protectorate over to South African rule, the United Kingdom granted the region its independence in 1966, and the Republic of Botswana was born. Today, Botswana is a democratic republic.

Government and people

Citizens who are at least 21 years old vote for candidates from several different parties to represent them as members of the National Assembly. The Assembly members then choose four additional members as well as a president. The president selects a Cabinet to help run the government. In addition, the House of Chiefs, made up of the leaders of Botswana's major ethnic groups, advises the government.

The vast majority of Botswanans are black Africans called Tswana who belong to eight main groups. The largest group is the Bamangwato, who make up nearly a third of the population. Most of the Tswana live in large rural villages and farm or herd for a living. Their main food crops are corn, millet, and sorghum.

Botswana also has about 10,000 San, or Bushmen, an African people with yellowish-brown skin whose ancestors have lived in the region since prehistoric times. Sometime before A.D. 1000, the San were pushed from fertile eastern Botswana into the Kalahari region by the Tswana, who had migrated from the north. A few San still live in the Kalahari, gathering food and hunting as their ancestors did, but many have been forced into settlements, and some work on cattle farms.

Several thousand whites also live in Botswana. Some own ranches, while others are technicians or managers in industry, business, or government. Generally, the whites earn more money and have a higher standard of living than black Botswanans. This situation has caused resentment, but the government insists that the country needs the skills and money of the whites to help the economy grow.

Economy

The economy of Botswana is developing rapidly. Copper, diamond, and nickel deposits

Fish from the Okavango River are a welcome addition to the diet of this Tswana villager.

FACT BOX

COUNTRY

Official name: Republic of Botswana
Capital: Gaborone
Terrain: Predominantly flat to gently rolling tableland; Kalahari Desert in southwest
Area: 231,804 sq. mi. (600,370 km²)
Climate: Semiarid; warm winters and hot summers

Main rivers: Okavango, Limpopo, Shashe
Highest elevation: Otse Mountain, 4,886 ft. (1,489 m)
Lowest elevation: Junction of the Limpopo and Shashe Rivers, 1,683 ft. (513 m)

GOVERNMENT

Form of government: Parliamentary republic
Head of state: President
Head of government: President
Administrative areas: 10 districts, 4 town councils

Legislature: Parliament consisting of the House of Chiefs, which is an advisory 15-member body, and the National Assembly with 44 members serving five-year terms
Court system: High Court; Court of Appeal
Armed forces: 9,000 troops

PEOPLE

Estimated 2002 population: 1,661,000
Population growth: 0.76%
Population density: 7 persons per sq. mi. (3 per km²)
Population distribution: 51% rural, 49% urban
Life expectancy in years: Male: 35 Female: 36
Doctors per 1,000 people: 0.2
Percentage of age-appropriate population enrolled in the following educational levels: Primary: 105* Secondary: 77 Further: 4

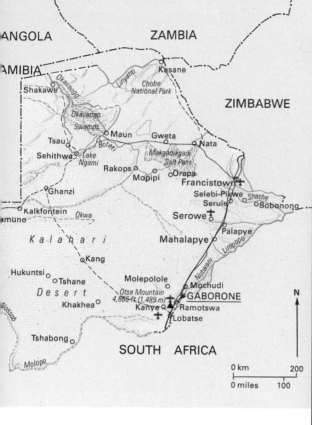

discovered in the late 1960's and 1970's are now being mined, and the nation also has deposits of coal and cobalt. Cattle raising is also important.

Botswana has little manufacturing, however, and unemployment is a major problem in the country. About 50,000 Botswanans, most of them young men, work in South

Botswana *above left* which lies in the center of southern Africa, is one of the most thinly populated countries on the continent. Most Botswanans live in the east.

A herd of elephants grazes in Chobe National Park, one of several wildlife reserves in Botswana, where these threatened animals are protected from ivory poachers. The Kalahari Desert covers the center and southwest of the country. The Okavango River forms a vast marshland in the northwest.

Africa for several months a year. While this arrangement brings badly needed money into Botswana, it separates families and causes other social problems.

Poor housing is also a major concern. About 50 per cent of Botswanans live in rural areas, but thousands move to the cities each year, hoping to find work and a better life. Unfortunately, many must live in crowded slums, especially in mining towns such as Orapa and Selebi-Pikwe.

The government of Botswana encourages private enterprise and foreign investment. Currently, the country's economy depends heavily on South African investments, markets, and technical skills. In addition, nearly all of Boswana's imports and exports travel on a railroad that runs through South Africa to the sea.

Languages spoken:
English (official)
Setswana

Religions:
Indigenous beliefs 85%
Christian 15%

Enrollment ratios compare the number of students enrolled to the population which, by age, should be enrolled. A ratio higher than 100 indicates that students older or younger than the typical age range are also enrolled.

TECHNOLOGY

Radios per 1,000 people: 155

Televisions per 1,000 people: 25

Computers per 1,000 people: 37.0

ECONOMY

Currency: Pula

Gross national income (GNI) in 2000: $5.3 billion U.S.

Real annual growth rate (1999–2000): 3.4%

GNI per capita (2000): $3,300 U.S.

Balance of payments (2000): $517 million U.S.

Goods exported:
Mostly: diamonds
Also: vehicles, copper, nickel, meat

Goods imported: Foodstuffs, machinery and transport equipment, textiles, petroleum products

Trading partners: European Union, Southern African Customs Union, Zimbabwe

Brazil

As the sun rises on Rio de Janeiro, another day begins in one of the world's most beautiful cities. Soon, sunbathers will flock to the world-famous Copacabana and Ipanema beaches. In the business district—also the center of Brazilian finance—stock market traders are already at their computer terminals. Along the city boulevards, shopkeepers prepare to open their elegant boutiques.

Bustling with activity by day, Rio de Janeiro quickens its pace even more after the sun sets. Festive partymakers crowd the city's exciting nightclubs, and colorful street festivals light up the darkness.

With its breathtaking setting, fascinating sights, and unique character, Rio de Janeiro is like Brazil itself, seemingly larger than life. Brazil—sprawled across almost half a continent and charged with an energy all its own—is a land that captures the visitor's imagination.

Brazil is South America's largest country in area, and it has more people than all the other countries combined. The course of its mighty Amazon River is longer than the highway route between New York City and San Francisco. Almost half of Brazil is covered by the largest tropical rain forest on earth. In other parts of the country, miles and miles of dry, grassy plains stretch across the countryside.

Cloud-capped mountains rise north of Brazil's forests and border the Atlantic Ocean in the southeast. The low plateaus of central and southern Brazil have fertile farmlands and lush grazing areas. Broad, white beaches line glistening seashores on the nation's Atlantic coast.

The forests, rivers, and mountains of Brazil have restricted inland travel, and the country's vast interior remains little developed. About 80 per cent of all Brazilians live within 200 miles (320 kilometers) of the Atlantic coast. One of the largest cities in Brazil's interior is Brasília, the nation's capital. It was built about 600 miles (970 kilometers) from the coast to help draw Brazilians inland.

Brazil is a land of many contrasts. Upper-class landowners enjoy the luxuries of modern life, while the nation's rural poor live in small huts made of mud or adobe with dirt floors and roofs of thatched palm leaves or clay tile. Brazil is a major industrial nation and a tremendous economic power, yet it has a staggering amount of debt. Every day, more of its precious rain forest is cleared for development, threatening not only the survival of animals and plant species, but also the well-being of our entire planet.

Despite its problems, however, Brazil has a spirit of warmth and liveliness unequaled on the South American continent. From the sandy beaches on its east coast to the tropical rain forests of the interior, this huge country offers much to see, explore, and appreciate.

Brazil Today

Brazil's great natural resources have made the country a potent and growing economic power. The nation's fertile farmland yields a huge coffee and banana crop, and its forests provide timber, nuts, and other products. Brazil's mines produce large quantities of iron ore, manganese, and other minerals needed by industry, while its rivers generate huge amounts of electricity.

Despite rapid industrial growth in the mid-1900's, Brazil is still making the difficult change from a developing to a developed country. Serious economic problems trouble the nation, including widespread poverty and unemployment. The military regime that ruled Brazil from the mid-1960's to the mid-1980's borrowed huge amounts of money from other nations to finance industrial development. As a result, Brazil's foreign debt has reached astronomical proportions of more than $100 billion.

The urban poor

Although the middle class is growing, a huge and widening gap still exists between the few who are enormously rich and the great mass of poor citizens. This extremely uneven distribution of wealth has been a serious obstacle to social progress.

Part of the problem stems from land policies dating from the 1600's, when wealthy plantation owners acquired huge tracts of land. In the 1980's, half of the land suitable for farming remained in the hands of just 1 per cent of the people.

Rural people with no land to farm continue to migrate to the cities, hoping to find work and a better life. But because many of these people are unskilled and uneducated, they can get only low-paying jobs—if they can find work at all. With little or no income, these rural migrants are forced to live in urban slums known as *favelas*.

Houses in the favelas are generally shabby shacks made of cardboard, metal, or wood. Because of the poor sanitation, many people suffer from diseases. Many parents abandon their children because they cannot afford to feed them. Millions of Brazilian children live on the streets—begging, stealing, or working long hours just to survive.

Democratic government

In 1985, Brazil returned to a civilian government after 21 years of military rule. When military leaders first took over the Brazilian government in 1964, the country's economy flourished. But the mid-1970's brought a worldwide business slump, and Brazil's economic growth slowed down. By 1979, the military administration faced such problems as high inflation rates and labor unrest.

FACT BOX

COUNTRY

Official name: Republica Federativa do Brasil (Federative Republic of Brazil)
Capital: Brasília
Terrain: Mostly flat to rolling lowlands in north; some plains, hills, mountains, and narrow coastal belt
Area: 3,286,488 sq. mi. (8,511,965 km²)

Climate: Mostly tropical, but temperate in south
Main rivers: Amazon, São Francisco, Araguaia, Paraná, Parnaíba
Highest elevation: Pico da Neblina, 9,888 ft. (3,014 m)
Lowest elevation: Atlantic Ocean, sea level

GOVERNMENT

Form of government: Federative republic
Head of state: President
Head of government: President
Administrative areas: 26 estados (states), 1 distrito federal (federal district)

Legislature: Congresso Nacional (National Congress) consisting of the Senado Federal (Federal Senate) with 81 members serving eight-year terms and the Camara dos Deputados (Chamber of Deputies) with 513 members serving four-year terms
Court system: Supreme Federal Tribunal
Armed forces: 291,000 troops

PEOPLE

Estimated 2002 population: 174,222,000
Population growth: 0.94%
Population density: 53 persons per sq. mi. (20 per km²)
Population distribution: 78% urban, 22% rural
Life expectancy in years: Male: 59 Female: 68
Doctors per 1,000 people: 1.3
Percentage of age-appropriate population enrolled in the following educational levels: Primary: 154* Secondary: 83 Further: 14

Brazil ranks among the largest, most populated countries in the world. Brazil is home to about half the population of South America. The country was named after the brazilwood trees that grow there.

Languages spoken:
Portuguese (official)
Spanish
English
French

Religion:
Roman Catholic (nominal) 80%

Enrollment ratios compare the number of students enrolled to the population which, by age, should be enrolled. A ratio higher than 100 indicates that students older or younger than the typical age range are also enrolled.

TECHNOLOGY

Radios per 1,000 people: 433

Televisions per 1,000 people: 343

Computers per 1,000 people: 44.1

ECONOMY

Currency: Real

Gross national income (GNI) in 2000: $610.1 billion U.S.

Real annual growth rate (1999–2000): 4.5%

GNI per capita (2000): $3,580 U.S.

Balance of payments (2000): -$24,632 million U.S.

Goods exported: Manufactures, iron ore, soybeans, footwear, coffee

Goods imported: Machinery and equipment, chemical products, oil, electricity

Trading partners: United States, Argentina, Germany

Military rule ended in January 1985, when the electoral college elected a civilian president, Tancredo de Almeida Neves. But Neves died only three months later, and José Sarney, who had been elected vice president, was named president. A constitutional amendment passed by Congress in 1985 provided for the direct election of future presidents by the people. In December 1989, the people elected Fernando Collor de Mello president.

In late 1992, minutes after his Senate impeachment trial began and facing criminal charges for corruption, Collor resigned his post. Itamar Franco became the new president. In December 1994, Collor was acquitted of corruption charges. Fernando Cardoso was elected president in 1995 and 1998. A previous finance minister, Cardoso was credited with reducing inflation and the deficit.

History

In 1493, the year after Christopher Columbus arrived in the New World, Pope Alexander VI drew an imaginary north-south line that divided the lands being explored and claimed by Spanish and Portuguese navigators. Known as the Line of Demarcation, it was intended to establish a boundary that would prevent disputes between Spain and Portugal over these lands. Land to the east of the line was declared Portuguese territory, while land to the west belonged to Spain. In 1494, through the Treaty of Tordesillas, Spain and Portugal moved the line westward to a point about 1,295 miles (2,084 kilometers) west of the Cape Verde Islands, giving Portugal what is now eastern Brazil.

Early settlements

In 1500, Pedro Álvares Cabral landed on the Brazilian coast to claim Portugal's new territory. But it was not until the 1530's that Portuguese colonists began to settle the region and establish huge sugar plantations.

The splendor of baroque design, *above,* lights up the church of Nossa Senhora do Pilar in the town of Ouro Prêto. According to local legend, the craftsmen who decorated the 300-year-old church mixed 182 pounds (400 kilograms) of gold dust in their paints.

The Indians tried to defend their native land against the Portuguese colonists, but many were killed in battle. Many others were forced to work as slaves on the plantations. When the Indian population was devastated by European diseases, the plantation owners replaced them with black slaves from Africa.

1500 Pedro Álvares Cabral lands on Brazil's east coast and claims the country for Portugal.
1530's Portuguese colonists settle in northeast and southern Brazil.
1549 Salvador is founded as the capital of the Brazilian colony.
1565 Portuguese establish a fort, which grows into the city of Rio de Janeiro.
1630 The Dutch invade Brazil.
1654 Portuguese drive the Dutch out of Brazil.
1700's Portuguese colonists travel to Brazil's interior in search of gold and diamonds.
1750 Portugal and Spain sign the Treaty of Madrid.
1763 Rio de Janeiro becomes the capital of Brazil.
1808–1821 Portuguese royal family rules Portugal and Brazil from Rio de Janeiro.
1822 Brazil declares its independence.
1831 Pedro I is forced to give up his throne, and 5-year-old Pedro II becomes emperor of Brazil.
Mid-1800's Thousands of European immigrants settle in southern Brazil.
1888 Pedro II abolishes slavery and frees about 750,000 slaves.
1889 Brazil becomes a republic.
Early 1900's Coffee becomes Brazil's chief export, bringing great wealth to the nation.
1917 Brazil joins the Allies in World War I (1914–1918).
1930 Military officers appoint Getúlio Vargas president.
1937 Vargas begins rule as dictator.
1942 Brazil joins the Allies in World War II (1939–1945).
1945 Brazil joins the United Nations.
1946 A new Constitution restores civil rights to the people.
1955 Juscelino Kubitschek is elected president.
1956 Construction of Brasília, the new capital, begins.
1960 The government moves from Rio de Janeiro to Brasília.
1964 Military officers take control of the government.
1974 General Ernesto Geisel becomes president.
1979 General João Baptista Figueiredo succeeds Geisel as president.
1985 Military rule ends, and José Sarney becomes president.
1989 Fernando Collor de Mello is elected president by the people.
1992 Collor resigns amid charges of corruption; Itamar Franco becomes president.

Pedro Álvares Cabral (1467?–1528?) was a Portuguese navigator who claimed Brazil for Portugal in 1500.

Getúlio Vargas (1883–1954), *far left,* was president of Brazil from 1930 to 1945 and from 1950 to 1954.

Pelé (1940–), *left,* is a Brazilian athlete and the greatest soccer player of his time.

During the 1600's and 1700's, many Portuguese settlers migrated to the interior and south of Brazil, where gold and diamonds had been discovered.

As colonists in the north began migrating into Brazil's interior, they crossed the Line of Demarcation. In 1750, Spain and Portugal signed the Treaty of Madrid, which gave Portugal almost all of what is now Brazil.

A new nation

In 1807, France invaded Portugal, and Prince John, Portugal's ruler, fled to Rio de Janeiro. In 1808, Rio became the capital of the Portuguese Empire, and Prince John raised Brazil to the status of a kingdom. When the royal family returned to Portugal in 1821, Prince John left his son Pedro to rule the new kingdom.

On Sept. 7, 1822, Pedro declared Brazil's independence from Portugal. A few months later, he was named emperor. But Pedro was a harsh ruler, and he became so unpopular that he was forced to resign in 1831. He left his throne to his 5-year-old son, Pedro II.

During the long reign of Pedro II, Brazil enjoyed a period of rapid development. The government built railways, telegraph systems, and schools. The growth of industry attracted thousands of European immigrants, who settled in southern Brazil where coffee growing spread rapidly. In addition, the worldwide demand for rubber products led to the development of the Amazon Region's vast natural rubber resources.

In 1888, Pedro II abolished slavery but refused to pay the plantation owners for their slaves. In 1889, the angry plantation owners supported the nation's military officers in removing Pedro from the throne and declaring Brazil a republic. General Manoel Deodoro da Fonseca was elected the first president.

But Deodoro and some of Brazil's other early presidents ruled the country as dictators. Getúlio Vargas, who became president in 1930, was hailed as a national hero when he increased wages and shortened work hours. But in 1937, he prepared a new Constitution that allowed him to censor the press, ban political parties, and take over Brazil's labor unions. Military officers removed Vargas from office in 1945, and the following year a new Constitution restored the people's civil rights.

Vargas was elected president again in 1950, but military officers overthrew his government four years later. In 1955, Juscelino Kubitschek was elected president. Political tension increased in the early 1960's, and military officers again took over the government in 1964.

Military rule ended in 1985. The electoral college elected a civilian president, and a 1985 constitutional amendment provided for the direct election of future presidents by the people.

The magnificent Opera House of Manaus opened in 1896.

People

The population of Brazil is the fifth largest in the world. Its 173 million people live in a *melting pot* society, where individuals from many different ethnic groups live together in relative harmony. While racial discrimination is far less widespread in Brazil than in many other countries, Brazilians of European descent usually have better educational opportunities and thus hold higher-level jobs in government and industry compared to Brazilians of non-European background.

Only about 7 per cent of Brazil's people live in the Amazon Region, which is larger than the United States west of the Mississippi, but mainly covered by thick forests. Most Brazilians live in the cities and urbanized regions along the Atlantic coastal zone. These cities suffer from overcrowding because Brazil has one of the fastest-growing populations in the Western Hemisphere and because many people continue to migrate to the cities from rural areas in search of work.

To solve the problems of overcrowding, Brazil's government has made many attempts to redistribute the population. In 1960, the capital was moved from the coastal city of Rio de Janeiro to Brasília, which is located about 600 miles (970 kilometers) inland on the central plateau. During the 1970's, the government began to offer free land to people willing to settle in the Amazon Region.

Catholics form about 80 per cent of Brazil's population. More Catholics live in Brazil than in any other country. About 10 per cent of Brazil's people, mostly blacks and people of mixed ancestry, practice such local religions as *macumba* and *candomblé*. These religions combine African spiritualist beliefs and Catholicism. Protestants make up about 5 per cent of Brazil's population.

Ethnic groups

About 1 million to 5 million Indians were living in Brazil when the first Europeans arrived in 1500, but the Indian population today totals only about 200,000, representing less than 1 per cent of the people of Brazil. Most Indians live in the forests of the Amazon Region and speak traditional Indian languages. About 180 Amazonian tribes can still be found in the forests, in settlements that are seldom larger than 200 people.

Followers of Macumba, *above,* a local religion that combines African spiritual beliefs with Roman Catholicism, prepare an offering to Iemanjá, the goddess of the sea. Many Brazilians who consider themselves Roman Catholics also worship the gods and goddesses of certain African religions.

A young lace maker works at her spindle, *above,* while colorful shawls and other items are displayed for prospective buyers. The making of *renda* (lace) is one of the traditional crafts still practiced in the states of Bahia and Ceará.

The blue eyes and dark skin of this mulatto, *left,* reflect the mixed ancestry of many Brazilians. The country's many ethnic groups are unified by a shared religion and a common language. About 85 per cent of the people are Roman Catholics, and almost all Brazilians speak Portuguese, the country's official language.

In addition to the Indians, Brazil has three main ethnic groups—whites, blacks, and people of mixed ancestry. Most of the whites are of European descent, and, according to the Brazilian government, make up about 60 per cent of the population. However, the government considers many light-skinned people of mixed ancestry as whites.

The white population in the north traces its ancestry to the Portuguese plantation owners who settled there in the 1600's and 1700's. The northeast also contains a distinctive group of blond, blue-eyed Brazilians, the descendants of Dutch colonists who held what is now the state of Pernambuco between 1630 and 1654.

Most European immigrants came to Brazil after the country declared its independence in 1822. People from Germany, Italy, Spain, and Portugal flocked to southeastern Brazil to work in the rapidly growing coffee industry. Today, Brazil has immigrants from about 30 nations. The largest groups include Italians, Portuguese, Spaniards, Japanese, Germans, Poles, and people from the Middle East and the former Soviet republics.

Caboclos and mulattoes

Caboclos (people of mixed white and Indian ancestry) and *mulattoes* (people of mixed black and white ancestry) make up about 30 per cent of Brazil's population. Blacks make up about 7 per cent of the population.

Black people were brought from Africa to Brazil as slaves, beginning in the mid-1500's. Many slaves were sold to sugar cane growers in the northeast. By about 1800, there were so many slaves in Brazil that they made up more than half the population. Many of the descendants of these African slaves still live in the coastal towns and cities, especially in the Northeast.

A fan waves the flag of Brazil in Rio de Janeiro before the start of the Brazilian Grand Prix, one of a series of international races for the world's Formula One championship. Automobile racing is a popular sport in Brazil.

Environment

From the lush vegetation of the tropical rain forests to the arid Northeast and fertile Mato Grosso, Brazil's landscape is beautiful and dramatic. Because all but the southernmost part of Brazil lies in the tropics, the climate is warm to hot the year around, with plenty of rainfall.

The Amazon Region

Extending across most of northern Brazil, the Amazon Region consists mostly of lowlands covered by jungle and tropical rain forest called *selva*. The region, which takes its name from the Amazon River that flows through it, also has two mountain areas—the Guiana Highlands in the far north and the Brazilian Highlands in the south.

The selva lies around the Amazon River and its tributaries, and it contains a tremendous variety of plant and animal life. More than 1,500 kinds of birds and more than 40,000 varieties of plants live in the forests. Scientists have found over 3,000 kinds of trees in 1 square mile (1.6 square kilometers) of the selva, and its animals include many kinds of monkeys as well as anteaters, jaguars, and sloths.

The climate in the western part of the Amazon Region is always hot and humid. Rain falls throughout the year, especially between December and May, for an annual total of about 160 inches (400 centimeters). The eastern part of the region receives less rain—about 40 to 80 inches (100 to 200 centimeters) annually.

The Northeast Region

The Northeast Region consists of the part of Brazil that juts out into the Atlantic Ocean. Although the region occupies less than one-fifth of Brazil's total land area, about 30 per cent of its people live there—mainly on the coastal plains, where the fertile red soil drew the first Portuguese colonists to establish sugar cane plantations. Today, farmers still grow sugar cane, as well as cacao and tobacco.

Fantastic rock formations, shaped by the wind and rain over thousands of years, are a feature of Vila Velha Park, in the southern state of Paraná. A human or animal form can be identified in most of the 23 different formations.

Spectacular Iguaçu Falls on the border between Brazil and Argentina is about 2 miles (3 kilometers) wide. The waters of some 30 rivers and streams plunge 237 feet (72 meters) down the cliffs in 275 separate waterfalls.

An Indian village, *right,* stands in a clearing of the dense Amazon forest in Xingu National Park. This protected area in northern Mato Grosso is home for many of Brazil's surviving Indian tribes.

Inland from the coastal plains lie the interior backlands, also known as the *sertão*. The sertão consists of plateaus and the hilly sections of the Brazilian Highlands. Agricultural production is low, due to the generally poor soil and the grazing land on the sertão and the variable rainfall, which may cause floods one year and droughts in another.

Central and Southern Plateaus

South of the Amazon Basin and the sertão lie the Central and Southern Plateaus, which include most of the Brazilian Highlands. A steep slope called the Great Escarpment runs along the Atlantic coast on the southeastern ridge of the highlands. This slope has been a partial barrier to the development of Brazil's interior.

The climate of the plateaus is cooler than the Amazon and Northeast regions. Winter frosts often occur in the state of Paraná, and light snow sometimes falls in the state of Santa Catarina. More than half of Brazil's people live in the region of the Central and Southern Plateaus, known as the nation's economic heartland, because of its fertile soil, fine cattle ranches, and rich mines. Farmers grow coffee on large plantations called *fazendas*.

The strong waves of the Atlantic, *below,* make the coast of Bahia a surfer's paradise. From the sandy white beaches of Rio de Janeiro to the peaceful bays and lagoons of Salvador, Brazil's coastline attracts tourists from all over the world.

Brazil's geography has strongly influenced the country's pattern of settlement. The hot, humid Amazon rain forest remains largely uninhabited, while the fertile soil and milder climate of southern Brazil have attracted most of the population.

165

Rio de Janeiro

Sugar Loaf Mountain, which rises above Guanabara Bay, offers a breathtaking, panoramic view of Rio de Janeiro—one of the most exciting and exotic cities in the world. Miles of white, sandy beaches and tall, graceful palm trees line the bay, and modern skyscrapers rise in the background.

Beautiful beaches

Rio de Janeiro—or simply Rio—lies nestled between forested mountains and the sparkling blue waters of the Atlantic Ocean and Guanabara Bay. Its name means *River of January,* which some historians believe refers to the month in 1503 when Portuguese seafarers first sailed into Guanabara Bay. Once the capital of Brazil, Rio is now the second largest city in South America, after São Paulo.

Rio's beautiful scenery provides an enchanting setting for its friendly, fun-loving citizens, who have been called *Cariocas* since the city's early years. This nickname may have come from a South American Indian expression meaning *white man's house.* Rio's long stretches of sunny beaches encourage an easygoing life style. Cariocas flock to the beaches to play volleyball and bask in the sun, or simply to enjoy the many music festivals and celebrations that take place on the sand.

Shantytowns

A world away from the glamorous beaches of Ipanema and Copacabana lies another, far less attractive side of Rio—the *favelas* (shantytowns). Here, thousands of people—about 25 per cent of Rio's population—live in run-down shacks on the hillsides and swampy shorelands.

The name *favela* comes from a lovely wild flower that once grew on the hills, but life in these neighborhoods is far from lovely. Poverty and violent crime are major problems, and many people suffer from malnutrition. Although the government has torn down a number of slum areas and replaced them with low-cost public housing, Rio still has nearly 300 favelas.

Samba and soccer

The lively spirit of Rio penetrates even the slums—in the form of music and dance. The driving *samba* beat echoes throughout the city, from the streets of the favelas to the elegant hotels along the Avenida Atlantica.

Samba was born as a musical form during the early 1900's when a group of young Carioca musicians began to combine traditional African rhythms with Portuguese folk songs popular at the time. It is often accompanied by the samba dance. Today, samba schools—dance clubs where dancers practice for months for the annual Carnival parade—can be found throughout the city.

The boundless energy of the Cariocas can also be seen in their love for soccer. Rio's huge Maracanã Stadium, with a seating capacity of 200,000, is one of the largest sports arenas in the world. A soccer game "Rio-style" is a lavish spectacle, with pounding drums, colorful flags, and firecrackers accompanying the action on the field.

Carnival

Held every year during the four days before the Christian observance of Lent, the Carnival of Rio de Janeiro symbolizes the lively spirit of the city. Although it began as a Chris-

Lavishly costumed samba dancers parade through the streets during the Carnival of Rio de Janeiro. Often called "the greatest party on earth," Carnival is a colorful, four-day spectacle of dancing, singing, and merry-making.

Luxurious hotels and apartment blocks overlook the crescent of Rio de Janeiro's Copacabana Beach. Situated on Guanabara Bay and the Atlantic Ocean, Rio is Brazil's chief seaport and an important center of finance, trade, and transportation.

A scene on Ipanema Beach, one of Rio's most glamorous resort areas, reflects two of the Cariocas' favorite activities—sunbathing and soccer. In the background, Sugar Loaf Mountain rises above Guanabara Bay to a height of 1,325 feet (404 meters).

tian festival, today's Carnival owes much of its character to African traditions, which have strongly influenced its music and dancing.

For many Cariocas, the Carnival is the most important event of the year. Preparations begin months in advance. Samba dancers and *baterias* (percussion bands) rehearse on the beach, while dressmakers create glittering, expensive costumes. Shops and street vendors stock up on colored streamers, and artists build huge *carros alegóricos* (parade floats).

When the Carnival finally begins, richly costumed Brazilians ride the floats through the boulevards of Rio, and samba schools compete for prizes in dazzling parades. Street parties, costume balls, and dancing on the beach add to the fun.

Rio de Janeiro became a major seaport in the mid-1700's, when prospectors shipped gold and diamonds to Portugal and imported many supplies. The gold trade attracted many new settlers to the city. New buildings and broad boulevards modernized Rio during the early 1900's, and today it is considered one of the most beautiful cities in the world. Important sights include the statue called *Christ the Redeemer* atop Corcovado Mountain (1); Copacabana Beach (2); the Botanical Gardens (3); the Federal University (4); Tijuca National Park (5); Maracanã Stadium (6). Civic buildings line the Avenida Rio Branco (8), and the massive Rio-Niterói Bridge (7) spans Guanabara Bay.

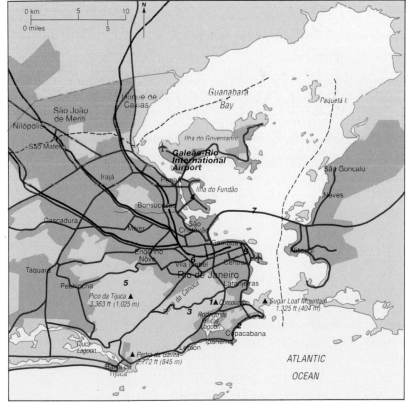

Cities Old and New

From the modern skyscrapers of São Paulo to the cobbled streets of Ouro Prêto, each of Brazil's cities reveals another fascinating chapter of the country's history. Traveling along the nation's 4,600-mile (7,400-kilometer) Atlantic coast is a journey back to Brazil's colonial past—and a glimpse of its vision for the future.

Colonial cities

Few cities capture Brazil's early colonial days as vividly as·Recife and Olinda. Situated on the northeast coast, Recife and Olinda were occupied by Dutch colonists during their attempt to stake a claim to Brazilian territory in the 1600's. Recife is often called *The Venice of Brazil* because it is built on three rivers, and many bridges connect its islands and peninsulas.

The influence of both the Dutch—and the Portuguese who drove them out—can be seen in Recife's historic downtown area, where many lavishly decorated churches from the 1600's and 1700's still stand. The Gold Chapel of the monastery of Saint Anthony, one of the most important examples of religious art in Brazil, has a baroque design covered in gold leaf.

In Olinda, now a suburb of Recife, narrow, winding streets twist up and down the hills overlooking the ocean. Many of the houses have the original latticed balconies, heavy doors, and pink stucco walls typical of the colonial period.

Farther south and hidden deep in the Brazilian Highlands is Ouro Prêto, the center of the gold and diamond trading in the 1700's. *Ouro Prêto* means *Black Gold,* and so much gold came from the hills around Ouro Prêto that the area was called *minas gerais* (general mines), which became the name for the modern state of Minas Gerais.

When the gold ran out, many people left Ouro Prêto, but the artistry of the brilliant mulatto sculptor of the period, António Francisco Lisboa da Costa (known as Aleijadinho), remains. Aleijadinho carved many human figures and church decorations out of soapstone.

Residents of a shantytown built over the river in Salvador, Bahia, cross a rickety bridge to their home. Founded in 1549, and now the third largest city in Brazil, Salvador served as the capital of the Portuguese colony of Brazil between 1549 and 1763.

skyscrapers and high-rise apartment blocks. Large parks and gardens provide a welcome sense of spaciousness in this crowded city.

A most contemporary capital

São Paulo is a sprawling city, growing faster every day with little direction from the government. In contrast, Brasília, the capital of Brazil, is one of the world's leading examples of large-scale city planning. Built in the east-central Brazilian wilderness in the late 1950's, Brasília is noted for its orderly development and impressive modern architecture.

The city was built as a link between the expanding south and the economically poor Northeast and as a launching point for settlement of the vast interior of the country. The government hoped that Brasília would attract people from the crowded coastal cities to the underpopulated interior. Today, Brasília is a hub of highways extending north to Belem in the Amazon Region and west to Peru.

Automobile traffic crowds an expressway in downtown São Paulo, *left.* The largest city in South America, São Paulo also has the second largest metropolitan area in the world. The city and surrounding area account for about half of Brazil's industrial output.

Twin towers in the capital city of Brasília, *above,* house congressional offices, while the Chamber of Deputies meets in the bowl-shaped structure to the left. Viewed from the air, Brasília is laid out in a pattern that resembles a drawn bow and arrow.

A modern metropolis

Unlike Brazil's colonial cities with their old buildings and winding streets, São Paulo is a thoroughly modern city. Although it was founded in 1554 as an Indian mission, São Paulo has a long tradition of tearing down the old and putting up the new. Most of São Paulo's buildings are less than 100 years old, and few of the old churches remain.

Today, São Paulo is the largest city in Brazil and its leading commercial and industrial center. The wide avenues of the downtown area are lined with imaginatively designed

Three-fourths of Brazil's people live in urban areas, mainly within 100 miles of the Atlantic coast and in the southeast. Some of Brazil's first cities were built along the northeast coast during the early days of Portuguese and Dutch exploration.

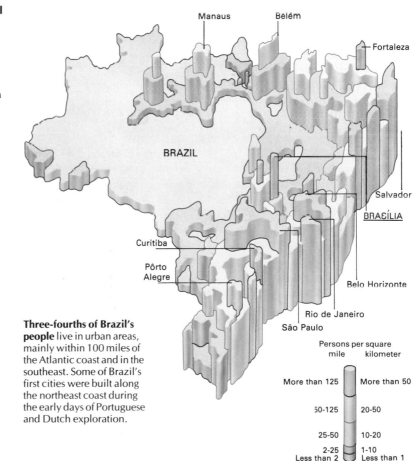

Manaus   Belém

Fortaleza

BRAZIL

Salvador

BRASÍLIA

Curitiba

Pôrto Alegre

Belo Horizonte

Rio de Janeiro

São Paulo

Persons per square	
mile	kilometer
More than 125	More than 50
50-125	20-50
25-50	10-20
2-25	1-10
Less than 2	Less than 1

Agriculture

Brazil has a vast amount of fertile farmland, and crops grown for export have been the main basis of the nation's economy since the earliest colonial days. Although factory production and service industries now contribute more to the GNP (gross national product), Brazil is still a world leader in crop and livestock production. Only the United States exports more farm products.

"Boom and bust" cycles

Beginning with the cultivation of sugar cane in the 1500's, Brazil's landowners have concentrated their efforts on growing a single crop for export in a series of "boom and bust" agricultural cycles. In each case, Brazilian farmers specialized in growing the crop that was in greatest demand on the world market at the time.

Brazil earned enormous profits during the "boom" of the crop demand, when prices were highest. But competition from other countries—or a decrease in demand—eventually brought prices tumbling down, resulting in a "bust."

In the late 1800's, for example, Brazil developed the Amazon Region's vast natural rubber resources in response to the worldwide demand for rubber products. But during the early 1900's, new rubber supplies from Asia reduced the great demand for Brazilian rubber. As rubber production decreased, coffee production increased. Then, in the 1920's, the price of coffee fell sharply, and thousands of plantation workers lost their jobs.

Crops and farming regions

During the 1980's, the Brazilian government encouraged farmers to grow a greater variety of crops. In addition to coffee, Brazil now leads all nations in growing bananas, cassava (a tropical plant with starchy roots), oranges, papayas, and sugar cane. It is also one of the world's top producers of cacao beans, cashew nuts, corn, cotton, lemons, pineapples, rice, soybeans, and tobacco.

Southern Brazil contains most of the nation's productive farmland. For many years, the state of São Paulo ranked as Brazil's chief

Brazilian laborers arrange cacao beans in an even layer to dry in the sun. Cacao beans, taken from the seed pods of an evergreen tree, are used in the production of chocolate and cocoa. Brazil is one of the world's largest suppliers of cacao.

Fishing crews in a *jangada* sailing raft, *right,* the traditional coastal fishing boat of northeast Brazil, brave the waters of the Atlantic. Despite excellent fishing grounds off the South Atlantic coast, large-scale commercial fishing in Brazil is undeveloped.

coffee-growing region, but the northern part of Paraná now supplies about half the coffee crop.

In addition to crops, Brazil is a leading producer of livestock, and cattle production has been a major source of wealth since World War I (1914–1918). Brazil ranks as one of the leading hog producers in the world today, and farmers also raise chickens, horses, and sheep.

In 1975, the traditional plantation crop of sugar cane became a source of fuel as well as of refined sugar. General Ernesto Geisel, who was president at the time, began a program to reduce Brazil's dependence on oil imports by substituting alcohol for gasoline made from oil. Today, nearly half of all Brazilian cars use alcohol distilled from sugar cane instead of gasoline.

Feeding the people

In addition to large cash crops of cacao beans, coffee, oranges, soybeans, sugar cane, and tobacco, Brazilian farmers grow such staples as cassava, beans, corn, rice, and potatoes for domestic use. However, the fast-growing population is outstripping the country's food supply. As a result, Brazil has had to import some food, particularly wheat, to feed its people.

Despite this situation, government policies—designed to reduce Brazil's huge foreign debt—encourage newly cultivated land to be used for growing high-profit cash crops. As a result, the increase in the percentage of land devoted to export crops was far greater than the increase in land used for domestic production during the 1980's.

Most of Brazil's chief farming and grazing areas are centered in the south and east of the country. Agriculture accounts for about 15 per cent of Brazil's economic output and employs about 30 per cent of the nation's workers.

Women gather the berries of the pepper plant, which will be dried and sold as peppercorns or ground black pepper. Most rural people work on the large plantations or ranches of corporations or wealthy landowners, but some work their own small farms with traditional tools.

A young boy, *below,* watches over a sugar cane field.

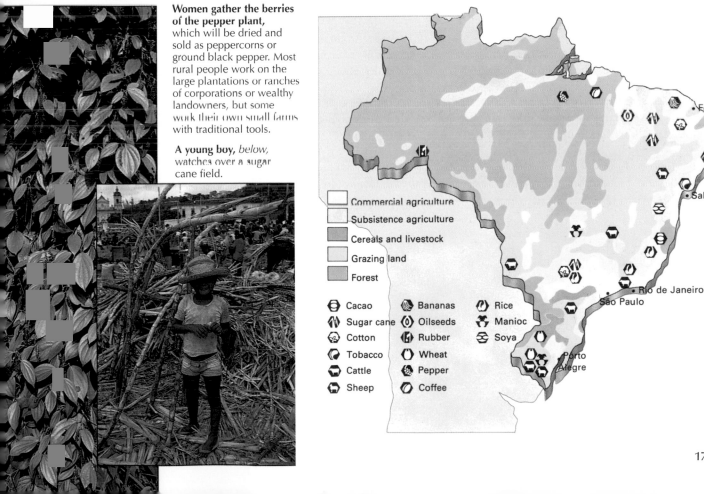

Commercial agriculture
Subsistence agriculture
Cereals and livestock
Grazing land
Forest

Cacao
Sugar cane
Cotton
Tobacco
Cattle
Sheep

Bananas
Oilseeds
Rubber
Wheat
Pepper
Coffee

Rice
Manioc
Soya

Fortaleza
Recife
Salvador
Rio de Janeiro
São Paulo
Porto Alegre

Industry

Brazil's natural resources, including its fertile farmland and rich mineral deposits, have been the backbone of the nation's economy through much of its history. However, rapid industrial growth during the mid-1900's has helped Brazil become one of the world's leading manufacturing nations.

Except for textile mills, industrial development did not actually begin to blossom until Brazil became an independent nation in 1889. Before that time, Portuguese rulers had discouraged industrial development in the colony because they wanted the Brazilians to buy Portugal's manufactured goods.

Once Brazil gained independence, industry enjoyed considerable growth under the leadership of Pedro II, who ruled for almost 50 years. Textile mills, breweries, chemical plants, and glass and ceramic factories were built, especially in São Paulo.

Between 1948 and 1976, the nation's greatest period of industrial growth, industrial production increased at an average rate of 9 per cent a year. In 1977, for the first time, manufactured products accounted for more than 50 per cent of the value of Brazil's exports. Manufacturing now accounts for about 27 per cent of Brazil's GNP (gross national product) and employs about 17 per cent of the nation's workers.

However, such tremendous growth has had its price. To speed industrial development, the Brazilian government borrowed heavily from foreign countries during the 1970's. Later, Brazil's huge foreign debt helped trigger hyperinflation. In 1990, President Fernando Collor de Mello froze larger bank deposits in an effort to slow down the inflation rate. He also began to sell some of the state-owned businesses to private corporations.

Plants and factories

Today, Brazil ranks among the world's major automobile producers, manufacturing more than 900,000 cars a year. Many international carmakers operate plants in Brazil. Latin America's largest iron and steel plant is located at Volta Redonda, near Rio de Janeiro. Brazil is also a major textile producer.

Other important industries include the manufacture of airplanes, cement, chemicals, electrical equipment, food products, machinery, pharmaceuticals, paper, and transportation equipment. Most manufacturing activity remains centered in the state of São Paulo.

Brazil's natural resources provide the power and raw materials for its industry. For example, the vast iron ore deposits in Minas Gerais have helped the steel industry expand; large hydroelectric power stations

Independent prospectors mine for gold, *right,* at *Serra Pelada* (Naked Mountain) in the Amazonian state of Pará. During the dry season, which lasts from June to November, up to 60,000 miners come here to seek their fortunes.

Workers wearing hardhats, *far right,* pause from their labors at the construction site of the Itaipú Dam, part of a long-term plan to harness Brazil's huge water resources. When it becomes fully operational, the Itaipú Dam will be one of the world's most powerful hydroelectric plants.

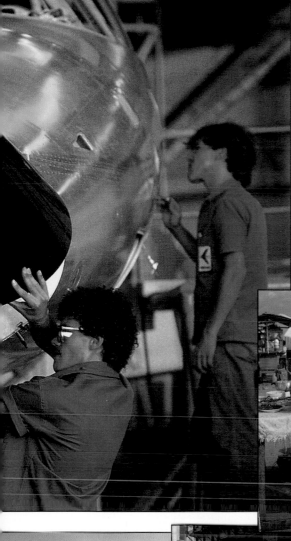

Technicians at an Embraer aircraft plant install the nose cone of an airplane. In contrast, a street vendor in Manaus, *below*, sells *churrasco*, a selection of charcoal-barbecued meats. Despite Brazil's industrial development, millions of its people are extremely poor and work in low-paying jobs, if they can find work at all.

operate on the Paraná, São Francisco, and Tocantins rivers; and hydroelectric power stations provide almost all of the nation's electricity.

Service industries

From 1940 to 1980, the percentage of Brazil's workers employed in service industries increased from 20 to 40 per cent. Today, service industries account for about 55 per cent of Brazil's economic output—more than industry and agriculture combined.

Many business services, such as banking, communications, insurance, and transportation, have developed to meet the needs of Brazil's industries. Another important area of growth has been among government agencies responsible for providing medical care and education.

The Itaipú Dam power plant on the Paraná River, a joint $20-billion project between Brazil and Paraguay, was designed to supply one-fifth of Brazil's energy needs.

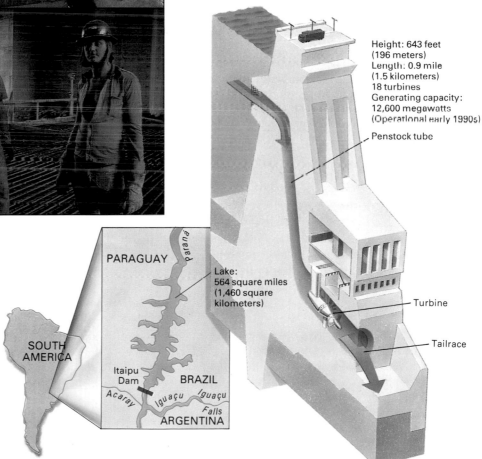

Height: 643 feet
(196 meters)
Length: 0.9 mile
(1.5 kilometers)
18 turbines
Generating capacity:
12,600 megawatts
(Operational early 1990s)

Penstock tube

Turbine

Tailrace

PARAGUAY

Paraná

Lake:
564 square miles
(1,460 square kilometers)

SOUTH
AMERICA

Itaipu
Dam

BRAZIL

Acaray   Iguaçu   Iguaçu
Falls

ARGENTINA

Brazil's Northeast

From Fortaleza in the north to Salvador in the south, Brazil has some of the most glorious, palm tree-fringed, unspoiled beaches in the world. A tropical climate, fanned by Atlantic breezes, attracts tourists by the thousands. And the fertile red clay soil of the coastal plains that lie inland from the white beaches is ideal for growing sugar cane, cacao, and tobacco.

In the plateaus and lowlands of the interior, beyond the sun-drenched sands and sugar cane fields, lies the dry, harsh face of tropical Brazil—the sertão. As British journalist James Cameron wrote, it is "known as the land of *miseria morte:* the sorrows of death." Together, the coastal plains and the sertão form Brazil's Northeast, home to more than 35 million people and Brazil's poorest region.

A land without mercy

The sertão is a desert that consists mainly of vast stretches of scrub forest known as *caatingas,* where droughts occur every 12–15 years and may last up to two years. During these times, the land becomes so dry that deep cracks form in the parched ground. Hot winds add to the dismal picture, as the lifeless soil swirls around the small, pitted hills that dot the landscape.

Stunted, thorny trees and cactus plants stand starkly against the sky, while others twist along the ground like huge snakes. Dwarf desert vegetation grows close to the ground to avoid the burning rays of the daytime sun. At night, the temperature drops sharply, and a chill sets in under the brilliant canopy of stars.

Eventually, the rains come, bringing relief to the drought-stricken land. Streams of water rush over the gaping cracks in the land and are swiftly absorbed. Thirsty vegetation springs to life, and the scent of blossoming flowers fills the air. Sometimes more damage is done by torrential rains than by droughts.

People of the backlands

In this harsh yet strangely beautiful land, millions of *Nordestinos* (northeasterners) struggle to make a living. Brazilians call those who try to work this often-shriveled, useless land *Flagelados* (The Beaten Ones)—because their life is difficult, and their rewards are few. Even in the best of seasons,

Small adobe houses with clay-tiled roofs line the main street of a village in the Northeast state of Ceará. Opportunities are few for the people of the Northeast, and many leave their villages to seek work in the cities of southern Brazil.

A street stall in Salvador, *far right bottom,* displays the food specialties of the Northeast. During colonial days, African slave cooks often created dishes using seafood, cassava flour, sweet potatoes, and coconuts, when meat and wheat flour were in short supply. The African cuisine also used more vegetables than the Portuguese did.

Coconut palms shade a wide, sandy beach near Fortaleza on Brazil's northeast coast, *bottom center.* Here, annual temperatures average a pleasant 80° F. (27° C), but the dry interior sertão suffers frequent droughts.

the Flagelados can hope for little beyond tending scrawny cattle and growing what crops they can in the region's poor soil, or begging.

Many Nordestinos will die before they reach their 50th birthday, and many cannot read or write, but they are fiercely loyal to the backlands. Even when they are forced to migrate to the cities to make a living, many return to the sertão when they have saved enough money to live on.

It was the sertão and the human misery that inspired one of Brazil's most famous books—*Os Sertões* (The Backlands), written in 1902 by Euclides da Cunha. The book described a peasant rebellion that took place there in the 1890's.

The poorest region in Brazil, the Northeast covers 9 of the nation's 26 states. A humid strip of coastal plains extends along the coastline, but most of the interior, or *sertão*, is semidry, with scrub forest, cactus, and thornbushes covering the land. In 1984, a five-year drought ended in huge downpours of rain that left 150 people dead or missing and 700,000 homeless. Many crops were destroyed and fields eroded.

The Cathedral Basilica, *left,* built in the 1600's, dominates the plaza of Terreiro de Jesus in Salvador, the capital of Bahia. During the 1600's, the sugar cane industry flourished in the Northeast. Many splendid churches and buildings still stand as a reminder of the region's former wealth.

On the outskirts of Fortaleza, Nordestinos (inhabitants of the Northeast) made homeless by one of the region's periodic droughts search for scraps in a city dump, *below.* The poverty of the Northeast stands in stark contrast to the wealthy, more developed southern region of Brazil.

Brunei

Brunei, a small country in Southeast Asia, lies on the north coast of the island of Borneo. The South China Sea borders Brunei on the north, and the rest of Brunei is surrounded by Malaysia. Most of the land is flat, and the interior is heavily wooded. Brunei's climate is tropical, with average monthly temperatures of about 80° F. (27° C). Rainfall averages about 100 inches (250 centimeters) a year along the coast and about 125 inches (320 centimeters) inland.

As early as the A.D. 600's, Brunei was mentioned in Chinese writings as an important trading center. The first sultan of Brunei came to power in the 1200's. During the 1400's and 1500's, Brunei was a powerful country that controlled most of the north coast of Borneo and parts of the southern Philippines. In the 1600's and 1700's, pirates used Brunei as a base for their attacks on European trading ships.

In the 1800's, in order to protect its shipping lanes between China and India, the United Kingdom took over most of northern Borneo, including Brunei. In 1888, the United Kingdom made the area a British protectorate. Brunei became an independent nation on Jan. 1, 1984.

Government

The country's official name is Negara Brunei Darussalam, which means Brunei, Abode of

Sir Muda Hassanal Bolkiah, the sultan of Brunei since 1967, led the country through independence. He is thought to be the world's richest man.

Bandar Seri Begawan, the capital of Brunei, lies on the north bank of the Brunei River. The city's many fine buildings include, at the right, the impressive Omar Ali Saifuddin Mosque with its gold dome.

Many Muslim women in Brunei wear traditional clothing—long skirts and long-sleeved blouses, *right*. About two-thirds of Brunei's people are Malays, and most are Muslims—followers of the Islam faith.

FACT BOX

COUNTRY

Official name: Negara Brunei Darussalam
Capital: Bandar Seri Begawan
Terrain: Flat coastal plain rises to mountains in east; hilly lowland in west
Area: 2,228 sq. mi. (5,770 km²)

Climate: Tropical; hot, humid, rainy
Main rivers: Belait, Tutong, Temburong
Highest elevation: Bukit Pagon, 6,070 ft. (1,850 m)
Lowest elevation: South China Sea, sea level

GOVERNMENT

Form of government: Constitutional sultanate
Head of state: Sultan
Head of government: Sultan
Administrative areas: 4 daerah-daerah (districts)

Legislature: Majlis Masyuarat Megeri (Legislative Council)
Court system: Supreme Court
Armed forces: 5,000 troops

PEOPLE

Estimated 2002 population: 350,898
Population growth: 2.06%
Population density: 151 persons per sq. mi. (58 per km²)
Population distribution: 67% urban, 33% rural
Life expectancy in years:
Male: 72
Female: 77
Doctors per 1,000 people: N/A
Percentage of age-appropriate population enrolled in the following educational levels:
Primary: N/A
Secondary: N/A
Further: N/A

BRUNEI

Peace. Its capital, Bandar Seri Begawan, is also its largest city. A monarch called a *sultan* heads the government and rules for life. In 1967, Sir Muda Hassanal Bolkiah was chosen as sultan. He also serves as the country's prime minister, minister of finance, and minister of home affairs. Several members of his family hold high positions in the government.

Resources

The discovery of oil off the coast in 1929 brought great wealth to Brunei. The income from oil exports has enabled the people of Brunei to enjoy a high standard of living. However, the nation's petroleum and gas reserves are expected to run out in the early 2000's.

Petroleum, petroleum products, and the natural gas often found with petroleum account for almost all of Brunei's exports, but the petroleum and gas industry employs only about 10 per cent of the country's labor force. The government employs about 50 per cent of the people and is by far the nation's largest employer.

People

About two-thirds of Brunei's people live in urban areas, and about one-third, in rural areas. About two-thirds of the people are Malays, and nearly all are Muslims—followers of the faith of Islam. The Chinese, the largest minority, make up about a fourth of the population. Most of the Chinese are Christians, and a small percentage are Buddhists. Most Bruneians speak Malay, the official language, but English and Chinese are also used.

In urban areas, most Bruneians wear Western clothing, but many Muslim women wear outfits of long skirts and long-sleeved blouses. In rural areas, many men and women wear loose shirts and *sarongs,* long pieces of cloth worn as a skirt and tied at the waist. Most city dwellers live in modern houses or apartment buildings made of brick or stone, while most rural homes are wooden and have thatched roofs.

The government provides free schooling and medical services for its people. Most Bruneian children complete elementary school, and many go on to high school. The nation's first university, the University of Brunei Darussalam, opened in 1985. Many Bruneians study at foreign universities, and the government pays for their education.

Languages spoken:
Malay (official)
English
Chinese

Religions:
Muslim (official) 67%
Buddhist 13%
Christian 10%
indigenous 10%

TECHNOLOGY

Radios per 1,000 people:
N/A

Televisions per 1,000 people: N/A

Computers per 1,000 people: N/A

ECONOMY

Currency: Bruneian dollar

Gross domestic product (GDP) in 2001: $6.2 billion U.S.

Real annual growth rate (2001): 3%

GDP per capita (2001): $18,000 U.S.

Balance of payments (2001): N/A

Goods exported: Crude oil, liquefied natural gas, petroleum products

Goods imported: Machinery and transport equipment, manufactured goods, food, chemicals

Trading partners: Japan, Singapore, United Kingdom

Brunei lies on the island of Borneo, with the South China Sea as its northern border and the Malaysian states of Sarawak and Sabah on its other sides. Most of Brunei's wealth comes from oil reserves discovered off its coast.

Bulgaria

Bulgaria lies on the Balkan Peninsula in southeastern Europe, and, like its neighbors, the nation experienced dramatic political upheaval during the late 1980's. In late 1989, human-rights activists and environmentalists challenged the dominance of Bulgaria's Communist Party in the largest demonstrations since the end of World War II (1939-1945).

Only a few days later, Todor Zhivkov, who had been head of state and leader of the Bulgarian Communist Party for the previous 27 years, was removed from office. Further demonstrations calling for democratic reforms and free elections were held in the capital city of Sofia.

In the elections of June 1990, many of the Communist Party's former representatives, now under the banner of the Bulgarian Socialist Party, were again brought to power. In August, the National Assembly elected Zhelyu Zhelev, a member of the Union of Democratic Forces—a coalition of 16 opposition parties—as president. But most of the political power remained in the hands of former Communists who claimed to have changed their views.

In the National Assembly elections of October 1991, the Union of Democratic Forces gained a slight lead over the Bulgarian Socialist Party. The Movement for

Bathed in light, the Alexander Nevsky Cathedral towers above the buildings of Sofia, Bulgaria's capital and largest city. The cathedral was built in the late 1800's to celebrate Bulgaria's liberation from Ottoman rule.

Once part of the Roman Empire, Bulgaria, *map far right,* became a kingdom in 681. The country was ruled by the Byzantines between 1018 and 1186. Bulgaria then kept its independence until 1396, when it was conquered by the Ottomans.

FACT BOX

COUNTRY

Official name: Republic of Bulgaria
Capital: Sofia
Terrain: Mostly mountains with lowlands in north and southeast
Area: 42,823 sq. mi. (110,910 km²)
Climate: Temperate; cold, damp winters; hot, dry summers

Main rivers: Danube, Iskŭr, Maritsa, Ogosta, Tundzha
Highest elevation: Musala, 9,596 ft. (2,925 m)
Lowest elevation: Black Sea, sea level

GOVERNMENT

Form of government: Parliamentary democracy
Head of state: President
Head of government: Chairman of the Council of Ministers (Prime minister)
Administrative areas: 9 oblasti (provinces)

Legislature: Narodno Sobranie (National Assembly) with 240 members serving four-year terms
Court system: Supreme Court, Constitutional Court
Armed forces: 80,760 troops

PEOPLE

Estimated 2002 population: 8,128,000
Population growth: -1.16%
Population density: 190 persons per sq. mi. (73 per km²)
Population distribution: 68% urban, 32% rural
Life expectancy in years: Male: 67 Female: 75
Doctors per 1,000 people: 3.5
Percentage of age-appropriate population enrolled in the following educational levels: Primary: 101* Secondary: 87 Further: 43

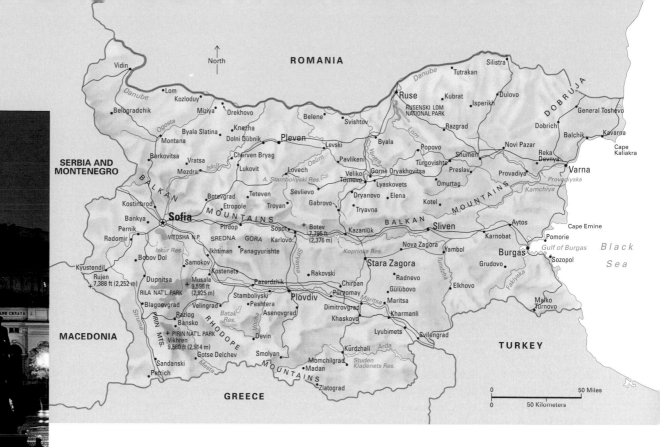

Rights and Freedom, a coalition representing Bulgaria's Muslim Turks, won about 7 per cent of the votes.

In December 1994, the Bulgarian Socialist Party won an absolute majority of 124 seats in the parliament. Bulgaria's economy showed little improvement. Unemployment stood at 16 per cent, wages dropped, and the cost of living increased.

The Communists gained complete control of Bulgaria between 1944 and 1947. The Communists changed Bulgaria from an agricultural country to an industrialized country.

This policy brought the nation some capital and international credit, but conditions for the working people remained poor. Wages were low, and food, housing, and consumer goods were in short supply. Today, Bulgaria is still a developing country.

About 85 per cent of the people are of Bulgarian ancestry, descended from Slavs and Bulgars. Bulgarian, the country's official language, is related to Russian and other Slavic languages and written in the Cyrillic alphabet.

Turks make up Bulgaria's largest ethnic minority and represent about 10 per cent of the population. Because Bulgaria suffered as part of the Ottoman Empire from the 1300's to the end of the 1800's, many Bulgarians resent the Turks.

In 1984 and 1985, the government tried to force the Turks to adopt Bulgarian names, and banned the use of the Turkish language in public. Some who ignored these new rules were killed by Bulgarian troops. In 1989, about 344,000 Turkish-speaking Bulgarians sought refuge in Turkey, but nearly one-third of them returned to Bulgaria after a few months. In 1990, the Bulgarian government ended its anti-Turkish program, but some ethnic disturbances continued.

Language spoken:
Bulgarian

Religions:
Bulgarian Orthodox 84%
Muslim 13%
Roman Catholic 2%

*Enrollment ratios compare the number of students enrolled to the population which, by age, should be enrolled. A ratio higher than 100 indicates that students older or younger than the typical age range are also enrolled.

TECHNOLOGY

Radios per 1,000 people:
543

Televisions per 1,000 people: 449

Computers per 1,000 people: 43.9

ECONOMY

Currency: Lev

Gross national income (GNI) in 2000: $12.4 billion U.S.

Real annual growth rate (1999–2000): 5.8%

GNI per capita (2000): $1,520 U.S.

Balance of payments (2000): -$701 million U.S.

Goods exported: Machinery and equipment; metals, minerals, and fuels; chemicals and plastics; food, tobacco, clothing

Goods imported: Fuels, minerals, and raw materials; machinery and equipment; metals and ores; chemicals and plastics; food, textiles

Trading partners: Germany, Italy, Russia, Greece

Environment

Bulgaria, a mountainous land broken by fertile valleys and plains, is bordered to the north by Romania, to the west by Serbia and Montenegro and Macedonia, and to the south by Greece and Turkey. The Black Sea lies to the east. Bulgaria's four main land regions are the Balkan Mountains, the Danubian Plateau, the Transitional Mountains and Lowlands, and the Rhodope Mountains. Because of the sharp contrasts in its terrain, Bulgaria's climate varies greatly from region to region.

The country's landscape is shaped chiefly by the Balkan Mountains, which stretch across Bulgaria from west to east, dividing the country in half. The northern half–the Danubian Plateau–has cold winters but warm and humid summers. The southern half–the Transitional Mountains and Lowlands–has cool winters and hot, dry summers.

In the mountain regions, weather conditions change yet again, depending on the altitude and the distance from the sea. The country's average rainfall is 25 inches (63 centimeters), and snowfall is light, except in the mountains. Near the Black Sea coast, winters are mild and summers are hot.

Northern Bulgaria

The Danubian Plateau, which covers northern Bulgaria from the Danube River south to the Balkan Mountains, is a vast sheet of limestone covered with river silt. As a result, this region has the country's most fertile farmland. The Danube River forms most of the border between Bulgaria and Romania, and several of its tributaries–including the Iskŭr and the Yantra–flow northward from the mountains.

The Danubian Plateau is partly flat, becoming more rolling as it approaches the foothills of the Balkans. In the valleys and flatter areas, where the climate is more humid, fruit, vegetables, and wine grapes flourish. The drier uplands are used for growing corn and wheat. In the northeast, the vast expanses of scrub grassland provide ideal pastures for sheep.

Most of the Balkan Mountains are not very high. The taller peaks lie mostly in the west, and some tower about 7,120 feet (2,170 meters) along the border with Serbia and

Montenegro. Generally, the Balkans form lengthy ridges and small plateaus where sheep graze and forests grow. Many mountain passes allow traffic to flow easily between the Danubian Plateau and the mountain regions of southern Bulgaria.

Immediately to the south of the Balkan Mountains lie a number of lower mountain chains, known as the Sredna Gora. A zone of fertile basins, where roses and wine grapes are cultivated, lies between the Balkans and these lower chains. Bulgaria's capital city of Sofia is situated in one of these basins, at an altitude of 1,800 feet (550 meters).

The mountainous south

The Rhodope Mountains stretch across southern Bulgaria, forming a natural boundary with Greece. Evergreen forests and alpine meadows are a dominant feature of this landscape. Northwest of the Rhodope, in the Rila Mountains, stands the Rila Monastery, a historic shrine revered by all Bulgarians and now the site of a national museum. West of the Rhodope rise the peaks of the Pirin Mountains, where bears, wolves, and wildcats are found among the abundant wildlife.

Bulgaria's coast extends about 175 miles (282 kilometers) along the Black Sea. The nation's sandy beaches, sunny climate, and fascinating historical ruins draw vacationers from all over Europe. Bulgaria's leading Black Sea ports are Varna and Burgas.

A small town occupies a sheltered valley in southeastern Bulgaria, *left*. The Maritsa and Tundzha river valleys support the cultivation of fruits and vegetables, such as apples, grapes, pears, tomatoes, and watermelons.

Snow-capped peaks rise above the Rila Monastery, hidden away in the Rila Mountains of southwestern Bulgaria. Bulgaria's highest peak, Musala, rises 9,596 feet (2,925 meters) along the northern tip of the Rhodope Mountains.

On the Black Sea coast, sandy beaches are interspersed with dunes, rocky cliffs, and forest-covered hills. The large coastal resorts of Varna and Burgas are known for their splendid beaches and parks. Broad expanses of reeds and water lilies mark the deltas of the Kamchiya and Ropotamo rivers, and farther north, monk seals bask on the rocks along the shore.

Rows of corn grow on the Danubian Plateau, in the region's fertile soil, aided by the humid summer conditions. In the southern part of Bulgaria, where the climate is drier, irrigation provides moisture for crops.

Economy

Following the Communist take-over in 1946, Bulgaria changed from an economy dominated by privately owned agricultural interests to one in which state-owned industry was of primary importance. During the period of industrialization, heavy industry was developed rapidly, and extremely high production goals were set by the government.

However, poor management and shortages of fuel and skilled labor have slowed economic growth in Bulgaria. At the same time, wherever an industry was allowed some degree of self-administration or profit-making, efficiency and productivity improved.

During the period of Communist rule, Bulgaria maintained exceptionally close ties with the Soviet Union, partly out of gratitude for Russia's help in 1878 when they gained freedom from Turkish rule. Because of its relationship to the Soviet Union, Bulgaria was given the responsibility for research, development, and production in the field of microelectronics for all Eastern bloc countries. Bulgaria's historic city of Plovdiv became the nation's center for high technology.

Beginning in 1985, Bulgaria's trade links with Eastern bloc countries were gradually abandoned, and Bulgaria began to seek greater cooperation with Western countries. However, the rigidly controlled and heavily subsidized economy of Bulgaria was unable to compete with the free markets of Western countries and corporations.

In 1989, the Bulgarian government announced plans to reform industry and agriculture. These reforms called for a decrease in centralized planning, permitting the establishment of small, private enterprises. Some foreign participation was to be allowed in these enterprises, and shares in newly formed companies were to be made available to foreign, as well as Bulgarian, investors.

Industry and energy

Today, manufacturing, mining, and energy production account for about half of Bulgaria's *net material product* (NMP)—the

Tank trucks await refueling at an oil storage depot at Varna, one of the country's leading ports on the Black Sea. Although Bulgaria has two oil fields, its reserves are very small, and the country imports most of its fuel.

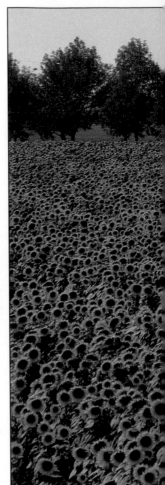

A field of golden sunflowers outside the town of Lom, in northwestern Bulgaria, is almost ready for harvest. The seeds of the sunflowers are crushed to extract a high-quality vegetable oil.

A *cooper* (barrel maker) produces wooden barrels for a local vineyard, *above.* Bulgaria produces red and white wines, as well as brandies, fruit liqueurs, and even a spirit made from roses. Some wine is exported to Western countries.

Roses are harvested by farmers in central Bulgaria for their *essence*—a fragrant oil made by distilling rose petals plucked from still-closed buds. Thousands of buds are harvested by hand to produce 2 pints (1 liter) of oil.

Bulgaria's Black Sea coast attracts millions of vacationers, *left,* primarily from Eastern European countries. Tourists who come to enjoy the coast's historic sites, mild climate, and sandy beaches have benefited the Bulgarian economy since the 1970's.

total value of goods, and of services used in the production of these goods, by a country in a year. This sector also employs about a third of the nation's workers. Bulgaria's major industrial centers are Sofia, Dimitrovgrad, Plovdiv, Ruse, and Varna. The top manufacturing industries produce chemicals, machinery, metal products, processed foods, and textiles.

Bulgaria has small deposits of many kinds of minerals. The country mines coal, copper, kaolin, lead, pyrite, salt, sulfur, and zinc. A nuclear power station at Koz-loduy produces nearly 25 per cent of the country's electricity. Bulgaria must import most of its fuel.

Agriculture

Despite the industrialization of Bulgaria, agriculture still accounts for about 20 per cent of the country's net material product and employs about 25 per cent of the country's workers. Farmland covers about 15 million acres (6 million hectares), or more than half of Bulgaria.

Bulgaria's chief farm product is grain. Wheat and corn are the leading crops, and other grains include barley, oats, rice, and rye. Bulgarian farmers also grow a wide variety of fruits and vegetables, including apples, grapes, potatoes, pears, sugar beets, tomatoes, and watermelons. Roses are grown for their sweet-smelling oil, which is used as the basis for many world-famous perfumes. Livestock production, including dairy and beef cattle, chickens, pigs, and goats, is also an important activity. Cow's milk is a major farm product.

Burkina Faso

The country of Burkina Faso in western Africa was known as Upper Volta until 1984, when the government changed the name to Burkina Faso, which means *land of the honest people*. It lies on the western bulge of Africa, about 600 miles (970 kilometers) east of the Atlantic Ocean.

Landlocked Burkina Faso is one of the least developed countries on the African continent. This dry, rocky plateau turns green for only a few months each year because its thin soil does not hold rain water well. Most of the rainfall quickly runs off into the country's many rivers. Because the country has poor soil and no mineral deposits, its people have only the bare necessities of life. Most make their living by raising cattle or farming.

Cattle raising is the most important economic activity in Burkina Faso. The country has between 6 million and 9 million cattle, goats, and sheep—and about 12 million people. Livestock exports make up from one-third to one-half of the national income.

In the river valleys, farmers raise such food crops as beans, corn, millet, rice, sorghum, and *fonio* (a grass whose seeds are used as a cereal). Cash crops include cotton, peanuts, and *shea nuts* (seeds that contain a fat used to make soap).

Because Burkina Faso lacks resources, many of its young men work in neighboring countries on plantations or as city laborers. The money they send home is important to the nation's income as well as to their families.

Most of the people of Burkina Faso belong to one of two major cultural groups—the Voltaic and the Mande. The Voltaic group includes the Mossi, the Bobo, the Gurunsi, and the Lobi peoples. The Mande group includes the Boussance, the Marka, the Samo, and the Senufo peoples.

The Voltaic Mossi, who make up about half the country's population, are mainly farmers who live in the central and eastern parts of the country. The typical Mossi family lives in a *yiri,* a group of mud huts built around a small court, where the family's sheep and goats are kept. For more than 800 years, the Mossi have had a kingdom in the region of Burkina Faso headed by the *Moro Naba,* or Mossi chief. A Moro Naba still holds court in the city of Ouagadougou.

The Voltaic Bobo, Gurunsi, and Lobi each make up less than 10 per cent of the population. The Bobo live in large villages in southwestern Burkina Faso. The Gurunsi live around the city of Koudougou and have

FACT BOX

COUNTRY

Official name: Burkina Faso
Capital: Ouagadougou
Terrain: Mostly flat to dissected, undulating plains; hills in west and southeast
Area: 105,869 sq. mi. (274,200 km²)
Climate: Tropical; warm, dry winters; hot, wet summers

Main rivers: Black Volta, Red Volta, White Volta
Highest elevation: Tena Kourou, 2,457 ft. (749 m)
Lowest elevation: Mouhoun (Black Volta) River, 656 ft. (200 m)

GOVERNMENT

Form of government: Parliamentary
Head of state: President
Head of government: Prime minister
Administrative areas: 30 provinces
Legislature: Assemblee des Deputes Populaires (National Assembly) with 111 members

serving five-year terms and the Chambre des Representants (Chamber of Representations) with 178 members serving three-year terms
Court system: Supreme Court; Appeals Court
Armed forces: 10,000 troops

PEOPLE

Estimated 2002 population: 12,600,000
Population growth: 2.71%
Population density: 119 persons per sq. mi. (46 per km²)
Population distribution: 85% rural, 15% urban
Life expectancy in years: Male: 46 Female: 47
Doctors per 1,000 people: Less than 0.05
Percentage of age-appropriate population enrolled in the following educational levels: Primary: 42 Secondary: 10 Further: N/A

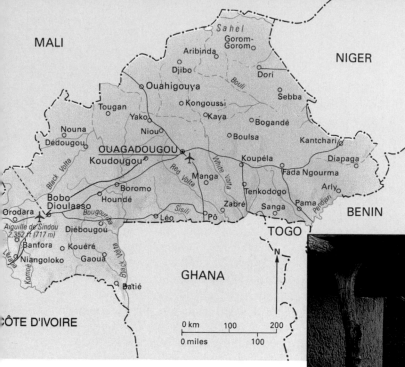

Burkina Faso lies about 600 miles (970 kilometers) east of the Atlantic Ocean on the western bulge of Africa. Consisting mostly of a wooded and grassy plateau, it is one of Africa's poorest nations.

A Bobo villager takes a break from her chores in the shade of thatch-roofed granaries. The Bobo people live in large villages in southwestern Burkina Faso, where they build castlelike structures with clay bricks and straw.

adopted modern changes fairly readily. The Lobi live in the Gaoua region and have turned from hunting and farming to migrant labor.

In addition to the Voltaic and Mande peoples, several hundred thousand Fulani and Tuareg live in Burkina Faso. These nomads roam the pastures in the north of the country with their goats, sheep, and other livestock.

The Mossi have the longest history among the people of Burkina Faso, but their kingdom was not discovered by Europeans until the 1800's. In 1897, France captured Ouagadougou, and the Moro Naba placed his kingdom under French protection. In 1919, France created the colony of Upper Volta in the region.

On August 5, 1960, Upper Volta became an independent republic. Since then, several civilian governments have been overthrown by army officers, who in turn have been overthrown in other military coups. Today, military leaders control the government of Burkina Faso. The president is a member of the military, and a Cabinet, whose members are appointed by the military, helps carry out government operations.

Languages spoken:
French (official)
native African languages belonging to Sudanic family 90%

Religions:
Indigenous beliefs 40%
Muslim 50%
Christian (mainly Roman Catholic) 10%

TECHNOLOGY

Radios per 1,000 people: 35

Televisions per 1,000 people: 12

Computers per 1,000 people: 1.3

ECONOMY

Currency: Communaute Financiere Africaine franc

Gross national income (GNI) in 2000: $2.4 billion U.S.

Real annual growth rate (1999–2000): 2.2%

GNI per capita (2000): $210 U.S.

Balance of payments (2000): -$65 million U.S.

Goods exported: Cotton, animal products, gold

Goods imported: Machinery, food products, petroleum

Trading partners: Côte d'Ivoire, France, Senegal, Taiwan

Burundi

Burundi, in east-central Africa, is one of the continent's smallest and most crowded countries. The nation has about 6 million people, with an average of 563 people per square mile (218 people per square kilometer).

Burundi has few minerals and little industry—most of the people are farmers who can raise only enough food to feed their families. The main crops are bananas, beans, cassava, corn, and sweet potatoes. Some farmers also raise cattle and other livestock. In addition, Lake Tanganyika provides an annual catch of thousands of tons of fish.

About 85 per cent of the people of Burundi belong to the Hutu ethnic group—mainly poor farmers—while some 14 per cent belong to the Tutsi group. Although the Tutsi are a minority, they dominate the nation politically and economically.

Most of the remaining 1 per cent of the population are Twa people, a Pygmy group. The Twa once hunted and gathered wild food, such as berries, but today many Twa make pottery and farm for a living.

The Twa, probably the first inhabitants of what is now Burundi, may have lived in the area since prehistoric times. It is not known when the Hutu arrived, but they were living there when the Tutsi invaded from the north,

and they eventually became the largest group in the region.

The Tutsi, who were more powerful than the Hutu, agreed to protect the Hutu if the Hutu would raise crops for them. However, the region was actually ruled by a small group, called the *Ganwa,* who ruled both the Tutsi and the Hutu and became wealthy. The people's king, called *mwami,* had little power.

In 1897, the Germans conquered the area that is now Burundi and Rwanda, the country to the north. Belgium later took control of the region, then called Ruanda-Urundi. In 1961, Urundi voted to become the independent monarchy of Burundi, while Ruanda voted to become the republic of Rwanda. The two became independent on July 1, 1962. By then, the power of the Ganwa had ended, and the Tutsi controlled Burundi.

After independence, political unrest and ethnic conflict troubled Burundi. The Hutu resented the power of the Tutsi. Political assassinations took place in 1965, and the king was overthrown in a military revolt in 1966. Then in 1972, the Hutu revolted. By the end of their unsuccessful rebellion, about 100,000 people, most of them Hutu, had died. A second army revolt in 1976 made Colonel Jean-Baptiste Bagaza president.

FACT BOX

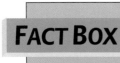

COUNTRY

Official name: Republika y'u Burundi (Republic of Burundi)
Capital: Bujumbura
Terrain: Hilly and mountainous, dropping to a plateau in east, some plains
Area: 10,745 sq. mi. (27,830 km²)

Climate: Equatorial; generally moderate; wet seasons from February to May and September to November with average yearly rainfall of about 59 in. (150 cm)
Main rivers: Rusizi, Ruvironza, Ruvubu
Highest elevation: Mount Heha, 8,760 ft. (2,670 m)
Lowest elevation: Lake Tanganyika, 2,533 ft. (772 m)

GOVERNMENT

Form of government: Republic
Head of state: President
Head of government: President
Administrative areas: 15 provinces (there may be a new province)

Legislature: Assemblee Nationale (National Assembly) with 121 members serving five-year terms
Court system: Cour Supreme (Supreme Court)
Armed forces: 45,500 troops

PEOPLE

Estimated 2002 population: 7,044,000
Population growth: 3.15%
Population density: 655 persons per sq. mi. (253 per km²)
Population distribution: 92% rural, 8% urban
Life expectancy in years: Male: 45 Female: 47
Doctors per 1,000 people: 0.1
Percentage of age-appropriate population enrolled in the following educational levels: Primary: 51 Secondary: 7 Further: 1

Burundi is a small, landlocked country whose location makes overseas trade difficult and expensive. Because the nation is situated far inland, goods must be loaded and unloaded from lake ships and railroad cars many times before reaching their destination.

Village women purify their water, *below left,* by pouring it through a gourd containing a purifying agent. Impure drinking water has caused illness in Burundi, and a government program designed to improve the rural water supply was begun in 1986.

On the highlands that cover much of Burundi, farmers have cleared the once-wooded plateaus. Poor farming methods and heavy rains have eroded once-fertile volcanic soils in the west.

ECONOMY

Languages spoken:
Kirundi (official)
French (official)
Swahili

Religions:
Roman Catholic 62%
indigenous beliefs 23%
Muslim 10%
Protestant 5%

Currency: Burundi franc

Gross national income (GNI) in 2000: $0.7 billion U.S.

Real annual growth rate (1999–2000): 0.3%

GNI per capita (2000): $110 U.S.

Balance of payments (2000): -$49 million U.S.

Goods exported: Coffee, tea, sugar, cotton, hides

Goods imported: Capital goods, petroleum products, foodstuffs

Trading partners: Benelux, France, Germany, United Kingdom

TECHNOLOGY

Radios per 1,000 people: 220

Televisions per 1,000 people: 30

Computers per 1,000 people: N/A

An elderly Tutsi man rests in the shade. Many Tutsi own livestock. Although a minority, the Tutsi hold most of Burundi's wealth and control its government and army. They are sometimes called the Watusi.

Bagaza restricted the Roman Catholic Church, which supported the rights of the Hutu. He was overthrown and replaced in 1987, but Hutu-Tutsi violence again broke out in 1988. Thousands of people died in the conflict or fled the nation.

In April 1994, Burundi's president was killed, along with Rwanda's president, in a suspicious airplane crash at an airport in the Rwandan capital of Kigali. His replacement was overthrown in 1996.

Outbreaks of ethnic violence occurred sporadically throughout the middle to late 1990's. Over 100,000 people have been killed in these conflicts.

187

Cambodia

Cambodia, known during the 1970's and 1980's as Kampuchea, is a Southeast Asian country that borders Thailand, Laos, and Vietnam. The Mekong River flows through the eastern part of the country, creating fertile valleys ideally suited to the production of rice. The land along the Mekong is a patchwork of rice fields. Most Cambodians live on the river's fertile plains or near the *Tonle Sap* (Great Lake) and Tonle Sap River northwest of Phnom Penh, the nation's capital.

The majority of the Cambodian people are Khmer, one of the oldest groups in Southeast Asia. They speak the Khmer language, which has its own alphabet. A large Chinese community of about 300,000 also lives in Cambodia. Most of the people living in Cambodia are Buddhists.

Cambodia's economy is based chiefly on agriculture, particularly the production of rice and corn. In the past, the country has also produced large quantities of rubber. However, many farms and rubber plantations were destroyed during the Vietnam War (1957-1975) and Cambodia's civil wars of the 1970's and 1980's. As a result, the nation's agricultural production has decreased sharply.

Early history

About 100 A.D., people in the southern part of what is now Cambodia established the kingdom of Funan, one of the greatest early powers of Southeast Asia. Funan gradually declined, and by the 600's a Khmer kingdom called Chenla had arisen north of Funan. Chenla broke up in the 700's.

Between the 800's and 1400's, the Khmer ruled a powerful Hindu-Buddhist kingdom in Cambodia. In Angkor, the capital of this empire, the Khmer built hundreds of beautiful stone temples, hospitals, and palaces. They also constructed roads, reservoirs, and canals. The Khmer empire prospered, and by the 1100's it commanded much of what is now Laos, Vietnam, and Thailand.

Internal and external conflicts eventually weakened the empire, however. In 1431, Thai forces captured Angkor, and the Khmer abandoned the city. But an inde-

pendent Khmer kingdom, with its capital near what is now Phnom Penh, survived until the mid-1800's. In 1863, the French, who occupied southern Vietnam, made Cambodia a protectorate.

Modern history

In 1953, France granted Cambodia its independence, and two years later the country's leader, King Norodom Sihanouk, gave up the throne to enter politics. He took the title of prince and became prime minister in 1955 and head of state in 1960.

In 1970, Lieutenant General Lon Nol, a member of the reigning government, overthrew Sihanouk. Lon Nol declared Cambodia a republic, and in 1971 he made himself president and assumed full control of the government.

Lon Nol's hold, however, was weakened by several factors. The United States, charging that North Vietnam had installed troops and supplies in Cambodia for use in the Vietnam War, began a series of bombing raids on Cambodia that continued through 1973. Meanwhile, a Cambodian Communist organization called the *Khmer Rouge* had been growing stronger. In April 1975, the Khmer Rouge seized power.

The Khmer Rouge, led by Pol Pot, dismantled all of Cambodian society. The government took control of all businesses and farms. The Khmer Rouge regime believed that Cambodia's economy should be based almost entirely on agriculture, so it forced most people in cities and towns to work on farms. After the Khmer Rouge evacuated Phnom Penh, its population of about 2 million fell to an estimated 20,000 people. Banks and currency were abolished, hospitals were closed, religion was almost completely abolished, education was limited to little more than political instruction, and people had to dress alike.

The Khmer Rouge remained in power until 1979, when invading Vietnamese and Cambodian allies seized control. Vietnam withdrew from Cambodia in 1989. In October 1991, government and opposition groups signed a peace treaty. Multiparty elections were held in May 1993.

Cambodia Today

Between 1975 and 1979, the Khmer Rouge killed large numbers of Cambodians, including many former government officials, intellectuals, and members of ethnic groups. In addition, conditions were so bad on the collective farms and work camps that many people died of exhaustion, starvation, and disease. Between 1 million and 3 million Cambodians may have died under the Khmer Rouge regime.

In 1977, disputes led to fighting between the Cambodian government and Vietnam. In January 1979, Vietnamese troops and Cambodian Communists ousted the Khmer Rouge from most of Cambodia.

The new pro-Vietnamese leaders reduced government control of the economy and discontinued many Khmer Rouge policies. However, Cambodia had been shattered by years of warfare, and the country could no longer produce enough food to feed its people. In addition, Western nations imposed an economic embargo on Cambodia, severely restricting trade. By the mid-1980's, thousands of Cambodians had fled to Thailand.

Vietnam supported Cambodia's new regime, and many Vietnamese troops remained in the country. The Khmer Rouge and

Phnom Penh, Cambodia's capital, *center,* lies on the Mekong River. This waterway serves as an important transportation network, since most of the country's roads and railways were destroyed during the conflicts of the 1970's and 1980's.

FACT BOX

CAMBODIA

COUNTRY

Official name: Preahreacheanachakr Kampuchea (Kingdom of Cambodia)
Capital: Phnom Penh
Terrain: Mostly low, flat plains; mountains in southwest and north
Area: 69,900 sq. mi. (181,040 km²)

Climate: Tropical; rainy, monsoon season (May to November); dry season (December to April); little seasonal temperature variation
Main rivers: Mekong, Tonle Sap
Highest elevation: Phnum Aoral, 5,938 ft. (1,810 m)
Lowest elevation: Gulf of Thailand, sea level

GOVERNMENT

Form of government: Multiparty liberal democracy
Head of state: King
Head of government: Prime minister
Administrative areas: 20 khett (provinces), 3 krong (municipalities)

Legislature: National Assembly with 122 members serving five-year terms and the Senate with 61 members serving five-year terms
Court system: Supreme Council of the Magistracy, Supreme Court, lower courts
Armed forces: 149,000 troops

PEOPLE

Estimated 2002 population: 12,269,000
Population growth: 2.27%
Population density: 165 persons per sq. mi. (64 per km²)
Population distribution: 84% rural, 16% urban
Life expectancy in years: Male: 54 Female: 59
Doctors per 1,000 people: 0.3
Percentage of age-appropriate population enrolled in the following educational levels: Primary: 119* Secondary: 22 Further: 1

some non-Communist groups continued to fight the new government, and in 1982 the opposition groups joined forces under Norodom Sihanouk. Although the Vietnamese-backed government was installed in Cambodia, only Vietnam, the Soviet Union, and their allies recognized it. Western nations and China backed the Sihanouk coalition's right to a seat in the United Nations (UN).

In 1989, Sihanouk met with Cambodian Prime Minister Hun Sen, a former Khmer Rouge official, to try to work out a settlement. To help put an end to the fighting between Hun Sen's regime and Sihanouk's coalition, Vietnam agreed to withdraw its troops from Cambodia.

The Vietnamese troops pulled out of Cambodia in September 1989, but leaders of the coalition charged that thousands of Vietnamese soldiers remained in Cambodia disguised as Cambodian soldiers. The Khmer Rouge and the non-Communist guerrillas then launched separate offensives against Hun Sen's forces, and the country plunged once again into civil war.

In October 1991, the warring groups within Cambodia signed a peace treaty. It called for a 12-member Supreme National Council, chosen from among all the opposing groups, to work with UN representatives to administer Cambodia until elections could be held.

A new constitution was put into effect in September 1993. A new democratically elected government headed by two prime ministers was established, and the office of king was restored as a ceremonial position. The Khmer Rouge boycotted the elections and did not join the new government.

Relations between Hun Sen and Prince Norodom Ranariddh, the two prime ministers, were strained. In July 1997, Hun Sen forced Ranariddh from office.

Elections for the National Assembly were held in July 1998. Hun Sen remained prime minister. In 1999, Cambodia established a new Senate.

Cambodia is a small Southeast Asian country on the Gulf of Thailand. Widespread death and emigration during the 1970's and 1980's seriously reduced its population.

Languages spoken:
Khmer (official) 95%
French English

Religion:
Theravada Buddhist 95%

Enrollment ratios compare the number of students enrolled to the population which, by age, should be enrolled. A ratio higher than 100 indicates that students older or younger than the typical age range are also enrolled.

TECHNOLOGY

Radios per 1,000 people: 119

Televisions per 1,000 people: 123

Computers per 1,000 people: 1.1

ECONOMY

Currency: New riel

Gross national income (GNI) in 2000: $3.1 billion U.S.

Real annual growth rate (1999–2000): 5.0%

GNI per capita (2000): $260 U.S.

Balance of payments (2000): -$19 million U.S.

Goods exported: Timber, garments, rubber, rice, fish

Goods imported: Cigarettes, gold, construction materials, petroleum products, machinery, motor vehicles

Trading partners: United States, Singapore, Vietnam, Japan

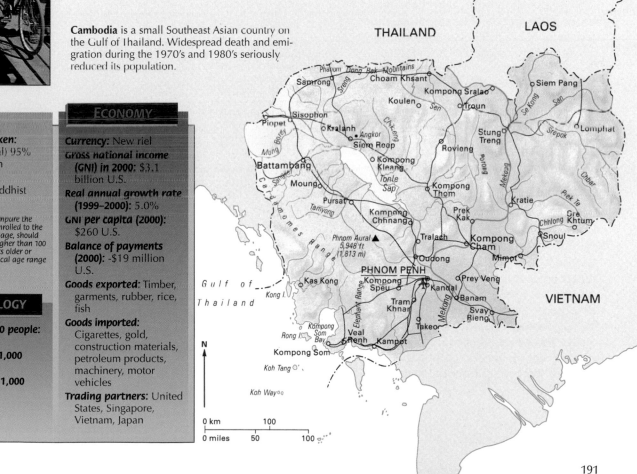

Environment and People

Cambodia, with its warm, wet climate, flat land, and fertile soil, is ideal for growing rice. Since the 1970's, however, the country has struggled to pursue its traditional agricultural ways despite the devastating effects of warfare and the terror of the Khmer Rouge.

Land and climate

Low mountains encircle most of Cambodia. Phnom Aural, Cambodia's highest mountain peak, rises in the Cardamomes Range in the southwest. Fertile plains cover about a third of Cambodia's land, and forests cover the remainder.

The great Mekong River flows south from Laos through Cambodia. During the dry season, the Tonle Sap River flows southeast from the shallow *Tonle Sap* (Great Lake) and joins the Mekong at Phnom Penh. During the *monsoon* (rainy) season, the river flows in the opposite direction because floods and melted snow from the Mekong's source in Tibet raise the river waters to a level higher than that of the lake.

Cambodia has a tropical climate. At Phnom Penh, the daily temperature averages about 85° F. (29° C) all year round. During the rainy season, which lasts from May to November, annual rainfall ranges from less than 60 inches (150 centimeters) in Phnom Penh to about 200 inches (510 centimeters) on the coast.

A transformed society

Years of warfare and Khmer Rouge rule shattered the Cambodian economy as well as many of its cherished traditions. However, since the Khmer Rouge regime was overthrown in 1979, Cambodians have begun to rebuild their society. But the principles of Communism still affect almost all aspects of Cambodian life.

Before the Khmer Rouge took over, most Cambodians were rice farmers, and rural families owned the land they lived on and farmed. However, the Khmer Rouge abolished private ownership of land and forced people to work on communal farms,

A worker in a textile factory manufactures cotton cloth. About 60 Cambodian state-owned factories produce plastics, tools, textiles, cigarettes, and other consumer goods. But the development of industry is slowed by lack of power and raw materials.

This village near Tonle Sap is typical of many rural communities in Cambodia. Many of the houses are built on stilts to protect against rising waters during the rainy season. Rice and fish make up the villagers' usual diet.

The Mekong River is the largest river on the Southeast Asian peninsula. As it flows through Cambodia, the Mekong waters many rice fields. In the rainy season, the river sometimes floods the flat, low-lying Cambodian landscape.

The Royal Palace in Phnom Penh, *far right*, was once the home of Khmer kings. The Cambodian people take pride in their distinguished past, but years of warfare have made the future uncertain.

where even rice for meals often was strictly rationed. Cultivation was greatly disrupted, and the country suffered grave food shortages.

Today, as before, most Cambodians are rice farmers, living in villages of between 100 and 400 people and working on paddies near their villages. Like the Khmer Rouge, the present government also prohibits private ownership of land. But some rural Cambodians may keep the rice they grow, and a few are allowed to occupy the land they owned before the Khmer takeover. Although the agricultural situation has improved somewhat, Cambodia still has serious problems with food production.

From the early 1900's until 1975, public education was widespread in Cambodia, and students learned a variety of subjects, including arithmetic, history, geography, health, language, and science. University education was also available. After 1975, the Khmer Rouge killed thousands of teachers and almost completely destroyed the educational system.

After the Vietnamese-backed government took over, education made a slow recovery, but it is still limited by lack of school buildings, teachers, and books and supplies. Children are required to attend school from the ages of 6 to 12. In 1975, the Khmer Rouge closed Phnom Penh University. But teaching in the fields of medicine and pharmacy resumed in 1980, and the university officially reopened in 1988.

Like education, religion also was violently suppressed under the Khmer Rouge. Many monks were killed, and others were taken from the monasteries and forced to perform hard labor. Temples were destroyed or converted to nonreligious uses. Today, however, the ban on Buddhism has been lifted. Although the government still limited religious practice in the 1980's, Buddhism was reinstated as the national religion in 1989.

Angkor

Angkor was an early Khmer civilization that flourished in northwestern Cambodia from the early 800's to the 1400's. The most famous capital of this civilization also was called Angkor. *Angkor* means *city,* or *capital.*

The Khmer built a huge imperial capital at Angkor. It may have had a million people, more than any European city at that time. Angkor included Angkor Thom, a "city within a city" that covered 4 square miles (10 square kilometers); Angkor Wat, a grand Hindu temple; and many other temples and palaces.

A number of building materials were used at Angkor, including brick, laterite, and sandstone. Laterite, a type of stone, provided material for foundations. Doorways, towers, and decorative details were built of sandstone, often carved in beautiful, complex designs.

Angkor Thom's central temple, the Bayon, an impressive structure with more than 200 giant stone faces adorning its towers, was erected in honor of Buddha and the reigning king. However, Angkor Wat was the most magnificent temple in Angkor.

Angkor Wat

Built in the early 1100's and dedicated to the Hindu god Vishnu, Angkor Wat was used as an astronomical observatory, as well as for religious purposes. It later became the tomb of the Cambodian king who had ordered its construction.

The vast scale of Angkor Wat reflects the enormous wealth of the Khmer empire. The monument covers nearly 1 square mile (2.6 square kilometers) and is surrounded by a moat.

Crossing a ceremonial causeway that extends over the moat, a Buddhist monk leaves Angkor Wat. The temple's main entrance is topped by three towers.

Angkor Wat consists of a group of temples constructed in a pyramidal form that imitates the mythological home of the Hindu gods. A series of staircases and terraces lead to the highest tower. The galleries that surround the central pyramid are decorated with carved scenes of Khmer history, as well as images from Hindu mythology.

The empire's decline

Many new temples and other buildings were built in the Angkor kingdom in the late 1100's and early 1200's. However, the great speed at which the temples were built often led to careless workmanship and faster deterioration. From that time to the end of the empire, little new construction was undertaken.

This deterioration perhaps symbolized the fate of the Angkor empire, which began to decline after the 1100's. Invasions from Thailand, epidemics of malaria, and disputes within the royal Cambodian family may have caused the empire's downfall. Thai forces captured the capital in 1431 but soon abandoned it. Looters overran the remaining temples, and years of forest growth gradually covered the once-beautiful city.

The roots of a large tree, left to grow during centuries of abandonment, push up through the pavement in Angkor.

The ancient Khmer capital of Angkor was built upon an elaborate network of canals and artificial lakes called *barays.* The canals irrigated the city's rice fields, and the barays served as reservoirs. The Bayon (A), built around 1200 and dedicated to Buddha, was the last great temple built within the capital. Angkor Wat (B), built in the 1100's and dedicated to the Hindu god Vishnu, is the largest and best preserved of the city's temples. Moats, which were part of the water system, surrounded Angkor Wat and other temples. Angkor Thom, where the Bayon is located, also was surrounded by a moat.

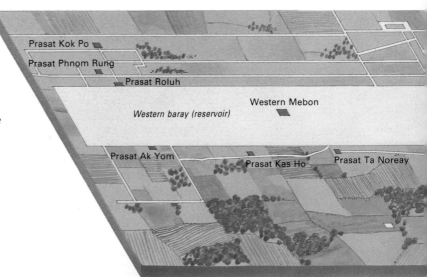

Prasat Kok Po
Prasat Phnom Rung
Prasat Roluh
Western Mebon
Western baray (reservoir)
Prasat Ak Yom
Prasat Kas Ho
Prasat Ta Noreay

Angkor's buildings were constructed of brick, laterite, and sandstone. Many of the city's temples have stood for more than 800 years.

Angkor remained abandoned for more than 400 years. However, interest in Cambodia's "lost city" was stirred by accounts of European explorers written in the 1600's. Early maps of the region eventually led to the ancient Khmer capital's rediscovery in 1860 by Henri Mouhot, a French naturalist.

Mouhot uncovered stone carvings and manuscripts that revealed much about daily life in Angkor. One manuscript described the magnificence and riches of one of Angkor's temples and noted that thousands of people were required to maintain it.

From the 1860's to the mid-1900's, French and Cambodian archaeologists restored and rebuilt many of Angkor's temples. A great deal of damage had been done by tree roots that had pushed up under the foundations, and rain had destroyed many of the exquisite sandstone carvings and statues. Nevertheless, even in their ruined state, the temples of Angkor probably represent the finest architectural monuments in Cambodia.

A Bayon

B Angkor Wat

Neak Pean

Ta Som

Siem Reap River

Preah Khan

Eastern Mebon

Eastern baray (reservoir)

Phimeanakas

Baphuon

Ta Keo

Pre Rup

Banteay Samre

A

ANGKOR THOM

Ta Prohm

Banteay Kdei

Phnom Bakheng

B

Cameroon

The west African country of Cameroon is home to more than 15 million people from about 200 different ethnic groups. The largest groups are the Bamiléké, who live in the western mountains of the country, and the Fulani, who live in the north. The Douala, the Ewondo, and the Fang inhabit the southern and central sections.

English and French are the official languages of Cameroon, holdovers from the time when the country was a colony of both Great Britain and France. But most Cameroonians speak 1 of the country's 24 African languages.

Many of these languages are *Bantu*—a term that refers to both the languages and the people who speak them. About 300 Bantu languages and dialects are spoken in Africa.

Several hundred years before Christ was born, the first Bantu people lived in the northern highlands of what is now Cameroon. About the time of Christ, the Bantu began one of the greatest migrations in history.

The migration occurred gradually, with small groups continually splitting off and moving to new regions as their population expanded. The groups eventually formed about 300 separate ethnic groups, and by the year 1500, Bantu peoples were living in most of central, eastern, and southern Africa. The Bassa, Douala, Ewondo, and Fang are among the Bantu peoples living in Cameroon today.

Cameroon's Pygmies are a small but special group of people, probably one of the first groups to live in Africa. Pygmies are only about 4 feet to 4 feet 8 inches (1.2 to 1.42 meters) tall, with reddish-brown skin and tightly curled brown hair.

The Pygmies' home has always been the thick tropical rain forests of central Africa, where they live in small bands, hunting and gathering. But today the Pygmies of Cameroon have a much smaller area to live in. Over hundreds of years, Bantu-speaking peoples in search of more land to farm invaded much of the Pygmies' territory and cut down the forests. Now, the Pygmies are losing even more land, as people build roads and towns in the forests. Fewer and fewer Pygmies in Cameroon and neighboring countries are able to follow their traditional way of life.

A Muslim religious leader leads worshipers in an ancient prayer, *bottom*. About 20 per cent of Cameroon's people are Muslims, and about 45 per cent follow traditional African religions.

Traditional clay huts, like the one in the photo below, have sheltered northern Cameroonians for hundreds of years. Many people in this hot, dry region belong to the Fulani ethnic group, one of more than 200 groups in Cameroon.

Colorful robes and a golden nose ring are part of the traditional dress of a woman in northern Cameroon.

Traders in a street market, *left,* conduct their business in the shade of leafy trees. Village markets are often social centers where many rural Cameroonians gather to exchange news and visit with friends.

Most of the other people in Cameroon also live off the land, much as their ancestors did. About two-thirds of the people make their homes in rural areas, mainly in villages or small towns, and many make their living as farmers or herders.

Houses in the northern towns and villages are round clay huts or rectangular brick houses. Herders who roam the north build light shelters from poles and woven mats so that they can move easily from place to place. Houses in the western mountains are usually square brick structures, while homes in the central and southern forests are typically rectangular houses made of wood, palm leaves, and clay. Along the coast, people build wooden houses and cover them with tree bark or sheets of metal. In the cities, some Cameroonians live in modern houses and apartments, but others live in rundown shacks in slum conditions.

The Cameroon government offers free public education, and private schools are given financial aid. However, due to a severe shortage of schools and teachers, many children do not attend school at all. Among Cameroonians 15 years or older, only about 4 of every 10 can read and write.

The slave trade became a triangular route across the Atlantic Ocean after the establishment of European plantations in the Americas during the 1500's led to a huge increase in the demand for African slaves. Food and manufactured goods were loaded onto cargo ships in European ports such as Liverpool, England, and Lisbon, Portugal. The ships sailed to the African coast, where they sold their cargoes and took on a new load—black African slaves. Then they sailed across the ocean to the Western Hemisphere. There the slaves were sold in markets to work on plantations. The ships then took on cargoes of plantation products, such as tobacco, sugar, and cotton, for transport back to Europe.

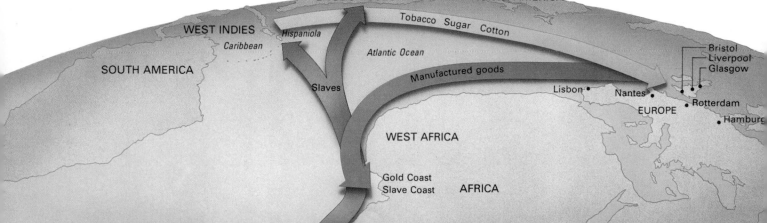

ENGLISH COLONIES   NORTH AMERICA
WEST INDIES
Hispaniola
Caribbean
Tobacco Sugar Cotton
Atlantic Ocean
SOUTH AMERICA
Manufactured goods
Slaves
Bristol
Liverpool
Glasgow
Lisbon
Nantes
Rotterdam
EUROPE
Hamburg
WEST AFRICA
Gold Coast
Slave Coast
AFRICA

Cameroon Today

Like many African countries, modern Cameroon is a blend of traditional ways and modern challenges. In rural areas, Cameroonians live much as their ancestors did, while in the cities the people face such problems as poverty and overcrowding as they work to develop Cameroon into a contemporary society.

Cameroon is a republic. A president heads the government and appoints a Cabinet to help run it. A 120-member National Assembly makes the laws. The people elect both the president and the Assembly.

Historical background

Portuguese explorers, who arrived in the 1400's, were the first Europeans to see Cameroon. They found huge schools of shrimplike animals, which they called *camarões* (shrimp), in the Wouri River. That Portuguese word eventually led to the country's name.

For the next 300 years, other Europeans flocked to the region. Many came to profit from the slave trade that flourished there. When the United Kingdom outlawed its slave trade in 1807—followed by other European nations in the early 1800's—traders turned to ivory and palm oil.

During the 1800's, three European countries—the United Kingdom, France, and Germany—competed for control of Cameroon. In 1858, British missionaries established Victoria, Cameroon's first permanent European settlement, at the base of Mount Cameroon. In 1884, however, two local chiefs of the Douala people in Cameroon signed a treaty with Germany that made the region a German protectorate.

Then, during World War I (1914-1918), Germany lost control of Cameroon to the United Kingdom and France, and in 1922 those two countries divided the land between them. The British section, called the British Cameroons, consisted of two separate parts along the western border. The French section, called French Cameroon, consisted of the remaining land—about 80 per cent of present-day Cameroon. Each section was governed by the laws of its ruling country and adopted that country's language.

Independence

On Jan. 1, 1960, French Cameroon became the independent Republic of Cameroon. In an election in February 1961, the United Kingdom asked the people in the British Cameroons whether they wanted to join the new republic or unite with neighboring Nigeria. Voters in the northern part chose to join Nigeria and became part of that country on June 1, 1961. Voters in the southern part

---

FACT BOX

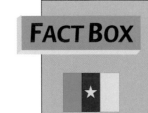

CAMEROON

COUNTRY

Official name: Republic of Cameroon
Capital: Yaoundé
Terrain: Diverse, with coastal plain in southwest, dissected plateau in center, mountains in west, plains in north
Area: 183,568 sq. mi. (475,440 km²)

Climate: Varies with terrain, from tropical along coast to semiarid and hot in north
Main rivers: Benue, Wouri, Sanaga
Highest elevation: Mt. Cameroon, 13,353 ft. (4,070 m)
Lowest elevation: Atlantic Ocean, sea level

GOVERNMENT

Form of government: Unitary republic
Head of state: President
Head of government: Prime minister
Administrative areas: 10 provinces

Legislature: Assemblee Nationale (National Assembly) with 180 members serving five-year terms
Court system: Supreme Court
Armed forces: 22,100 troops

PEOPLE

Estimated 2002 population: 15,855,000
Population growth: 2.47%
Population density: 86 persons per sq. mi. (33 per km²)
Population distribution: 56% rural, 44% urban
Life expectancy in years:
 Male: 54
 Female: 56
Doctors per 1,000 people: 0.1
Percentage of age-appropriate population enrolled in the following educational levels:
 Primary: 85
 Secondary: 27
 Further: 4

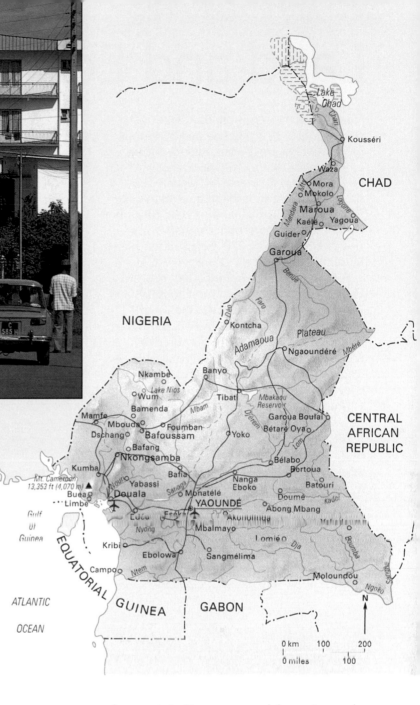

Modern apartment build-
ings line a broad street in
a residential section of
Yaoundé, capital of
Cameroon.

Cameroon is a country in
western Africa, where the
continent's Atlantic coastline turns from an east-
west direction to north-
south.

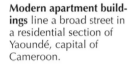

ECONOMY

Languages spoken:
English (official)
French (official)
24 major African
language groups

Religions:
Indigenous beliefs 40%
Christian 40%
Muslim 20%

Currency: Communauté
Financière Africaine
franc

**Gross national income
(GNI) in 2000:** $8.6
billion U.S.

**Real annual growth rate
(1999–2000):** 4.2%

GNI per capita (2000):
$580 U.S.

**Balance of payments
(2000):** -$153 million
U.S.

Goods exported: Crude
oil and petroleum prod-
ucts, lumber, cocoa
beans, aluminum, cof-
fee, cotton

Goods imported:
Machines and electrical
equipment, transport
equipment, fuel, food

Trading partners: France,
Italy, Spain

TECHNOLOGY

Radios per 1,000 people:
163

**Televisions per 1,000
people:** 34

**Computers per 1,000
people:** 3.3

chose to join Cameroon, and that union took
place on Oct. 1, 1961. Ahmadou Ahidjo became president.

From then until early 1972, Cameroon
operated as a federation of two states—East
Cameroon and West Cameroon. In May
1972, Cameroon adopted a new Constitution
that united the two states.

Ahidjo retired in 1982, and Paul Biya succeeded him. Until 1991, Cameroon only allowed one political party. But late that year,
the government legalized opposition parties.
In October 1992, Biya was declared the winner of a presidential election. The election
was seen as fraudulent, however, and many
believed that Biya's opponent was the true
winner.

Land and Economy

Cameroon covers more than 180,000 square miles (470,000 square kilometers) of mountains, grasslands, and forests in west-central Africa. The mountains and hills run along Cameroon's western border, from the seacoast in the south to Lake Chad in the north. Near the coast, Mount Cameroon—Cameroon's highest point—rises 13,353 feet (4,070 meters) above sea level.

A grassy, thinly wooded plain, or *savanna,* in northern Cameroon contains a wildlife reserve called Waza National Park, the home of a great variety of African animals, including elephants, giraffes, monkeys, and antelopes. This northern savanna region is hot and dry most of the year. The average temperature is about 82° F. (28° C), but daytime temperatures sometimes reach as high as 120° F. (49° C).

A forested plateau covers central Cameroon. The central plateau is cooler than the savanna, with an average temperature of about 75° F. (24° C).

South of the plateau, a tropical forested lowland lies along the coast. This coastal region is hot and humid, with an average temperature of about 80° F. (27° C). Some areas receive up to 200 inches (500 centimeters) of rain each year.

Huge numbers of wild animals once roamed the forests of southern Cameroon, but they have become scarce. Many were killed by hunters, and others by farmers trying to protect their crops.

A developing economy

Although Cameroon is a developing country, and quite poor by Western standards, its economy is strong and varied compared to other countries in western Africa.

Cameroon's economy still depends heavily on agriculture, and most of the nation's people are farmers or herders. Farmers grow such food crops as cassava, corn, millet, yams, and sweet potatoes, mainly for their own use. They also raise such cash crops as bananas, cacao beans, coffee, cotton, and peanuts.

Petroleum is Cameroon's most important natural resource. Since the 1970's, when the country began producing petroleum

A modern truck delivers goods to a Cameroon village of traditional round, thatched huts, *far right.* Most of the nation's roads are unpaved, but railroads connect the largest cities and towns.

Rural villages or small towns are home to about two-thirds of Cameroon's people. Villagers raise food crops for their families or tend livestock. Cameroon is still a developing nation.

Carrying their burdens on their heads in traditional style, two women walk along a hot, dusty road in Cameroon's northern savanna region. There, daytime temperatures may reach 120° F. (49° C), and little rain falls.

Passengers reach dry land, *far right,* after a journey across the Sanaga River in southern Cameroon. Some of the energy needed for the country's developing industries comes from hydroelectric projects on rivers such as the Sanaga.

Lake Nios

On Aug. 21, 1986, a cloud of carbon dioxide gas escaped from the waters of Lake Nios in rural western Cameroon. This colorless, odorless gas, normally present in very small amounts in the atmosphere, is heavier than oxygen. As the cloud of gas left the lake, it flowed downhill toward a number of small villages, displacing the air as it went. As a result, more than 1,700 Cameroonians, unable to breathe oxygen, died of suffocation. The bodies of their cattle lay scattered across the fields, and even birds and insects were killed. The gas apparently had been dissolved in water deep in the lake, but no one knows what caused the gas to be released. Witnesses reported hearing a low rumble right before the disaster, and some scientists think that an earth tremor or some kind of volcanic activity beneath the lake triggered the violent release of carbon dioxide.

Lake Nios lies in the mountainous region of western Cameroon, near the Nigerian border.

from wells drilled in the Gulf of Guinea, oil exports have greatly aided the economy. Together with hydroelectric power, the petroleum has also helped the country meet its energy needs.

Cameroon's other mineral products include limestone and *pozzuolana* (a rock used to make cement). The country also has deposits of bauxite, iron ore, diamonds, and other minerals, but these are not mined commercially. Cameroon's natural resources also include its vast forests, which provide palm oil, rubber, and timber.

Most of Cameroon's manufacturing industries are based on the processing of the nation's resources. Some plants, for example, process agricultural raw materials, such as animal hides, cacao, and sugar cane. Petroleum refining and the manufacture of cement from limestone and pozzuolana are also important. Other factories manufacture products using raw materials or parts imported from other countries. For example, aluminum is produced from bauxite imported from nearby Guinea. Other factories in Cameroon manufacture consumer products such as beer, cigarettes, shoes, soap, and soft drinks.

City life

These manufacturing industries and some service industries provide jobs in Cameroon's urban areas, where about a third of the people live. Each year, large numbers of rural people move to the towns and cities to find jobs, causing problems with overcrowding and housing.

Yaoundé and Douala, the largest cities, have elegant hotels, fine office buildings, and fashionable modern houses. But they also have slum areas where many poorer people live in wretched conditions.

Little industry is located in Yaoundé, the capital of Cameroon, but the city is a busy commercial and transportation center. Railroads connect it with Douala, the country's largest city and the Gulf of Guinea's major port. Road transportation is difficult in Cameroon because most roads are unpaved.

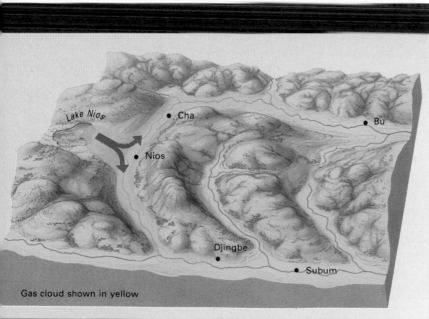

Gas cloud shown in yellow

Canada

Canada is a land of many contrasts. It is the second largest country in the world, but it ranks thirty-sixth in population, with about 31 million people. It is slightly larger than the United States, but has less than one-tenth as many people.

Canada spans the continent of North America from Newfoundland on the Atlantic Ocean to British Columbia on the Pacific, and from the Arctic Ocean in the north to the United States in the south. Yet 75 per cent of the Canadian people live within 100 miles (150 kilometers) of the country's southern border. Few people live in the rest of the country because of its rugged terrain and harsh climate.

The Canadian landscape includes towering mountains in the west; vast, flat prairies inland; and sandy beaches on the eastern coast. In the north, lush forests cover huge areas of land, and beyond the woodlands lies the frozen, barren Arctic.

Canada is wealthy in natural resources. Beginning in the 1500's, Europeans came to fish in its coastal waters and trap fur-bearing animals in its forests. The forests also became a resource as settlers used their wood for building and fuel. Fertile soil attracted immigrant farmers. Today, Canada's mighty rivers supply water and power, and the nation's rich deposits of petroleum and other minerals provide raw materials for manufacturers.

Canada's people are as varied as its landscape. Nearly half are of British descent, and about one quarter are the descendants of French settlers. Both English and French are official languages today. Other major groups include people of German, Italian, and Ukrainian descent. Large numbers of Asian immigrants have settled in western Canada and 11 per cent of Canadians are of Asian descent. American Indians and Inuit make up about 4 per cent of the population, while people of African descent make up less than 1 per cent.

More than three-fourths of Canada's people live in cities and towns. Many of these urban areas lie near the Great Lakes and the St. Lawrence River, including Montreal and Toronto, the largest cities in Canada. Inuit and Indians make up almost half the population of the Arctic north.

Canada is an independent, self-governing nation with strong historic ties to the United Kingdom. It has a close and friendly relationship with the United States but strives to keep its Canadian identity. The name *Canada* probably came from an Iroquois word meaning *community,* though keeping a sense of community over such a vast area continues to challenge the Canadian people.

Canada Today

Canada is a member of the Commonwealth of Nations, an association of countries once governed by the United Kingdom. Today, it is an independent democracy with a federal form of government like the United States, combined with a cabinet system and Parliament like the United Kingdom.

The national government in Ottawa takes care of matters that affect the nation as a whole. Canada is made up of 10 provinces and 3 territories. Each province has its own government; the national government helps administer the territories.

Because Canada is a member of the Commonwealth, the queen of England is also queen of Canada, but a governor general acts as her representative. The governor general once had great power but now performs only formal and symbolic duties. The prime minister heads the government.

The cabinet system of Canada combines the legislative and executive branches of government. Parliament is the national legislature. It has two houses: the House of Commons and the Senate.

Members of the House are elected by the people to five-year terms unless a new election is called earlier. The prime minister is the leader of the majority party in the House of Commons. The prime minister recommends people for the Senate, and they are appointed by the governor general.

The office of prime minister is not established by law. It became a custom long ago when people saw that a leader was needed in this kind of government. The prime minister chooses as many as 40 ministers to head departments in the Cabinet. The prime minister and the Cabinet run the government with the support of Parliament.

Parliament can control the actions of the prime minister by withholding support. Then the prime minister must resign or ask the governor general to call a new election. In turn, the prime minister can control the actions of Parliament by asking for a new election.

The judicial branch of government has two high courts—the Supreme Court and the Federal Court. There are other federal courts, and each province and territory has its own court system.

Canada's government is based on a constitution that is partly unwritten and partly written. The unwritten part is based mainly on custom, such as the cabinet system and the office of prime minister. The written part consists of the Constitution Act of 1982, the British North America Act, and various laws

FACT BOX

COUNTRY

Official name: Canada
Capital: Ottawa
Terrain: Mostly plains with mountains in west and lowlands in southeast
Area: 3,851,809 sq. mi. (9,976,140 km²)
Climate: Varies from temperate in south to subarctic and arctic in north

Main rivers: St. Lawrence, Fraser, Mackenzie, Nelson
Highest elevation: Mount Logan, 19,551 ft. (5,959 m)
Lowest elevation: Atlantic Ocean, sea level

GOVERNMENT

Form of government: Confederation with parliamentary democracy
Head of state: British monarch, represented by governor general
Head of government: Prime minister
Administrative areas: 10 provinces, 3 territories

Legislature: Parliament or Parlement consisting of the Senate or Senat with 104 members serving until age 75 and the House of Commons or Chambre des Communes with 301 members serving five-year terms
Court system: Supreme Court
Armed forces: 60,600 troops

PEOPLE

Estimated 2002 population: 31,698,000
Population growth: 1.02%
Population density: 8 persons per sq. mi. (3 per km²)
Population distribution: 80% urban, 20% rural
Life expectancy in years:
Male: 76
Female: 83
Doctors per 1,000 people: 2.1
Percentage of age-appropriate population enrolled in the following educational levels:
Primary: 97
Secondary: 105*
Further: 58

Arctic Ocean

Cape Columbia
QUTTINIRPAAQ NATIONAL PARK
Mt. Barbeau 8,584 ft (2,616 m)

NORTH MAGNETIC POLE

North

GREENLAND (Denmark)

ICELAND

Canada's 10 provinces include the Atlantic Provinces of Newfoundland and Labrador, Prince Edward Island, New Brunswick, and Nova Scotia; Quebec; Ontario; the Prairie Provinces of Manitoba, Alberta, and Saskatchewan; and British Columbia. The country also has three territories—the Northwest Territories, Nunavut, and the Yukon.

Ellef Ringnes I.
Prince Patrick I.
Queen Elizabeth Islands
Melville I.
Bathurst I.
Axel Heiberg
Ellesmere Island

Baffin Bay

Beaufort Sea

UNITED STATES (Alaska)

IVVAVIK N.P.
VUNTUT N.P.
Mackenzie Bay
Tuktoyaktuk
Cape Kellett
AULAVIK NATIONAL PARK
Banks Island
Viscount Melville Sound
Prince of Wales I.
Somerset I.
SIRMILIK NATIONAL PARK
Bylot I.
Devon Island

Inuvik
Eskimo Lakes
Victoria Island
King William I.
BOOTHIA PENINSULA
Gulf of Boothia
Prince Charles I.
Baffin Island
Admiralty Inlet
Home Bay
AUYUITTUQ NATIONAL PARK

Dawson
TUKTUT NOGAIT N.P.
Norman Wells
Kugluktuk
Coronation Gulf
MELVILLE PENINSULA
Foxe Basin
Davis Strait

Mt. Logan 19,551 ft (5,959 m)
Yukon
Whitehorse
Mt. Sir James MacBrien 9,062 ft (2,762 m)
Great Bear Lake
Northwest Territories
Yellowknife
Baker Lake
Chesterfield Inlet
Coats I.
Mansel I.
Puvirnituq
UNGAVA PENINSULA
Ungava Bay
Kuujjuaq
Cape Chidley
Nain
Labrador Sea

KLUANE N.P.
NAHANNI N.P.
Fort Simpson
Fort Liard
Great Slave Lake
Fort Resolution
Arviat
Hudson Strait
Akpatok I.
TORNGAT MTS.

Newfoundland and Labrador

Mt. Fairweather 15,300 ft (4,663 m)
Hay River
WOOD BUFFALO NATIONAL PARK
Nueltin Lake
Churchill
Southampton I.
UKKUSIKSALIK N.P.

Prince Rupert
Kitimat
British Columbia
Fort Nelson
Lake Athabasca
Fort McMurray
Reindeer Lake
Wollaston Lake
Southern Indian Lake
Hudson Bay
Cape Tatnam
Belcher Islands
Kuujjuarapik
Grande Rivière de-la-Baleine
Schefferville
LABRADOR PENINSULA
Happy Valley-Goose Bay
Smallwood Res.
LABRADOR
TRANS-CANADA HIGHWAY
GROS MORNE N.P.
Corner Brook
TERRA NOVA N.P.
St. John's

GWAII HAANAS N.P.
Queen Charlotte Islands
Prince George
Fort St. John
Dawson Creek
Grande Prairie
Alberta
Saskatchewan
Flin Flon
Lynn Lake
Thompson
Nelson
James Bay
Akimiski I.
Fort Albany
Moosonee
LG-4 Res.
La Grande
LG-2
LG-3 Res.
Chisasibi
Labrador City
Gagnon
Sept-Îles
MINGAN ARCHIPELAGO N.P.
Gulf of Saint Lawrence
ST. PIERRE AND MIQUELON (France)
Island of Newfoundland

Mt. Waddington 13,104 ft (3,994 m)
Williams Lake
Mt. Robson 12,972 ft (3,954 m)
JASPER N.P.
Edmonton
ELK ISLAND N.P.
PRINCE ALBERT N.P.
Prince Albert
The Pas
Eastmain
Mistassini
Chibougamau
Quebec
FORILLON N.P.
Gaspé

Vancouver Island
Nanaimo
Kamloops
Red Deer
Danff
BANFF N.P.
Saskatoon
Yorkton
L. Winnipeg
Chicoutimi
Jonquière
LA MAURICIE N.P.
Matane
Bathurst
New Brunswick
Moncton
Prince Edward Island
Charlottetown
Amherst
Nova Scotia
Truro
Sydney
CAPE BRETON HIGHLANDS N.P.

PACIFIC RIM NAT'L PARK
Victoria
Vancouver
GLACIER N.P.
KOOTENAY N.P.
YOHO N.P.
Calgary
Medicine Hat
Moose Jaw
Regina
RIDING MOUNTAIN N.P.
Winnipeg
Thunder Bay
Timmins
Val-d'Or
Amos
Trois-Rivières
Drummondville
Quebec
Sherbrooke
Fredericton
Saint John
KEJIMKUJIK NATIONAL PARK
Halifax
Cape Sable

GULF ISLANDS N.P.
WATERTON LAKES N.P.
GRASSLANDS N.P.
Lake of the Woods
Selkirk
TRANS-CANADA HIGHWAY
Brandon
PUKASKWA N.P.
Kirkland Lake
North Bay
Ottawa
Cornwall
Kingston
Bay of Fundy

UNITED STATES
Sault Ste. Marie
Greater Sudbury
Georgian Bay
Peterborough
Montreal
Atlantic Ocean

500 Miles
500 Kilometers

Lake Superior
Lake Huron
Toronto
Kitchener
London
Hamilton
St. Catharines
Niagara Falls
L. Ontario
Lake Erie
Windsor
Lake Michigan

Languages spoken:
English 59.3% (official)
French 23.2% (official)

Religions:
Roman Catholic 43%
Protestant 29%
Other groups include Buddhists, Eastern Orthodox, Hindus, Jews, Muslims, and Sikhs,.

*Enrollment ratios compare the number of students enrolled to the population which, by age, should be enrolled. A ratio higher than 100 indicates that students older or younger than the typical age range are also enrolled.

TECHNOLOGY

Radios per 1,000 people:
1,047
Televisions per 1,000 people: 715
Computers per 1,000 people: 390.2

ECONOMY

Currency: Canadian dollar
Gross national income (GNI) in 2000: $649.8 billion U.S.
Real annual growth rate (1999-2000): 4.5%
GNI per capita (2000): $21,130 U.S.
Balance of payments (2000): $18,014 million U.S.
Goods exported: Motor vehicles and parts, wood, newsprint, wood pulp, crude petroleum, precious metal, wheat
Goods imported: Machinery, motor vehicles and parts, computers, appliances, scientific equipment
Trading partners: United States, China, Germany, Japan, Mexico, United Kingdom

and court decisions. The Constitution Act of 1982 ended formal British control over amendments to Canada's constitution.

The British North America Act, which governed Canada from 1867 to 1982, established a powerful national government. Through the years, however, the provinces became stronger and richer. Arguments about the division of power between federal government and provincial governments increased. Each province now controls such matters as education, administration of justice, town and city institutions, property, and civil rights.

Environment

Canada's vast and varied land covers most of the northern half of North America, extending 3,223 miles (5,187 kilometers) from east to west, over six time zones. It stretches 2,875 miles (4,627 kilometers) from north to south; only Greenland lies nearer to the North Pole.

Forests cover 47 per cent of Canada's land area, while mountains and the frozen Arctic make up another 41 per cent. Only about 12 per cent of the land has been settled, mostly in the south and along the coasts. Canada has eight major land regions.

Land regions

The Pacific Ranges and Lowlands form the region farthest west. The Coast Mountains rise up along the Pacific coast. This mountain chain includes the highest peak in Canada—Mount Logan, which reaches a height of 19,524 feet (5,951 meters) in the Yukon.

The coast of British Columbia is cut by *fiords* (long, narrow inlets) that reach the dense forests on the lower slopes of the mountains. The tall western red cedars, Douglas firs, hemlocks, and other evergreens here are a valuable Canadian resource. East of the Coast Mountains is a mineral-rich area of grassy plains, fertile valleys, and smaller mountains.

The Rocky Mountains form the region to the east of the Pacific Ranges and Lowlands. The snow-capped peaks and sky blue lakes of the Rockies offer some of the world's most beautiful scenery. Thousands of tourists visit the mountains of British Columbia and western Alberta every year.

The Interior Plains stretch east of the Rockies. This region covers the northeast corner of British Columbia and most of the Prairie Provinces of Alberta, Saskatchewan, and Manitoba; the plains extend north to the Northwest Territories and the Arctic. The southern plains, once vast natural grasslands, are now dotted with wheat farms and cattle ranches. Evergreen forests cover the northern plains.

The Arctic Islands, numbering in the hundreds, are uninhabited. The islands are *tundras*—areas too cold and dry for trees to

Canada spreads over most of the northern half of North America. It covers 3,849,674 square miles (9,970,610 square kilometers), including inland water such as Great Bear Lake, Great Slave Lake, and thousands of other lakes. The country also has one of the longest coastlines of any country. Hudson Bay and James Bay form a huge inland sea. Hudson Bay, which remains frozen for about eight months of the year, serves as a summer waterway to Canada's vast interior. The Coast Ranges and Rocky Mountains in western Canada are sometimes called the Cordillera. A great northern forest sweeps across Canada from Alaska to Labrador. Near the Arctic Ocean, the forests gradually give way to treeless, mossy tundra that lies over frozen soil called *permafrost*. Crops are grown mainly on the southern Interior Plains and in the St. Lawrence Lowlands.

The climate of Canada is generally cool. Winter, *top,* is long and cold in much of the country. Average summer temperatures, *middle,* range from about 40ºF. (4ºC) in the Arctic Islands to more than 70ºF. (21ºC) in southern Ontario. Precipitation, *bottom,* is heavy in the southeast and on the west coast.

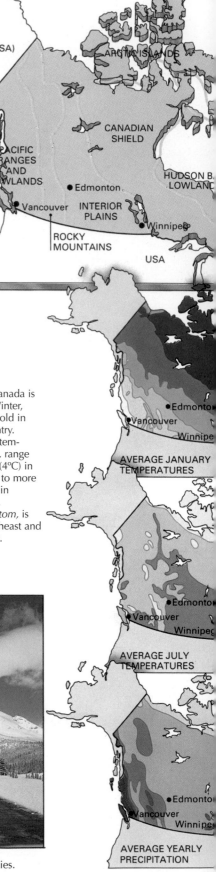

The Banff-Jasper Highway runs along the Rockies.

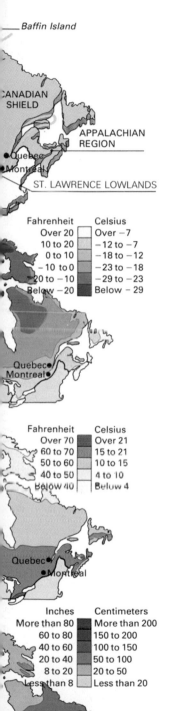

Baffin Island

CANADIAN SHIELD

APPALACHIAN REGION

Quebec
Montreal

ST. LAWRENCE LOWLANDS

Fahrenheit	Celsius
Over 20	Over −7
10 to 20	−12 to −7
0 to 10	−18 to −12
−10 to 0	−23 to −18
−20 to −10	−29 to −23
Below −20	Below −29

Quebec
Montreal

Fahrenheit	Celsius
Over 70	Over 21
60 to 70	15 to 21
50 to 60	10 to 15
40 to 50	4 to 10
Below 40	Below 4

Quebec
Montreal

Inches	Centimeters
More than 80	More than 200
60 to 80	150 to 200
40 to 60	100 to 150
20 to 40	50 to 100
8 to 20	20 to 50
Less than 8	Less than 20

Quebec
Montreal

The Horseshoe Falls is the Canadian half of Niagara Falls.

Forests cover the hills near Haliburton, Ont.

Rolling prairies blanket south-central Canada.

grow. Minerals have been discovered there, but so far most have proved too costly to mine.

South of the Arctic is the Canadian Shield, a huge region of ancient rock. The Shield covers about half of Canada and curves in a horseshoe shape around Hudson Bay. The low hills of the Canadian Shield are actually very old mountains worn down by glaciers. The glaciers also scraped away most of the soil and left behind thousands of lakes, which are the source of many rivers. Valuable evergreen forests cover much of the Canadian Shield, and the region is rich in minerals as well.

The Hudson Bay Lowlands are a flat, swampy region extending southwest from Hudson Bay. Few people live in this area of forests and vast deposits of *peat* (the decayed remains of plants).

The St. Lawrence Lowlands, Canada's smallest land region, are home to more than half of all Canadians. The area includes the St. Lawrence River Valley and southern Ontario, where crops thrive on the flat or gently rolling land. Canada's major cities of Quebec, Montreal, and Toronto are located here, along with many industries, making the region Canada's manufacturing center.

The Appalachian Region includes south-eastern Quebec as well as all the Atlantic Provinces except Labrador. The rounded Appalachian Mountains dominate this region. Most of the people live along the Atlantic coast, where hundreds of inlets provide excellent harbors for fishing fleets.

Climate

Canada's northern location gives the country a generally cold climate with average January temperatures below 0°F. (-18°C) in more than two-thirds of the country. Northern Canada has short, cool summers, but in southern Canada, summers are long enough and warm enough for raising crops. Precipitation is heaviest along the Pacific coast, where lush forests grow. Southeastern Canada also receives plentiful precipitation, including heavy snow in the winter months.

The First Canadians

Canada's history begins with the Asiatic peoples who crossed into what is now North America at least 20,000 years ago. These people moved southward and became the first North Americans. In Canada today, they are known as "Indians" or "Native peoples."

The ancestors of the Inuit also came from Asia, probably about 5,000 years ago, and settled in the Arctic area. *Inuit* means *people* in the Inuit language. Some people call them *Eskimos,* which comes from an Indian word meaning *eaters of raw meat.*

Traditional ways

People living in different parts of Canada eventually developed different ways of life. The Inuit and Indian peoples of Canada have been grouped into six main culture areas, determined by their traditional ways of life—the Arctic, Subarctic, Northwest Coast, Plateau, Plains, and Northeast (also called Eastern Woodlands) areas.

These two groups of people developed different ways of life. The Inuit had to survive in the harsh environment of the Arctic. The sea provided most of their food—seals, walruses, whales, and fish. The Inuit also hunted polar bears and caribous. They used animal skins to make clothing, summer tents, and boats. In the winter, they made sod houses or snowhouses, and traveled by dog sled.

Most Indians who lived in northern regions belonged to two major language groups: the Athabaskan in the west and the Algonquian in the east. These people lived mainly by hunting, gathering, and fishing. They used wood from the northern forests to make utensils, houses or wigwams with wooden frames, and bark canoes and snowshoes.

The Huron, part of the Northeast (also called Eastern Woodlands) group, lived in what is now southeastern Canada. The Huron were mainly farmers and feared the raiding Iroquois from the southeast.

Such tribes as the Blackfeet and the Assiniboine lived on the southern prairies. They farmed along rivers and hunted the vast buffalo herds. They used buffalo skins and deerskins to make tepees and clothing.

The Tlingit and the Haida lived on the western coast where the ocean and rivers teemed with fish and seafood. These Indians hunted game and gathered berries in the

Beautiful Dancing Blankets such as this one, *right*, are used by the Tlingits of British Columbia. The blankets are used as ceremonial robes, and as the dancers move, the fringe provides an exciting image. The blankets' abstract patterns represent clan symbols or forms from nature.

Northwest Coast Indians created totem poles (1), dugout canoes (2), rich dress (3), and masks (4). Inuit used harpoons (5) to hunt.

Plains Indians hunted buffalo (6) and used their hides for clothing (7). Some Plains Indians wore a twisted topknot (8). Feather headdresses (9), beaded jackets (10), and the tepee (11) were also characteristic of Plains culture. Cree hunters used trumpets (12) to lure moose.

huge forests. The trees provided wood for their lodges and canoes.

The traditional life of these first Canadians began to change when Europeans arrived. Eastern groups such as the Algonquin slowly changed their way of life by trading furs for food, weapons, and traps. The various groups took different sides in the wars between the French and English, and fought among themselves as well. Those who managed to survive the wars and the diseases brought by Europeans lost their land to the settlers. Some moved west, and others moved onto reservations.

The Indians on the west coast adapted to the Europeans' ways better than most. Some bought boats and started to sell their fish. Others took jobs in canneries.

The Inuit way of life began to change during the 1800's. They started working with the Europeans, first in whaling and then in fur trapping. They traded with the colonists for goods—especially guns, which helped the Inuit hunt. But increased whaling, trapping, and hunting killed enormous numbers of the animals on which the Inuit depended.

By the mid-1900's, more and more Inuit were moving to communities around trading posts, government offices, and radar sites. Some Inuit found construction work, but many began to need help from the government.

Indians and Inuit today

Nearly 550,000 Indians live in Canada today. Most live on the country's 2,200 reserves, which are owned by the Indians but held in trust for them by the government. The government is also responsible for education, housing, and health care on the reserves. Some Indians have protested the living conditions on the reserves. Others have sued the government to halt projects they believe would harm their rights.

Most of the Inuit who live in Canada inhabit Nunavut. In 1992, an agreement between Canada, the Inuit, and the Northwest Territories established a new national homeland for the Inuit. Nunavut, meaning "our land," became a territory in April 1999. It consists of 800,000 square miles (2 million square kilometers) carved out of the Northwest Territories.

History

About A.D. 1000, Vikings landed on the northeast coast of North America in Newfoundland. The Vikings called the region *Vinland* and founded a small settlement, but it was short-lived.

Lasting contact between Europe and Canada began in 1497, when John Cabot landed in eastern Canada and claimed the region for England. In the 1530's, Jacques Cartier sailed into the Gulf of St. Lawrence and traveled up the St. Lawrence River. He claimed the land for France.

Fishing and, later, the fur trade brought the French to Canada. The growth of the colony known as New France established French culture in the country.

Meanwhile, English seamen explored Canada. In 1610, Henry Hudson sailed into the bay that was later named for him. England claimed large parts of Canada because of Cabot's and Hudson's voyages. But France also claimed this land on the basis of extensive explorations and surveys by the French explorer Samuel de Champlain. From 1689 to 1763, the English and French colonists fought each other in four wars.

The last of these wars was called the *Seven Years' War* in Canada and the *French and Indian War* in the English colonies. British troops seized Quebec City in 1759 and Montreal in 1760. The fighting ended in 1763, and France surrendered most of New France to the British.

Great Britain gave the name *Quebec* to its new territory. Prodded by Quebec Governor Guy Carleton, Britain passed the Quebec Act in 1774. This law gave the French Canadians in Quebec political and religious rights.

Quebec's many British loyalists then became unhappy. The British tried to solve the problem by dividing Quebec into two colonies in the Constitutional Act of 1791. Lower Canada, along the lower St. Lawrence River, remained largely French in population and law. Upper Canada, along the Great Lakes, was British in population and law.

Canada began to grow as fur traders explored the northwest and thousands of immigrants arrived. Trouble brewed, however. French Canadians in Lower Canada resented the power of British Canadians. Led by Louis Papineau, many French Canadians

Yukon
Territory
1898

Northwest
Territories
1870

Saskatchev

British
Columbia
1871

Alberta
1905

9

10

1000 Vikings reach Vinland.
1497 John Cabot claims Newfoundland for England.
1534 Jacques Cartier claims Canada for France.
1604 Acadia founded.
1608 Champlain founds Quebec.
1642 Montreal founded.
1670 Hudson's Bay Company founded.
1689–1763 British and French fight wars; Britain wins New France.

1774 Quebec Act gives French Canadians rights.
1791 Constitutional Act splits Quebec.

1812–1814 War with United States.
1837 Revolts break out in Upper and Lower Canada.
1841 Act of Union joins Upper and Lower Canada.
1848 Province of Canada and Nova Scotia gain self-government.
1857 Gold Rush on Fraser River.
1867 British North America Act establishes the Dominion of Canada.
1869 Riel leads Red River Rebellion.
1870 Province of Manitoba created; Northwest Territories established.
1871 British Columbia joins Confederation.
1873 Prince Edward Island joins Confederation.
1885 Second Riel revolt.
1885 Canadian Pacific Railway completed.
1897 Klondike Gold Rush.

1905 Provinces of Saskatchewan and Alberta created.
1914–1918 Canadians serve in World War I.
1931 Complete independence granted.
1939–1945 Canadians serve in World War II.
1949 Newfoundland becomes 10th province.
1959 St. Lawrence Seaway opens.
1962 Trans-Canada Highway completed.
1967 Centennial celebration.
1969 Official Languages Act establishes services in both French and English.
1976 Separatists elected in Quebec.
1982 Constitution Act ends British control over amendments to Canada's Constitution.
1989 Free trade pact with United States.
1992 North American Free Trade Agreement.
1999 Nunavut becomes a territory.

Samuel de Champlain founded the city of Quebec in 1608.

John A. Macdonald, *far left,* became Canada's first prime minister in 1867.

Jeanne Sauvé took office as governor general in 1984, the first woman to hold that office in Canada.

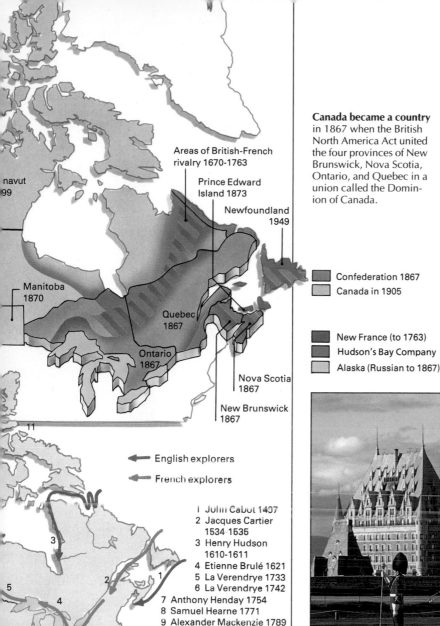

Areas of British-French
rivalry 1670-1763

Prince Edward
Island 1873

Newfoundland
1949

navut
99

Manitoba
1870

Quebec
1867

Ontario
1867

Nova Scotia
1867

New Brunswick
1867

11

← English explorers

← French explorers

1 John Cabot 1497
2 Jacques Cartier
1534-1535
3 Henry Hudson
1610-1611
4 Etienne Brulé 1621
5 La Verendrye 1733
6 La Verendrye 1742
7 Anthony Henday 1754
8 Samuel Hearne 1771
9 Alexander Mackenzie 1789
10 Alexander Mackenzie 1793
11 Sir John Franklin 1845

Canada became a country in 1867 when the British North America Act united the four provinces of New Brunswick, Nova Scotia, Ontario, and Quebec in a union called the Dominion of Canada.

Confederation 1867
Canada in 1905

New France (to 1763)
Hudson's Bay Company
Alaska (Russian to 1867)

The exploration of Canada began with John Cabot in 1497. Jacques Cartier sailed up the St. Lawrence, but fur trappers and traders opened up the interior.

A red-coated band plays in Quebec City's Citadel. Here in 1759, British troops under General James Wolfe captured the city from the French. Montreal fell in 1760, and New France became British.

(once Lower Canada). Macdonald became Canada's first prime minister. His chief goal was to extend the country to the west coast. Some settlers in a western settlement called Red River feared this expansion. They were *métis*—people of mixed European and Indian ancestry. In 1869 and again in 1885 Louis Riel led his fellow métis in unsuccessful revolts against the government.

The completion of the Canadian Pacific Railway in 1885 triggered a great rush to settle the western prairies. Wilfred Laurier became the first French Canadian prime minister in 1896, and Canada prospered under his leadership. Huge wheat crops were traded in Europe, steel and textile industries expanded, and mining areas opened up.

revolted in 1837. British Canadians in Upper Canada who wanted reforms followed William Mackenzie in revolt one month later. Finally, in 1841, the British united Lower and Upper Canada as the Province of Canada.

In the mid-1800's, trade and transportation routes grew as Canada prospered. But in the Province of Canada problems remained. John A. Macdonald and George Cartier headed a campaign for a self-governing federal union. Canadian officials presented a plan to Britain, and in 1867 the British North America Act established the Dominion of Canada. The new Dominion had four provinces—New Brunswick, Nova Scotia, Ontario (once Upper Canada), and Quebec

With the addition of new provinces and the expansion of others, Canada grew. In 1931, the nation won full independence. Canadians helped the Allies fight World War I (1914-1918) and World War II (1939-1945). The country's economy thrived after World War II. In 1959, the St. Lawrence Seaway opened the Great Lakes to oceangoing ships. In 1962, the Trans-Canada Highway—Canada's first ocean-to-ocean road—was completed.

In 1982, the Constitution Act ended British control over amendments to Canada's Constitution and included a bill of rights. Today, Canadian leaders continue to work for national unity, but problems between French- and English-speaking Canadians still flare.

Conflict and Opportunity

In 1967, Canada celebrated the 100th anniversary of Confederation—the union of the provinces. But maintaining that feeling of unity has often been difficult due to Canada's vast geographical area and many differences among the people and the provinces. The proximity of the United States—with its larger population and greater economic power—keeps Canadians careful in protecting their national identity.

Quebec and Canada

About 65,000 French colonists lived in Quebec when France lost its colony to Britain in 1763. Since that time, Canada's French population has grown to about 8 million, including more than 7 million in Quebec. These French Canadians, who call themselves *Québécois,* try to preserve their French language and culture.

In 1960, the Quebec government started the Quiet Revolution, a movement to defend French Canadian rights. The Quiet Revolution led some Québécois to approve of *separatism,* the demand that the province separate from Canada and become an independent nation. The Parti Québécois organized as a separatist political party in 1968, and in 1976 it won control of Quebec's provincial government.

However, in 1980, the separatist movement suffered a major setback. Voters defeated a proposal that would have allowed Quebec to work out an agreement with the Canadian government to separate. An agreement worked out in 1987 stated that Quebec would be recognized as a distinct society in Canada. This agreement, known as the Meech Lake Accord, died in June 1990, after the provinces failed to ratify it.

In October 1992, a nationwide referendum was held on proposals to recognize Quebec as a separate society and to grant native peoples self-government. A majority of voters rejected the proposals. In September 1994, Quebecers again voted the Parti Québécois into provincial office. On October 30, 1995, Quebecers in a referendum voted against independence by 50.6 per cent to 49.4 per cent.

Regionalism

Quebec is not the only Canadian province to seek more control over its own affairs. Dur-

A war veteran shows his opposition to Quebec's Bill 101, the law making French the single official language of the province. Queen Elizabeth II signs the Constitution Act of 1982, witnessed by Prime Minister Pierre Trudeau (seated). The Charter of Rights and Freedom, *bottom left,* was an important addition to the Canadian Constitution.

ing the 1970's, the energy-rich provinces of Alberta, Saskatchewan, and British Columbia benefited from a boom in petroleum and natural gas. There was talk of independence for Alberta by westerners who objected to the national government's control over oil prices.

On the other hand, the Altantic Provinces suffer from economic problems. This region has a lower standard of living, lower wages, and a higher rate of unemployment than any other part of Canada.

Industry and the environment

Canada is rich in natural resources, including forests, petroleum, and water power. These resources have helped make Canada a leading manufacturing nation. However,

recovering the resources and turning them into manufactured goods also has resulted in damage to Canada's natural environment.

For example, acid rain, caused by pollutants from factories as far away as the Midwestern United States, is damaging forests and streams in southeastern Canada. Oil exploration in the far northwest could harm the fragile Arctic plant and animal life. The giant James Bay hydroelectric project, designed to harness water power, has also disrupted animal and human life in the area. In Canada, as elsewhere in the world, there is a growing awareness of environmental problems.

A sign in French advertises a riding school in the province of Quebec, *top*. Canada is bilingual by law, but French predominates in Quebec, where over 7 million Canadians of French ancestry live.

Mennonite women sew quilts in Ontario, *above*. Dutch and German Mennonites came to Canada in the 1800's, along with many other Europeans, but two out of three Canadians have British or French ancestors.

Autumn colors in Riding Mountain National Park in Manitoba display the riches of Canada's forests. They provide lumber for industry and also serve as recreation areas. Some Canadian forestland has been harmed by acid rain, which forms when water vapor in the air reacts with chemical compounds given off by cars, factories, and power plants.

A Greenpeace activist prepares a banner, *above*, aboard one of the group's vessels. Founded in Vancouver in 1969, Greenpeace uses nonviolent methods to protest seal hunts, whaling, and nuclear testing.

Economy and Resources

Fish and, later, fur brought Europeans to Canada. Settlers also farmed and cut down trees in the forests. Some Canadians still make their living in these ways, but the major economic activities today are the service and manufacturing industries.

In August 1992, Canada, the United States, and Mexico announced a comprehensive plan for free trade across North America. Known as the North American Free Trade Agreement, the accord was designed to bind together the economies of the three countries in a regional trading block with more people and more economic production than the European Community. The agreement was ratified by all three countries in 1993.

Service and manufacturing industries

About 70 per cent of Canadian workers are employed in service industries, and one of every three workers performs a community, social, or personal service. Such workers include teachers, doctors, data processors, and hotel employees.

Other service workers are involved in finance, insurance, or real estate. Toronto and Montreal are the leading financial centers. The federal and provincial governments participate in this area of the service economy by providing insurance that guarantees medical care for all Canadians.

Service industries also include transportation, communication, and utilities. The federal and provincial governments play a role in these services too. They own transportation firms such as Canadian National Railways, some television and radio companies, and utilities.

The St. Lawrence Lowlands are at the heart of Canadian manufacturing. Factories in Ontario and Quebec produce more than three-fourths of the value of all of Canada's manufactured goods.

Transportation equipment ranks first in Canada's manufacturing industry. The Canadian plants of U.S. automakers produce about a million cars every year, as well as trucks, subway cars, and airplanes.

The food-processing industry handles chiefly meat and poultry products. Other important food products include baked goods, dairy products, canned fruits and vegetables, fish, and beverages.

Dairy farms in Quebec, *above,* produce great quantities of milk on fairly small plots of land. The huge wheat and cattle ranches of Alberta are on average more than four times larger than Quebec's farms.

Bound for paper mills, a tug pulls log booms down the Saint John River in New Brunswick. With almost half its land covered by forests, Canada is a leading producer of forest products.

Canadians also manufacture chemicals, medicines, machinery, metal products, steel, and paper. Canada leads the world in the production of newsprint.

Mining

Canada is one of the world's top mineral exporters. Petroleum and natural gas are the country's most important minerals. The Prairie Provinces have large deposits of these valuable resources. Alberta produces about 80 per cent of Canada's petroleum and 90 per cent of its natural gas. Deposits have also been found in the Arctic Islands, but these are difficult to recover and transport. The federal government created a company called Petro-Canada to gain some control over oil prices within the country.

A Nova Scotia fishing village, *top,* waits for the fishing boats to return. Fishing is one of Canada's oldest industries.

A steel mill in Sydney, Nova Scotia, *center,* is one of the few heavy industries in the Atlantic Provinces.

A railway yard in British Columbia, *bottom,* handles freight from around the country. The province also owns its own railway.

The Canadian Shield holds much of Canada's mineral wealth. About 85 per cent of the country's iron ore comes from mines near the Quebec-Newfoundland border. Ontario is Canada's leading producer of metal ores, including cobalt, copper, nickel, and platinum mined near Sudbury.

Gold attracted miners to British Columbia in the 1800's. This province, along with Ontario, Quebec, and the Northwest Territories, makes Canada the fourth largest producer of gold in the world. British Columbia is also the leading coal-mining province.

Agriculture, fishing, and forestry

Many of the raw materials used in manufacturing come from Canada's farms, waters, and forests.

The Prairie Provinces provide most of Canada's wheat and much of its beef. Farmers in the St. Lawrence Lowlands produce a variety of goods, including grains, milk, vegetables, and fruits. Farmers in the Atlantic Provinces raise potatoes and dairy cattle.

Fishing is Canada's oldest industry. The Grand Banks area off Newfoundland is among the world's best fishing grounds. Pacific waters yield salmon.

Canada's forests provide logs for processing into lumber, paper, plywood, and wood pulp. About 90 per cent of the forests are owned by the national and provincial governments, who lease them to private companies.

Canadian Cities

In the second half of the 1900's, Canada became an urban society. Today, more than 80 per cent of its people live in urban areas, and over 30 metropolitan areas have a population of more than 100,000.

Ottawa—the capital city

Ottawa was a small lumbering town on the south bank of the Ottawa River in Ontario when Queen Victoria chose it as the capital of the United Province of Canada. With Confederation in 1867, Ottawa became the capital of the Dominion.

Today, Canada's Parliament buildings rise atop Parliament Hill. Attractive parks and scenic drives add to the beauty of the city. More than 800,000 people live in the Ottawa metropolitan area, and more than 100,000 of them work for the federal government.

Montreal—city of Mount Royal

Montreal, the largest French-speaking city in the world after Paris, is one of North America's most interesting cities. It lies on an island in Quebec where the St. Lawrence and Ottawa rivers meet, and a tree-covered mountain rises in its center. Montreal's downtown area includes the world's largest network of underground stores and restaurants, and its fascinating waterfront area has old stone buildings, cobblestone streets, and monuments.

Montreal has more people than any other Canadian city, though Toronto's metropolitan area is larger in population than Montreal's. Montreal is Canada's chief transportation hub and a major center of Canadian business, industry, culture, and education.

Quebec—Canada's oldest city

In 1608, the French explorer Samuel de Champlain founded the settlement of Quebec where the St. Lawrence River narrows. That settlement is now a major city, the capital of Quebec Province, and an important port. Thousands visit the city each year to see "the cradle of French civilization in the New World."

Quebec has many landmarks that help give it the charm of an old European city. The Notre-Dame-des-Victoires Church, built in 1688, stands on the site of Champlain's first

Sidewalk cafes and shops attract tourists to Quebec City. Such landmarks as Place Royale, a historic square dating from the 1600's, and the Citadel, a walled fortress, are also popular with tourists.

The Parliament buildings in Ottawa take on a golden tinge as twilight settles on the city. The wooded slopes and tended lawns of Parliament Hill offer a dramatic view of Canada's capital.

log cabin. The Citadel, a walled fortress, overlooks the city, and the Chateau Frontenac, a castlelike hotel, rises dramatically from the skyline.

Toronto—a dynamic city

The name *Toronto* is a Huron word meaning *meeting place*. Today, so many people have come to live in and around this Ontario city that Toronto is now Canada's largest metropolitan area. Lying on the northwest shore of Lake Ontario, the city is the chief manufacturing, financial, and communications center of the country, as well as one of the busiest Canadian ports on the Great Lakes.

Toronto is also noted for its cultural life and boasts Canada's largest museum and public library system. Today, only about 40 per cent of the city's people trace their roots to Britain. Immigrants from many other countries came to the area after World War II

(1939-1945), and the city now includes many people of Chinese, East Indian, Eastern European, French, Greek, Italian, and Portuguese ancestry.

Vancouver—gateway to the Pacific

Vancouver is the busiest port in all Canada and one of its largest cities. The people who live in the Vancouver metropolitan area make up about half the entire population of British Columbia. The city is the province's major center of commerce, culture, industry, and transportation.

About 25 miles (40 kilometers) north of the United States, Vancouver lies in a beautiful setting near the Coast Mountains and the Pacific Ocean. The protective mountains and warm Pacific winds give Vancouver a mild climate, but the city's chief asset is its natural harbor, which never freezes. Vancouver handles nearly all of Canada's trade with Asia.

Edmonton and Calgary—boom towns

Edmonton is the capital of the Prairie Province of Alberta and the northernmost major city in North America. Although its location makes Edmonton a distribution point for goods traveling to Alaska and the northwest, it was the discovery of oil that lured thousands of people to Edmonton. Many of Alberta's principal oil wells are within 100 miles (160 kilometers) of the city. Petroleum distributing and processing and the production of petroleum products are Edmonton's leading industries.

Calgary, in the foothills of the Rockies in southwest Alberta, grew up as a cattle town and is still a major cattle center. The Calgary Exhibition and Stampede, a world-famous rodeo, is a celebrated annual event. As in Edmonton, oil has dramatically affected the city of Calgary. The petroleum industry has made Calgary one of the country's fastest-growing cities and the oil center of Canada.

Halifax—maritime city

The largest city in Canada's Atlantic Provinces is Halifax in Nova Scotia. The city's large natural harbor makes it Canada's main naval base and busiest east coast port. Halifax is also one of the nation's most historic cities. The oldest parliament building in Canada stands in downtown Halifax.

Toronto, *left,* has become Canada's chief center of industry and finance. The CN Tower on the left is a communications tower 1,815 feet (553 meters) high, is the world's tallest free-standing structure.

Skiers flock to the slopes overlooking North Vancouver. The Vancouver metropolitan area is now the third largest in Canada. Its mild climate makes it attractive the year around.

The Canadian Wilderness

Canada is a land of magnificent natural beauty. Towering mountains, crystal-clear lakes, rocky coastlines, and lush, green forests mark its wilderness areas, which cover about nine-tenths of Canada. Most of the Canadian people live near the southern border in about one-tenth of the country's land area.

To preserve some of this great wilderness and the wildlife it supports, Canada has established an extensive system of national parks. The system began in 1885, when Banff National Park was established in Alberta. Today, the system has a total of 35 national parks, plus about 700 national historic parks and sites. All the provinces and territories have at least one national park. Each province also has its own park system.

Canadians enjoy a wide variety of recreational activities, such as canoeing, fishing, hiking, and snowshoeing. Many of these activities take place in their national parks.

Eastern wilderness

The Atlantic, or Maritime, Provinces include a number of superb natural areas. Gros Morne National Park, for example, on the west coast of Newfoundland, has fiordlike lakes, waterfalls, a rugged seacoast, and the scenic Long Range Mountains. At Sir Richard Squires Memorial Park, also in Newfoundland, Atlantic salmon make spectacular jumps up the Big Falls to reach their egg-laying grounds upstream. The Cape Breton Highlands National Park in Nova Scotia marks the rugged coast and forested hills where John Cabot landed.

A well-known wilderness area in Quebec is the Gaspé Peninsula. This rugged arm of land attracts artists, hikers, and mountain climbers. Bonaventure Island, off the coast of Gaspé, is one of the largest water-bird refuges open to visitors. The Laurentian Mountains, or Laurentides, form the southeastern edge of the Canadian Shield in Quebec. Low ranges in the provincial parks of Laurentides and Mont Tremblant attract skiers.

Ontario has more people than any other Canadian province, but almost all of them live in the extreme southeast section. Huge forests cover much of the land, and wild flowers are plentiful. Woodland caribou, moose, shy white-tailed deer, and black bears roam these northern woodlands. Ontario has 6 national parks and more than 200 provincial parks. The densely forested Quetico Provincial Park, for example, draws many canoeists to its beautiful lakes.

Western wilderness

Stretching west, Canada's landscape changes, and the wilderness areas and parks change too. In Saskatchewan, Grasslands National Park protects the short-grass prairie that is native to the area, as well as the wildlife it supports. Riding Mountain National Park in Manitoba features grasslands, lakes, and forests around a ridge that rises above the flat, rolling land.

Farther west, the majestic Canadian Rockies erupt boldly from the prairie. Some of the best-known parks in the world are located here. Alberta has more square miles of na-

The forests and flat tundra of Canada's wilderness areas provide a habitat for large mammals such as moose (1), caribou (2), and bears (3). Small fur-bearing mammals include raccoons (4), gray squirrels (5), and beavers (6). Birds include cardinals (7), snowy owls (8), Canada geese (9), hairy woodpeckers (10), and mallard ducks (11). The many lakes and rivers in the country are home to northern pike (12), perch (13), and rainbow trout (14).

more than 6,560 ft (2,000 m)
3,280-6,560 ft (1,000-2,000 m)
1,640-3,280 ft (500-1,000 m)
656-1,640 ft (200-500 m)
less than 656 ft (200 m)

National parks of Canada

1 Algonquin
2 Auyuittuq
3 Banff
4 Cape Breton Highlands
5 Cypress Hills
6 Dinosaur
7 Fundy
8 Gaspesie
9 Glacier
10 Gros Morne
11 Jasper
12 Kluane
13 La Verendrye
14 Mont Tremblant
15 Mount Revelstoke
16 Naikoon
17 Nahanni
18 Pacific Rim
19 Polar Bear
20 Prince Albert
21 Pukaskwa
22 Quetico
23 Riding Mountain
24 Tweedsmuir
25 Wells Gray
26 Willmore Wilderness
27 Wood Buffalo

tional parks than any other province. Banff National Park and Jasper National Park attract millions of tourists to their peaks, glaciers, hot springs, and resorts.

Alberta also lies along three of the major North American flyways used by birds migrating between their winter and summer homes. Wetlands are managed to help ensure the success of nesting waterfowl. Wood Buffalo National Park in the northeastern part of the province protects the largest buffalo herd in North America and the nesting grounds of rare whooping cranes.

The wilderness of British Columbia is also a favorite with tourists from all across Can-

ada and the United States. South Moresby National Park on Queen Charlotte Islands protects rare plant and animal life on the islands. Pacific Rim National Park on Vancouver Island features sea lions. British Columbia also has national and provincial parks throughout its mountain areas.

The Far North

The Far North of Canada is itself one vast wilderness. The territories make up more than one-third of Canada's land area, yet less than 1 per cent of its people live there. Forest-covered mountains spread over the Yukon and part of the Northwest Territories. Kluane National Park in the Yukon contains the highest peak in Canada—Mount Logan. Large glaciers lie in its mountains, and Dall sheep roam their slopes. Nahanni National Park in the Northwest Territories features deep canyons, hot springs, and the Virginia Falls.

Much of the rest of the Far North is tundra—cold, dry, treeless land that is home to caribou, bears, foxes, and other northern animals. Although this environment is harsh, it is also fragile.

Cape Verde

The republic of Cape Verde is an island nation off the western coast of Africa. Its 15 islands were formed by volcanic eruptions that took place 2-1/2 million to 65 million years ago. Most of the islands are ruggedly mountainous, with steep cliffs rimming their coastlines.

Portuguese explorers discovered the uninhabited islands of Cape Verde about 1460. Settlers came about two years later, planting cotton, fruit trees, and sugar cane. They also brought slaves from the African mainland to work the land.

The slave trade eventually became the most important economic activity on the islands, and Cape Verde prospered. Slaves were "trained" on plantations there before being shipped elsewhere. But the slave trade declined in the late 1600's, and prosperity disappeared with it.

Portugal ruled Cape Verde and what is now Guinea-Bissau on mainland Africa under one government. In 1879, Cape Verde became a separate Portuguese colony, and in 1951, an overseas province. The African Party for the Independence of Guinea and Cape Verde, or PAIGC (its initials in Portuguese), fought for full independence, and achieved it in 1975.

Until 1991, the PAIGC—now the African Party for the Independence of Cape Verde

Cape Verde children enjoy a swim in the Atlantic waters that surround the islands.

FACT BOX

COUNTRY

Official name: Republica de Cabo Verde (Republic of Cape Verde)
Capital: Praia
Terrain: Steep, rugged, rocky, volcanic
Area: 1,557 sq. mi. (4,033 km²)

Climate: Temperate; warm, dry summer; precipitation meager and very erratic
Highest elevation: Mt. Fogo, a volcano on Fogo Island, 9,281 ft. (2,829 m)
Lowest elevation: Atlantic Ocean, sea level

GOVERNMENT

Form of government: Republic
Head of state: President
Head of government: Prime minister
Administrative areas: 14 concelhos (districts)

Legislature: Assembleia Nacional (National Assembly) with 72 members serving five-year terms
Court system: Supremo Tribunal de Justia (Supreme Tribunal of Justice)
Armed forces: 1,100 troops

PEOPLE

Estimated 2002 population: 447,000
Population growth: 0.98%
Population density: 287 persons per sq. mi. (111 per km²)
Population distribution: 56% rural, 44% urban
Life expectancy in years:
Male: 66
Female: 72
Doctors per 1,000 people: N/A
Percentage of age-appropriate population enrolled in the following educational levels:
Primary: N/A
Secondary: N/A
Further: N/A

A village on Santo Antão, the northernmost island of the Cape Verde group, nestles at the foot of an ancient volcanic peak. The islands were formed by volcanic eruptions, but only one volcano, on Fogo Island, remains active.

(PAICV)—was the only legal political party in the country. But in that year, multiparty elections were held, and the PAICV was voted out of office.

Cape Verde, an underdeveloped nation, relied almost entirely on Portugal for economic support before its independence. Since 1975, Cape Verde has received food aid from the United Nations and financial aid from various countries. The country's chief economic activities—farming and fishing—provide only a very low income, and many of its people cannot find work.

However, with the help of foreign aid, the government is working to strengthen the economy. One area that is open to expansion is the fishing industry. Catches of some species could be increased by as much as 80 per cent. Tourism is another promising enterprise. Cape Verde's cool breezes, white sand beaches, and clean, sparkling water offer a tempting destination for vacationers.

Cape Verde has a warm, dry climate, and the lack of rainfall makes most of the land too dry to farm. Since the late 1960's, drought has increased the problems of the nation's farmers, causing a drop of about 90 per cent in agricultural production, and killing most of the livestock. The nation's chief crops are bananas and other fruits, coffee, sugar cane, and vegetables.

Cape Verde fishing crews catch mainly lobsters and tuna. The mining industry produces salt and pozzuolana, a volcanic rock used to make cement.

Because of their country's underdeveloped economy, the people of Cape Verde have a low standard of living, and many are undernourished due to drought and low agricultural production. Since the mid-1900's, hundreds of thousands of Cape Verdeans have emigrated to Brazil, Portugal, the United States, and other countries.

Today, the population of the islands is slightly more than 400,000. About 70 per cent of the people have mixed black African and Portuguese ancestry, and most of the rest are black Africans. Cape Verdeans speak a local dialect based on Portuguese and African languages. Most are Roman Catholics, but many practice *animism*—the belief that everything in nature has a soul.

Languages spoken:
Portuguese Crioulo (a blend of Portuguese and West African words)

Religions:
Roman Catholic mixed with indigenous beliefs
Protestant

TECHNOLOGY

Radios per 1,000 people: N/A

Televisions per 1,000 people: N/A

Computers per 1,000 people: N/A

ECONOMY

Currency: Cape Verdean escudo

Gross national income (GNI) in 2000: $588 million U.S.

Real annual growth rate (1999–2000): 6.8%

GNI per capita (2000): $1,330 U.S.

Balance of payments (2000): N/A

Goods exported: Fuel, shoes, garments, fish, bananas, hides

Goods imported: Foodstuffs, industrial products, transport equipments, fuels

Trading partners: Portugal, Germany, Netherlands, Spain, France

Cape Verde consists of 10 main islands and 5 tiny ones, including 6 that are not inhabited. Cape Verde lies about 400 miles (640 kilometers) west of the African mainland. Praia, its capital city, is on São Tiago, the largest island.

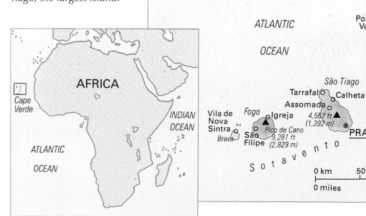

Central African Republic

The Central African Republic is a land-locked country in the center of the continent. Most of the country is a vast, rolling plateau, covered by grass and scattered trees and broken by river valleys. The northeast is arid, but thick rain forests blanket the southwest.

In the north, the rivers run northward into the Chari River, while the rivers in the center and south form part of the Congo River Basin. Many flow into the Ubangi River, a major branch of the Congo.

The rivers are the most important transportation routes in the Central African Republic. The nation has no railroads, and many roads are impassable during the rainy season.

Economy

The Central African Republic is an extremely poor, underdeveloped country, where most of the people farm for a living. The country has a few factories, including a textile mill, and diamond mining is the only important mining industry.

In addition to raising food crops, rural Central Africans hunt, fish, and gather insects and caterpillars to feed their families. They also tend some goats, pigs, sheep, and poultry. A few farmers raise livestock in regions where there are no *tsetse flies*—insects that spread a disease called *sleeping sickness*.

Most of the people of the Central African Republic are black Africans, but they belong to many ethnic groups and speak many languages. French is the official language, but Sango is most widely spoken. Most adults are unable to read or write.

History

The people in what is now the Central African Republic lived in small settlements before the arrival of Europeans in the 1800's brought slave raids and turmoil to the region. In 1889, France set up an outpost at Bangui, which is now the capital. In 1894, the French made the region a territory called Ubangi-Shari, which later became part of French Equatorial Africa.

In 1958, Ubangi-Shari gained internal self-government as the Central African Republic, and the country became fully independent on Aug. 13, 1960. David Dacko became the new nation's first president.

Dacko was elected to a seven-year term in 1964, but in 1966 he was overthrown by army officers, and Jean-Bedel Bokassa, head of the army, took over. In 1972, Bokassa was named president for life, and in 1976 he declared himself emperor and changed the name of the country to the Central African Empire.

FACT BOX

CENTRAL AFRICAN REPUBLIC

COUNTRY

Official name: Republique Centrafricaine (Central African Republic)
Capital: Bangui
Terrain: Vast, flat to rolling, monotonous plateau; scattered hills in northeast and southwest
Area: 240,535 sq. mi. (622,984 km²)

Climate: Tropical; hot, dry winters; mild to hot, wet summers
Main rivers: Ubangi, Mbomou, Sangha, Kotto
Highest elevation: Mont Ngaoui, 4,659 ft. (1,420 m)
Lowest elevation: Oubangui River, 1,099 ft. (335 m)

GOVERNMENT

Form of government: Republic
Head of state: President
Head of government: Prime minister
Administrative areas: 14 prefectures, 2 prefectures economiques (economic prefectures) 1 commune

Legislature: Assemblee Nationale (National Assembly) with 109 members serving five-year terms
Court system: Cour Supreme (Supreme Court), Constitutional Court
Armed forces: 4,950 troops

PEOPLE

Estimated 2002 population: 3,746,000
Population growth: 1.77%
Population density: 16 persons per sq. mi. (6 per km²)
Population distribution: 61% rural, 39% urban
Life expectancy in years:
Male: 42
Female: 46
Doctors per 1,000 people: Less than 0.05
Percentage of age-appropriate population enrolled in the following educational levels:
Primary: 57
Secondary: N/A
Further: 2

Pygmy people of the rain forest live by hunting wild animals and gathering wild plants.

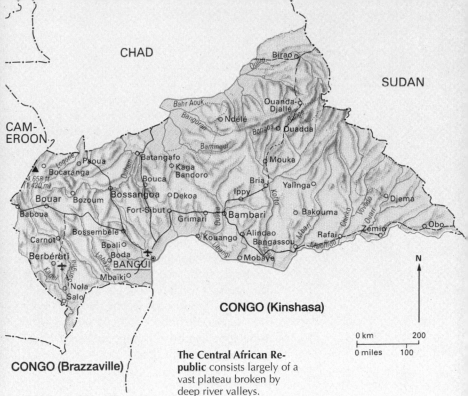

The Central African Republic consists largely of a vast plateau broken by deep river valleys.

When Bokassa was overthrown by supporters of Dacko in 1979, the nation's name was changed back to the Central African Republic. In March 1981, Dacko was elected president. But in September, he was overthrown by Chief General André Kolingba. In 1993, the constitution was revised to permit a multiparty democracy, and in presidential and parliamentary elections held that year, Ange-Félix Patasse became president.

During the mid-1990's, rebel soldiers staged several revolts against the government of Patasse. Hundreds of people were killed and forced from their homes during the fighting. A cease-fire agreement ended the hostilities in mid-1997.

The Ubangi River, below, forms much of the Central African Republic's southern boundary with Congo (Kinshasa).

Languages spoken:
French (official)
Sangho (lingua franca and national language)
Arabic
Hunsa
Swahili

Religions:
Indigenous beliefs 24%
Protestant 25%
Roman Catholic 25%
Muslim 15%

TECHNOLOGY

Radios per 1,000 people: 80

Televisions per 1,000 people: 6

Computers per 1,000 people: 1.7

ECONOMY

Currency: Communaute Financiere Africaine franc

Gross national income (GNI) in 2000: $1.0 billion U.S.

Real annual growth rate (1999–2000): 2.5%

GNI per capita (2000): $280 U.S.

Balance of payments (2000): $0 million U.S.

Goods exported: Diamonds, timber, cotton, coffee, tobacco

Goods imported: Food, textiles, petroleum products, machinery, electrical equipment, motor vehicles, chemicals, pharmaceuticals

Trading partners: Benelux, France, Côte d'Ivoire, Cameroon

223

Chad

Chad is a large and thinly populated country in north-central Africa. It is a landlocked nation, but Lake Chad lies on its western border. Today, Chad is one of the poorest nations in the world. Desert covers much of Chad in the north. A small fertile region in the south was called "Useful Chad" by the French because the rest of the country had infertile soil and few other resources.

Between the northern desert and the southern fertile strip lies a *savanna,* or grassy plain. The savanna is part of a larger region called the Sahel. Severe droughts hit the Sahel from the late 1960's to the 1980's, destroying crops and killing livestock. Famine followed, and millions of Africans died.

Modern life

Droughts and a lack of resources are not the only problems that trouble Chad. Sharp religious, social, and economic differences between the people of the north and south have kept the country in an almost constant state of civil war since the mid-1960's.

Most of the people in northern Chad are Muslims, while most of the people in the south follow African or Christian religions. About 80 per cent of the country's schools are in the south. Although Chad has very little industry, most of its few factories are located in the south too.

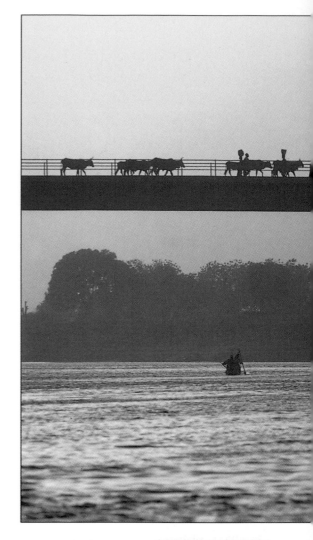

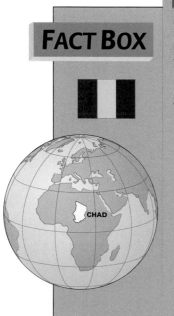

FACT BOX

COUNTRY

Official name: Republique du Tchad (Republic of Chad)
Capital: N'Djamena
Terrain: Broad, arid plains in center, desert in north, mountains in northwest, lowlands in south
Area: 495,755 sq. mi. (1,284,000 km²)

Climate: Tropical in south, desert in north
Main rivers: Chari, Logone, Bahr Salamat
Highest elevation: Emi Koussi, 11,204 ft. (3,415 m)
Lowest elevation: Djourab Depression, 525 ft. (160 m)

GOVERNMENT

Form of government: Republic
Head of state: President
Head of government: Prime minister
Administrative areas: 14 prefectures

Legislature: National Assembly with 125 members serving four-year terms
Court system: Supreme Court, Court of Appeal, Criminal Courts, Magistrate Courts
Armed forces: 30,350 troops

PEOPLE

Estimated 2002 population: 8,081,000
Population growth: 3.31%
Population density: 16 persons per sq. mi. (6 per km²)
Population distribution: 78% rural, 22% urban
Life expectancy in years:
Male: 49
Female: 53
Doctors per 1,000 people: Less than 0.05
Percentage of age-appropriate population enrolled in the following educational levels:
Primary: 67
Secondary: 11
Further: N/A

The huge gap in education and economic development, along with the religious difference, increases the tension between the north and south. People in the north believe they do not have equal opportunity. Southern Chadians called the Sara remember that for hundreds of years northern raiders seized their people as slaves.

History

A kingdom called Kanem arose along the desert trade routes northeast of Lake Chad about the A.D. 700's. Islam was introduced into the region around 1100. Later, two smaller kingdoms—Baguirmi and Ouaddai—developed near Kanem in the 1500's and 1600's. All three kingdoms became powerful and prosperous by trading goods and slaves they had captured from the Sara.

In the late 1800's, France claimed Chad as its own. In 1920, Chad became a French colony. The Sara people suffered more than any other group under colonial rule. When Chad gained its independence from France in 1960, a Sara government took over.

In 1962, a group of northern rebels formed a group called the *Front de Libération National* (National Liberation Front), or *Frolinat.* When civil war broke out between Frolinat and government troops, Chad's government turned to France for help. Frolinat received aid from Libya because Libyan leader Muammar al-Qadhafi hoped to make Chad part of Libya. A military coup took over the government in 1975.

Fighting continued into the 1980's. One group was headed by Hissene Habré, a former Frolinat leader who won control of the capital and was declared president in 1982. The groups finally agreed to a truce in 1987. However, some Libyan troops remained in Chad until 1994, when the United Nations settled a final dispute.

In 1990, a rebel group overthrew Habre's government. Chad set up an interim government in 1993. In 1996, the country adopted a new constitution and held multiparty presidential elections, which were followed by legislative elections in 1997.

Longhorn cattle plod across a bridge over the Chari River in southern Chad. This area was called "Useful Chad" by the French.

ECONOMY

Languages spoken:
French (official)
Arabic (official)
Sara and Sango (In south)
more than 100 different languages and dialects
Religions:
Muslim 50%
Christian 25%
indigenous beliefs (mostly animism) 25%

Currency: Communaute Financiere Africaine franc
Gross national income (GNI) in 2000: $1.5 billion U.S.
Real annual growth rate (1999–2000): 0.6%
GNI per capita (2000): $200 U.S.
Balance of payments (2000): -$158 million U.S.
Goods exported: Cotton, cattle, textiles
Goods imported: Machinery and transportation equipment, industrial goods, petroleum products, foodstuffs, textiles
Trading partners: France, Portugal, Germany, Nigeria

TECHNOLOGY

Radios per 1,000 people: 236
Televisions per 1,000 people: 1
Computers per 1,000 people: 1.3

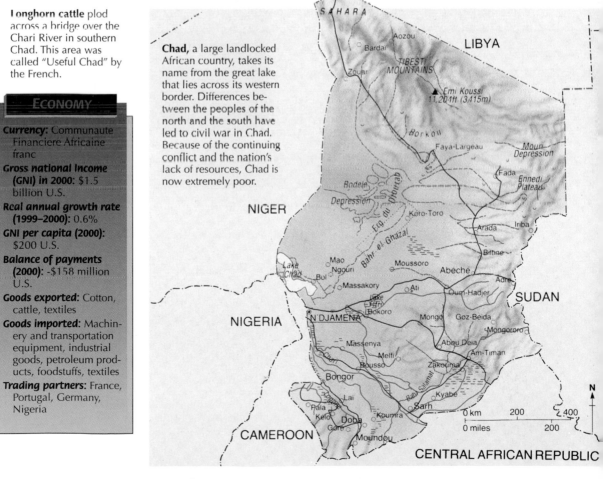

Chad, a large landlocked African country, takes its name from the great lake that lies across its western border. Differences between the peoples of the north and the south have led to civil war in Chad. Because of the continuing conflict and the nation's lack of resources, Chad is now extremely poor.

Land and People

In Chad, differences between the north and the south exist not only in the landscape, but also in the people. However, the north and south alike are affected by Chad's under-developed economy.

Only about a sixth of all Chadian adults can read and write. The country has no railroads and few paved roads. There is limited phone, telegraph, and postal service, and no television. A few factories and cotton- and peanut-processing mills are located in the south, but civil war has closed down most of these businesses. The people of Chad rely on aid from France, the United States, and other countries.

The north

In the great Sahara that stretches across northern Chad, temperatures often reach 120° F. (49° C), and the annual rainfall is less than 5 inches (13 centimeters). In north-western Chad, the Tibesti Mountains rise more than 11,000 feet (3,000 meters).

Most of the people in northern Chad are dark-skinned Arabs or members of a black African group called the Toubou. The majority are Muslims and speak Arabic.

Most northern Chadians are cattle traders who raise cattle, camels, goats, and sheep. While milk and meat are the basis of their diet, they also eat dates and vegetables grown in oases. The northern Chadians travel through the desert in small groups with their herds. They construct tents out of sticks and woven mats.

Northern men usually wear loose gowns with turbans or skullcaps. Some also wrap white cloths around their faces for protection during sandstorms. The women wear light blue or black robes. In the north, less than 10 per cent of the children go to school.

The south

Southern Chad is a tropical forest, warm and much wetter than the north. Such wild animals as lions, elephants, and giraffes roam parts of the south. Large rivers flow northeast across the region into Lake Chad. Cranes, crocodiles, and hippopotamuses live in the marshes around the lake.

The soil and climate of the south are ideal for raising cotton, and the area has the richest farmland in Chad. Most Chadians live in this fertile region.

Toubou gather palm fronds to weave into baskets and mats. The Toubou are Arabic-speaking nomads who live in northern Chad. They roam the desert with their herds, searching for pasture and water.

The town of Faya-Largeau south of the Tibesti Mountains, *right,* is a crossing point of two Saharan caravan routes. Here, northern nomads trade their livestock for food. Their robes and turbans are traditional clothing in northern Chad.

Round *granaries* (grain storehouses), like the one at the right, are a common sight in southern Chad. In this small but fertile region, the soil and climate are good for growing cotton and other crops. Southern Chad may further benefit from future development of oil deposits in the region.

Chadians fish in Lake Chad, *below,* as well as southern rivers, but fishing is seasonal. Deposits of *natron,* a mineral, lie near the lake, and uranium is found in the north. These resources may one day improve Chad's economy.

Most of the people of southern Chad are members of black African ethnic groups, including the Sara—the largest group. The majority of southern Chadians follow traditional African religions, but many have converted to Christianity. Sara is the most widely spoken language in the south, but many other languages are spoken too.

Most southern Chadians farm for a living. Their main cash crops are cotton and peanuts. Farmers raise millet, sorghum, and rice for their own use. Meals occasionally include vegetables, fish, or meat.

In the rural south, Chadians live in round huts made of adobe brick or dried mud and covered with a straw roof. Some huts are made entirely of straw.

The men usually wear cotton trousers or shorts and loose shirts, and the women dress in brightly colored blouses and skirts.

About 75 per cent of Chad's people live in N'Djamena or other cities, located mainly in the south. Most of the country's business people, teachers, traders, and government workers live in the south.

Chile

The most striking geographical feature of Chile is its unusual shape—it is 10 times as long as it is wide. Like a ribbon stretching down the western coast of South America, Chile is about 2,650 miles (4,265 kilometers) long but only 265 miles (427 kilometers) wide at its widest point. But to those who have explored Chile, its shape is only part of its fascination.

Spectacular scenery

Because of its great length, Chile is a land of extremes in both landscape and climate. The Atacama Desert in the north is one of the driest places on the earth. Here, in this remote, barren land—free from the interference of bright artificial lights and polluted air—astronomers at the Cerro Tololo Inter-American Observatory study the stars and planets. The observatory's reflecting optical telescope, with a mirror 158 inches (400 centimeters) in diameter, is the largest in the Southern Hemisphere.

Far from the northern desert, the lonely, windswept coast of the icy southern regions is an equally desolate but different landscape of snow-capped volcanoes, thick forests, and glaciers. To the east, the mighty Andes Mountains extend along Chile's border with Argentina and Bolivia. Nestled between the Andes and the lower mountains on the west coast lies the Central Valley. Several rivers flow through this mild, fertile region—the heartland of Chile and the center of its population.

A history of conflict

Isolated from the rest of the world by mountains, deserts, and glaciers, the Chilean people have a long history of resisting invasion. The early Indian inhabitants of the area fought bravely to protect their land—first against Inca forces and later against the Spanish conquistadors.

Long before the first white people arrived, several different Indian groups inhabited what is now Chile. The Atacama, Diaguita, and other tribes lived along the north coast and at the southern edge of the Atacama

Desert. Chile's largest Indian group was the Araucanians, a fierce, warlike tribe that inhabited the Central Valley.

In the late 1400's, much of northern Chile fell under the rule of the Inca empire. However, their triumphant march south to the Central Valley ended in defeat when the Araucanians routed the Inca armies.

After the Spanish conquistadors defeated the Inca and seized their gold and silver, they headed south in search of more riches. In 1535, Diego de Almagro and his men reached the area around present-day Santiago but turned back after finding only scattered Indian settlements with no gold and silver.

In 1540, another Spaniard, Pedro de Valdivia, led an expedition from what is now Peru to Chile's Central Valley. On Feb. 12, 1541, Valdivia and his men founded Santiago. The Araucanians destroyed the settlement only six months later, but the Spaniards rebuilt Santiago and later founded the cities of La Serena, Valparaíso, Concepción, Valdivia, and Villarrica.

In the end, however, the Spaniards fared no better than the Inca against the Araucanians. In 1553, the Araucanians killed Valdivia and most of his men in battle. These fierce warriors never weakened in their resistance to Spanish rule, making Chile a bloody battleground for almost 300 years.

Spain ruled Chile from the 1500's to the early 1800's. Chile was part of a large Spanish colony called the Viceroyalty of Peru, which included other parts of Spanish South America. During the colonial period, the Roman Catholic Church sent missionaries to Chile to convert the Indians to Christianity. In time, the church became a powerful institution in the colony.

Early in the 1800's, Chile joined the other New World colonies in rebellion against Spain. After an eight-year struggle, led first by José Miguel Carrera and later by Bernardo O'Higgins and the Argentine general José de San Martín, Chile won its independence in 1818.

Chile Today

National elections in 1989 brought democratic government back to Chile after 16 years of harsh military rule. Patricio Aylwin Azócar, the candidate who represented a coalition of 17 political groups, won the people's vote. Aylwin's victory reawakened the hope of democracy for many Chileans, but serious economic and social problems remain an obstacle to the nation's progress. Chile's lower-class people are still in desperate need of jobs, decent housing, health care, and better nutrition.

Allende's Chile

During the 1960's, President Eduardo Frei Montalva gave Chile's people a glimmer of hope for a better life. After he was elected in 1964, Frei introduced limited land reforms and improved standards of health and housing. He also convinced the American owners of Chilean copper mines to give his government greater control of the nation's copper industry.

Frei's first modest steps toward reform did not please his opponents, however. Leftist groups thought his measures were not strong enough, while conservatives condemned them as being too radical. In 1970, Salvador Allende Gossens, who headed a coalition of Communist and other left wing parties, was elected president. Allende became the first Marxist to win a democratic presidential election in the Western Hemisphere.

Allende attempted to reshape the nation along socialist lines. He increased the minimum wage and redistributed land among rural farmers. The Allende government also took over many of Chile's private banks, the huge copper mines, and numerous industries.

But when the Allende government increased the minimum wage, it was also trying to hold down the prices of consumer goods. As a result, food shortages became widespread, and inflation soared from about 20 per cent in 1971 to more than 350 per cent in 1973. Strikes became widespread, productivity declined, and many educated professional people fled the country. Political tensions increased as both supporters and opponents took to the streets in violent demonstrations.

Military government

On Sept. 11, 1973, military leaders overthrew Allende's weakened government. After the coup, they claimed that Allende committed suicide rather than resign. The military leaders formed a junta, led by Augusto Pinochet Ugarte, to rule Chile. At first, the people fiercely opposed the new military government—many died in street fighting, and thousands more fled the country.

FACT BOX

COUNTRY

Official name: Republica de Chile (Republic of Chile)
Capital: Santiago
Terrain: Low coastal mountains; fertile central valley; rugged Andes in east
Area: 292,260 sq. mi. (756,950 km²)

Climate: Temperate; desert in north; Mediterranean in central region; cool and damp in south
Main rivers: Loa, Maipo, Maule, Bió-Bió
Highest elevation: Ojos del Salado, 22,572 ft. (6,880 m)
Lowest elevation: Pacific Ocean, sea level

GOVERNMENT

Form of government: Republic
Head of state: President
Head of government: President
Administrative areas: 13 regiones (regions)

Legislature: Congreso Nacional (National Congress) consisting of the Senado (Senate) with 48 members serving eight-year terms and the Camara de Diputados (Chamber of Deputies) with 120 members serving four-year terms
Court system: Corte Suprema (Supreme Court), Constitutional Tribunal
Armed forces: 93,000 troops

PEOPLE

Estimated 2002 population: 15,572,000
Population growth: 1.17%
Population density: 53 persons per sq. mi. (21 per km²)
Population distribution: 85% urban, 15% rural
Life expectancy in years:
Male: 72
Female: 79
Doctors per 1,000 people: 1.1
Percentage of age-appropriate population enrolled in the following educational levels:
Primary: 106*
Secondary: 85
Further: 34

CHILE

Police officers hold back demonstrators during the 1988 referendum, which rejected the military government under General Augusto Pinochet Ugarte.

The Pinochet government imprisoned many of its opponents, dissolved the Congress, restricted freedom of the press, and banned political parties. It returned many of the state-owned industries to private control and checked inflation. In 1988, the people rejected Pinochet's bid to extend his term in office, paving the way for a democratic government.

In January 2000, Chile's voters elected Ricardo Lagos Escobar of the Socialist Party as president. Lagos was the first Socialist elected president of Chile since Salvador Allende in 1970.

Chile extends along the west coast of South America from the Peruvian border to Cape Horn. Easter Island and the Juan Fernández Islands are also part of Chile, and the country claims a portion of the Antarctic Peninsula, although few other countries acknowledge the claim.

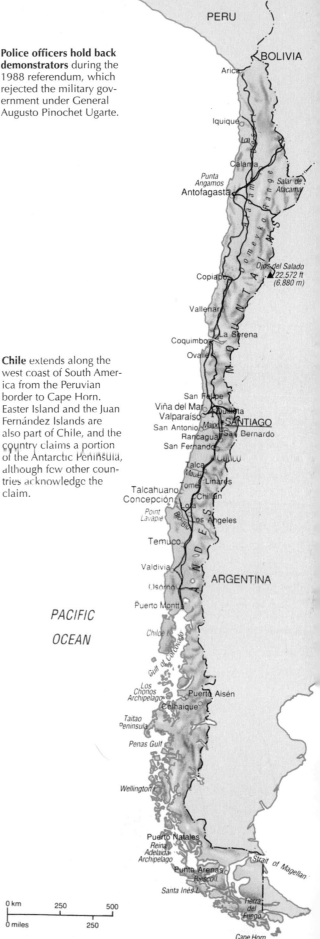

Language spoken:
Spanish

Religions:
Roman Catholic 89%
Protestant 11%
Jewish (negligible)

Enrollment ratios compare the number of students enrolled to the population which, by age, should be enrolled. A ratio higher than 100 indicates that students older or younger than the typical age range are also enrolled.

TECHNOLOGY

Radios per 1,000 people:
354

Televisions per 1,000 people: 242

Computers per 1,000 people: 82.3

ECONOMY

Currency: Chilean peso

Gross national income (GNI) in 2000: $69.8 billion U.S.

Real annual growth rate (1999–2000): 5.4%

GNI per capita (2000): $4,590 U.S

Balance of payments (2000): -$991 million U.S.

Goods exported: Copper, fish, fruits, paper and pulp, chemicals

Goods imported: Consumer goods, chemicals, motor vehicles, fuels, electrical machinery, heavy industrial machinery, food

Trading partners: European Union, United States, Japan, Argentina

Environment

Chile is a land of extreme contrasts in its climate, geography, and plant life. Its mainland landscape ranges from barren deserts to green valleys and lush rain forests, from treeless plains to gleaming glaciers. Far off Chile's western coast in the South Pacific Ocean lies Easter Island, its three extinct volcanoes a silent reminder of the island's fiery origins.

While Chile's three land regions—the Northern Desert, the Central Valley, and the Archipelago—have their own unique characteristics, they share one common feature—the frequent occurrence of violent natural activity. Flash floods caused by the sudden melting of mountain snows often endanger lives and property in the farming villages of the Andean valleys. On the Pacific coast, storms and unpredictable offshore currents are a constant challenge to sailors and fishing crews.

But the country's most serious natural activities are earthquakes. Chile lies along a major earthquake belt, and well over 100 quakes, many accompanied by massive tidal waves, have been recorded since 1575. In the early 1900's, an earthquake almost leveled the city of Valparaíso, and 20,000 people were killed by a quake that struck Concepción in 1939.

Deserts and valleys

Chile's Northern Desert region stetches from the Peruvian border in the north to the Aconcagua River, just north of Valparaíso. It includes the Atacama Desert, a region so arid that a 1971 rainfall was the first precipitation recorded in the desert town of Calama in 400 years.

Because of the lack of rainfall, the Atacama Desert has almost no plant life, except for the typical tola desert brush. Any moisture comes from subsurface water. The desert oases support small farming communities.

In the south, the Atacama gradually gives way to a slightly less arid area called the *Norte Chico* (Little North). Farmers there raise livestock and grow crops in irrigated river valleys.

A few charred tree limbs, *above,* are all that remain of a forest that stood in the path of a lava flow from Llaima Volcano. Located in the Central Valley, Llaima is one of several volcanoes in the western Andes whose eruptions have frequently altered Chile's landscape.

Icebergs and ice floes, formed when massive glaciers plunge into the sea, create a floating hazard for ships along Tierra del Fuego's coastline. Ferdinand Magellan discovered the islands in the early 1500's while trying to find a passage to the Pacific.

In contrast to the desolate Northern Desert, the Central Valley is Chile's chief population, agricultural, and industrial center. Orchards, vineyards, pastures, and croplands cover much of the Central Valley.

The region south of the Bió-Bió River, known as the Lake Country, is especially beautiful. Snow-capped volcanoes rise on the western Andean slopes, while thick forests of laurel and magnolia trees blanket the mountains. Sparkling lakes and deep valleys add to the spectacular beauty of this area, and ocean winds ensure a mild climate, making the Lake Country a popular tourist destination.

The stormy south

The trees of the Lake Country gradually become smaller and eventually disappear in the bitter, damp cold of the Archipelago. This region, which extends for about 1,000 miles (1,600 kilometers) from the Central Valley to Cape Horn, is a wild, windswept area of dense forests, snow-covered glaciers, and icy lakes.

Cold rains, piercing winds, and violent storms frequently pound the coastline of the Archipelago. The region's western edge is broken into thousands of tiny islands. At the southern tip of Chile lie the islands of *Tierra del Fuego* (Land of Fire). They were named by the famous Portuguese explorer Ferdinand Magellan in 1520 for the fires that Indians lit on the shores to keep themselves warm. Chile and Argentina each own some of the Islands of Tierra del Fuego.

Chile also governs the Juan Fernández Islands, situated 400 miles (640 kilometers) off the mainland's west coast. Of the three islands in this group, Róbinson Crusoe Island is perhaps the most famous. A Scottish sailor named Alexander Selkirk lived alone on the island for more than four years between 1704 and 1709, and his adventures became the basis for Daniel Defoe's novel *Robinson Crusoe*. About 2,300 miles (3,700 kilometers) westward in the South Pacific, huge stone statues carved hundreds of years ago still stand on Easter Island's volcanic slopes.

A geyser fed by an underground spring spurts hot water and steam above the barren landscape of the Atacama Desert. Only the Loa River crosses the Atacama Desert. It flows from the Andes Mountains to the Pacific Ocean through one of the world's driest areas.

A small farming settlement in Chile's Lake Country, *above,* stands in the shadow of the snow-capped Andes. The Lake Country's mountainous landscape, dense forests, and crystal-clear lakes have led tourists to call it *Little Switzerland.*

The narrow land of Chile extends from just north of the Tropic of Capricorn to the icy waters of Cape Horn. Chile is sandwiched between the towering Andes Mountains in the east and the Pacific Ocean on the west.

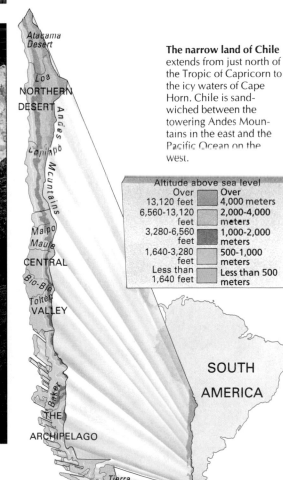

Altitude above sea level	
Over 13,120 feet	Over 4,000 meters
6,560-13,120 feet	2,000-4,000 meters
3,280-6,560 feet	1,000-2,000 meters
1,640-3,280 feet	500-1,000 meters
Less than 1,640 feet	Less than 500 meters

People

Much of Chile remains uninhabited because of its harsh environment. Relatively few people live in the Northern Desert and the Archipelago. Most Chileans make their home in the Central Valley, where the climate is pleasant and the soil is rich. About 86 per cent of all Chileans live in cities and towns. The rest live in rural areas.

About 75 per cent of Chile's people are *mestizos* (people of mixed Spanish and Indian ancestry). About 20 per cent of the population is of unmixed European descent, mostly Spanish or British. About 3 per cent of the people are of unmixed Indian ancestry.

Ethnic groups

The Araucanians—descendants of the brave warriors who defended their land against the Inca and the Spanish conquistadors—form the largest Indian group. During the 1800's, the Araucanians controlled huge areas of the Lake Country, but the 250,000 who survive today live on reservations in the Temuco area.

A few other Indian tribes remain scattered in various parts of the country. As many as 20,000 Aymara, Quechua, and Atacama Indians survive in oases in the Northern Desert region. The Aymara and Quechua probably migrated to the region from Bolivia and Peru in the 1900's. A few smaller groups are nomads roaming the Archipelago. Before the Spanish conquest, many other Indian tribes lived in the Archipelago, but they either were killed by the invading Spanish armies or died of diseases brought by the Spaniards, to which they had no natural resistance.

City life

Living in isolated regions or on reservations, much of the Indian population exists outside the mainstream of Chilean society. Most Indians who live in cities and towns are part of the lower class—Chilean society is based on wealth, not ancestry. Nearly all members of the small, rich upper class are of European descent. Well-to-do mestizos make up most of the middle class, while poor mestizos, along with most of the Indians, belong to the lower class.

Chile's lower class is concentrated in the crowded *callampas* (shantytowns) surrounding Santiago and other large cities. These slums are called *callampas*—the Spanish word for mushrooms—because they seem to spring up overnight.

The people who live in the callampas have moved to the cities from rural areas in search of higher-paying jobs and a better life, but there is not enough work or low-income housing to meet the needs of the huge population.

The small Chilean upper class, on the other hand, lives in luxurious high-rise apartment buildings or spacious houses with well-kept lawns and gardens. Members of the middle class, whose ranks include government, industrial, and professional workers, also enjoy comfortable housing in modern apartments or single-family homes.

Rural people

Most of the Chileans who remain in the rural areas are farmers. They own small farms or work as laborers or sharecroppers on large

Past and present meet in Santiago's Plaza de Armas, where a modern office block towers above a cathedral built in the Spanish colonial style. The capital and largest city in Chile, Santiago is also the nation's cultural, economic, and transportation center.

Most of Chile's remaining Araucanian Indian population, like this elderly woman, *above,* live on reservations.

234

A shepherd, *below*, displays wool taken from his sheep. Sheep production is particularly high in the cold, wet climate of southern Chile, where the sheep grow a thick, heavy wool coat.

Cheerful merchants in a Santiago seafood market, *top left*, offer the day's fresh catch. Chile's Pacific waters, particularly off the north coast, are rich in anchovettas, jack mackerel, and sardines. Although it employs only about 1 per cent of all the nation's workers, Chile's fishing industry is one of the largest in the world. Most of the fish are processed into fish meal and fish oil for export. Chileans also enjoy eating fish in such dishes as *empanadas* — stuffed turnovers.

A heavy cloud of smog hangs over the Santiago Valley. Air pollution caused by exhaust fumes and industrial gases is one of the city's major modern-day problems. The situation is made worse in winter, when there are few breezes to blow the smog away.

farms. Although conditions have improved somewhat since the 1960's, life is still difficult for these farmers, who barely make enough to support their families.

Before the 1960's, most poor Chileans worked as *inquilinos* (farmworkers) on huge estates called *fundos,* which were owned by a few wealthy families. In exchange for their labor, the inquilinos received a small plot of land to farm for themselves, but these plots were often too small to provide enough food for a family. In the 1960's, the Chilean government divided up many huge estates, enabling some inquilinos to own their own small farms.

Economy

High in the mountains of the Atacama Desert, at an altitude of 9,900 feet (3,000 meters), the Chuquicamata mine gouges a huge scar in the earth. The largest open-pit copper mine in the world, Chuquicamata yields more than 550,000 short tons (500,000 metric tons) of copper a year. Southeast of the Atacama Desert, in the Central Valley, lies El Teniente, the world's largest underground copper mine. Along with Chuquicamata and other mines, El Teniente produces large amounts of the reddish ore that Chile depends on for so much of its export.

With about a fifth of the world's known copper reserves, Chile is the world's leading copper-producing nation. The nation's mineral wealth also includes coal, gold, iron ore, lead, lithium, manganese, molybdenum, petroleum, and silver.

But too much dependence on the profits from copper and other mining interests is dangerous to the nation's overall economy. Since the worldwide depression of the 1930's, when the market for copper almost completely dried up, Chile has tried to develop other sources of revenue.

Service industries and manufacturing

Today, service industries account for about 63 per cent of the *gross domestic product*— the value of all goods and services produced yearly within the country. Many of Chile's service workers are employed by stores, restaurants, hotels, banks, health care facilities, social service organizations, and government agencies. Others are involved in transportation, communication, and such professions as teaching and law.

Manufacturing also contributes to the nation's economy, and Concepción, Santiago, and Valparaíso are the leading industrial centers. Chile's plants and factories produce a variety of consumer goods, including beverages, clothing, processed foods, textiles, and wood products. Other manufactured goods include cement, chemicals, paper products, steel, and transportation equipment.

Agriculture

The mild climate and fertile soil of the Central Valley provide good growing conditions,

A lumber worker in Chile's fast-growing forest industry saws through logs. About a third of the land in Chile is covered with forests. Timber, paper, pulp, and other wood products hold great promise for Chile's economy.

236

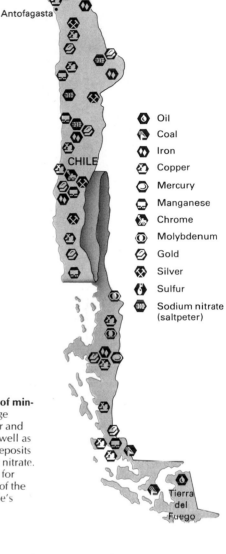

In copper production, ore is first ground into small pieces (1). Then water is added to the crushed ore, and the mixture, called slurry, passes into ball mills (2), rotating drum-shaped cylinders half filled with iron balls. The slurry next goes into flotation cells, which concentrate the mineral-bearing particles. Smelting (4) removes most of the remaining impurities. The new mixture, called copper matte, then goes through a converter (5), where blowers force air through it and silica is added to it. The mixture is readied for casting (6) or electrolytic refining.

Oil
Coal
Iron
Copper
Mercury
Manganese
Chrome
Molybdenum
Gold
Silver
Sulfur
Sodium nitrate (saltpeter)

About 80 per cent of the copper from Chuquicamata, *top left,* and other mines is produced by the state-run *Corporación del Cobre de Chile* (Chilean National Copper Corporation). Because minerals have long made up a large percentage of Chile's exports, the nation's economic health has long been closely linked to the world market price for copper and other metals.

Chile's rich store of minerals includes large deposits of copper and molybdenum, as well as the only known deposits of natural sodium nitrate. Minerals account for about three-fifths of the total value of Chile's exports.

Young Chileans pack fresh strawberries for export. Fruit crops grown in the Central Valley include apples, citrus fruits, table and wine grapes, peaches, pears, and plums. The Central Valley is known as Chile's heartland.

and the farmers in this region grow barley, corn, oats, rice, and wheat. Beans, potatoes, sugar beets, and other vegetables, as well as apples, citrus fruits, nuts, peaches, and wine and table grapes, are also grown in the Central Valley.

The harsh climate and rugged terrain of Chile's other land regions make agriculture less profitable. As a result, only 5 per cent of the land in Chile can be cultivated. Chile's farmers are unable to grow enough food to feed all its people, and the nation must rely on massive food imports.

Chile's land policies also limit agricultural production. In the 1960's, when the government began to break up the huge fundos and redistribute the land among poor farmers, many of the new plots were barely large enough to support a family. Today, about 60 per cent of Chile's farms cover less than 12 acres (5 hectares)—too small to afford the investment in modern equipment that would increase production.

Today, the value of Chile's export income is not nearly enough to cover the cost of its imports. Chile's economy also suffers from high rates of inflation and unemployment. But even with all its current problems, Chile has great potential for economic wealth through careful management of its natural resources.

China

China, a huge country in eastern Asia, is the world's third largest nation in area and the largest in population. About 20 per cent of the world's people live in China.

This vast country is marked by an extraordinary variety of climates and landscapes. China's climatic regions range from tropical conditions in the southeast to severe, freezing weather in the north, and its landscapes range from some of the world's driest deserts and highest mountains to some of its richest farmland. The beautiful limestone hills near the city of Guilin on the Li River are among the most unusual features of this enormous country.

China has the world's oldest living civilization, and a written history that goes back about 3,500 years. The Chinese were the first people to develop the compass, gunpowder, movable type, paper, porcelain, and silk cloth. Numerous schools of philosophy and religion, including Confucianism and Taoism, began in China. The Chinese also built great cities and created magnificent works of art. Over the centuries, Japan, Korea, and other Asian lands have borrowed from Chinese art, language, literature, religion, government, and technology.

The Chinese call their country *Zhongguo*, which means *Middle Country* and probably originated from the ancient Chinese belief that their country was the geographical and cultural center of the world. The name *China* was given to the country by foreigners and may have come from Qin (pronounced *chihn*), the name of an early Chinese *dynasty* (series of rulers).

Today, China's official name is Zhonghua Renmin Gongheguo (People's Republic of China). The Chinese Communist Party gave the country this name in 1949 when they set up China's present government.

Since the Communists came to power, China has undergone many major changes. For example, most of the country's industries, trade, and finance have been placed under government control in an effort to make the nation an industrial power. As a result, the Communists have dramatically increased industrial production and expanded and improved education and medical care.

In spite of the government's efforts to modernize the country, China remains essentially a rural nation, and agriculture employs about 70 per cent of all Chinese workers. Although Chinese farmers grow sufficient food to feed the nation's people, China remains a poor country by world standards.

China Today

China in the 1990's tried to move toward an open-market economy while retaining its Communist political system. Chinese leader Deng Xiaoping was credited with decentralizing economic decisions and introducing "socialism with Chinese characteristics." The decentralization led to great economic expansion. For example, in 1992 China's economy grew by nearly 13 per cent, the fastest rate in the world. This economic boom improved the living standards of many of China's nearly 1.3 billion people.

The vibrant economy created much prosperity, but it did so unevenly. In 1994, Premier Li Peng warned of the danger of public disorder stemming from corruption and the disparities of wealth. He told China's parliament that the country needed to fight "money-worship, ultraindividualism, and decadent lifestyles."

The economic changes displaced an estimated 100 million to 150 million rural workers, who moved around the country seeking work. With so many available workers, entrepreneurs could keep wages low. Inflation was rampant, reaching 27 per cent in big cities in 1994. Crime appeared to rise in China, especially corruption. In 1993, for example, three bookkeepers and five others were executed for embezzlement.

Tensions arose as China's leaders allowed economic autonomy but retained political control. These tensions had come to a head on April 18, 1989, when about 2,000 students rallied in Tiananmen Square, a huge open area in the center of Beijing next to the former imperial residence, the Forbidden City. There, the students held pro-democracy demonstrations. For six weeks, thousands of students set up camp in the square, boycotted classes, and continued the demonstrations.

Early in the morning of June 4, about 100,000 soldiers entered the square, shooting at students and setting fire to their tents. Occasional shootings continued for several days as the troops established control. Although the actual death toll is unknown, Western sources estimate that between 700 and 2,000 people died.

After the massacre, the government arrested thousands of people suspected of being involved in the demonstrations. Some were tried and executed immediately. The

FACT BOX

COUNTRY

Official name: Zhonghua Renmin Gongheguo (People's Republic of China)
Capital: Beijing
Terrain: Mostly mountains, high plateaus, deserts in west; plains, deltas, and hills in east
Area: 3,705,407 sq. mi. (9,596,960 km²)

Climate: Extremely diverse; tropical in south to subarctic in north
Main rivers: Huang He, Yangtze, Xi Jiang, Amur
Highest elevation: Mount Everest, 29,035 ft. (8,850 m)
Lowest elevation: Turpan Pendi, 505 ft. (154 m) below sea level

GOVERNMENT

Form of government: Communist state
Head of state: President
Head of government: Premier
Administrative areas: 23 sheng (provinces)†, 5 zizhiqu (autonomous regions), 4 shi (municipalities)

Legislature: Quanguo Renmin Daibiao Dahui (National People's Congress) with 2,979 members serving five-year terms
Court system: Supreme People's Court
Armed forces: 2,480,000 troops

†China considers Taiwan to be one of its provinces.

PEOPLE

Estimated 2002 population: 1,303,875,000
Population growth: 0.9%
Population density: 352 persons per sq. mi. (136 per km²)
Population distribution: 69% rural, 31% urban
Life expectancy in years: Male: 70 Female: 73
Doctors per 1,000 people: 1.7
Percentage of age-appropriate population enrolled in the following educational levels: Primary: 106* Secondary: 85 Further: 34
Languages spoken: Standard Chinese or Mandarin (Putonghua, based on the Beijing dialect)

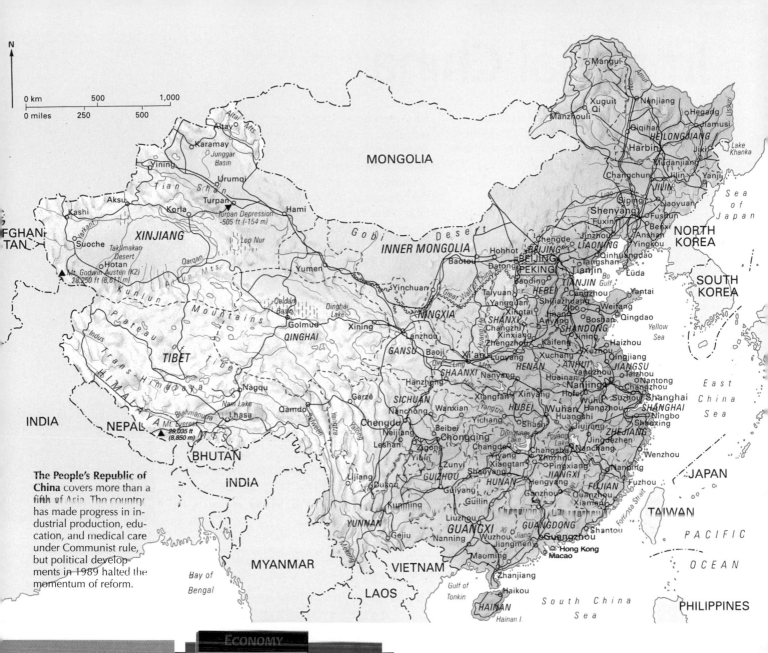

The People's Republic of China covers more than a fifth of Asia. The country has made progress in industrial production, education, and medical care under Communist rule, but political developments in 1989 halted the momentum of reform.

Yue (Cantonese), Wu (Shanghaiese), Minbel (Fuzhou), Minnan (Hokkien-Taiwanese), Xiang, Gan, Hakka dialects

Religions:
atheist (official)
Daoist/Taoist
Buddhist
other 4%

Enrollment ratios compare the number of students enrolled to the population which, by age, should be enrolled. A ratio higher than 100 indicates that students older or younger than the typical age range are also enrolled.

TECHNOLOGY

Radios per 1,000 people:
339

Televisions per 1,000 people: 293

Computers per 1,000 people: 15.9

ECONOMY

Currency: Yuan

Gross national income (GNI) in 2000: $1,062.9 billion U.S.

Real annual growth rate (1999–2000): 7.9%

GNI per capita (2000): $840 U.S.

Balance of payments (2000): $20,518 million U.S.

Goods exported: Machinery and equipment; textiles and clothing, footwear, toys and sporting goods; mineral fuels, chemicals

Goods imported: Machinery and equipment, plastics, chemicals, iron and steel, mineral fuels

Trading partners: Japan, United States, Hong Kong, Taiwan

Chinese government then instituted repressive controls within the country, urging citizens to inform against one another.

China's violent suppression of the pro-democracy movement was denounced by most other countries. The nation's economy briefly suffered as the result of economic sanctions and a decline in tourism. In time, though, most nations (including the United States) resumed trade with China, and the country enjoyed an economic boom.

In 2001, China became a member of the World Trade Organization, which promotes trade among its members. China's entry into the organization marked progress in freeing the Chinese economy from government control.

241

Imperial China

The first distinctly Chinese civilization emerged from two cultures that developed about 10,000 B.C. in what is now northern China. China's first dynasty, the Shang, arose from one of these cultures during the 1700's B.C.

Around 1122 B.C., the Zhou people of western China overthrew the Shang and ruled until 256 B.C. During the early Zhou period, about 500 B.C., the philosopher Confucius developed a system of moral standards that influenced Chinese society for more than 2,000 years.

Early empires

In 221 B.C., the Qin state defeated the Zhou dynasty and other states that were struggling for control. Although the Qin dynasty only lasted until 206 B.C., it founded the first Chinese empire controlled by a strong central government.

After the Qin dynasty collapsed, the Han dynasty gained control of China in 202 B.C. and ruled until A.D. 220. Arts and sciences thrived during this period, and Buddhism was introduced into China from India. A rebellion in 220 ended the Han dynasty, and China split into three rival kingdoms. The Sui dynasty reunified China in 581.

During the Tang dynasty, which replaced the Sui in 618, China enjoyed nearly 300 years of prosperity and cultural accomplishment. Another rebellion led to the collapse of the Tang empire in 907, and many dynasties fought for control of the shattered empire. The Song dynasty reunified China in 960, and developed *Neo-Confucianism,* which combined Confucianism with elements of Buddhism and Taoism, and made it the state philosophy.

During the 1200's, Mongol armies invaded China from the north. In 1279, the Mongol leader Kublai Khan established the Yuan dynasty and made China part of the vast Mongol Empire, which extended over most of Asia. Around this time, enthusiastic reports about the country from Marco Polo, a trader from Venice who lived in China from 1275 to 1292, helped stimulate European interest in China.

The Qin dynasty abolished the local states in 221 B.C. and set up a strong central government. The Qin also ordered the construction of the Great Wall of China and standardized the Chinese writing system.

During the Han dynasty, which lasted from 202 B.C. to A.D. 220, *far right map,* Confucianism became the philosophical basis of government. In addition, overland trade routes were developed that linked China with Europe for the first time.

The Qing dynasty (1644-1912) was established by the Manchus who, like the Mongols, were foreigners. However, unlike the Mongols, the Manchus adopted many elements of Chinese culture, including Neo-Confucianism.

c. 500,000-c. 200,000 B.C. Prehistoric human beings live in northern China.
c. 10,000 to c. 1700 B.C. New Stone Age cultures, including Yangshao and Longshan, flourish.
c. 1766-c. 1122 B.C. China's first dynasty, the Shang, arises from Longshan culture.
c. 1122 B.C. The Zhou overthrow the Shang and establish new dynasty that rules until 256 B.C.
c. 500 B.C. Philosopher Confucius develops system of moral values.
221-206 B.C. Qin dynasty establishes China's first strong central government. Great Wall constructed.
202 B.C.-A.D. 220 China becomes powerful empire under Han dynasty.
A.D. 105 Chinese invent paper.
220-581 China divided. Buddhism spreads.
581-618 Sui dynasty reunifies China.
618-907 Tang dynasty rules China during period of prosperity and cultural achievement.
960-1279 Gunpowder, compass, and movable type for printing invented under Song dynasty.
1126 Invaders from Manchuria conquer north.
1275-1292 Marco Polo visits China.
1279-1368 Mongols rule China under Yuan dynasty.
1368-1644 The Ming dynasty governs China.
1644 The Manchus establish Qing dynasty and rule for 268 years.
1842 Treaty of Nanjing gives Hong Kong to Great Britain and opens five other ports to British trade.
1851-1864 Millions die during the Taiping Rebellion.
1894-1895 Japan defeats China and gains control of Korea and Taiwan.
1900 Boxer Rebellion—an anti-Western campaign waged by Chinese secret societies— crushed by troops from eight nations.
1912 Republic of China established.

Confucius developed a system of moral values.

Kublai Khan, *far left,* a Mongol leader, conquered China in 1279.

Sun Yat-sen worked for the unification of China in the early 1900's.

In

Beijing's Forbidden City—so called because only the emperor's household could enter it—includes the palaces of former Chinese emperors. The Forbidden City was built during the 1440's on the site of the palace of Mongol leader Kublai Khan.

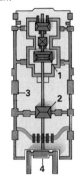

1 Palace of Great Peace

2 Gate of Great Peace

3 Pavilions and Galleries

4 Meridian Gatehouse

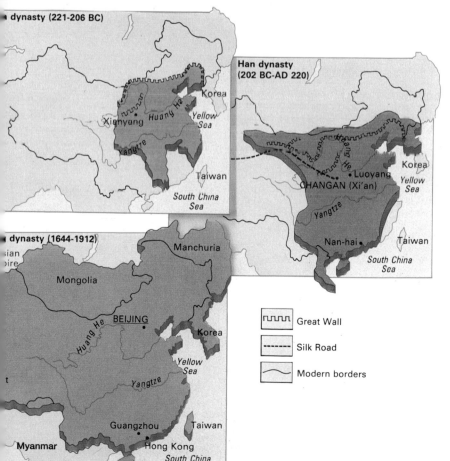

dynasty (221-206 BC)

Korea

Xianyang Huang He Yellow Sea

Yangtze

Taiwan

South China Sea

Han dynasty (202 BC-AD 220)

Luoyang Korea

CHANGAN (Xi'an) Yellow Sea

Yangtze

Nan-hai Taiwan

South China Sea

dynasty (1644-1912)

Manchuria

Mongolia

Huang He BEIJING

Korea

Yellow Sea

Yangtze

Guangzhou Taiwan

Myanmar Hong Kong

South China Sea

⊓⊔⊓⊔ Great Wall

- - - - Silk Road

Modern borders

The Mongols were driven out of China in the mid-1300's. The authoritarian Ming dynasty, established in 1368, ushered in a period of stability, prosperity, and flourishing arts that lasted until 1644.

Manchu rule and Western powers

In 1644, the Manchu people of Manchuria invaded China and founded the Qing dynasty, which lasted until 1912. The empire enjoyed stability until 1796, when political corruption touched off a rebellion that lasted until 1804 and weakened the Qing dynasty.

In the 1800's, European merchants began to smuggle opium into China. When the Chinese tried to stop British merchants from conducting the illegal trade, the Opium War broke out between China and Great Britain. Britain easily won the war, which ended in 1842 with the Treaty of Nanjing—an agreement that gave Hong Kong to Great Britain and opened five other Chinese ports to British trade. During the 1800's, China signed similar treaties with other Western nations.

The Taiping Rebellion, which lasted from 1851 to 1864, threatened the survival of the Qing dynasty, and though the rebellion was put down, millions of people were killed. Then China was defeated in a war with Japan in 1894 and 1895, further weakening the country.

In 1899, in order to prevent a single Western power from becoming dominant in China, the United States established the Open-Door Policy, which guaranteed the rights of all nations to trade with China on an equal basis. However, some Chinese opposed the spread of Western influences in China, and in 1900 a secret society called the Boxers led a rebellion in which Westerners and Chinese Christians were attacked and killed. Troops from eight nations crushed the Boxer Rebellion of 1900.

In the years following the rebellion, the Manchus tried to reform the Chinese government and economy, but these reforms did not save the dynasty. In the early 1900's, a movement to set up a republic began to grow, led by a Western-educated physician named Sun Yat-sen. The revolution that began on Oct. 11, 1911, eventually overthrew Manchu rule and established the Republic of China.

Modern History

In 1912, the republican revolution forced the last Manchu emperor — a 6-year-old boy named Pu Yi — from China's throne. Yuan Shikai became president of the Republic of China in place of Sun Yat-sen, who agreed to step down, but Yuan's presidency soon became a dictatorship. In 1913, the republicans established the Kuomintang (Nationalist Party) and tried to overthrow Yuan. The revolt failed, however, and the Kuomintang leaders fled to Japan.

When Yuan died in 1916, the central government weakened, and the real power in northern China passed into the hands of *war lords* (local military leaders). Sun Yat-sen set up a rival government in Guangzhou in southern China, but by 1922 his republic had failed and civil war was widespread.

Meanwhile, Sun had begun to reorganize the Kuomintang in 1919 and to recruit students who had formed Communist groups. In 1923, the Soviet Union sent advisers to aid the Nationalists and enlist the help of Chinese Communists.

After Sun Yat-sen died in 1925, the Nationalist Party was lead by its military commander, Chiang Kai-shek. In 1926, Chiang set out to reunite China, but tensions developed between the Nationalists and the Communists. In 1927, Chiang and his troops turned against the Communists, who retreated to the hills in southern China. The Nationalists captured Beijing and united China under one government in 1928.

Nationalist rule

The Nationalist government was plagued from the start by Communist opposition and Japanese aggression. Then, in 1931, the Japanese seized Manchuria and extended their military influence into other parts of northern China. In 1934, Chiang's armies forced the Communists to evacuate their bases in southern and central China, but they established a new base in Shaanxi in northern China, after marching more than 6,000 miles (9,700 kilometers) in the famous *Long March*. During that fateful journey, Mao Zedong became the leader of the Chinese Communist Party.

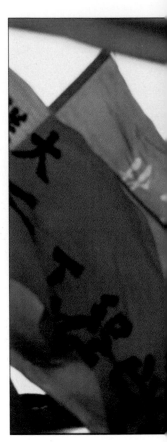

Chinese students and workers demonstrated in support of democratic reforms in 1989 at Beijing's Tiananmen Square and in other Chinese cities, *above right*. Their bold challenge to the country's Communist leaders brought a brutal military crackdown.

During the famous Long March, Chinese Communists marched 6,000 miles (9,700 kilometers) from southeastern China to Shaanxi province. Of the approximately 100,000 Communists who began the march, only a few thousand reached the final destination.

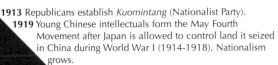

1913 Republicans establish *Kuomintang* (Nationalist Party).
1919 Young Chinese intellectuals form the May Fourth Movement after Japan is allowed to control land it seized in China during World War I (1914-1918). Nationalism grows.
1928 The Nationalists, led by Chiang Kai-shek, unite China under one government.
1931 The Japanese seize Manchuria and set up a puppet state called Manchukuo.
1934-1935 Mao Zedong leads the Chinese Communists on their Long March to Shaanxi.
1937-1945 War with Japan shatters China. Chinese Communists expand forces.
1946 Civil war between Nationalists and Communists breaks out.
1949 Chinese Communists defeat Nationalists and establish People's Republic of China.
1958 Communists launch Great Leap Forward, which severely weakens China's economy.
1960's Friendly relations between China and the Soviet Union end.
1962 Chinese troops fight border war with India.
1966-1969 Cultural Revolution disrupts education, government, and daily life.
1971 China admitted to the United Nations.
1972 U.S. President Richard M. Nixon visits China.
1976 Mao Zedong dies.
1979 China and United States establish normal diplomatic relations.
1984 Economic reforms lessen government control of business and increase trade and cultural exchanges with Western nations.
1989 Army troops kill hundreds of pro-democracy demonstrators in Tiananmen Square.
1997 Deng Xiaoping dies.
2001 China becomes a member of the World Trade Organization.

Yaun Shikai ruled China from 1912 to 1916.

Zhou Enlai, *far left,* served as premier under Mao Zedong.

Deng Xiaoping brought about sweeping changes in China during the 1970's and 1980's.

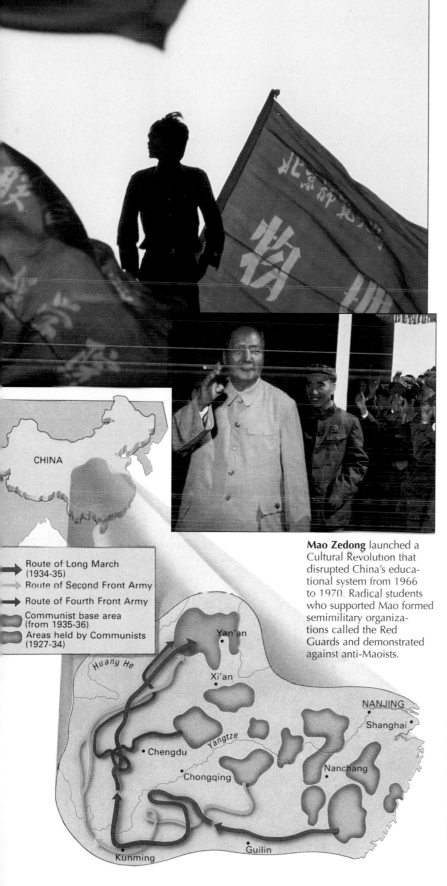

In 1937, the Japanese launched a major attack against China, and the Nationalists and Communists formed a united front to oppose them. In World War II (1939-1945), China fought with the Allies against Japan. By the end of that war in 1945, the Chinese Communists held an area in northern China and commanded a large army. In 1946, a full-scale civil war broke out between the Nationalists and the Communists. The superior military tactics of the Communists and the social revolution they conducted in the countryside gradually turned the tide against the Nationalists. Mao Zedong established the People's Republic of China on Oct. 1,1949, and Chiang and his followers fled to Taiwan.

Communist rule

The Communists, under Party Chairman Mao Zedong, initiated an economic plan based on state control and the development of heavy industry. The new government also redistributed farmland among the peasants and combined the landholdings into large cooperatives.

In 1958, the Communists launched the Great Leap Forward, a campaign designed to accelerate economic development. The program shattered China's economy, however, resulting in food shortages and a decline in industrial production.

In 1966, Mao launched the Cultural Revolution, another disastrous campaign aimed at preserving Communist principles. During the Cultural Revolution, radicals warred against moderate party members, and China came close to civil war.

When Mao Zedong died in 1976, the moderates came to power and liberalized some of Mao's strict policies. In 1979, the new leaders established normal diplomatic relations with the United States.

By 1980, Deng Xiaoping, a moderate, had become China's leader. He began economic reforms and increased cultural contact with Western nations, but in 1989 many students demonstrated for increased freedoms. Chinese soldiers attacked the students gathered in Beijing's Tiananmen Square and killed hundreds. Although Deng Xiaoping resigned later that year, he remained China's most influential leader until his death in 1997.

Mao Zedong launched a Cultural Revolution that disrupted China's educational system from 1966 to 1970. Radical students who supported Mao formed semimilitary organizations called the Red Guards and demonstrated against anti-Maoists.

CHINA

Route of Long March (1934-35)
Route of Second Front Army
Route of Fourth Front Army
Communist base area (from 1935-36)
Areas held by Communists (1927-34)

Huang He
Yan'an
Xi'an
NANJING
Shanghai
Chengdu
Yangtze
Chongqing
Nanchang
Guilin
Kunming

Chinese Civilization

China has the world's oldest living civilization, and many other countries have benefited from Chinese technology, philosophy, and culture over the centuries. About 1,000 years ago, Chinese scientists invented the compass and gunpowder. Movable type for printing was also invented in China during this period—approximately 400 years before its development in Europe. Many Asian lands adopted Confucian and Taoist values, and Marco Polo's tales of the country's fine silk cloth and other riches helped introduce China to the Western world.

Throughout the centuries, Chinese civilization has been heavily influenced by Confucianism, Taoism, and Buddhism. Confucianism offered a set of moral values stressing order, discipline, and rules of behavior that benefited society. Taoism, on the other hand, dealt with more personal problems, such as a person's ability to live in harmony with nature. Buddhism, which originated in India, encouraged spiritual thinking, right living, and detachment from worldly things. China's literature, art, and music reflect all these traditional religions and values.

Sculpture and pottery

The oldest known Chinese works of art include pottery and jade carvings from the 5000's B.C. Bronze urns and vases were used before the 1500's B.C. in religious ceremonies that included ancestor worship.

Excavations of tombs and dwellings have yielded many other ancient works of Chinese art. In 1974, for example, archaeologists uncovered thousands of life-sized clay figures of soldiers and horses in burial pits near the city of Xian. These figures stood guard over the tomb of emperor Shi Huangdi who ruled during the Qin dynasty in the 200's B.C. In March 1990, about 25 miles (40 kilometers) from that site, a road crew discovered a network of vaults that extend over an area about the size of 10 football fields and contain tens of thousands of terra-cotta sculptures of men, boys, horses, and carts.

After Buddhism reached China from India during the Han dynasty (202 B.C.-A.D. 220), sculptors carved images of Buddha to decorate the temples. Some of

Porcelain, the most delicate type of pottery, was developed by the Chinese during the Tang dynasty (618-907). Fine porcelain dishes and vases are among the greatest treasures of Chinese art.

A scroll from the Tang dynasty shows a court scene in ancient China, *right*. The artist has used calligraphy to enhance the beauty of the painting and describe the circumstances under which it was created.

these sculptures were made of stone or clay, while others were cast in bronze and coated with gold. In rural areas, elaborate Buddhist chapels were hollowed out of cliffsides and decorated with figures of Buddha.

Painting, literature, and drama

As early as the 5000's B.C., Chinese potters decorated their works with sophisticated painted designs. Painting on silk has been an art in China since about 400 B.C., while painting on paper began later. Most of the early paintings show people, gods, or spirits, but by the A.D. 900's, many artists painted landscapes. In these paintings, called *shanshui* (mountain-water), artists used towering mountains and vast expanses of water to communicate a feeling of Taoist-inspired harmony between nature and the human spirit.

In China, *calligraphy* (fine handwriting) is a branch of painting and considered an art form. During the 1200's, an inscription or poem in exquisite calligraphy often formed part of a painting's overall design.

A clay army of about 10,000 terra-cotta soldiers and horses was excavated near Xian in 1974 by local farmers. In the 1100's B.C., the soldiers and servants of a ruler were buried alive in their master's tomb when he died. Over time that custom was modified, and clay images were substituted for living people.

Chinese literature dates back almost 3,000 years and includes many great works. Some, inspired by Confucianism, teach moral lessons, while poems that celebrate the beauties of nature reflect the influence of Taoism. One of China's greatest poets, Wang Wei, lived during the Tang dynasty (A.D. 618-907). His works, which emphasize quietness and contemplation, demonstrate the influence of Buddhism. Before the 1900's, almost all of China's greatest writers were given important government jobs, due to their skill with words. For this reason, many masterpieces of Chinese literature deal with history, politics, and science.

Chinese drama developed around the 1200's. However, since the 1800's, the most popular form of Chinese drama has been *Beijing opera*— plays based on Chinese history and folklore. Dressed in elaborate and colorful costumes, the actors of the Beijing opera combine dialogue and songs with dance and symbolic gestures.

In traditional Chinese houses, large tile roofs with elegant, curved edges are supported by wooden columns. The design and location of Chinese buildings express the ideal of harmony between people and nature.

A huge statue of Buddha, *above right,* watches over a cliffside chapel in the Yunggang Grotto near Datong. More than 51,000 statues of Buddha and his attendants grace this magnificent grotto.

1 Entrance door
2 Living rooms divided
  by light partitions
3 Galleries link rooms
4 Wooden support posts
5 Tiled roof
6 Courtyard

The Great Wall

The Great Wall of China is the only man-made object visible from the moon. With a total length of about 4,000 miles (6,400 kilometers), it is the longest structure ever built and was erected entirely by hand. The Chinese built the wall to protect their northern border from invasion. In times of war, troops and horses could march quickly along the wall, avoiding difficult mountain passes. Today, the Great Wall is truly one of the treasures of world civilization.

The Great Wall begins in the east near the North Korean border and winds its way to Jiayuguan in the west. Watchtowers, placed every 100 to 200 yards (91 to 180 meters) along the wall, once served as lookout posts. Although parts of the wall have crumbled through the years, much of it remains, and some sections have been restored.

In the east, the wall winds through a mountainous region called the Mongolian Border Uplands. Granite blocks form the foundation of this part of the Great Wall, while the sides are made of stone or brick, and the inside of the wall is filled with earth. Layers of brick placed on top of the earth to prevent water seepage form a roadway.

Farther west, the Great Wall runs through hilly areas and along the borders of deserts. Stone and brick were scarce in these areas, so the workers built this section of the wall out of earth, moistened and pounded to make it solid.

The first sections of what was to become the Great Wall of China were probably built during the 400's B.C. by the peoples of small, warring states. Some states constructed long walls of packed earth to serve as borders marking their territory.

In 206 B.C., the Qin dynasty conquered these smaller states, and Qin Emperor Shi Huangdi planned the Great Wall, building new sections of the wall to connect with the older ones. The wall was constructed at huge expense—and at the cost of many lives. Thousands of workers toiled for years to build the Great Wall.

Work on the wall continued through the Han dynasty (202 B.C.-A.D. 220) and the Sui dynasty (581-618), but much of the wall

gradually fell into ruin after these periods. The structure continued to provide protection against minor attacks, but in the 1200's, Mongol warriors led by Kublai Khan swept across the wall and conquered much of China.

The Great Wall was rebuilt during the Ming dynasty (1368-1644), which followed the Mongol rule. To prevent further invasion from hostile foreigners, the Ming emperors had soldiers on guard in the watchtowers at all times. At particularly vulnerable points, several walls were built—one behind the other—to strengthen the defenses. Almost all of the Great Wall as it appears today dates from the Ming period.

Over the centuries, much of the Great Wall again collapsed. However, the Chinese Communists have restored three sections of it since 1949, when their rule began. These

Views of the Great Wall from various locations are a reminder of its enduring significance. A graceful watchtower marks the western end of the wall, *bottom left*. At Datong, farmers in need of handy building material have stolen the wall's stone facing, *below left*. A restored section near Badaling, *below right,* once defended a strategic mountain pass—and now fascinates visitors.

sections are near the east coast, outside Beijing, and in the province of Gansu in north-central China. Near Beijing, a monumental gateway marks a restored section of the wall at Badaling, where the roadway atop the wall is wide enough for five horses to gallop side by side.

The Chinese no longer depend upon the Great Wall to keep enemies out, but rather to bring visitors in. Thousands of tourists from China and other countries come to see the wall every year. The Great Wall is also of interest to historians, who study the structure's fortifications, and to scientists, who study the effects of earthquakes on the wall.

The Great Wall of China, *far left,* represents one of the world's great engineering feats. The wall stands about 25 feet (7.6 meters) high. The main part of the wall is about 2,150 miles (3,460 kilometers) long.

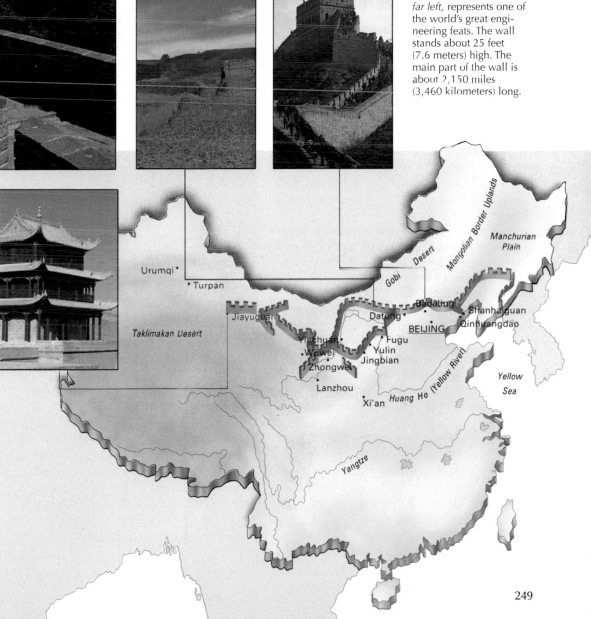

The Great Wall of China can even be seen from outer space, as shown by this satellite photo. The thin orange line running from the upper left to the lower left is a section of the Great Wall about 434 miles (700 kilometers) west of Beijing. The dark blue areas in the photo are dry lakebeds used for salt extraction, and the rectangular patterns are primarily wheat fields.

Urumqi

Turpan

Jiayuguan

Taklimakan Desert

Gobi Desert

Mongolian Border Uplands

Manchurian Plain

Badaling

Datong

BEIJING

Shanhaiguan

Qinhuangdao

Yinchuan

Fugu

Yulin

Wuwei

Jingbian

Zhongwei

Lanzhou

Xi'an

Huang He (Yellow River)

Yellow Sea

Yangtze

Western Land Regions

China, the world's third largest country, spans about 2,500 miles (4,023 kilometers) from north to south, and approximately 3,000 miles (4,828 kilometers) from east to west. This vast land has a remarkably wide variety of landscapes and climates.

Western China is a land of high mountain ranges and vast areas of deserts and *steppes* (dry grasslands). Mountains form natural boundaries along much of China's southern and western border regions, which are sparsely populated. The Gobi, Mu Us, Ordos, and Taklimakan deserts lie in northern and northwestern China. These areas are also thinly populated. Western China can be divided into two large land regions—the Tibetan Highlands and the Xinjiang-Mongolian Uplands.

The Tibetan Highlands

The Tibetan Highlands lie in southwestern China. The region contains the high, cold Plateau of Tibet, bordered by towering mountains—the Himalaya on the south, the Pamirs on the west, and the Karakoram Range and the Kunlun on the north. This region includes Tibet, which has been part of China since the 1950's.

Tibet stands at an average elevation of 16,000 feet (4,880 meters) and the highest mountain in the world—Mount Everest—rises 29,028 feet (8,848 meters) in the Himalaya in southern Tibet. In the north, many peaks of the Kunlun range rise more than 20,000 feet (6,000 meters). Two of China's most important rivers, the Huang He and Yangtze, begin in the mountains of the Tibetan Highlands and flow eastward across China to the sea.

Tibet's harsh climate is characterized by drought and long, bitterly cold winters, while violent winds sweep the region the year around. Most of the Highlands is a wasteland of rock, gravel, snow, and ice, though a few areas provide limited grazing for hardy *yaks*—hairy oxen that furnish food, clothing, and transportation for the Tibetan people. Most of the land cannot support agriculture due to the poor soil and cold climate. However, crops can be grown in some fertile valleys in the south.

Farming villages in Qinghai province, *above*, nestle in the mountain valleys of the Tibetan Highlands. Crops such as barley and wheat can be grown in these sheltered valleys.

Xinjiang-Mongolian Uplands

The Xinjiang-Mongolian Uplands cover the vast desert areas of northwestern China, and Xinjiang lies in the western part of the region. Although Xinjiang covers about 17 per cent of China's land area, only about 1 per cent of China's people live in the region. However, Xinjiang is an important region economically, with vast

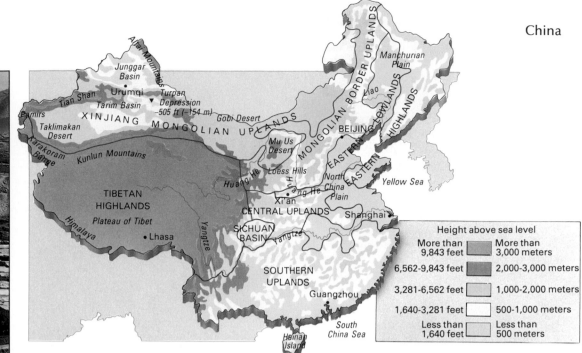

Western China has some of the highest mountains in the world. The land of Tibet in the Tibetan Highlands of southwestern China is often called the *Roof of the World.*

Camel caravans once transported silk and other goods on the Silk Road, an overland trade route from China to the West that crossed the forbidding wastes of the Taklimakan Desert.

A Kazakh campsite, *left,* with its warm felt tents and peaceful animals, makes a cozy scene on the lower slopes of the Altai Mountains in the Xinjiang-Mongolian Uplands. The Kazakh people, one of China's minority groups, are herders in northwestern China.

deposits of coal, iron ore, oil, and uranium.

The Tian Shan mountains divide the Xinjiang region into two areas—the Taklimakan Desert to the south and the Dzungarian Basin to the north. The Taklimakan is one of the world's driest deserts, receiving less than 4 inches (10 centimeters) of rain a year. Most of the people of this region live on or near natural or artificially created desert oases. The Turpan Depression, an oasis near the northern edge of the Taklimakan, is the lowest point in China, lying 505 feet (154 meters) below sea level. The remote Dzungarian Basin north of the Tian Shan stretches northward to the Altai Mountains along the Mongolian border.

The eastern part of the Xinjiang-Mongolian Uplands contains part of the Gobi Desert and the Mu Us Desert. The Gobi consists mainly of dry, rocklike or sandy soil surrounded by steppes. Summers are hot in the Gobi, with daytime temperatures exceeding 100° F. (38° C). Nighttime lows in the winter, however, can fall to −30° F. (−34° C). The dry, sandy Mu Us Desert lies in a region known as Inner Mongolia, bordering the Loess Hills in the Mongolian Border Uplands.

Eastern Land Regions

Eastern China contrasts sharply with the barren, thinly populated regions of western China. Most of China's people live crowded together in the eastern third of the country, which has nearly all the land suitable for farming and most of China's major cities.

Eastern China can be divided into six major land regions. In northeastern China, they are the Mongolian Border Uplands, the Eastern Highlands, and the Eastern Lowlands. In southeastern China, they are the Central Uplands, the Sichuan Basin, and the Southern Uplands.

The Mongolian Border Uplands lie between the Gobi Desert and the Eastern Lowlands, with the rugged Greater Hinggan Mountains to the north. Little agriculture is carried out in this area.

The southern part of the region is thickly covered with *loess,* a fine, yellowish soil of tiny mineral particles that is deposited by the wind and easily eroded. The *Huang He,* which means *Yellow River,* takes its name from the large amounts of loess it carries.

The Eastern Highlands consist of eastern Manchuria and the mountainous Shandong Peninsula, a region with excellent harbors and rich coal deposits. China's finest forestland covers the hills of eastern Manchuria, and timber is one of the region's major products.

The Eastern Lowlands consist of the Manchurian Plain, the North China Plain, and the Yangtze River Valley. This region lies between the Mongolian Border Uplands and the Eastern Highlands and extends south to the Southern Uplands. The Eastern Lowlands have China's most productive farmland and many of the country's largest cities, including Beijing and Shanghai.

The Manchurian Plain has fertile soils and large deposits of coal and iron ore. Wheat is the main crop in the wide, flat North China Plain south of the Manchurian Plain in the Huang He Valley, a highly productive agricultural area.

The Yangtze Valley has the best combination of level land, fertile soil, and suffi-

A rural village in the Sichuan Basin, *above,* is surrounded by fertile hills. Land travel is difficult in the region, and rivers provide transportation routes for small boats.

The city of Yan'an in the province of Shaanxi lies on a tributary of the Huang He in the fertile Loess Hills area of the Mongolian Border Uplands. The Huang He and its tributaries have carved out hills and steep-sided valleys in the soft loess soil.

The limestone hills near the city of Guilin, *left,* owe their unusual shape to erosion and weathering. Many isolated limestone hills rise 100 to 600 feet (30 to 182 meters) almost straight up. Some people say the hills resemble rows of dragons' teeth.

The course of the Huang He River has shifted several times during the last several hundred years. Major flooding formerly occurred every few years in the Huang He Valley, earning the river the nickname "China's Sorrow." Today, a system of dams and dikes controls most floods. Loess carried by the river fertilizes the North China Plain in the Eastern Lowlands.

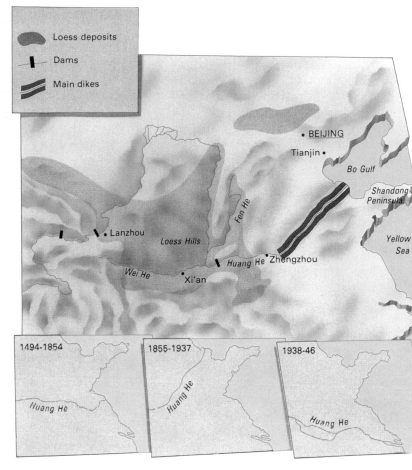

Loess deposits
Dams
Main dikes

BEIJING
Tianjin
Bo Gulf
Shandong Peninsula
Yellow Sea
Lanzhou
Fen He
Loess Hills
Zhengzhou
Huang He
Wei He
Xi'an

1494-1854 — Huang He
1855-1937 — Huang He
1938-46 — Huang He

cient rainfall in China, and rice is the region's chief crop. In addition, the Yangtze River and its many tributaries are the country's most important trade routes.

The Central Uplands are an area of hills and mountains between the Eastern Lowlands and the Tibetan Highlands. The Qin Ling Mountains, which cross the region from east to west, are China's most significant geographic boundary because they form a natural barricade against the monsoons that carry dust from the north and rain from the south. North of the mountains, the dry weather is beneficial in the cultivation of wheat, while rice is the major crop in the warm, humid areas to the south.

The Sichuan Basin, which lies south of the Central Uplands, is a region of hills and valleys surrounded by high mountains. With its mild climate and long growing season, the Sichuan Basin is one of China's major agricultural regions. The name *Si-chuan* means *Four Rivers* and refers to the four streams that flow into the Yangtze in this region. The rivers have carved out deep gorges in the red sandstone, making land travel difficult.

The Southern Uplands, a region of green hills and mountains, cover southeastern China and include the island of Hainan. The delta of the Xi Jiang (West River), is the only level area and also the most densely populated part of the region. Guangzhou (also called Canton), southern China's largest city, lies near the mouth of the Xi Jiang. Deep, rich soils and a tropical climate help make the delta an extremely productive agricultural region.

Much of the Southern Uplands, however, is so hilly and mountainous that farming is largely impossible. The Guilin Hills, one of the strangest and most beautiful sights in China, rise in the central part of the region.

Wildlife

China's wildlife includes a great variety of animal species. The takin, a mammal that resembles a musk ox, inhabits the dense bamboo forests of central, western, and southwestern China, and the Himalaya. The Chinese alligator and the giant salamander live in the Yangtze River Valley. China is also home to many species of birds, including the rare Himalayan monal and Lady Amherst's pheasant—found only in the foothills of the Himalaya.

Many other rare and endangered animals also live in China. The giant panda, a black-and-white bearlike animal, lives only in western and southwestern China. Other rare animals include the snow leopard, which lives on the cold Plateau of Tibet, and several species of cranes. The Chinese dolphin, a small freshwater whale, is found in Dongting Lake in Hunan province.

Endangered species

Many animal species in China are close to extinction, and in many cases their survival is threatened by the activities of human beings. For example, people hunt and kill the snow leopard for its beautiful fur, Asian rhinoceroses are killed for their horns, and tigers in China have been hunted for food.

People have also seriously harmed and even destroyed many animal habitats to clear land for agriculture and industry. Marshes that serve as breeding grounds for cranes have been drained for farming and for settlements. In the Sichuan Basin, bamboo and rhododendron forests as well as many broadleaved and coniferous trees have been cut and burned to extend the region's agricultural land. Animals that live in the area—such as the antelope, shrew, golden monkey, and giant panda—depend on these plants for their food.

The destruction of bamboo forests has particularly threatened the survival of the giant panda, which feeds chiefly on bamboo shoots. However, the growth cycle of the bamboo plant has also contributed to its scarcity. Since the 1970's, some of the bamboo species eaten by the giant panda have been going through periodic die-offs. Every 40 to 100 years, bamboo plants flower, produce seeds, and then die. It takes several years for the seeds to grow into plants that can provide food for pandas, and as a result hundreds of pandas have died. Scientists estimated that only about 600 pandas remained in the wild in the late 1980's.

Wildlife preservation

In an effort to save the remaining giant pandas and increase their population, pandas are now protected by law in China. In addition, the Chinese government has loaned giant pandas to various zoos in the United States, hoping that the animals will breed in captivity. Unfortunately, most such attempts have failed.

By 1990, China had also set up about 468 *nature reserves*—refuge areas where

The rare giant panda lives in bamboo forests on the upper mountain slopes of western and southwestern China.

China's wildlife includes animals that live in high, mountainous regions, such as the yak **(1)** and the snow leopard **(2).** The golden monkey **(3),** red panda **(4),** Père David's deer **(5),** musk deer **(6),** giant panda **(7),** and tiger **(8)** all live in forested areas. Tiny shrews **(9)** and the giant salamander **(10)** make their home in and along China's rivers. The country's birds include such exotic specimens as the black-throated crane **(11),** the northern goshawk **(12),** the collared Scops owl **(13),** the Asian flycatcher **(14),** and Temminck's tragopan **(15).**

plants and animals are protected. The southern province of Yunnan is known as China's "plant and animal kingdom" because of its many protected areas.

Some of China's nature reserves protect an entire ecological system from people and pollution, conserving the natural balance between plants and animals and their habitat, while other areas have been designed to protect particular animal and plant species. For example, a small preserve near Lüda (Dalian) in northeastern China protects tens of thousands of venomous Halys snakes. In the past, many of these animals had been killed for their meat, which some Chinese consider a delicacy. In some nature reserves, trees such as the silver cypress are grown to replenish forests that have been cleared.

China's major conservation areas, *below,* preserve distinct ecological environments or protect endangered animals and plants. In the late 1980's, China began to devote more of its resources to conservation.

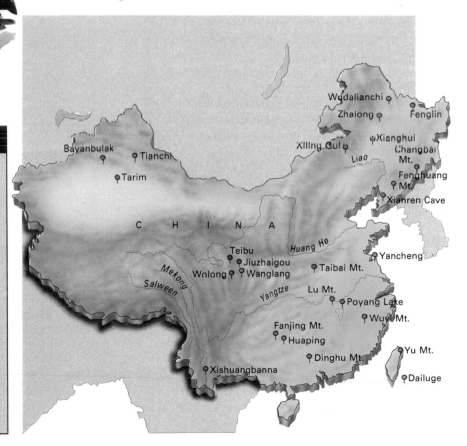

The giant panda

The giant panda is one of the world's most endearing and popular animals. Zoologists disagree about how to classify the giant panda because these chubby creatures resemble bears but also have some characteristics in common with raccoons. Research conducted during the 1980's, however, revealed that the giant panda's *chromosomes* (the parts of a cell that carry genes) are chemically more like those of bears than those of raccoons. As a result, most zoologists now consider the giant panda to be a bear. Panda cubs are extremely tiny, weighing only about 5 ounces (140 grams) at birth. Adults, on the other hand, weigh up to 350 pounds (160 kilograms). A giant panda can grasp an object between its fingers and its so-called extra thumb. This thumb, which is actually a bone covered by a fleshy pad, grows from the wrist of each forepaw. Pandas use their true thumbs as fingers.

The Han

China has more than 1 billion people, and about 94 per cent of them belong to the Han ethnic group, which has been the largest nationality in China for centuries. The Chinese call themselves Han people in recognition of China's achievements during the Han dynasty.

All the Han people speak Chinese, but spoken Chinese has many dialects that differ enough in pronunciation to be considered separate languages. About 70 per cent of the nation's people speak Mandarin, or *putonghua* (common language), the country's official language. Other major dialects include Wu (spoken in Shanghai) and Yue (also called Cantonese). However, although the dialects differ in pronunciation, all the people who speak Chinese write the language in the same way.

Changes under Communism

Family life has always been extremely important in Han Chinese culture, but family life has changed greatly since the Communists came to power in 1949. In the past, children were expected to obey their parents without question in all matters, and a father could legally kill his children if they disobeyed him. Parents also decided who their children would marry. Today, relationships within Chinese families are more flexible and more democratic.

Before 1949, families valued sons far more than daughters, and girls were sometimes killed at birth because they were considered useless. Today, the sexes are regarded more equally. Most women work outside the home, and many men share in the housekeeping.

The Communist government has also made great progress in education. Adult education classes are available for older people, and all children must attend school for at least six years. However, a modern industrial society needs well-educated people, and the Communist ideal of equality in education conflicts with their desire to provide talented students with better facilities. Education in China has alternated between supporting the Communist principle of equality and providing high-quality education for outstanding students.

City and country life

In general, people in China's urban areas have a higher standard of living than people in the countryside. In the cities, most households have at least two wage earners, and the cost of food and rent are low. However, housing can be a problem in China's crowded cities. Families live in apartments assigned to them by their employers, and sometimes two families must share a small apartment.

About 75 per cent of China's people live in rural villages and small towns. Most rural families live in three- or four-room houses made of mud bricks, clay bricks, or stone, with roofs of tile or straw. Farmers work many hours a day and attend night

Female welders, *above,* at an industrial plant reflect the increasing equality between the sexes in the Chinese workplace. The government believes that women should contribute to the family income and participate in social and political activities.

The day begins with exercises for these students at a middle school. Children enter middle school in China around age 12.

China's population is concentrated mainly in the eastern half of the country. In an attempt to reduce population growth, the government launched a program in the 1980's that rewarded couples who limited their family to just one child.

BEIJING
Tianjin
Shenyang
Zibo
Harbin
Shanghai
Nanjing
Xi'an
Wuhan
Chengdu
Chongqing
Guangzhou

Population density by province

Persons per square mile	per square kilometer
more than 1,000	more than 400
500–1,000	200–400
250–500	100–200
125–250	50–100
25–125	10–50
less than 25	less than 10

Cities with more than 2,000,000 inhabitants

News printed on wall posters provides absorbing reading for these citizens of Shanghai, *left,* though one elderly man prefers to practice his taijiquan exercises. For years, people have used these posters to express their opinions.

Out for a stroll on a sunny day, a man takes care of his grandchildren while their parents work outside the home. Although this arrangement is widespread in China, a growing number of children attend nursery school and kindergarten.

classes and political meetings, but they still have time for recreation. Most villages provide facilities for basketball and table tennis, a small library, and a center for television viewing, and some have a small orchestra or theater group.

City life offers a greater variety of cultural opportunities. People who live in cities have more classes to choose from. City dwellers also enjoy restaurants, parks, museums, theaters, and sporting events. Stores in the city provide a wider selection of foods and merchandise.

Many Han people—both city and rural dwellers—perform ancient Chinese exercises called *taijiquan* every morning. Taijiquan emphasizes relaxation, balance, and proper breathing techniques and is also a form of self-defense.

Most Han people throughout China dress for comfort rather than style. Both men and women usually dress in Western-style shirts and loose-fitting trousers, and generally prefer short hair styles, though permanents and more fashionable styles are becoming popular for women.

Minority Groups

About 8 per cent of China's people are members of minority groups. Kazakhs, Mongols, Tibetans, and Uigurs are a few of the country's approximately 55 ethnic minority groups. Most of China's minority peoples live in the border regions and in the western half of the country. Many of these ethnic groups retain their own way of life, culture, and language, in spite of government efforts to impose the ways of the Han Chinese on them.

Tensions between the minorities and the Han Chinese have sometimes led to open revolts. Many minority groups resent what they perceive as China's attempts to absorb their cultures, while many Han Chinese have a deep-seated prejudice against the minorities.

Pressure to conform

The Chinese Communist government has tried to integrate the minority groups into the country's mainstream way of life. At times, this effort has included pressure to adopt practices of the majority, such as particular farming methods. Since 1976, however, policies toward the minority groups have become more moderate.

The Communists have also tried to encourage members of ethnic groups to participate in the Communist Party and in government. Today, although Han Chinese hold the key positions, minority members occupy some positions within their local governments.

A clash of cultures

The government has also had moderate success in integrating the Mongols who live in northern China—a region sometimes called *Inner Mongolia*. The Mongols have traditionally been nomadic herders, roaming the land in search of pasture for their sheep and goats. The traditional Mongolian customs are still followed in nomadic camps, where people live in felt tents called *yurts* and hold horse races, archery contests, and wrestling matches. Today, however, many Mongol people have settled down on government-owned cooperative farms.

However, the government has had far less success in Tibet and Xinjiang, where

Horse races and hunting are popular pastimes among the nomadic Kazakh people of northwestern China.

Mongol boys in Hohhot, *right,* dress much like other schoolchildren in China. Mongols live along the Mongolian border but make up only a small percentage of Inner Mongolia's population.

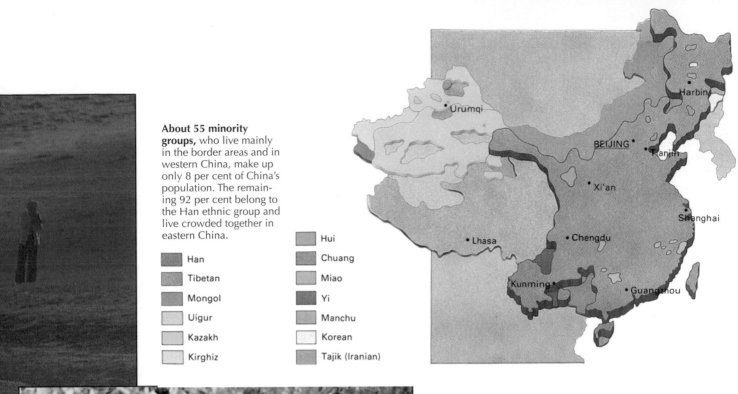

About 55 minority groups, who live mainly in the border areas and in western China, make up only 8 per cent of China's population. The remaining 92 per cent belong to the Han ethnic group and live crowded together in eastern China.

- Han
- Tibetan
- Mongol
- Uigur
- Kazakh
- Kirghiz
- Hui
- Chuang
- Miao
- Yi
- Manchu
- Korean
- Tajik (Iranian)

A group of Uigurs, *above,* listens to a musician playing a stringed instrument called a *rawap.* The Uigurs, who live in western Xinjiang province, are of Turkic origin.

A Hani woman in a brightly colored headdress pauses to pose for a photographer at a market place in Yunnan, along the border with Vietnam. The Hani people are among the many minority groups living in this part of southwestern China.

minorities form the majority of the population. The Tibetan people, who live in China's southwestern highlands, have fiercely resisted Chinese rule, and their language, culture, and religion differ radically from those of the Han Chinese. Most Tibetans, who constitute about 96 per cent of their region's population, are barley farmers or nomadic herders. They resent the Chinese government's attempts to change their agricultural methods.

The Uigurs and Kazakhs, who live in the deserts of northwestern China in the Xinjiang region, have also rebelled against the

Chinese. The Uigurs raise livestock and grow a wide variety of crops on oases in the deserts, while the Kazakhs herd sheep and goats. Both groups follow Islam—the major religion in the Middle East. Their language, clothing, architecture, and music also show Middle Eastern influence. Although Xinjiang is officially called a self-governing region, the Chinese government actually controls the area.

Many other minority groups live in the far southern parts of China. Although some of these groups speak Chinese dialects and live much like the Han Chinese, ethnic differences are strong among others. Many of these groups are related to the peoples of Myanmar, Laos, Vietnam, and Thailand. The people in several of these areas have adopted some aspects of Chinese culture, but more out of a fear of official displeasure than a fondness for the Han way of life.

For example, the T'ai people in the province of Yunnan, who are related to the people of Thailand, celebrate agricultural festivals and other special occasions with songs and dancing. However, during Mao Zedong's rule, dances that had been traditionally performed around harvest foods were done instead around a large picture of Mao.

Chinese Cities

Two of China's cities are among the largest in the world. The metropolitan area of Shanghai is second largest with more than 13 million people, and Beijing ranks fifth in the world with almost 11 million. These cities are also important manufacturing centers. Although the Communist government modernized many of China's cities to make way for factories, offices, and apartment buildings, some still preserve traces of their ancient past.

Xi'an

Xi'an lies in central China at the eastern end of the Silk Road, the great overland trade route that linked Rome to Chang'an (now called Xi'an). The ancient city of Chang'an, which means *eternal peace,* served as the capital of the Han (202 B.C.-A.D. 220), Sui (581-618), and Tang (618-907) empires. Chang'an had more than 1 million residents during the Tang period, making it the largest city in the world.

Chang'an declined after the fall of the Tang dynasty, and attempts to restore the city during the Ming dynasty (1368-1644) were short-lived. Two Buddhist temples—the Little Wild Goose Pagoda and the Big Wild Goose Pagoda—are among the buildings that have survived from the Tang dynasty. The massive Bell Tower standing at the crossroads of Xi'an's two main streets was built during the Ming dynasty.

Nanjing

People have lived in what is now the Nanjing area since about the 400's B.C. Nanjing, which means *southern capital,* was the seat of government during the first part of the Ming dynasty. It also served as the capital of the Republic of China from 1928 to 1937 and then again in 1946. Today, the city is the capital of Jiangsu Province and an important center of industry, transportation, and government in east-central China.

Nanjing lies on the Yangtze River, and wharves that can handle oceangoing ships line its banks. A 3-mile (5-kilometer), double-deck bridge completed in 1968 takes trains and motor vehicles across the Yangtze.

Suzhou

Sometimes called the "Venice of the East" for its many canals, Suzhou is best known for its beautiful classical gardens. The walled gardens were each created in a different style by Chinese scholars and artists between the 900's and 1900's. In the gardens, covered walks wind past ornamental ponds, summer houses, bamboo plants, and stones that are grouped to form tiny mountain ranges. The perfect harmony of the gardens expresses the Taoist ideal of achieving balance with nature and also reflects the quiet contemplation of Buddhism.

Shanghai

Shanghai, China's largest city, lies on the Huangpu River about 14 miles (23 kilometers) from the Yangtze River. The city's location near these important waterways helps make it China's leading port and industrial city.

Bicycles throng a tree-lined street in Suzhou during the early morning rush hour. Many of Suzhou's citizens work in silk factories, where they weave beautiful silk cloth. Silk manufacture in Suzhou began during the Song dynasty (960-1279).

The tomb of Sun Yat-sen, *right,* lies on Zijin Mountain, east of Nanjing. Sun, a Nationalist leader, helped establish the Republic of China in 1912. When the Nationalists, under Chiang Kai-shek, united China under one government in 1928, they made Nanjing their capital.

Tall buildings lining the Huangpu River in the northern part of Shanghai are a reminder of the city's past as an international free port. Shanghai was the center of European influence in China from about the mid-1800's to the early 1900's. Western powers made the city a world leader in trade and banking. South of the foreign section lies the original Chinese settlement—sometimes called the "Chinese City"—an area of residential and commercial buildings and narrow, twisting streets.

The heart of Shanghai lies in the old foreign section called the Bund, named after a broad boulevard near the Huangpu. When Great Britain forced China to open its doors to foreign trade in 1842, people from Britain, France, the United States, and other countries settled in this section of Shanghai. They built homes, churches, and office buildings in the Bund, giving much of the area a Western appearance. Today, many of the buildings constructed by Europeans and Americans in the 1920's stand empty or serve as schools.

A train crosses the double-deck bridge over the Yangtze River in Nanjing. China and the Soviet Union began joint construction of the bridge in the 1950's. However, when friendly relations between the two nations ended in the early 1960's, the Chinese completed the bridge on their own.

A street vendor sells soft drinks in the shadow of a statue of Mao Zedong, *left,* in a busy square in Chengdu. The city, the capital of Sichuan Province and a major industrial center in southern China, still has some of its traditional wooden houses and bustling markets.

261

Beijing

Beijing, also spelled *Peking,* is China's capital and second largest city with a population of about 6 million residents—only Shanghai has more people. Most of Beijing's residents belong to the Han ethnic group and speak Mandarin. Many of the minority groups in the city have adopted the customs and clothing of the Han.

Beijing, founded as a trading center nearly 4,000 years ago, has served as a center of government on and off for more than 2,000 years. *Beijing* means *northern capital.*

The city is part of the Beijing special municipal district, which has a population of about 9-1/2 million. The district includes the central city, called the Old City, and a series of suburbs with farmland beyond.

The Old City

The Old City consists of two large rectangular areas called the Inner City and the Outer City. Walls once surrounded both areas, but they are gradually being torn down.

The Forbidden City and the Imperial City lie within the Inner City. The Forbidden City includes the palaces of former emperors. Only members of the emperor's household could enter the Forbidden City—hence its name. The buildings in this part of Beijing are now preserved as museums.

The Imperial City, which surrounds the Forbidden City, includes lakes, parks, and the residences of China's Communist leaders. At the southern edge of the Imperial City stands the imposing *Gate of Heavenly Peace* (Tiananmen). This gate overlooks a huge square, the site of parades, fireworks displays, and many historic gatherings. On Oct. 1, 1949, Mao Zedong proclaimed the establishment of the People's Republic of China, with Beijing as its capital, to a crowd of thousands in Tiananmen Square. In June 1989, the square was the scene of another historic event—a massacre—when pro-democracy demonstrations led by Chinese students were crushed by the nation's army.

Commercial areas, residential areas, and parks make up much of Beijing's Outer

Shaded by a large umbrella, a policeman directs traffic in Beijing's Tiananmen Square. As in other Chinese cities, bicycles make up most of the traffic. The Great Hall of the People stands in the background.

Boating on the lake in Beihai Park near Beijing's Forbidden City is a favorite summertime activity.

The Temple of Heaven, or *Tiantan,* is a monument from China's imperial past. Architects from the Ming dynasty built the temple and many other buildings that still stand in Beijing's Old City.

The Beijing Zoo lies just outside of the Inner City. The giant panda, found only in western and southwestern China, is one of the zoo's main attractions.

City. The Temple of Heaven, where Chinese emperors used to pray for a good harvest, stands at the southern end of the Outer City.

The Summer Palace, which served as an imperial residence during the summer, lies northwest of the Old City of Beijing. The tombs of Ming emperors and Beijing University are also located in the northwest suburbs.

Many people in the Old City live in old, one-story houses that border the *hutongs* (narrow, treelined alleys) that branch out from the main streets. Vendors walk up and down the hutongs selling such foods as fish, noodle soup, and vegetables.

Modern Beijing

After the Communists took over in 1949, China's new rulers modernized the city. By the end of the 1950's, several new buildings had been erected around Tiananmen Square. These included the Great Hall of the People (China's parliament building), the Museum of the Revolution, and the Historical Museum.

Modern apartment buildings were constructed to house Beijing's growing population. The city's planners also built Beijing's main railroad station, an underground commuter line, and a new traffic system.

The development of industry after 1949 accounted for much of the city's growth. Today, its factories produce chemicals, electronic equipment, farm machinery, iron and steel, and textiles. In the 1980's, tourism also became an important industry in Beijing, but tourism in Beijing—and throughout China—dropped dramatically following the crackdown against the pro-democracy demonstrators in 1989.

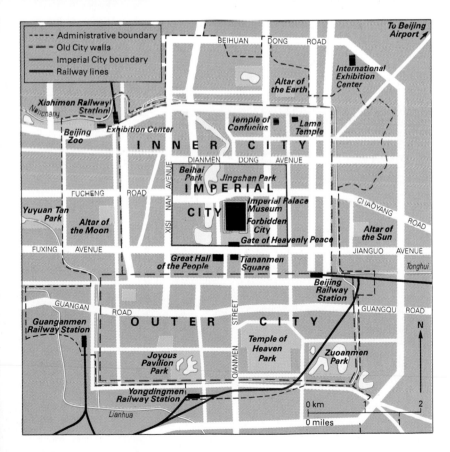

Beijing's Old City consists of the Inner City and the Outer City. East and south of the Old City lie suburbs, where many of Beijing's factories are located. Part of the Great Wall of China runs just north of Beijing. A major earthquake, centered in the nearby city of Tangshan, struck the Beijing area in 1976. The earthquake caused about 240,000 deaths and widespread property damage throughout China's northern region.

263

Hong Kong

Hong Kong is a special administrative region of China. It lies on the southern coast of China, near the mouth of the Zhu Jiang (Pearl River), about 90 miles (140 kilometers) southeast of China's Guangzhou Province.

Hong Kong consists of a peninsula, which is attached to mainland China, and more than 235 islands. The mainland area has two sections—the New Territories in the north and the Kowloon peninsula in the south. The main island, Hong Kong Island, lies south of the peninsula. Hong Kong covers a land area of only about 410 square miles (1,061 square kilometers), but about 6 million people live there. Hong Kong is one of the world's most densely populated places, with about 14,000 people per square mile (5,500 per square kilometer).

Rugged mountains and rolling hills cover much of Hong Kong. Some mountains in the New Territories rise more than 3,000 feet (910 meters) above sea level. Victoria Peak, on Hong Kong Island, is 1,818 feet (554 meters) high.

Only about 10 per cent of Hong Kong's land is suitable for agriculture. Throughout the New Territories, fields of rice, vegetables, and flowers lie crowded between areas of poor vegetation and rocky hillsides. Hong Kong's mountainous areas contain some mineral deposits, but mining has yielded very little.

About 95 per cent of Hong Kong's people live in urban areas and have jobs in factories, commerce, or the government. Most of the urban people live in Hong Kong City and Kowloon, the main centers of trade, finance, industry, and tourism. Many stores, open-air markets, hotels, and restaurants line the narrow streets of these crowded areas. Hong Kong City and Kowloon, which lie on opposite sides of Victoria Harbor, are connected by ferries that carry thousands of commuters every day.

People in rural areas of Hong Kong live in villages and raise crops and livestock. Although some farmers still plant and harvest crops by hand or with simple tools, modern farming methods and machinery have enabled many to increase their production.

An economic center

Hong Kong ranks among Asia's major ports, and serves as an important center of trade, finance, manufacturing, and tourism. Most of Hong Kong's economic activity takes place in two heavily populated urban areas—the northern part of Hong Kong Island, sometimes called Hong Kong City, and Kowloon on the southern part of the mainland. Victoria, the dependency's capital and financial center, lies on Hong Kong Island.

Hong Kong's status as a *free port* makes it an attractive trading partner. As a free port, Hong Kong collects no import duties on imported goods, and as a result many products can be bought and sold more cheaply there than in most other parts of the world. Also, with more than 100 foreign banks and an important stock exchange, Hong Kong ranks as the third busiest financial center in the world.

Hong Kong's history

Hong Kong was part of China from ancient times until the 1800's. Through treaty agreements, Hong Kong became a British dependency. Hong Kong came under Chinese control again on July 1, 1997.

About 90 per cent of Hong Kong's nearly 6 million people are Chinese. The non-Chinese residents include people from Australia, the United Kingdom, India, Japan, the United States, and Vietnam. For many years, English

Chinese and Western advertising dominates a wide shopping street in Hong Kong. The double-decker buses draw power from overhead cables and do not pollute the crowded urban areas.

The density of the skyline along the north shore of Hong Kong Island reflects how crowded Hong Kong is along the beautiful Victoria Harbor.

Street markets in Hong Kong sell clothing, jewelry, textiles, and a wide variety of other items to local residents and the more than 2 million tourists that visit Hong Kong each year.

was Hong Kong's official language, but few of the Chinese residents understood it. As a result, the government made Chinese the second official language in 1974.

British control of Hong Kong began when the United Kingdom acquired Hong Kong Island in 1842 and the Kowloon Peninsula in 1860 through treaty agreements with China. In 1898, China leased the New Territories to the United Kingdom for 99 years.

In 1842, Hong Kong had only about 5,000 people, but its population increased dramatically during the 1900's, when several waves of immigrants flooded the region. Many Chinese fled to Hong Kong during periods of upheaval in China. For example, Hong Kong's population grew to 500,000 after revolutionaries overthrew China's Manchu dynasty and established the Republic of China in 1911. After the Communists took over China in 1949, Chinese immigrants pushed the number of people in Hong Kong up to about 2 million. Then, in the late 1970's, thousands of Vietnamese fled Communist rule in their country and migrated to Hong Kong.

The Chinese Communist government never formally recognized the United Kingdom's control of Hong Kong, but it did not oppose it either because Hong Kong was of great value to China's economy. China earned money by selling food, water, raw materials, and manufactured products to Hong Kong. The Chinese government also owned a great deal of property in the region.

Nonetheless, in 1984, China and the United Kingdom agreed to transfer Hong Kong from British to Chinese rule in 1997, when the lease of the New Territories expires. Under the agreement, Hong Kong became a special administrative region (SAR) of China with a high degree of control over its affairs, except in foreign policy and defense. Hong Kong will also be allowed to preserve its capitalistic economy. These arrangements are to be in effect for at least 50 years after 1997.

The Hong Kong SAR retains its own executive, legislative, and judicial power. It may issue its own currency and passports, maintain its own customs force and police, and remain a free port.

Macao

Macao, a special administrative region of China, lies at the mouth of the Zhu Jiang (Pearl River), about 40 miles (64 kilometers) west of Hong Kong. The territory has an area of only about 6-1/2 square miles (17 square kilometers) and consists of the city of Macao, which occupies a peninsula, and three small islands. More than 90 per cent of the territory's 436,000 people are Chinese. Most of the rest are Portuguese or of Portuguese descent.

Some sections of Macao include modern high-rise hotels and apartment buildings. Gambling casinos, racetracks, and night clubs attract many tourists, mainly from Hong Kong. Macao's economy is based on tourism and light industry, chiefly the manufacture of fireworks and textiles.

A blend of cultures

Much of Macao combines both Chinese and Portuguese influences. In some areas of Macao, cobblestone streets are lined with old, pastel-colored houses much like those in Lisbon, the capital of Portugal. However, the Chinese *pedicab,* a two-wheeled cart pulled by a large tricycle, often bumps its way along these streets.

Roman Catholic churches in Macao resemble those built between the 1400's and the 1600's during Portugal's golden age of art. The facade of the São Paulo Cathedral, which is all that remains of the church after a fire in 1835, is one of the territory's most famous sights. Roman Catholic churches, however, are often located near Buddhist shrines, such as the ancient temple dedicated to A-Ma, the goddess of sailors and fishermen. Christian Portuguese settlers named Macao after this goddess. In addition, both Catholic and Buddhist festivals are celebrated in Macao.

Even the different cuisines of the two regions have been combined. Restaurants serve Chinese specialties with Portuguese wine and traditional Portuguese fish stew is eaten with chopsticks.

Past, present, and future

The Portuguese were the first Europeans to establish trade with China. In 1557, they leased Macao from China and established a

The ruined São Paulo Cathedral is one of Macao's most famous landmarks. Only the cathedral's ornate facade survived the fire that destroyed the rest of the building in 1835.

Macao's pastel-colored buildings, *right,* recall Lisbon, but the pedicabs parked in front of the buildings are typical of the Far East.

Portuguese settlement in the territory. Macao soon became the chief port for Portugal's trade operations in China and Japan and also served as the headquarters for Catholic missions in East Asia. A Portuguese governor was appointed to rule Macao's Portuguese settlers in 1680, but the Chinese retained complete authority over the territory itself and its native population.

Although Portugal's power had begun to decline by the 1600's, it held on to much of its empire—including Macao—well into the 1900's. During China's Cultural Revolution of the late 1960's, Portugal offered to return Macao to the Chinese, but China's Communist rulers refused the offer.

In the 1970's, Portugal's government ended the country's control of its colonies, but Macao remained a Portuguese territory. China allowed Portugal to retain Macao because Macao was contributing to China's economy. Macao bought almost all its food

Macao's casinos attract many visitors to the "Las Vegas of the East."

A busy cook, *right,* prepares Chinese and Portuguese snacks at a roadside stand in Macao's "night market."

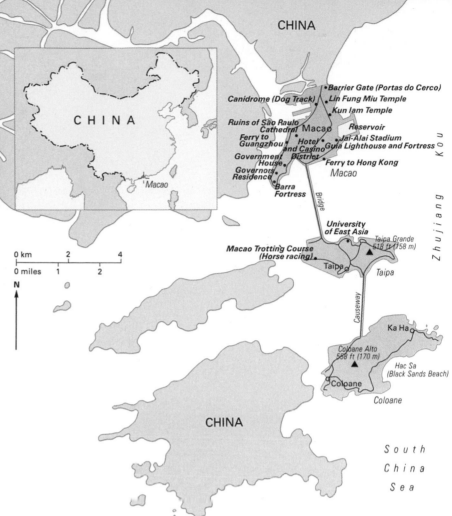

A Chinese astrologer, *below,* in Macao offers her predictions to customers at an outdoor stand. Although about 90 per cent of Macao's population is Chinese, both Chinese and Portuguese are the territory's official languages.

Macao, *map above,* lies at the mouth of the Zhu Jiang (Pearl River) on China's southeastern coast.

and drinking water from China, and these purchases provided China with foreign currency for international trade.

Portugal returned Macao to China in December 1999 under an agreement signed by both countries in 1987. As a special administrative region of China, Macao maintains separate political, judicial, and social systems from the rest of the country. China, however, appoints the chief executive of Macao.

The Yangtze River

The Yangtze River, also called Yangtze Kiang, runs for about 3,915 miles (6,300 kilometers) across China. The Yangtze is the third longest river in the world, and the longest and most important river in China. To most Chinese, the Yangtze is known as the *Chang Jiang,* or *long river.*

The Yangtze River has been called "China's equator" because it divides the wheat-growing northern half of the country from the rice-growing south. A large percentage of China's rice is grown along the Yangtze, as well as much of the country's cotton, corn, and wheat.

This great river has been one of China's most important transportation waterways for hundreds of years. In the 1200's, Marco Polo marveled at the number of ships on the Yangtze loaded with precious cargo, and ships and boats of all sizes loaded with cargo still travel the Yangtze today. About half of China's ocean trade is distributed over the Yangtze and its branches. Ocean steamers reach Wuhan—680 miles (1,090 kilometers) by river from the coast. Cargo boats and small wooden sailing craft called *junks* also travel the river, and thousands of Chinese live on the Yangtze in junks.

The river begins in the Tanggula Mountains of Qinghai Province near Tibet at an altitude of about 16,000 feet (4,880 meters). After crossing much of China, its waters empty into the East China Sea just north of Shanghai.

The Yangtze begins as little more than a trickle of water, flowing across the Plateau of Tibet in a shallow, wide valley. The high mountains at the Yangtze's source cause it to flow rapidly for most of its length. When the river goes south from the plateau to Yunnan, the rapid drop in elevation increases the speed at which the water moves. Deep gorges have been cut by the fast-flowing river in its upper course above Yichang.

From Yunnan, the Yangtze flows northeast across the Sichuan Basin. Here, too, the river has carved great gorges that make

The Yangtze River, the third longest river in the world, has many potential hydroelectric sites. The Gezhouba Dam near Yichang was the first hydroelectric plant constructed in China.

Towering gorges cut by the upper parts of the Yangtze River, *right,* make it one of the most beautiful rivers in the world. Mountains more than 1 mile (1.6 kilometers) high form the riverbanks in some areas.

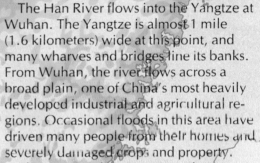

Yellow Sea

Grand Canal

Yangzhou • • Zhenjiang — Nantong
Nanjing • • Changzhou
Ma'anshan • • Wuxi • Suzhou
• Wuhu • Shanghai
• Fanchang
• Tongling
Grand Canal

Vanxian • Fengjie • Wushan • Xiling Gorge — Gezhouba Dam
Qutang Gorge • Wu Gorge • Badong • Yichang — Han Shui — Wuhan • — Anqing •
• Huangshi
Shashi • — Yangtze
Jiujiang • —
• Yuenyang — Poyang Lake
Dongting Lake — Nanchang •
Zi Shui — Gan Jiang
Changsha •

In Wuhan, a flight of steps takes travelers down to a wharf on the Yangtze. Ocean-going ships travel about 680 miles (1,090 kilometers) by river to reach Wuhan from the coast.

land travel difficult. Ships can travel east on the Yangtze into western Sichuan, but only small craft can navigate the four swift-flowing tributaries that flow into the river in this region.

In Sichuan, the Yangtze passes through Chongqing, a major center of industrial activity in western China. From the city's inland port, passenger ferries carry sight-seers east through the scenic landscape of the Three Gorges region and its steep lime-stone cliffs to the industrial center of Wu-han. The hydroelectric plant at Gezhouba Dam near Yichang also lies along the Yangtze River.

The Han River flows into the Yangtze at Wuhan. The Yangtze is almost 1 mile (1.6 kilometers) wide at this point, and many wharves and bridges line its banks. From Wuhan, the river flows across a broad plain, one of China's most heavily developed industrial and agricultural regions. Occasional floods in this area have driven many people from their homes and severely damaged crops and property.

The Yangtze then moves northeast to Nanjing and enters the Yangtze River Delta, which has the best combination of level land, fertile soil, and sufficient rain-fall in all China. The so-called Fertile Tri-angle between Nanjing, Shanghai, and Hangzhou is one of the most densely pop-ulated rural areas in the world with more than 5,000 people per square mile (1,900 per square kilometer).

Near Nanjing, the Grand Canal, a water-way built during the A.D. 500's and 600's, links the Yangtze with the Yellow River and China's northern cities. About 14 miles (23 kilometers) north of Shanghai, the Yangtze and the Huangpu rivers meet and empty into the East China Sea.

269

Agriculture

Agriculture is the foundation of China's economy, and about 70 per cent of all workers are farmers. In southern China, rice, sweet potatoes, and tea are the major crops. Wheat is the chief crop in the north, followed by corn and *kaoliang* (sorghum). China produces more cotton, pears, potatoes, rice, and tobacco than any other country and grows 75 per cent of the world's sweet potatoes. In addition, it is also a leading producer of apples, cabbages, carrots, corn, melons, rubber, sugar beets, sugar cane, tea, tomatoes, and wheat. Chinese farmers also raise a wide variety of other crops, including millet, peanuts, and soybeans. Farmers on Hainan Island grow tropical crops, such as bananas and pineapples.

Bountiful harvests

Although only about 13 per cent of China's land is suitable for farming, the country produces almost enough food for its huge population. The long growing season in southern China, where two or more crops can be grown on the same land each year, is an important factor in this achievement. Chinese farmers also practice *terracing*— growing crops on level strips of land cut out of hillsides—to utilize the fertile land in hilly or mountainous areas. In addition, they make extensive use of irrigation and organic fertilizers and practice soil conservation.

China's farm output has greatly expanded since the Communists took control of China. Although economic growth was slow at first, a series of reforms launched in 1978 vastly increased productivity.

Reforms and counter-reforms

During the 1950's, the Communists seized control of China's farmland and organized the peasants to farm the land cooperatively in units called *communes*. However, the commune system was not a success. Between 1957 and 1978, grain production rose only slightly, and China had to import large quantities of grain to feed its huge and increasing population. In addition, the standard of living on farms had not improved, and Chinese farmers were discouraged.

Commune farmers work together to gather in the wheat harvest. In the late 1980's, family-owned farms replaced many of the communes and only a few remain in existence in the 1990's.

A bridge spans a stream between terraced rice fields in southern China. Farmers use every bit of land they have to support themselves and feed the huge population of China.

In December 1978, the government decided that fundamental reforms in agriculture were needed and began loosening some of its control. Many months of discussions led to the adoption of a new policy that allowed individual families to farm more of the land. Under this system, each household received a plot of land and entered into a contract with the commune production team. According to the contract, the household gave a certain amount of its crops to the commune as its production quota and as payment for the use of the land. The farmer could then sell crops produced in excess of that amount on the free market.

The government also worked to increase farm production by using higher-yielding seeds, more machinery, more irrigation, and more chemical fertilizers. In addition,

rural workers were encouraged to specialize in crops, livestock, fisheries, or forestry.

As a result of these radical reforms, productivity rose sharply. In 1987, China produced 50 per cent more rice and wheat than it had under the commune system, and the production of eggs and livestock also increased. Most important, the standard of living in rural areas was greatly improved.

During 1988, however, China once again struggled with economic problems. Damage caused by droughts and floods destroyed more than 30 per cent of the country's crops, and grain had to be imported. China was not making enough money on exports to pay for all the imported goods that its people wanted. As a result, prices rose and runaway inflation followed.

The government reacted to the situation by cutting back on its economic reform program. Investments in industrial projects were decreased, and price controls on some staple foods were reimposed. In 1989, China's economy declined further due to the international reaction to the massacre in Tiananmen Square. As the economy slid into recession, conservative Chinese leaders called for greater government control and cuts in the people's private economic activity.

Farmers sell their own produce at an open market. Under the new economic system, each farm family assumes full responsibility for the entire process of production—from selecting the seeds to gathering the harvest.

China's huge farm output makes it the world's largest producer of agricultural products, *map below*. However, the country's average *per capita* (per person) income is very low. Economists consider China a developing country because it ranks low in per capita production.

Corn- and wheat-growing areas

Rice-growing areas

Northern limit of rice cultivation

Sorghum
Soybeans
Barley
Wheat
Cotton
Silk
Tobacco
Tea
Sugar cane

Intensive cultivation
Mainly cultivated
Grazing land
Forests
Unproductive

Shenyang
BEIJING
Shanghai
Chongqing
Guangzhou

Industry

In the early 1950's, China's industrial structure was modeled after the system that was in use in the Soviet Union. The government owned and operated all public enterprises and emphasized the development of heavy industry. Since 1949, China's industrial production has grown at an average annual rate of more than 12 per cent. Today, China has one of the world's largest and most rapidly growing steel industries. The machine-building industry provides metalworking tools and other machines for new factories. Other heavy industrial products include cement, fertilizer and other chemicals, irrigation equipment, locomotives, military equipment, ships, tractors, and trucks.

China has much of the energy and raw materials it needs to run these industries. The country is one of the world's largest producers of coal, and it also has rich deposits of oil. In addition, China is a leading producer of antimony, gold, iron ore, and tin. China also mines bauxite, lead, manganese, salt, uranium, and zinc.

Limited growth

Although the Chinese government achieved some industrial growth under its hard-line Communist policies, the Communist system also hampered efficiency, productivity, and incentive. All the workers were paid the same wage—regardless of the quality of their work—and all factories were supported by the government regardless of their performance.

In 1978, to help China's workers reach their full potential, the government developed a plan for restructuring industries similar to the strategy they had used in the agricultural sector.

Industrial reforms

Under the new reforms, an industrial enterprise paid a quota of its profit to a supervisory board but kept a share of any profits over and above the quota. These profits could be used for bonuses, employee benefits, and industrial improvements.

In 1984, a decree affirmed the government's intention to loosen its control of industry. The government, led by moderate reformers, envisioned a mixed econ-

The Chinese art of jade carving dates back to the 5000's B.C. Today, the principal jade-carving centers are Beijing, Shanghai, and Guangzhou. China imports nephrite, the chief source of jade, from New Zealand.

Construction of a dam on the Huang He nears completion. The construction industry boomed following the industrial reforms of the late 1970's and 1980's.

Artists put the finishing touches on richly decorated carpets, *above*. The production of textiles, such as these carpets, is one of China's major export industries.

A textile worker weaves silk yarns into fabric on an automatic power loom. China produces more raw silk than any other country, and silk cloth is an important product of China's textiles industry.

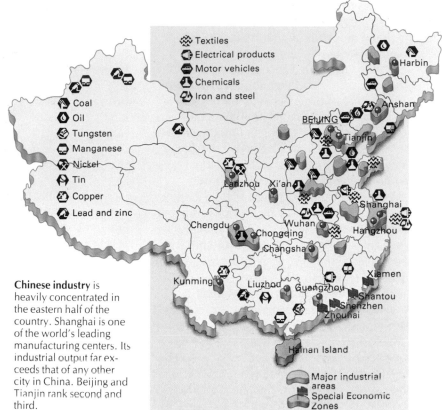

Chinese industry is heavily concentrated in the eastern half of the country. Shanghai is one of the world's leading manufacturing centers. Its industrial output far exceeds that of any other city in China. Beijing and Tianjin rank second and third.

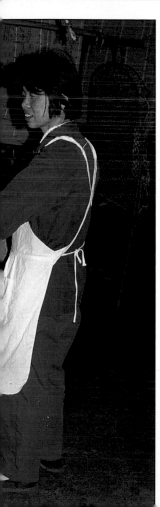

omy composed of both state-owned and privately owned enterprises. China also launched a more open foreign-trade program designed to help finance the modernization of its industries.

As industry rapidly progressed, the industrial workers' standard of living improved and their demand for such consumer goods as television sets, refrigerators, washing machines, and tape recorders grew. Many of these items had to be imported because China's own consumer goods production was basically limited to textile manufacturing and food-processing.

By mid-1988, however, China was not making enough money on exports to pay for all the imported goods that consumers wanted. Too much money was chasing too few goods—a classic cause of inflation.

Moderate Communist Party leaders argued that bolder reforms and increased free enterprise would solve China's economic problems. Conservative leaders, on the other hand, wanted more cautious changes that would ensure continued state control of the economy.

In June 1989, the student demonstrations in Beijing brought the debate to a head. The conservatives felt that the students were challenging China's Communist leadership, and they saw a clear connection between the economic reforms and the protests.

The military put down the demonstration by force, killing hundreds of demonstrators. Some foreign investment was suspended but later restored. China entered an economic boom that raised living standards for most of its people. In 1994, the Chinese economy was expected to grow by 11.5 per cent. But inflation continued, averaging 19.5 per cent in 1994.

By the mid-1990's, the Chinese government still owned about 100,000 businesses, mostly in heavy industry. The number of privately owned service industries has increased rapidly. Manufacturing is a large part of the economy, and Shanghai is one of the world's leading manufacturing centers. Amid growing demand for such consumer items as radios and watches, China is increasing production of these items.

273

Tibet

Tibet, a land in south-central Asia, is often called the *Roof of the World.* Its snow-covered mountains and its vast, windswept plateau are the highest in the world, and even the valleys in Tibet are higher than the mountains of most other countries. Some of Asia's greatest rivers begin in the Tibetan mountains, including the Brahmaputra, Indus, Mekong, Salween, and Yangtze rivers.

Although Tibet has been a part of China since the 1950's, it was an independent or semi-independent state for many years. While Tibet carried on some trade with other lands, its mountain ranges generally isolated the nation from the outside world. Many foreigners believed that Tibet was a hidden paradise, a land of mystics and magicians. The mysterious Tibetans themselves have sometimes been called the *hermit people.*

Myths about the land probably originated from tales of its people's culture and religion. Tibetans are intensely religious people who even turn prayer wheels and recite prayers on the streets. Tibet's religion is a branch of Buddhism called *Lamaism,* and the region was traditionally a *theocracy* (religious kingdom). Before China took control, Buddhist monks had a strong voice in the rule of Tibet.

Tibet has an area of 471,662 square miles (1,221,600 square kilometers)—much of it covered by a high, cold plateau called the Plateau of Tibet. High mountains border the plateau, including the snowy Himalaya along its southern end. The Himalaya, which rises higher than any other mountain chain in the world, includes Mount Everest, the world's highest mountain at 29,035 feet (8,850 meters) above sea level. Ka-erh, located more than 15,000 feet (4,570 meters) above sea level in western Tibet, is one of the highest towns in the world.

The Plateau of Tibet is dotted with hundreds of salt lakes and marshes, but many of them have a high salt content and barren shores. Tibet also has hilly grasslands and forests in its northern sections. However, large parts of the region are wastelands of gravel, rock, and sand where only the hardy Tibetan reed grass grows.

Tibet, part of China since the 1950's, lies in south-central Asia. It is bordered by India, Nepal, and Bhutan on the south and west.

Because of the poor soil and cold climate, most of the land cannot be farmed, but fertile areas in southern Tibet allow some farming and livestock raising. In the shadow of towering mountain peaks, farmers grow their crops—chiefly barley—and raise cows, goats, horses, poultry, and sheep. Most Tibetans live in the sheltered valleys of the south and southeast, and Lhasa, Tibet's capital and largest city, stands in this region.

Nomads roam the northern grasslands with their sheep and yaks. The domesticated yak is

Green fields line a fertile valley in southern Tibet. Most Tibetans live in the south, where the climate is less harsh and the soil is more suitable for farming.

The snow-covered peaks of the Himalaya, *right,* enclose the sparkling waters of a mountain lake in southern Tibet. Many peaks of the Kunlun range in northern Tibet rise more than 20,000 feet (6,000 meters).

The ruins of the Gandan monastery perch on the Plateau of Tibet. Many Lamaists left Tibet after the Chinese invaded the land in 1950 and removed the Buddhists from power.

Domestic yaks can carry heavy loads for 20 miles (32 kilometers) a day. The yak—well-suited for traveling across Tibet's rugged terrain—can slide down icy slopes, swim swift rivers, and cross steep rockslides.

used as a beast of burden in Tibet. The yak also supplies butter, cheese, meat, and milk, as well as hides for tents and shoes. Tibet's wild creatures include deer, gazelles, tigers, bears, monkeys, pandas, and wild horses. Some of these animals feed on the more than 5,000 different kinds of plants in Tibet. Dense forests of oak, pine, and bamboo flourish in the east and southeast.

Tibet has a severe climate. Winter brings sudden blizzards and snowstorms that can last for days, while fierce windstorms sweep Tibet in all seasons. January temperatures average 24° F. (−4° C), but often drop as low as −40° F. (−40° C). July temperatures average 58° F. (14° C). In addition, because the towering Himalaya shuts out moisture-bearing winds from India, much of Tibet receives less than 10 inches (25 centimeters) of rain annually.

Tibetan People and History

Tibet has a population of about 2 million people. About 96 per cent of the people are Tibetans, while most of the rest are Chinese. Most of the people live in southern Tibet, and many work as farmers. In Lhasa, which ranks as the region's largest city with a population of about 84,000, many people hold jobs in government, light industry, or tourism.

Although Mandarin Chinese is the official language, Tibet's main traditional language is Tibetan. Both languages are taught in schools, and all government documents are written in both languages.

Most Tibetan people live in small, one-floor homes with stone or brick walls and flat roofs. Houses built for the wealthy have three or four floors—animals are housed on the ground floor. Many Tibetans work in their homes in such traditional household industries as cloth weaving and carpet making. Wool is a major export.

Much of Tibetan life revolves around Lamaism. Religion is an important part of life, and festivals in Tibet are religious in character. Many people make long pilgrimages to important temples in Lhasa or Xigaze. The traditional emphasis on religious life has decreased, however, as a result of Communist Chinese rule.

Early history

During the A.D. 600's, Tibet became a powerful kingdom that played an important role in central Asia for 200 years. During this period, Buddhism and writing were introduced from India, and Lhasa was founded. Buddhism was eventually combined with traditional Tibetan religious beliefs to form Lamaism. The Lamaists built monasteries called *lamaseries,* which became political and educational centers in Tibet.

Between 900 and 1400, several Lamaist sects developed in Tibet. The most powerful was the Yellow Hat sect—so called because its monks wore yellow uniforms. Their leader, the Dalai (High) Lama, became the spiritual and political leader of Tibet in 1642.

A carpet seller, warmly bundled against the cold Tibetan winds, displays his wares on a street in Lhasa. Carpets are woven from yak wool, which is also used to make winter clothing. Lighter garments are made of hemp and cotton.

The Potala Palace in Lhasa, *right,* has gold-leaf roofs and more than 1,000 rooms. Formerly a residence of the Dalai Lama and other monks, it now houses a museum that has many art treasures.

Prayer flags and religious paintings decorate the rocks near a Tibetan monastery. Many of Tibet's monasteries were destroyed by the Chinese in the 1960's and 1970's, and many monks now work in agriculture and handicrafts.

A Tibetan potter fashions a bowl on a potter's wheel. The art of pottery making spread to Tibet from China. Much of Tibetan culture reflects both Chinese and Indian influences.

A rural trader fills a bucket with rich yak milk, *left*. In Tibet, yaks serve many of the same purposes served by cows in Western countries. The domestic yak even provides butter, which, together with salt and soda, is used to flavor tea.

China controlled Tibet from the early 1700's until 1911, when Tibetans forced out the Chinese troops. However, in 1950, China—under Communist rule—once again invaded Tibet. The Chinese claimed that they wished to liberate Tibetan farmers from serving the nobility and monks who owned the farmland. Most farmers were *serfs*—workers who were not free to leave the land—and much of what they produced had to be given to the landowners. In 1951, Tibet surrendered its sovereignty to the Chinese government, and China broke up the large estates of the monks and the nobility and distributed them among farmers.

Communist Chinese rule
The Communists agreed to allow Tibet

regional self-government, and they also promised to guarantee the Tibetans freedom of religious belief. However, by 1956, China had begun tightening its control of the region. The Chinese army forced the Tibetan peasants, who were used to growing barley, to grow wheat to feed the Chinese soldiers. China seized control of Tibet's media, banks, and food stores. The Chinese also took most of the best jobs, such as government administrators and teachers. In 1959, Tibet rebelled against Chinese rule. About 87,000 Tibetans were killed in the uprising, and the Dalai Lama fled to exile in India.

The people of Tibet continued to stage riots against the Chinese in the 1960's. The Chinese retaliated by closing or destroying most of Tibet's monasteries during the 1960's and 1970's.

In the 1980's, the Communist Chinese adopted a more liberal policy toward Tibet. Some monasteries were reopened, and farmers were allowed to decide for themselves which crops they would grow and sell. However, Tibetan demonstrations against the Chinese government in the late 1980's halted these reforms. Many Tibetans were killed in a demonstration in Lhasa in 1989, and hundreds of monks and nuns were imprisoned.

Colombia

The fourth largest South American country in area, Colombia is situated on the extreme northwest part of the continent. It is a nation with a troubled history. Years of suffering and devastation under Spanish rule were followed by periods of political disorder, as the country struggled to establish an orderly society and a democracy.

In addition, natural disaster struck Colombia in 1985, when an eruption of the Nevado del Ruiz volcano killed 25,000 people. Also in the 1980's, the illegal activities of the country's infamous drug dealers have caused a serious breakdown in law and order and many other problems for Colombia.

Colombia boasts some of the most varied and magnificent scenery in all of South America. Miles of sandy beaches lined with graceful palm trees stretch along its Caribbean and Pacific coasts, while the snow-covered peaks of the Andes tower high above the landscape. Banana, cotton, and sugar-cane plantations dot the sun-drenched lowland plains, and in the south, tropical rain forests rise up along the rivers that feed into the great Amazon.

A rich heritage

Adding to the charm of the Colombian countryside is the rich cultural heritage of its people. In the southern Andean region, for example, gigantic earthen mounds, stone statues, and tombs around San Agustín date from about the first 700 years A.D.—the relics of an advanced civilization.

Today, many exquisite works created hundreds of years ago by Indian goldsmiths are preserved in the famed *Museo del Oro* (Gold Museum) in Bogotá, Colombia's capital city. These masterpieces, including small statues and pieces of jewelry, are ranked among Latin America's greatest artistic treasures.

The most famous goldsmiths were the Chibcha Indians, who made *tunjos*—flat, stylized human figures with long bodies, large heads, and decorations of gold wire. The Chibcha were a peaceful tribe of farmers who lived in the eastern chain of the Andes, near the center of what is now Colombia. During Chibcha coronation ceremonies, the

new ruler was covered with gold dust to represent a god. Then he was rowed out to the middle of a lake and washed free of the gold dust to represent a human ruler.

The legend of El Dorado—a kingdom filled with gold and riches—grew out of this custom. Under the leadership of Gonzalo Jiménez de Quesada, Spanish explorers in search of El Dorado mercilessly conquered the peace-loving Chibcha and founded the city of Bogotá in 1538. Jiménez de Quesada named Bogotá the capital of what he called the New Kingdom of Granada.

From there, the Spaniards gradually spread throughout the region. The conquerors used the Indians as slave laborers, forcing them to mine emeralds, gold, and platinum. Along the Caribbean coast, black African slaves were brought in to work on the sugar-cane and cacao plantations.

Independence

Colombia finally broke free from Spanish rule in 1819 when the Venezuelan general Simón Bolívar defeated Spain in the Battle of Boyacá, near Bogota. The republic of Gran Colombia was established, which included what are now Colombia, Ecuador, Venezuela, and Panama. By 1830, Ecuador and Venezuela had become separate nations. Colombia lost Panama in 1903.

Almost from the beginning, the new nation was torn by disputes over how strong the central government should be. Those who favored a strong central government and a powerful role for the Roman Catholic Church became the Conservative Party. Members of the Liberal Party preferred strong regional governments.

Over the years, fighting between the groups often led to civil unrest and rioting, reaching a climax between 1948 and the 1960's. About 200,000 Colombians died during that period, known as *La Violencia* (The Violence).

Colombia Today

Unlike most other Latin-American countries, Colombia has had a government elected by the people through much of its history. Colombia is a republic, headed by a president who is elected to a four-year term. There is no vice president; instead, a presidential alternate, chosen by Congress every two years, performs executive duties in the absence of the president.

A history of violence

Despite its long tradition of democracy, Colombia has suffered years of political disorder and civil strife. By 1957, the turmoil created by *La Violencia* forced the Liberal and Conservative parties to form a *coalition* (joint government) to restore order in the country.

Violence erupted again in the 1970's and 1980's, however, as various groups protested against economic inequalities and the lack of government reforms. The death squads of the *Movimiento 19 de Abril* (M-19), an antigovernment guerrilla group that rose up in 1970, were responsible for a number of terrorist attacks.

In January 1994, gunmen thought to belong to *Fuerzas Armadas Revolucionarias de Colombia* (FARC) attacked rivals, killing 35 people. In July, FARC attacked government forces, leaving about 50 soldiers and 100 rebels dead. In February and April, about 800 guerrillas belonging to other groups disarmed in return for amnesty and low-interest loans.

Liberals and conservatives

The Liberal and Conservative parties were violently opposed to each other when they were founded in the 1800's, but the two parties have come to share many beliefs since the formation of the coalition. Nevertheless, their traditional differences remain. The Liberal Party continues to support regional government, religious tolerance, and the social and economic demands of the masses, while the Conservative Party prefers a highly centralized government managed by a small elite. In August 1994, Ernesto Samper Pizano became president after defeating the Conservative Party's candidate in the closest election in Colombian history.

Drug wars

It is estimated that about 80 per cent of the world's cocaine supply comes from Colombia, and a powerful organization of drug dealers operates from the city of Medellín. The activities of these "cocaine barons" are a constant threat to the political and economic stability of Colombia. Since the 1980's, the government has actively campaigned against

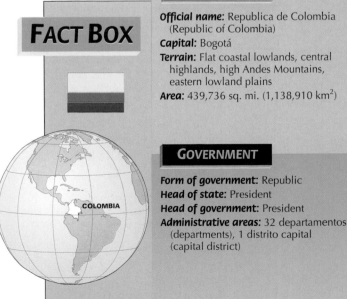

FACT BOX

COUNTRY

Official name: Republica de Colombia (Republic of Colombia)
Capital: Bogotá
Terrain: Flat coastal lowlands, central highlands, high Andes Mountains, eastern lowland plains
Area: 439,736 sq. mi. (1,138,910 km²)

Climate: Tropical along coast and eastern plains; cooler in highlands
Main rivers: Cauca, Magdalena, Guaviare, Meta, Caquetá
Highest elevation: Cristóbal Cólon, 18,947 ft. (5,775 m)
Lowest elevation: Pacific Ocean, sea level

GOVERNMENT

Form of government: Republic
Head of state: President
Head of government: President
Administrative areas: 32 departamentos (departments), 1 distrito capital (capital district)

Legislature: Congreso (Congress) consisting of the Senado (Senate) with 102 members serving four-year terms and Camara de Representantes (House of Representatives) with 166 members serving four-year terms
Court system: Corte Suprema de Justicial (Supreme Court of Justice), Council of State, Constitutional Court
Armed forces: 144,000 troops

PEOPLE

Estimated 2002 population: 43,755,000
Population growth: 1.68%
Population density: 100 persons per sq. mi. (38 per km²)
Population distribution: 71% urban, 29% rural
Life expectancy in years:
Male: 66
Female: 74
Doctors per 1,000 people: 1.2
Percentage of age-appropriate population enrolled in the following educational levels:
Primary: 112*
Secondary: 53
Further: N/A

Situated in the extreme northwest region of the continent, Colombia has been called the "Gateway to South America." It is the only South American country to have both Atlantic and Pacific coastlines.

High-rise office and apartment buildings are changing the skyline of Colombia's cities. The Spanish-style homes built during the colonial era—adobe structures with red tile roofs and patios—are rapidly disappearing.

the drug traffickers, but their efforts have been met with severe and violent resistance. In 1989, the U.S. government sent military advisers and equipment to help the Colombians in their fight against drug trafficking.

But in 1994, the campaign against the drug trade faltered. Leftist guerrillas and right-wing paramilitary groups further destabilized the government, which was accused of drug payoffs and political corruption. By late 1997, guerrillas controlled an estimated 50 per cent of Colombia.

In 1998, Andres Pastrana Arango was elected president and soon began peace talks with the FARC and the National Liberation Army (ELN), another left-wing guerrilla group. He withdrew government forces from about 16,000 square miles (41,400 square kilometers) of territory in southern Colombia, giving the FARC control over the area. Despite Pastrana's efforts to negotiate peace, the FARC and ELN continued to enlarge their forces and launch terrorist attacks. In 2002, Pastrana broke off talks with FARC rebels and sent Colombian military forces back into the FARC-held area in southern Colombia. That same year, Alvaro Uribe Velez was elected president of Colombia.

Land and Economy

Colombia's great variety in climate and landscape make it a land of seemingly endless contrasts. Although the country is situated entirely within the tropics—the equator crosses its southern region—parts of Colombia are quite chilly because of their high altitude. From the snow-capped peaks of the Andes Mountains in the west to the tropical rain forests in the south, Colombia's scenic landscape makes it a fascinating country to explore.

Landscape and climate

The Coastal Lowlands, the Andes Mountains, and the Eastern Plains make up Colombia's three main land regions. Most of the country's people live in the valleys and basins of the Andes. Many of Colombia's jungles are so remote that they have yet to be explored and mapped in detail.

The Coastal Lowlands lie along the Caribbean Sea and the Pacific Ocean. The two coasts differ greatly in character. The Caribbean Lowlands have about 20 per cent of Colombia's people and the nation's busiest seaports. The bustling cities of Barranquilla, Cartagena, and Santa Marta handle most of Colombia's foreign trade. Inland, large banana, cotton, and sugar-cane plantations, as well as cattle ranches and small farms, dot the landscape. By contrast, the Pacific Lowlands consist mostly of swamps and dense forests where heavy rains fall almost every day.

Three ranges of the Andes Mountains, separated by Colombia's two major rivers, cover about a third of the country. The Magdalena River separates the middle and eastern ranges of the Andes, while the Cauca River flows between the middle and western ranges. About 75 per cent of Colombia's people live within these mountain valleys and river basins. The region's rich mines, fertile farms, and large factories produce most of the country's wealth.

About 60 per cent of Colombia's land is covered by the warm, humid Eastern Plains—a sparsely populated area. Many rivers flow eastward across these plains to join the Orinoco and Amazon systems. In the north, cattle and sheep graze on the rolling grasslands known as the *llanos*, while the southern forests are home to scattered Indian tribes.

Economy

Colombia is still a developing country. Its economy has long been dependent on agriculture, and coffee is by far the leading export crop. Other major crops include bananas, cassava (a tropical plant with starchy roots), corn, cotton, potatoes, rice, and sugar cane.

Although agriculture still accounts for more than half of Colombia's export earn-

Blue waters and sunny beaches make Colombia's Caribbean coast a popular tourist spot. Since the 1970's, both government programs and private enterprises have been developing resort hotels and other tourist facilities in Colombia.

Swift-flowing rivers cut deep valleys through the soaring Andes peaks, *right,* where pure mountain waters tumble over the massive rocks. Farmers grow a wide variety of crops in the rich soil of the river valleys.

A coffee farmer removes the husks from beans to prepare them for market. Coffee shrubs thrive in the mild climate of the steep Andes slopes at altitudes of 4,200 to 6,000 feet (1,300 to 1,800 meters). Colombia is the world's second largest producer of coffee, surpassed only by Brazil, its huge neighbor to the east. Coffee-growing farms—many under 15 acres (6 hectares)—account for about 55 per cent of Colombia's cultivated land.

ings, government leaders have made some progress in decreasing the country's dependence on agriculture. Since the 1950's, manufacturing has grown steadily. Today, major manufactured products include cement, chemicals, metal products, processed foods and beverages, and textiles and clothing.

Colombia is rich in minerals, and mining is rapidly growing in importance. More than 90 per cent of the world's emeralds come from Colombia. The country also has valuable gold and platinum deposits, and its substantial copper, iron, nickel, lead, and other mineral reserves are important in the development of the nation's economy. For example, salt is mined for use in the chemical industry, and coal, petroleum, and natural gas provide fuel for the textile, food-processing, and cement industries.

Cowhands known as *llaneros* herd their cattle across a river in northeastern Colombia. Livestock breeding has long been an important industry in Colombia. Cattle and sheep are raised on large ranches for both meat and dairy products.

People

Like the people of most other South American countries, Colombians have widely different ethnic origins. A large Indian population lived in what is now Colombia when the first Spanish colonists arrived in the 1500's. After the Spaniards conquered the territory, they brought blacks from Africa to work alongside the Indians as slave laborers.

Ethnic groups

Over the years, many Indians, Spaniards, and blacks intermarried. *Mestizos*—people of mixed white and Indian ancestry—make up 50 to 60 per cent of Colombia's population. Between 15 and 25 per cent of Colombians are *mulattoes*—people of mixed white and black ancestry, while about 3 per cent are *zambos*—people of mixed black and Indian descent. About 4 per cent of Colombia's people are of unmixed black ancestry, and about 1 per cent are of unmixed Indian ancestry.

The remaining population consists of people of unmixed European ancestry, mainly descended from Spanish colonists. These people form most of the country's small upper class. Upper-class Colombians tend to socialize only with other upper-class Colombians. Traditionally, their wealth has come chiefly from large rural landholdings, but an increasing number of upper-class Colombians now earn their incomes from business and industry.

Each group has its own cultural heritage, but together these ethnic groups weave the rich, varied tapestry that makes up the Colombian national character. For example, the lively Afro-Caribbean rhythms of *La Cumbia*, the national dance, are a fascinating contrast to the haunting melodies played by the southern Andean Indians on flutes, stringed instruments, and drums.

Despite their ethnic differences, almost all Colombians speak Spanish, the country's official language. Rich or poor, mestizo or mulatto, the people of Colombia are very proud of their language. They consider it closer to the pure Castilian Spanish of Europe than the Spanish spoken in other Latin-American countries. They have even passed a law to protect their language from unnecessary change.

The central square in Silvia, a large town south of Cali in the Andes, provides a convenient spot for these Colombians to chat. Their traditional skirtlike garments and felt hats are now seen only rarely among Indians in Colombia's rural areas.

An Indian paddles a canoe along the Putumayo River, which forms Colombia's southern border with Peru. Only a few Indian tribes remain in Colombia, mostly in remote areas of the country.

City life

Most of Colombia's people live in the valleys and basins of the Andes Mountains in western Colombia. Only about 2 per cent of the population live in the warm, tropical lowlands of eastern Colombia.

A few small Indian tribes inhabit the great forests bordering the Amazon Basin, where they fish, hunt animals for food, and gather wild rubber. Indians who live in larger settlements on the dry La Guajira Peninsula, in the

Simón Bolíva[r]

1783	Born in Venezuela.
1810	Participates in throwing off Spanish rule in Caracas.
1811	Works for formal declaration of Venezuelan independence, which is made on July 5.
1813	Becomes dictator of Venezuela.
1814	Seizes Bogotá, Colombia.
1819	Defeats the Spaniards at Boyacá, Colombia, thereby liberating Colombia. Become[s] president of Gran Colombia[.]
1821	Defeats Spaniards at Carabobo, Venezuela.
1823	Becomes dictator of Peru.
1828	Survives assassination attem[pt.]
1830	Dies while leaving for Europ[e.]

extreme northwest, make their living by selling handcrafted textiles and hammocks.

The Colombian population is increasing rapidly, although the infant death rate among the nation's Indian population remains high. According to recent estimates, more than half of all Colombians were under 25 years old in 1990.

The rapid population growth, along with the massive wave of migration to the cities, has created serious social problems for Colombia. Unskilled rural laborers, seeking an escape from their backbreaking, low-paying work on the land, continue to pour into the

Most rural families in the Colombian Andes earn their living by growing crops on a small plot of land. They often live together in extended family groups, with several generations under one roof.

Bales of *agave* plant fibers await shipment from a Colombian warehouse. The agave is a desert plant with rigid, fleshy leaves that is grown on the dry plateau between the Andes ranges. Long, tough fibers separated from the leaves are used to make rope and cord.

nation's urban areas. There, they settle in huge, sprawling slums called *tugurios,* only to face unemployment or a low-paying job.

These urban poor raise large families in shacks made of tin, cardboard, and other scrap materials. Many parents abandon their children because they cannot afford to feed them.

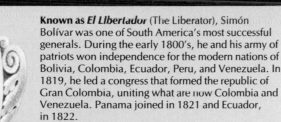

Known as *El Libertador* (The Liberator), Simón Bolívar was one of South America's most successful generals. During the early 1800's, he and his army of patriots won independence for the modern nations of Bolivia, Colombia, Ecuador, Peru, and Venezuela. In 1819, he led a congress that formed the republic of Gran Colombia, uniting what are now Colombia and Venezuela. Panama joined in 1821 and Ecuador, in 1822.

Bolívar became dictator of Peru in 1823. His army won a victory over the Spaniards at Ayacucho in 1824, which ended Spanish power in South America. Upper Peru became a separate state, named Bolivia in Bolívar's honor, in 1825.

Bolívar hoped to form a union of the new South American nations against Spain, having close relations with the United States. But his hopes were not achieved. By 1830, the republic of Gran Colombia had split into three separate countries.

Feelings against Bolívar grew violent. He resigned as president of Colombia in 1830.

Colombian Gold

In the 1530's, when Gonzalo Jiménez de Quesada led his expeditions into the highland valleys of the Andes, he and his fellow conquistadors had one goal: to find the legendary riches of El Dorado. Although the kingdom of El Dorado was never found, the quest for this mythic land of gold altered the course of South American history. Fired by greed and hungry for glory, the Spanish conquistadors marched boldly over the mountains and across the plains—and changed the face of Colombia forever.

The legend of El Dorado may have grown out of a Chibcha Indian coronation ceremony, during which, according to tradition, the new ruler was covered in gold dust and rowed out to the middle of the lake. It was said that the boat contained many objects made of gold and emeralds. According to legend, as the gold dust was washed off the new ruler, the priceless objects were cast into the lake as offerings to the gods.

Other Indian tribes told stories about this custom to the Spanish conquistadors. The Spanish assumed that any land with such a custom must be full of treasures. They called the Indian ruler in the stories *El Dorado* (the Golden One). Later, the legendary kingdom also came to be called El Dorado.

Numerous expeditions into South American territory in search of El Dorado's wealth were led by explorers, including Gonzalo Pizarro, who left Quito (in present-day Ecuador) to strike out across the Andes, and Francisco de Orellana, who followed the course of the Napo and Amazon rivers.

By then, the Chibcha, whose coronation ceremony had created such a powerful myth, had been conquered by Jiménez de Quesada's armies. Their people were enslaved, their culture was devastated, and the Chibcha civilization was soon destroyed by the invaders' invincible greed.

Given time, the Chibcha might have developed an empire as great as that of the Incas of Peru. No one will ever know. All that remains of their culture today is the magnificent goldwork that somehow escaped the Spanish melting pots. Now displayed in the Gold Museum in Bogotá, the beauty of these

masterpieces is especially haunting because it was the Chibcha's remarkable talent as goldsmiths that helped bring about their downfall.

When the Spaniards first swarmed over the rocky hills into Chibcha territory, they found fortified towns, organized into two loose confederations. The wooden houses of the Chibcha were covered inside and out with clay and cane to keep out the mountain cold. Some—perhaps those of the wealthier families—even had cotton curtains in the windows and ornamental gold plates above the doorways.

The Chibcha were a farming people who cultivated fields of beans, corn, cotton,

Only 8 inches (20 centimeters) long, this small golden replica of a raft, *above,* was found at the edge of Lake Siecha, one of the Chibcha's sacred lakes. It appears to depict the coronation ceremony that grew into the legend of El Dorado.

potatoes, and tobacco. They were also accomplished weavers and potters. But their greatest skill was their exquisite goldworking, and they cast, welded, and hammered this precious metal into magnificent earrings, necklaces, nose ornaments, masks, pendants, breastplates, bells, and bracelets.

The Chibcha also sculpted a variety of small figures out of pure gold, such as frogs,

Stunning artifacts, *right,* from Bogotá's Gold Museum display the artistry of the Chibcha Indians. The pieces show distinctive stylistic markings, including large ear disks.

Lake Guatavita is believed by some historians to be the site of the ceremony that inspired the legend of El Dorado. Beginning in 1562, several attempts were made to drain the lake, and gold objects were found buried in its muddy bottom. In 1965, the Colombian government prohibited all further privately sponsored "treasure hunts."

A present-day inhabitant of the Colombia highlands displays her gold teeth, *above*. The gold-working for which her ancestors were famous led early explorers to believe that the Andes contained large deposits of the precious metal.

birds, snakes, and fish. Using the simplest tools, they created objects that even the artisans of today find difficult to reproduce.

The Chibcha way of life ended in the 1530's when, forced to defend their land against the Spanish invaders, they were quickly and brutally defeated. Tales of Chibcha chiefs weighed down by gold ornaments, face masks, and breastplates as they marched into battle—desperate to save their land and liberty—have kept the myth of El Dorado alive for hundreds of years.

Comoros

The small African nation of Comoros consists of three main islands—Anjouan, Grande Comore, and Moheli—and several smaller ones. A fourth main island—Mayotte—is claimed by Comoros, but remains under French rule.

The first people who lived on the Comoros Islands came from mainland Africa, Madagascar, and Malaysia. In the 1400's, Arabs took over the islands and ruled each one as a separate kingdom. France seized Mayotte in 1843 and had gained control of the rest of the island group by 1886.

The French granted the Comoros Islands self-rule in 1961. In 1974, Anjouan, Grande Comore, and Moheli voted for complete independence. But Mayotte voted to keep French rule then, and again in 1976.

In 1978, Ahmed Abdallah Abderemane was elected president, but he actually was installed in the office with the help of European *mercenaries* (hired soldiers) who held much power themselves. In 1989, Abderemane was assassinated. French troops took control of Comoros and expelled the mercenaries. Said Mohamed Djohar was elected president in March 1990.

In 1997, separatists on Anjouan and Moheli each declared independence, claiming the central government had neglected their political and economic needs. The central

government did not recognize the independence claims. In April 1999, military leaders overthrew the elected government of Comoros. In December 2001, voters approved a new constitution that was designed to give greater autonomy to the three main islands of Comoros.

Comoros is one of the world's poorest nations. The country spends more than twice as

The beautiful islands of Comoros, *right,* have many exotic plants and animals that are found nowhere else but nearby Madagascar. Most of the islands were formed by volcanic activity.

FACT BOX

COUNTRY

Official name: Republique Federale Islamique des Comores (Federal Islamic Republic of the Comoros)
Capital: Moroni
Terrain: Volcanic islands, interiors vary from steep mountains to low hills

Area: 863 sq. mi. (2,235 km²)
Climate: Tropical marine; rainy season (November to May)
Highest elevation: Le Kartala, 7,746 ft. (2,361 m)
Lowest elevation: Indian Ocean, sea level

GOVERNMENT

Form of government: Independent republic
Head of state: President
Head of government: Prime minister
Administrative areas: 3 islands with 4 municipalities

Legislature: Comoros's Federal Assembly was dissolved following the coup of April 30, 1999
Court system: Cour Supremes (Supreme Court)
Armed forces: N/A

PEOPLE

Estimated 2002 population: 582,000
Population growth: 3.05%
Population density: 674 persons per sq. mi. (260 per km²)
Population distribution: 71% rural, 29% urban
Life expectancy in years:
Male: 54
Female: 59
Doctors per 1,000 people: N/A
Percentage of age-appropriate population enrolled in the following educational levels:
Primary: N/A
Secondary: N/A
Further: N/A

COMOROS

Most of the Comoros Islands were formed by volcanoes, and lava from the volcanic peaks has created plateaus and valleys. Swamps lie along almost all the shorelines. Heavy rains from November through April provide the islands with their only natural source of drinking water. The people store the rain water for use from May through October.

Hunger and disease are major problems on the Comoros Islands. Illness and malnutrition occur frequently due to poor diet, and the people suffer from a shortage of doctors and hospitals.

Most of the people of Comoros have mixed ancestry. They are descendants of Arabs, black Africans, and other groups. Most Comorans are Muslims and speak Arabic or the African language of Swahili. Many also understand French, the country's official language, even though most Comorans do not speak or write it.

The population lives mainly in rural villages. Moroni, the capital and largest city, lies on the west coast of Grande Comore Island. The city has just over 17,000 people, but Muslims from many countries come to visit Moroni's beautiful *mosque*.

The people of Comoros have mixed ancestry. They are largely descendants of Arabs, black Africans, and other groups.

much money for imports as it earns from exports. It has no major industry, and no valuable minerals have been found there.

The economy of Comoros depends almost entirely on agriculture. About 85 per cent of its workers farm for a living, raising such food crops as bananas, coconuts, and rice. In addition, the country must import large amounts of rice and other food because good farmland is scarce.

Comoros is an island nation that lies in the Indian Ocean between the African mainland and the large island of Madagascar. Both Comoros and France claim the island of Mayotte.

Languages spoken:
Arabic (official)
French (official)
Comoran (a blend of Swahili and Arabic)

Religions:
Sunni Muslim 98%
Roman Catholic 2%

TECHNOLOGY

Radios per 1,000 people: N/A

Televisions per 1,000 people: N/A

Computers per 1,000 people: N/A

ECONOMY

Currency: Comoran franc

Gross national income (GNI) in 2000: $212 million U.S.

Real annual growth rate (1999–2000): -1.1%

GNI per capita (2000): $380 U.S.

Balance of payments (2000): N/A

Goods exported: Vanilla, ylang-ylang, cloves, perfume oil, copra

Goods imported: Rice and other foodstuffs, consumer goods; petroleum products, cement, transport equipment

Trading partners: France, United States, South Africa

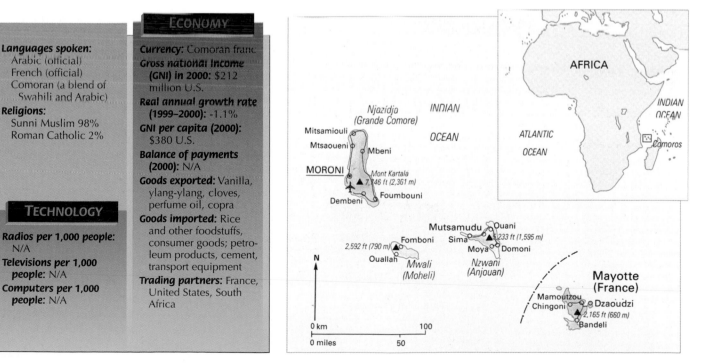

Congo (Brazzaville)

The hot, humid country of Congo lies in west-central Africa, directly on the equator. The country takes its name from the Congo River, which flows along much of its eastern border. Its name in French, the official language, is Républic du Congo (Republic of the Congo). It is called Congo (Brazzaville) to distinguish it from its neighbor Congo (Kinshasa).

Land and economy

Thick tropical rain forests of tall trees, tangled bushes, and lush vines cover the northern half of Congo. Many exotic animals live in this section of the country, which forms part of the Congo River Basin.

South of the river basin, in central Congo, is the Batéké Plateau, a grassy plain divided by deep, forested valleys. Still farther south lies Stanley Pool, a lake formed where the Congo River widens. Brazzaville, the capital city of Congo, is located on Stanley Pool.

To the west of Stanley Pool is the Niari Valley, a farming region covered by both woods and grassland. At the Mayombé Escarpment, a series of ridges and plateaus west of the valley, the land drops down to the Coastal Plain. This 40-mile (64-kilometer) stretch of land is cooler and drier than the rest of Congo because of the cold Benguela ocean current.

A gold-mining camp on the Mayombé Escarpment consists of tin-roofed shacks amid dense tropical woods, *right*. Congo has poor soil but several mineral resources, including petroleum, lead, natural gas, potash, and zinc.

FACT BOX

CONGO (BRAZZAVILLE)

COUNTRY

Official name: Republique du Congo (Republic of the Congo)
Capital: Brazzaville
Terrain: Coastal plain, southern basin, central plateau, northern basin
Area: 132,047 sq. mi. (342,000 km²)

Climate: Tropical; rainy season (March to June); dry season (June to October); constantly high temperatures and humidity; particularly hot and humid along the Equator
Main rivers: Congo, Ubangi, Kouilou
Highest elevation: Mount Berongou, 2,963 ft. (903 m)
Lowest elevation: Atlantic Ocean, sea level

GOVERNMENT

Form of government: Republic
Head of state: President
Head of government: President
Administrative areas: 9 regions, 1 commune

Legislature: National Transitional Council with 75 members
Court system: Cour Supreme (Supreme Court)
Armed forces: 10,000 troops

PEOPLE

Estimated 2002 population: 3,105,000
Population growth: 2.23%
Population density: 24 persons per sq. mi. (9 persons per km²)
Population distribution: 59% rural, 41% urban
Life expectancy in years: Male: 44 Female: 50
Doctors per 1,000 people: 0.3
Percentage of age-appropriate population enrolled in the following educational levels: Primary: 57 Secondary: N/A Further: N/A
Languages spoken: French (official) Lingala and Monokutuba (lingua franca trade languages)

Although building and maintaining roads in Congo is difficult because of the heavy rains and thick forests, the country has one of the longest transportation systems in Africa, mainly because of the Congo-Ubangi river system. Boats carry goods between countries to the north and as far south as Stanley Pool. At that point, rapids prevent boats from getting to the ocean, so the Congo-Ocean railroad was built to link Brazzaville on Stanley Pool with Pointe-Noire on the Atlantic.

People

Most of Congo's people live near Brazzaville or Pointe-Noire. They raise bananas, corn, rice, and other crops.

The Congolese belong mainly to four black African ethnic groups. About 45 per cent are Kongo farmers who live west and southwest of Brazzaville, about 20 per cent are Batéké hunters and fishermen who live north of the capital, and about 10 per cent are M'Bochi people, who work mainly as clerks and technicians. The fourth major group, the Sangha, live in the north.

Politics

Congo was part of French Equatorial Africa from 1880 until it became an independent nation on Aug. 15, 1960. Fulbert Youlou became the country's first president. But he was forced to resign in 1963, and a socialist government led by Alphonse Massamba-Debát took control. A military coup removed Massamba-Debát from office in 1968, and a one-party state was established. Congo remained a one-party state until Jan. 1, 1991, when opposition political parties were legalized.

In 1992, voters approved a new constitution and elected Pascal Lissouba as president. In December 1993, ethnic strife broke out and continued through January 1994. Violence flared up again in June, raising fears that the new democracy could unravel.

In 1997, rebels led by former dictator General Denis Sassou-Nguesso overthrew Lissouba's government. Sassou-Nguesso declared himself president. In 1998, delegates from many of the country's political parties elected 75 members to a National Transitional Council to act as the country's legislature until national elections could be held. A new constitution was to be drafted and voted on before the elections.

many local languages and dialects with Kikongo having the most users

Religions:
Christian 50%
animist 48%
Muslim 2%

ECONOMY

Currency: Communaute Financiere Africaine franc

Gross national income (GNI) in 2000: $1.7 billion U.S.

Real annual growth rate (1999–2000): 7.9%

GNI per capita (2000): $570 U.S.

Balance of payments (2000): N/A

Goods exported:
Mostly: petroleum
Also: lumber, plywood, sugar, cocoa, coffee, diamonds

Goods imported: Petroleum products, capital equipment, construction materials, foodstuffs

Trading partners: United States, France, Benelux

TECHNOLOGY

Radios per 1,000 people: 123

Televisions per 1,000 people: 13

Computers per 1,000 people: 3.5

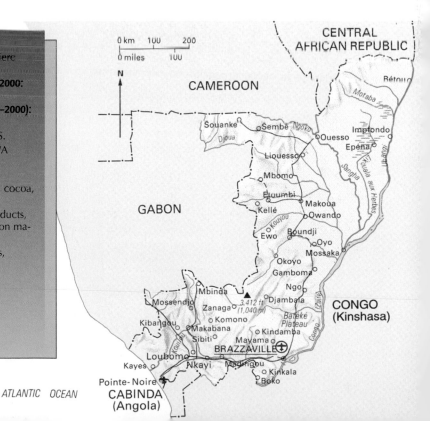

Congo (Kinshasa)

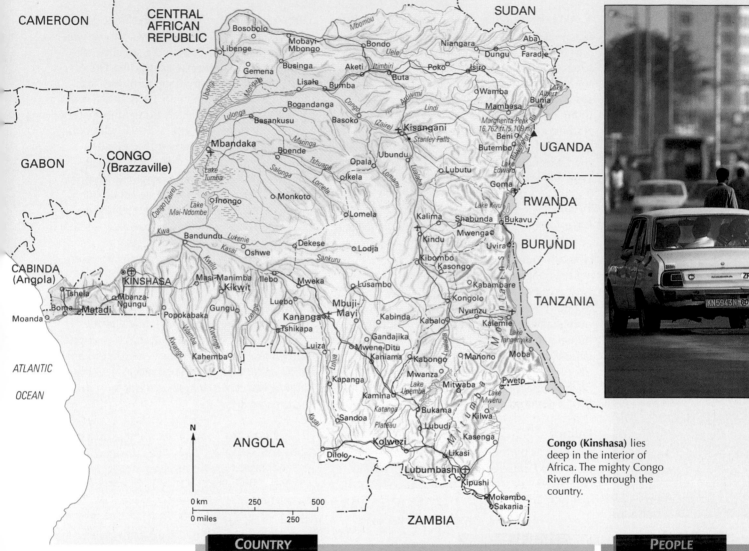

Congo (Kinshasa) lies deep in the interior of Africa. The mighty Congo River flows through the country.

FACT BOX

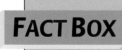

CONGO (KINSHASA)

COUNTRY

Official name: Republique Democratique du Congo (Democratic Republic of the Congo)

Capital: Kinshasa

Terrain: Vast central basin is a low-lying plateau; mountains in east

Area: 905,568 sq. mi. (2,345,410 km²)

Climate: Tropical; hot and humid in equatorial river basin; cooler and drier in southern highlands; cooler and wetter in eastern highlands; north of Equator, the wet season is April to October, dry season December to February; south of Equator, the wet season is November to March, dry season April to October

Main rivers: Congo, Ubangi, Aruwimi, Lomami, Kasai

Highest elevation: Pic Marguerite on Mont Ngaliema (Mount Stanley), 16,765 ft. (5,110 m)

Lowest elevation: Atlantic Ocean, sea level

GOVERNMENT

Form of government: Dictatorship

Head of state: President

Head of government: President

Administrative areas: 10 provinces, 1 city

Legislature: Transitional Constituent Assembly with 300 members established in 2000.

Court system: Cour Supreme (Supreme Court)

Armed forces: 55,900 troops

PEOPLE

Estimated 2002 population: 54,768,000

Population growth: 3.19%

Population density: 60 persons per sq. mi. (23 per km²)

Population distribution: 71% rural, 29% urban

Life expectancy in years: Male: 47 Female: 51

Doctors per 1,000 people: 0.1

Percentage of age-appropriate population enrolled in the following educational levels: Primary: 46 Secondary: 18 Further: 1

The huge country of Congo (Kinshasa) lies in the heart of Africa. Only a narrow strip of land that stretches west to the Atlantic Ocean keeps the country from being landlocked.

One of the world's largest and thickest tropical rain forests covers most of northern Congo. Its extraordinary variety of trees and plants grow so close together that sunlight seldom reaches parts of the forest floor. Grassy savannas cover much of southern Congo. The country is known as Congo (Kinshasa) to distinguish it from neighboring Congo (Brazzaville). The nation was known as Zaire from 1971 to 1997.

History

People have lived in Congo since prehistoric times. At least 2,000 years ago, other Africans began moving into the area.

Beginning in the early 1500's, thousands of Africans in the area were enslaved and sold to the Portuguese and other Europeans. The slave trade ended in the early 1800's. In 1878, King Leopold II of Belgium hired a British explorer, Henry M. Stanley, to set up Belgian outposts along the Congo River. Leopold eventually gained control of the entire region and made it his personal colony, called the Congo Free State.

The people of the Congo Free State suffered horribly under Leopold's rule. Other countries protested, and in 1908, the Belgian government responded by taking control from the king.

Belgium refused to give the people any voice in their government. In 1959, rioting broke out against Belgian rule, and on June 30, 1960, the colony was granted independence. The name of the new nation was Congo.

Civil war followed independence, as rival groups fought for power. Then in 1965, the Congolese army took control of the government, and General Joseph Désiré Mobutu became president. In 1971, he changed the name of the country to Zaire.

A troubled government

Etienne Tshisekedi, an opponent of Mobutu, was elected prime minister in October 1991. Mobutu tried to remove Tshisekedi and, in 1994, named Kengo wa Dondo as a new prime minister. Tshisekedi claimed he was still the legal prime minister.

In 1996, the government attempted to repatriate millions of Rwandans and many thousands of Burundians who were living in refugee camps. But fighting broke out as government troops fought refugee militias. Rebel militias opposed to the Mobutu regime also engaged government troops.

In May 1997, the rebels, led by Laurent Kabila, marched into Kinshasa. Mobutu fled the country, and Kabila was sworn in as president on May 29. Kabila renamed the country the Democratic Republic of Congo.

In 1998, Congo suffered through the second civil war in three years. As in 1996, the rebellion began when the Congolese Tutsi community fought against persecution by government-controlled Hutu forces. The rebels were backed by troops from Rwanda and Uganda.

In 1999, Congo, the rebels, and the other countries involved in the conflict signed a cease-fire agreement. In 2000, the United Nations sent a peacekeeping force to Congo.

In 2001, Kabila was assassinated. Kabila's son, Joseph, succeeded him and tried to establish peace.

By October 2002, nearly all foreign troops on both sides of the war, including all Rwandan troops, had left Congo. In December, the Kabila government signed a power-sharing agreement with the Rwandan- and Ugandan-backed rebel groups and political opposition groups. However, some fighting continued in northeastern Congo.

Kinshasa, *above*, is a busy, thriving city, but modern road transportation is rare in Congo. Fewer than 1 per cent of the people own an automobile, and most roads are unpaved.

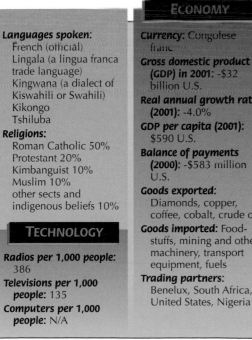

Languages spoken:
French (official)
Lingala (a lingua franca trade language)
Kingwana (a dialect of Kiswahili or Swahili)
Kikongo
Tshiluba

Religions:
Roman Catholic 50%
Protestant 20%
Kimbanguist 10%
Muslim 10%
other sects and indigenous beliefs 10%

TECHNOLOGY

Radios per 1,000 people: 386

Televisions per 1,000 people: 135

Computers per 1,000 people: N/A

ECONOMY

Currency: Congolese franc

Gross domestic product (GDP) in 2001: -$32 billion U.S.

Real annual growth rate (2001): -4.0%

GDP per capita (2001): $590 U.S.

Balance of payments (2000): -$583 million U.S.

Goods exported: Diamonds, copper, coffee, cobalt, crude oil

Goods imported: Foodstuffs, mining and other machinery, transport equipment, fuels

Trading partners: Benelux, South Africa, United States, Nigeria

People and Economy

When Congo became independent in 1960, Europeans greatly influenced the country's cultural life and economy. Deep divisions existed among the various ethnic groups, and the country faced severe economic problems. Since independence, Congo's leaders have worked to reduce European influence, unite the people, and improve the economy.

More than 99 per cent of Congolese are black Africans, but they belong to many different ethnic groups. Tension between these groups has caused a great deal of conflict.

Congo's people also include the Pygmies, whose ancestors lived in the region thousands of years ago, and Europeans, especially Belgians. In addition, about a million refugees who have fled from neighboring war-torn countries, such as Angola, Burundi, Rwanda, and Uganda, live in Congo.

French is the nation's official language. It is used by government officials and taught in many schools, but most of the country's ethnic groups have their own language that the people use in their everyday lives. About 200 languages are spoken, but most belong to the Bantu language group and thus are closely related. In addition, most Congolese speak one of the country's four regional languages—Kikongo, Lingala, Swahili, and Tshiluba.

About 7 of every 10 Congolese live in rural areas, mainly in small villages that range from a few dozen to a few hundred people. Their houses are made from mud bricks or dried mud and sticks. Most of the homes have thatched roofs, but the houses of more well-to-do rural families have metal roofs. In some areas, people pound out rhythms on drums to send messages from village to village.

The great majority of rural families farm small plots of land and grow almost all their own food, including bananas, cassava, corn, peanuts, and rice. The basic Congolese dish

Congolese dancers sport fantastic costumes that express the ferocity of jungle beasts. Many local African religions include the *animistic* belief that all things in nature have a spirit.

A young miner, *left,* at Kalima, in east-central Congo, removes tin from ore by repeated washings. Tin is just one of the country's many valuable mineral resources.

A Congolese villager, *below,* bathes in one of the many small rivers that flow into the Congo. Many rural people suffer from malnutrition because their diet often lacks protein.

is a porridge of grain and cassava, served with a spicy sauce.

Crops raised for sale include cacao, coffee, cotton, and tea. Few farmers can afford modern equipment. As a result, production is low, and most farm families are poor.

Since independence, large numbers of Congolese—especially young people—have moved to urban areas seeking work. Today about 30 per cent of Congolese live in cities, and this rapid urban growth has caused such problems as unemployment and crowded living conditions. Government officials and business people live in attractive bungalows, but large numbers of urban factory and office workers are crowded into small, flimsy houses made of cinder blocks or mud bricks.

Congo is a poor country with a developing economy. Urban factory workers produce relatively small amounts of manufactured goods, mainly beer, cement, processed foods, soft drinks, steel, textiles, and tires. Many manufactured goods are imported.

Copper is the country's most important mineral resource. Congo ranks among the leading copper-producing nations and leads the world in producing industrial diamonds, its second most important mineral. Oil deposits lie off the coast, and the nation also has deposits of cadmium, cobalt, gold, manganese, silver, tin, and zinc.

Civil war throughout the late 1990's brought Congo's economy almost to a standstill. Most exports stopped, the mining industry almost shut down, and most cities lacked electricity. Inflation ran at an annual rate estimated at up to 12,000 per cent. Widespread malnutrition and a substantial increase in AIDS cases added to the woes of Congo's people.

A thick blanket of mist covers the dense tropical rain forest of Congo. Because of the lack of open space, few people live in the forest, but its trees yield palm oil, rubber, and timber.

The Congo River

The fifth longest river in the world, the Congo River flows 2,900 miles (4,667 kilometers) through the heart of Africa. Carrying more water than any other river except the Amazon, it drains an area of about 1.4 million square miles (3.6 million square kilometers). The Congo is the main waterway of Congo (Kinshasa).

The first European to see the river was Portuguese navigator Diogo Cão, who reached its mouth in 1483. Portuguese settlers established an outpost on the Congo's southern bank near the Atlantic Ocean in the 1490's. But Europeans knew little about the rest of the great river until after the British explorer Henry M. Stanley completed an expedition from its source to its mouth in 1877.

The Congo begins south of Kabalo, Congo (Kinshasa), where the Lualaba and Luvua rivers meet. The river is often called the Lualaba from this point until it tumbles over Stanley Falls, when it is known as the Congo.

Near Stanley Falls, the river turns westward and flows through the rain forest of northern Congo (Kinshasa), where several major rivers empty into the Congo, including the Aruwimi, Lomami, and Ubangi. Near the town of Mbandaka, the Congo turns southwestward to form a natural boundary between the countries of Congo (Kinshasa) and Congo (Brazzaville) for about 500 miles (800 kilometers).

Near Kinshasa, the Congo widens so much that it forms a lake called Stanley Pool. The river then drops about 800 feet (240 meters) in altitude, forming a series of spectacular waterfalls between Kinshasa and Matadi. These falls prevent riverboats from sailing all the way to the Atlantic Ocean.

The Congo empties into the Atlantic about 90 miles (140 kilometers) west of Matadi. Unlike the Mississippi and the Nile, the Congo does not form a delta at its mouth. Instead, the river's muddy waters flow into a deep trench that extends far into the ocean.

Commercial ships sail the Congo between the Atlantic and Matadi and between Kinshasa and Kisangani, and the river also serves as a major transportation route for local people. Fishing ranks as the most important economic activity in all areas of the Congo River Basin, but little agricultural activity is possible in the dense forest.

People have settled in areas where the riverbanks are relatively firm and permanent. But elsewhere, swampy conditions and the possibility of floods make living conditions much more difficult. In the densely forested, hard-to-reach northern areas of the Congo River Basin, pygmies carry on their traditional ways, hunting and gathering food as they travel in small groups from one area to another.

The rain forests that lie along the mighty Congo are also home to a remarkable variety of wild animals. Crocodiles and hippopotamuses live in or near the river, while baboons, chimpanzees, gorillas, and monkeys thrive in the forests. The okapi, a forest-dwelling animal related to the giraffe, lives nowhere else in the world but the Congo River Basin. The okapi was unknown to Europeans until the year 1900, more than 400 years after the first European saw the river itself.

The Congo River, *right,* drains a vast area of equatorial Africa. Despite its many waterfalls and rapids, the river is Congo's main waterway and an important transportation route. Oceangoing ships use the river between the Atlantic and Matadi, and other commercial ships navigate its waters between Kinshasa and Kisangani. Goods are transported between Kinshasa and Matadi by railroad.

Canoe travel, *center,* is widespread on the Congo because of the lack of bridges and roads in the forests that border the river. Rapids and waterfalls prevent navigation in some sections of the Congo, however.

Barge passengers and their belongings travel on the upper course of the Congo River, above Kisangani. Here, the great river is usually known as the Lualaba. The waters of the Congo and its branches are navigable for about 7,200 miles (11,500 kilometers), making it one of the country of Congo's most important transportation systems.

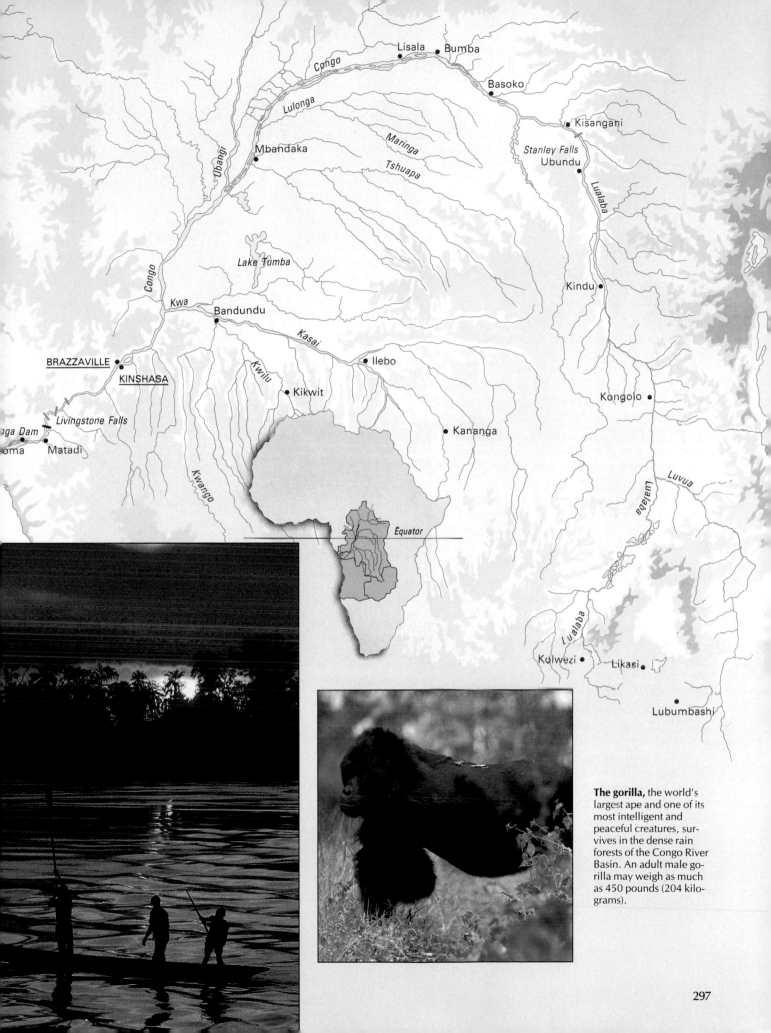

The gorilla, the world's largest ape and one of its most intelligent and peaceful creatures, survives in the dense rain forests of the Congo River Basin. An adult male gorilla may weigh as much as 450 pounds (204 kilograms).

Congo
Lisala
Bumba
Basoko
Kisangani
Lulonga
Stanley Falls
Ubundu
Maringa
Tshuapa
Ubangi
Mbandaka
Lualaba
Lake Tumba
Kindu
Congo
Kwa
Bandundu
Kasai
Kwilu
Ilebo
Kongolo
Kikwit
Kwango
Kananga
Lualaba
Luvua
BRAZZAVILLE
KINSHASA
nga Dam
Livingstone Falls
oma
Matadi
Equator
Lualaba
Kolwezi
Likasi
Lubumbashi

Cook Islands

The 15 islands of the Cook group are spread out over 850,000 square miles (2.2 million square kilometers) in the South Pacific Ocean, about 1,800 miles (2,900 kilometers) northeast of New Zealand. The Cook Islands form two groups—the Southern Group and the Northern Group. Most of the islands of the Southern Group are raised volcanic islands. Rarotonga, the principal island of the Cooks, is in the Southern Group. Most islands of the Northern Group are coral atolls.

People

The Cook Islanders, who are mainly Polynesians, call themselves *Maori*. Their language is closely related to that of the New Zealand Maori, as are many of their customs. The Cook Islands have a population of about 17,000, including about 600 Europeans. The only large settlement, Avarua on Rarotonga, is also the capital and commercial center.

Attending church services is important to the people of the Cook Islands. Most islanders belong to the Cook Islands Christian Church. This church follows the teachings of the former London Missionary Society, which sent the first missionaries to the islands in the 1820's.

Economy

Traditionally, the economy of the Cook Islands has been based on agriculture. Many islanders grow bananas, citrus fruits, coconuts, and pineapples. In the northern islands, divers collect mother-of-pearl shell. Rarotonga has three clothing factories, while other factories produce local handicrafts. A canning factory in Rarotonga processes oranges, pineapples, and other tropical fruits.

Cook Island government policy calls for "controlled development" of tourism. For example, to preserve the landscape and the environment, local regulations forbid camping and spearfishing, and no structure may rise higher than a coconut palm tree. Rarotonga has a number of hotels and motels, and Aitutaki, also in the Southern Group, has a motel. Tourists are often entertained by local dancers, and they sail between islands on small ships or fly on Cook Islands Airways.

Wearing the traditional grass skirt, an islander makes music on a slit-drum. Many traditional customs have disappeared from the Cook Islands as a result of European influence, but some of the old ways persist.

Cook Islanders, *far right,* assemble for church. Most islanders are members of the Cook Islands Christian Church. This church follows the teachings of the London Missionary Society, which introduced Christianity to the islands in the 1820's.

A jagged, rocky outcrop rises from lush, coastal vegetation in the Southern Group of the Cook Islands, *left*. Most of the Southern Group consists of raised volcanic islands whose fertile soil yields rich harvests.

The Cook Islands sprawl over a wide expanse of the South Pacific. The largest of the 15 islands is Rarotonga in the Southern Group.

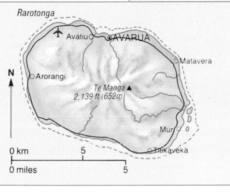

The Kermadec Islands, *below*, a dependency of New Zealand, lie south-west of the Cooks. Raoul, the largest of the group, is uninhabited because of volcanic eruptions there.

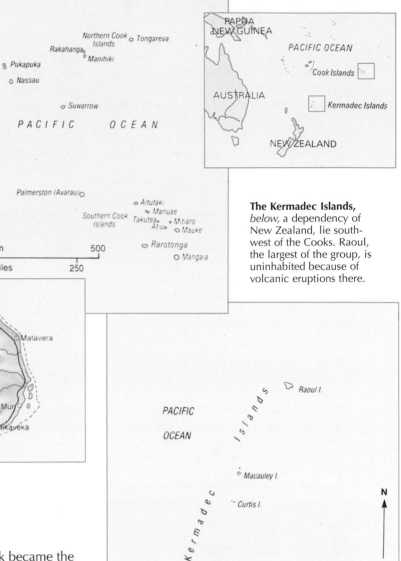

History and government

In 1773, Captain James Cook became the first known European to reach the islands. Great Britain took control of the islands in 1888 and gave administrative control to New Zealand in 1891. A new Constitution gave the islanders control of their internal affairs in 1965.

Today the islands have an arrangement with New Zealand called *free association*. Under free association, the Cooks are self-governing, but the people are citizens of New Zealand. That nation offers the islands military support for defense and provides economic assistance. However, the population of the Cook Islands has decreased in recent years because of migration to New Zealand.

A New Zealand representative, with an office in Avarua, handles that nation's relations with the Cook Islands. A representative of the British monarch also resides in the Cook Islands and serves as head of state. The islands have a 24-member Parliament, which chooses the prime minister, who appoints a Cabinet of 6 ministers. An Executive Council made up of the Cabinet and the monarch's representative ratifies Parliament's decisions.

Costa Rica

Costa Rica is a small but rapidly growing Central American country. In 2000, its population of about 3.7 million people was increasing at a rate of about 1.7 per cent a year.

Ancestry

Indians were the first people to live in what is now Costa Rica. The Corobici tribe settled in the northern valleys, and the Boruca lived in the south. The Carib, Chorotega, and Nahua Indians moved into the area in the 1400's.

In the 1500's, the Spaniards arrived and colonized the land. Many Spanish colonists and Indians intermarried, and their descendants are called *mestizos*. Today, mestizos and whites of unmixed ancestry make up more than 97 per cent of Costa Rica's population.

About 10,000 Indians live in isolated communities in the highlands and along the Pacific and Caribbean shores. They follow their ancestors' traditional ways of life.

About 70,000 blacks live along the Caribbean coast. Their ancestors came to Costa Rica from the Caribbean island of Jamaica in the late 1800's to build railroads and work on banana plantations.

Nearly all Costa Ricans speak Spanish, but many blacks still speak a Jamaican *dialect* (local form) of English. About 93 per cent of the Costa Rican people can read and write—the highest literacy rate in Central America.

The economy

About half of Costa Rica's people live on farms or in rural towns, and about one-fourth of its workers are employed in farming or ranching. Costa Rica's most valuable natural resource is its fertile volcanic soil.

The chief agricultural products are bananas, beef cattle, *cacao* (seeds used to make chocolate), coffee, corn, rice, and sugar cane. Farmers also grow a wide variety of fruits and vegetables, including oranges, beans, and potatoes.

Although manufacturing employed only about a fifth of the nation's workers in the late 1980's, that number is increasing rapidly.

The leading manufactured products include cement, clothing, cosmetics, fertilizer, furniture, machinery, medicines, processed foods, and textiles.

Rich forests of oaks, pines, and tropical hardwoods such as mahogany and cedrela cover about a third of the land. Costa Rica also has small deposits of bauxite and manganese. In addition, many foreign tourists, who come to enjoy the sunshine and beauty of the land, also help boost the economy.

Costa Rica's economy depends heavily on foreign exports, particularly coffee. The nation belongs to the Central American Common Market, an economic union that encourages trade among its members.

During the early 1980's, Costa Rica's economy began to decline due to a high unemployment rate, low earnings from exports, and a large foreign debt. In response, the United States increased its financial aid to the country.

Coffee plants, *far left,* produce Costa Rica's leading export. Hillsides covered with coffee plants surround San José, the capital. Coffee beans, bagged in 132-pound (60-kilogram) burlap sacks, *left,* are ready for shipping from the *beneficio* (processing plant) to the roasting plant. There, they are blended, roasted, ground, and packed for market.

Poás volcano, *above,* is easily accessible to tourists with a paved road leading up to its smoky crater. Such volcanoes help make the soil of Costa Rica rich and fertile.

Some of Costa Rica's younger generation owe their distinctive culture to their black Jamaican ancestors. Black Africans were originally brought to Jamaica as slaves. In the 1800's, some came to Costa Rica to build railroads or work on banana plantations. Today, many black Costa Ricans speak a Jamaican form of English.

Costa Rica Today

Costa Rica is a land of rugged mountains, fertile soil, and lush forests. Its name, meaning *rich coast* in Spanish, came from explorers who heard tales of precious metals in the region. However, the land has little mineral wealth.

The land

High mountain ranges called *cordilleras* cross Costa Rica from northwest to southeast. The cordilleras divide the country into three land regions.

In the Central Highlands lie two large, fertile areas—the *Meseta Central* (Central Plateau) and the *Valle del General* (Valley of the General). Steep cordilleras surround each area.

The Meseta Central is the heartland of Costa Rica. About 75 per cent of Costa Rica's people live there, and the capital, San José, stands on the plateau. The Meseta's rich volcanic soil and favorable climate make it the country's chief coffee-growing region.

The Valle del General lies to the southeast of the Meseta. Slightly warmer and wetter than the Meseta, it is an agricultural region of hills and plains.

The Caribbean Lowlands form a second major land region of Costa Rica. This wide band of swampy tropical jungles lies along the east coast.

FACT BOX

COSTA RICA

COUNTRY

Official name: Republica de Costa Rica (Republic of Costa Rica)
Capital: San Jose
Terrain: Coastal plains separated by rugged mountains
Area: 19,730 sq. mi. (51,100 km²)

Climate: Tropical and subtropical; dry season (December to April); rainy season (May to November); cooler in highlands
Main rivers: Grande de Térraba, San Carlos, Tempisque
Highest elevation: Chirripó Grande, 12,530 ft. (3,819 m)
Lowest elevation: Pacific Ocean, sea level

GOVERNMENT

Form of government: Democratic republic
Head of state: President
Head of government: President
Administrative areas: 7 provincias (provinces)

Legislature: Asamblea Legislativa (Legislative Assembly) with 57 members serving four-year terms
Court system: Corte Suprema (Supreme Court)
Armed forces: None

PEOPLE

Estimated 2002 population: 4,188,000
Population growth: 1.69%
Population density: 212 persons per sq. mi. (82 per km²)
Population distribution: 55% rural, 45% urban
Life expectancy in years: Male: 73 Female: 78
Doctors per 1,000 people: 0.9
Percentage of age-appropriate population enrolled in the following educational levels: Primary: 104* Secondary: 48 Further: 33

Lush tropical vegetation blankets the hills overlooking the port of Golfito on Costa Rica's Pacific coast. Annual rainfall totals about 130 inches (330 centimeters) along the Pacific, and from 150 to 200 inches (381 to 510 centimeters) along the swampy eastern Caribbean coast.

Costa Rica is a small Central American republic, bordered by Nicaragua on the north and Panama on the south. A plateau in the Central Highlands is home to most of its people.

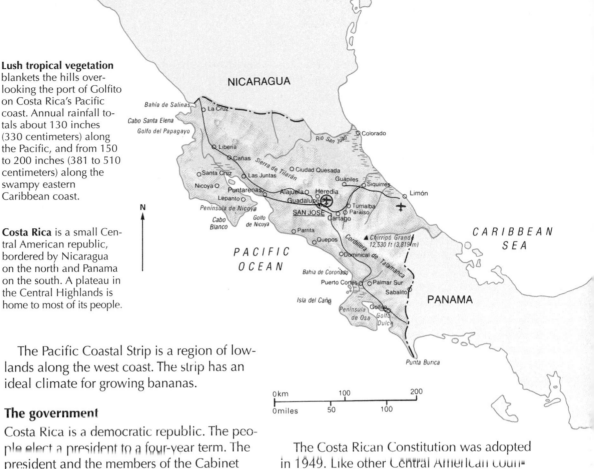

The Pacific Coastal Strip is a region of lowlands along the west coast. The strip has an ideal climate for growing bananas.

The government

Costa Rica is a democratic republic. The people elect a president to a four-year term. The president and the members of the Cabinet make up the Council of Government. The council, which conducts foreign affairs and enforces federal laws, may also veto bills passed by the 57-member Legislative Assembly. The people elect the legislators to four-year terms.

Languages spoken:
Spanish (official)
English spoken around Puerto Limon

Religions:
Roman Catholic 85%
Evangelical Protestant 14%

Enrollment ratios compare the number of students enrolled to the population which, by age, should be enrolled. A ratio higher than 100 indicates that students older or younger than the typical age range are also enrolled.

TECHNOLOGY

Radios per 1,000 people: 816

Televisions per 1,000 people: 231

Computers per 1,000 people: 149.1

ECONOMY

Currency: Costa Rican colon

Gross national income (GNI) in 2000: $14.5 billion U.S.

Real annual growth rate (1999–2000): 1.7%

GNI per capita (2000): $3,810 U.S.

Balance of payments (2000): -$649 million U.S.

Goods exported: Coffee, bananas, sugar; textiles, electronic components, electricity

Goods imported: Raw materials, consumer goods, capital equipment, petroleum, electricity

Trading partners: United States, European Union, Central America, Japan, Mexico

The Costa Rican Constitution was adopted in 1949. Like other Central American countries, Costa Rica has had a series of dictators and revolutions, and like other Central American states, it has a history of Spanish colonization.

The region was a Spanish colony for about 300 years after Columbus landed in Costa Rica in 1502. In 1821, Costa Rica and other Central American states broke away from Spain. They became part of Mexico, but in 1823 formed the United Provinces of Central America. When the union began to collapse in 1838, Costa Rica declared its independence and fell under the dictatorship of Braulio Carrillo.

But Costa Rica has also had strong, effective leaders in its history. From 1849 to 1859, President Juan Rafael Mora established the country's first national bank, its first streetlight system, and many public schools. Julio Acosta became president in 1919, and under Acosta and his successors, Costa Rica became a model of democracy and social reform.

Since 1974, Costa Rica has had an orderly succession of democratic governments. President Oscar Arias Sánchez, who served from 1986 to 1990, won the 1987 Nobel Peace Prize for his Central American peace plan.

Tourism

The gold-hungry Spanish explorers who gave Costa Rica the name *rich coast* found neither gold nor silver. But today, Costa Rica offers riches of another kind. Costa Rica's favorable climate, natural beauty, and culture attract hundreds of thousands of tourists every year.

Cultural attractions

San José is Costa Rica's bustling capital and largest city. Lying in a valley in the mountainous interior, the city has a mild climate. Daytime temperatures range from 75° to 80° F. (24° to 27° C) the year around.

San José is a picturesque mix of old and new—with Spanish-style churches and houses standing among modern stores and office buildings. The National Theater and Gran Hotel Costa Rica dominate the Culture Plaza—a large, beautiful square in the capital. The city's National Monument is an impressive statue dedicated to the five Central American republics who ousted William Walker, an American who tried to take control of Nicaragua in the 1800's.

Colorful festivals on religious holidays are also a tourist attraction. During the annual Christmas festivals in San José, for example, thousands of tourists as well as Costa Ricans come to enjoy the bullfights, fireworks, and parades of masked merrymakers.

Natural attractions

Many tourists also come to enjoy the natural beauty of Costa Rica. Rugged mountains and lush tropical forests cover most of the land, and warm ocean waters roll onto its sandy beaches.

Many national parks have been created to preserve these natural wonders. The country's park system includes beaches where sea turtles come to lay their eggs, tropical rain forests that provide a habitat for chattering monkeys and colorful birds, and several active volcanoes.

Coco Island (Isla del Coco) is a small island that lies about 200 miles (320 kilometers) southwest of Costa Rica in the Pacific Ocean. The entire island is a national park. Rare sea birds nest there, and waterfalls spill out of the evergreen forest into the sea.

Coco Island, off the Costa Rican mainland in the Pacific Ocean, is home to unusual species of birds. To preserve their habitat, Costa Rica has made the island a park.

Dazzling religious festivals in traditional settings, *below,* attract tourists and residents alike.

The National Theater, *above right,* one of San José's most famous landmarks, is a glittering showcase for plays, operas, and ballets. A levy on every sack of coffee exported from Costa Rica in the late 1800's financed the construction of the theater. The building is now a national monument.

Wildlife

National Parks in Costa Rica	
1 Santa Rosa	6 Poás volcano
2 Rincón de la Vieja	7 Braulio Carrillo
3 Palo Verde	8 Irazú volcano
4 Barra Honda	9 Manuel Antonio
5 Tortuguero	10 Chirripó
	11 La Amistad
	12 Corcovado
	13 Cahuita
	R Nature reserves

2,000 m	6,560 ft
1,000 m	3,280 ft
500 m	1,640 ft
200 m	656 ft
0 m	0 ft

Cahuita National Park, near Puerto Limón on the Caribbean coast, is one of the parks that preserve the rain forest. Like rain forests throughout the world, the rain forests of Costa Rica are a precious natural resource with a wealth of plant and animal life. A tropical rain forest has more kinds of trees than any other area in the world. And more species of amphibians, birds, insects, mammals, and reptiles live in tropical forests than anywhere else.

In the Central American rain forest of Costa Rica, squirrel monkeys scamper along tree branches and climb vines. Glittering emerald-green-and-crimson birds called *quetzals* perch high in the trees. And *jaguars*—large, powerful wild cats—live and hunt in the forests too.

Poás and Irazú are two active volcanoes in the Cordillera Central of Costa Rica—the mountain range that rings the plateau where San José lies. Tourists and scientists alike can view the two volcanoes at close range.

A rich variety of wildlife makes its home in Costa Rica's national parks, providing enjoyment for tourists and residents alike.

1 Quetzal
2 Spider monkey
3 Pygmy anteater
4 Squirrel monkey
5 Mouse opossum
0 Jaguar

7 Agrias scardanapalus
8 Nessaea obrinus
9 Atlantic green turtle
10 Tarantula
11 Alligator

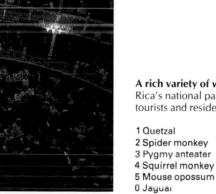

Côte d'Ivoire

République de Côte d'Ivoire lies along the Gulf of Guinea on the western bulge of Africa. The land rises gradually from the Atlantic Ocean to a tropical forest in the interior. In the north, the forest changes to grassland with scattered trees.

Low, rocky cliffs line the southwestern coast of the country, while the southeastern coast is flat and sandy. A sand bar that runs for 180 miles (289 kilometers) along this section of the coast is bordered by deep lagoons.

Yamoussoukro is the capital of Côte d'Ivoire. However, most government offices are in Abidjan, the administrative center and former capital of the country. Abidjan is also Côte d'Ivoire's largest city and main port.

The Côte d'Ivoire Democratic Party (PDCI) is the country's largest political party. Until 1990, it was the nation's only party.

Côte d'Ivoire received its name from French sailors who came to the region in the late 1400's to trade for ivory. Before that time, great African kingdoms had ruled there. After the Europeans arrived, the slave trade became important.

In 1842, the French took control of the area on the coast around Grand-Bassam, and later they made treaties with African chiefs to expand the area under French protection. Côte d'Ivoire became a French colony in 1893 and was made part of French West Africa in 1895.

After World War I (1914-1918), France built ports, roads, and railroads in Côte d'Ivoire. After World War II (1939-1945), the French began developing the region's resources, and Côte d'Ivoire became the richest colony in French West Africa. France made Côte d'Ivoire a territory in the French Union in 1946.

In 1958, Côte d'Ivoire voted to become a self-governing republic within the French Community, an organization that linked France with its overseas territories, and on August 7, 1960, Côte d'Ivoire declared itself an independent republic. However, the nation kept close economic ties with France, and it joined neighboring African nations in the Council of the Entente.

The movement for independence among French territories in western Africa was led by Félix Houphouët-Boigny. Houphouët-Boigny was elected president of Côte d'Ivoire for seven 5-year terms beginning in 1960.

Houphouët-Boigny helped unite the country's many ethnic groups and brought political stability and economic progress. After he died in 1993, the constitution called for the Speaker of the National Assembly, Henri Konan Bedie, to take over as president for the rest of the term. In 1995, Bedie was

FACT BOX

COUNTRY

Official name: Republique de Côte d'Ivoire (Republic of Côte d'Ivoire)
Capital: Yamoussoukro
Terrain: Mostly flat to undulating plains; mountains in northwest
Area: 124,504 sq. mi. (322,463 km²)

Climate: Tropical along coast, semiarid in far north; three seasons—warm and dry (November to March), hot and dry (March to May), hot and wet (June to October)
Main rivers: Bandama, Cavelly, Komoé, Sassandra
Highest elevation: Mont Nimba, 5,748 ft. (1,752 m)
Lowest elevation: Gulf of Guinea, sea level

CÔTE D'IVOIRE

GOVERNMENT

Form of government: Republic
Head of state: President
Head of government: Prime minister
Administrative areas: 58 departements (departments)

Legislature: Assemblee Nationale (National Assembly) with 225 members serving five-year terms
Court system: Cour Supreme (Supreme Court)
Armed forces: 13,900 troops

PEOPLE

Estimated 2002 population: 15,417,000
Population growth: 2.58%
Population density: 124 persons per sq. mi. (48 per km²)
Population distribution: 54% rural, 46% urban
Life expectancy in years:
Male: 44
Female: 47
Doctors per 1,000 people: 0.1
Percentage of age-appropriate population enrolled in the following educational levels:
Primary: 78
Secondary: 23
Further: 7

Côte d'Ivoire lies on the Gulf of Guinea, a part of the Atlantic Ocean, on the western bulge of Africa. It received its name in the 1400's from French sailors who traded for ivory in the area.

The skyline of Abidjan, Côte d'Ivoire's largest city, is reflected in the calm waters of a lagoon. In 1983, the country's legislature voted to move the capital from Abidjan to Yamoussoukro, but most government offices remain in Abidjan.

elected president. In 1999, military officers led by General Robert Guei ousted Bedie and set up a transitional government.

In July 2000, voters approved a new constitution designed to return the country to civilian rule. A presidential election was held, and when it appeared that candidate Laurent Gbagbo would defeat General Guei, Guei shut down the election commission and declared himself the winner. But mass protests forced Guei to leave office, and Gbagbo was sworn in as president. Former Prime Minister Alassane Ouattara was barred from running in both the elections because of questions about his nationality. In late 2000 and early 2001, violent clashes took place between Ouattara's supporters and Gbagbo's supporters.

In September 2002, rebels staged a violent uprising in Abidjan against the Gbagbo government and seized control of parts of northern and central Cote d'Ivoire. Later that year, two separate rebel uprisings began in western Cote d'Ivoire, killing hundreds of people. In January 2003, representatives of the three rebel groups and the Ivorian government reached a power-sharing agreement. However, thousands of Ivorians protested against the agreement and some violence continued.

ECONOMY

Languages spoken:
French (official)
60 native dialects with Dioula the most widely spoken

Religions:
Muslim 60%
Christian 22%
indigenous 18% (some of these are also numbered among the Christians and Muslims)

Currency: Communaute Financiere Africaine franc

Gross national income (GNI) in 2000: $9.6 billion U.S.

Real annual growth rate (1999–2000): -2.3%

GNI per capita (2000): $600 U.S.

Balance of payments (2000): -$13 million U.S.

Goods exported: Cocoa, coffee, tropical woods, petroleum, cotton, bananas, pineapples, palm oil, cotton, fish

Goods imported: Food, consumer goods; capital goods, fuel, transport equipment

Trading partners: France, U.S., Netherlands, Italy

TECHNOLOGY

Radios per 1,000 people: 137

Televisions per 1,000 people: 60

Computers per 1,000 people: 6.1

People and Economy

Almost all the people of Côte d'Ivoire are black Africans. They belong to four major ethnic groups. The Akan live in the southeast, the Kru in the southwest, the Voltaic in the northeast, and the Mandingo in the northwest.

These major groups are actually made up of many smaller ethnic groups. French is the nation's official language, but more than 60 languages are spoken in Côte d'Ivoire.

Most Ivorians, as Côte d'Ivoire's people are called, used to practice ancient local religions, but now about 60 per cent of the people are Muslims, and about 22 per cent are Christians. The largest Christian church in Africa and one of the largest in the world, Our Lady of Peace, is located in the city of Yamoussoukro. Construction was completed in 1989, and the church was dedicated in 1990.

Rural and urban life

More than 50 per cent of Ivorian people are farmers who live in small villages. Each village family has its own *compound,* or group of huts. The number of huts in the compound varies according to the size of the family. The huts have mud walls and roofs made of thatch or metal. The farmers raise cassava, corn, rice, and yams as food crops.

Agriculture is also the country's chief source of income. Côte d'Ivoire leads the world in the production of *cacao beans,* which are used to make cocoa, and ranks fifth in the production of coffee beans. Cacao, coffee, and palm oil are the country's chief exports. Bananas, pineapples, and rubber are other important agricultural products.

Côte d'Ivoire factories process palm oil, pineapples, sugar, timber, tuna, and manufacture textiles. In addition, small amounts of petroleum from offshore wells are refined in Côte d'Ivoire facilities. Since the 1960's,

Workers handle sacks of coffee beans at Abidjan, one of western Africa's major ports. Coffee and cacao have long been Côte d'Ivoire's chief cash crops. The French grew coffee and cacao trees in their colony after World War I.

A member of one of the Akan ethnic groups of southeastern Côte d'Ivoire is marked by a pattern of traditional facial scars. Unlike the ethnic groups in some African nations, Côte d'Ivoire's ethnic groups live in harmony with one another.

Drummers beat out of rhythm for Ivorian dancers. Most Ivorians practice traditional African religions, and their dances often have religious significance.

Mud huts with cone-shaped thatched roofs cluster together in a typical village in Côte d'Ivoire, where village compounds are family-based. About 54 per cent of the people live in such rural villages, but a growing number are moving to the cities to seek work.

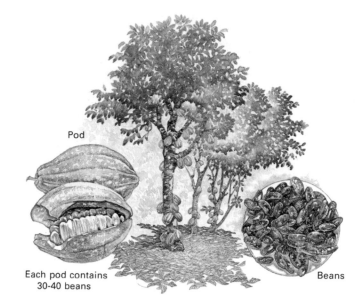

Pod

Each pod contains 30-40 beans

Beans

Cacao (*Theobroma cacao*)

Cacao trees are the source of the beans used to make cocoa and cocoa butter. The light brown to purple cacao beans develop inside melonlike fruits that grow from the tree's trunk and branches.

many young rural Ivorians have moved to the cities to find work in these industries, and almost 50 per cent of the people now live in urban areas.

Like rural Ivorians, most people in the cities live in mud huts. A few wealthy Africans, along with nearly all the non-Africans in the nation, live in modern houses and apartments.

Coping with economic growth

Côte d'Ivoire receives much support from France and other Western European nations. Its economy is rapidly becoming one of the strongest among the developing African nations, but this growth has also led to some

problems. As an increasing number of people move to urban areas in search of work, the cities have become seriously overcrowded. Since 1960, Abidjan's population has increased more than tenfold, from about 180,000 to about 1,900,000. In addition, non-Africans hold most of the higher-level jobs in industry and government, and this inequality displeases many Ivorians.

Transportation and education

Côte d'Ivoire has one of Africa's best transportation systems. A railroad operates between Abidjan and Ouagadougou, Burkina Faso. It handles large numbers of passengers and hundreds of thousands of tons of freight every year.

Côte d'Ivoire also has several harbors, the two largest at Abidjan and San Pedro. In addition, an international airport also operates at Abidjan, and a number of smaller airports serve other parts of the country.

Some young Ivorians attend colleges in other countries, and the National University of Côte d'Ivoire in Abidjan enrolls about 13,000 students. However, although the overwhelming majority of children attend elementary school, only about 25 per cent of Ivorians even go to high school.

Croatia

The republic of Croatia lies in the Balkan Peninsula in southeastern Europe. Formerly one of the six republics of Yugoslavia, Croatia broke away from the federation and declared its independence in 1991.

Croatia's varied and beautiful landscape includes the Adriatic coastlands along its western border, the scenic slopes of the Dinaric Alps running through its interior, and the fertile Pannonian Plains bordering Hungary to the north. Croatia's two principal rivers, the Drava and the Sava, flow into the Danube, the second longest river in Europe after the Volga.

Zagreb, Croatia's capital, is the chief manufacturing center in this highly industrialized country. Croatia produces chemicals, food products, petroleum, ships, and textiles. Grapes thrive in the mild climate of the coastal region.

Most of Croatia's people belong to a Slavic group called Croats, who speak Croatian, a form of Serbo-Croatian, and follow the Roman Catholic religion. Present-day Croats are descended from Slavic tribes that began to settle in what is now Croatia during the A.D. 600's. Throughout the 900's and 1000's, Croatia flourished as an independent kingdom.

After about 1100, Croatia formed a political association with Hungary, and in 1526 and 1527, the Habsburgs gained control of much of Hungary and Croatia. In 1867, Croatia became part of Austria-Hungary, and in 1918, Croatia united with neighboring territories to form a new country—the Kingdom of the Serbs, Croats, and Slovenes. In 1929, the kingdom's name was changed to Yugoslavia.

In May 1991, Serbia blocked the election of a Croat to the head position in the *Presidency,* Yugoslavia's chief policymaking body. This action heightened tension, and in June, Croatia declared its independence from Yugoslavia.

Fierce fighting broke out when the national government, which strongly opposed Croatia's declaration of independence, sent government troops into the republic.

However, bloody violence in the republic continued. In August 1991, heavy fighting broke out between the Croat militia and ethnic Serbs living in Croatia who claimed part of the republic for Serbia. The Yugoslav military fought on the side of the Serbs. Within a few months, Serbian forces had taken over about 30 per cent of Croatia's land. A cease-fire in January 1992 ended most of the fighting, but some fighting continued between Serbs and Croats in Serb-occupied Croatian lands.

In mid-1995, Croatian forces began taking back the territory that had been seized by the

FACT BOX

COUNTRY

Official name: Republika Hrvatska (Republic of Croatia)
Capital: Zagreb
Terrain: Geographically diverse; flat plains along Hungarian border, low mountains and highlands near Adriatic coastline and islands
Area: 21,829 sq. mi. (56,538 km²)

Climate: Mediterranean and continental; continental climate predominant with hot summers and cold winters; mild winters, dry summers along coast
Main rivers: Drava, Sava
Highest elevation: Dinara, 6,004 ft. (1,830 m)
Lowest elevation: Adriatic Sea, sea level

GOVERNMENT

Form of government: Presidential/parliamentary democracy
Head of state: President
Head of government: Prime minister
Administrative areas: 20 zupanije (counties), 1 grad (city)

Legislature: Sabor (Assembly) consisting of the Zupanijski Dom (House of Counties) with 68 members serving four-year terms and the Zastupnicki Dom (House of Representatives) with 151 members serving four-year terms
Court system: Supreme Court, Constitutional Court
Armed forces: 61,000 troops

PEOPLE

Estimated 2002 population: 4,460,000
Population growth: 0.93%
Population density: 204 persons per sq. mi. (79 per km²)
Population distribution: 54% urban, 46% rural
Life expectancy in years:
Male: 70
Female: 78
Doctors per 1,000 people: 2.3
Percentage of age-appropriate population enrolled in the following educational levels:
Primary: 87
Secondary: 82
Further: 28

Serbs. The Croatian government and the leaders of the Croatian Serbs made peace later that year. In 1996, Croatia signed an agreement with Yugoslavia to normalize relations and joined the Council of Europe. In January 1998, the remaining land that had been seized by Croatian Serbs was reunited with Croatia. Elections in 2000 brought the Social Democrats to power.

Formerly one of the federal republics of Yugoslavia, Croatia declared its independence in 1991. Zagreb, its capital and largest city, is also a major trade, industrial, and cultural center.

Croatian women stop for a chat on Susak, a remote island off Croatia's Adriatic coast. Susak, the only place where the ancient Croatian dialect is still spoken, has no electricity or automobiles.

Languages spoken:
Croatian 96% (official) other 4% (including Italian, Hungarian, Czech, Slovak, and German)

Religions:
Roman Catholic 76.5%
Orthodox 11.1%
Muslim 1.2%

TECHNOLOGY

Radios per 1,000 people: 340

Televisions per 1,000 people: 293

Computers per 1,000 people: 80.7

ECONOMY

Currency: Croatian kuna

Gross national income (GNI) in 2000: $20.2 billion U.S.

Real annual growth rate (1999-2000): 3.7%

GNI per capita (2000): $4,620 U.S.

Balance of payments (2000): -$399 million U.S.

Goods exported: Textiles, chemicals, foodstuffs, fuels

Goods imported: Machinery, transport and electrical equipment, chemicals, fuels and lubricants, foodstuffs

Trading partners: Italy, Germany, Slovenia, Bosnia and Herzegovina

Workers tend the grapevines in a vineyard in the coastal region of Dalmatia, now part of Croatia. Citrus fruits, figs, olives, and tobacco also flourish in this region.

Cuba

Christopher Columbus claimed Cuba, an island country in the Greater Antilles, for Spain in 1492. In the 1500's, Spanish settlers established plantations on the island and forced the native Indians to work on them. Many Indians died of diseases or harsh treatment. As the Indian population declined, the Spaniards began to bring blacks from Africa to work as slaves.

Struggle for independence

In 1812, a group of slaves headed by José Antonio Aponte planned a revolt. The Spaniards discovered the plan and hanged Aponte, but various other groups continued to plot against Spain.

Cuba's struggle to end Spanish rule led to the Ten Years' War, which began in 1868. The war ended with a treaty that promised the abolition of slavery. Slavery ended in 1886, but many Cubans still wanted independence. A revolution broke out in 1895, led by José Martí. By 1898, Spain had lost control of all of Cuba except the major coastal cities.

United States President William McKinley told Spain to either crush the revolution or give up Cuba, and sent the U.S. battleship *Maine* to Havana to protect U.S. citizens in Cuba. When the *Maine* mysteriously blew up, the United States blamed the Spanish and declared war on Spain.

Spain lost the war and rights to Cuba in 1898. The United States then set up a military government on the island, which angered many Cubans and Americans alike.

U.S. involvement

Under strong pressure from the Cuban people, the United States decided to let Cubans govern themselves, and Cuba adopted a Constitution in 1901. However, the United States insisted that the document allow the United States to intervene in Cuban affairs. The United States was also allowed to buy or lease land for naval bases in Cuba. In 1903, the United States leased Guantánamo Bay and built a large naval base there, which remains today.

The United States removed its troops in 1902, but it sent armed forces into Cuba on three subsequent occasions when revolts threatened the Cuban government. Many businesses, factories, and farms in Cuba were owned by U.S. companies, and the U.S. troops were sent to protect this property.

In 1933, an army sergeant named Fulgencio Batista helped overthrow the government, and eventually removed the president of the new government because the United States did not support him. Batista felt his best hope for power lay in winning U.S. support for himself.

From 1934 to 1940, Batista ruled Cuba as dictator through presidents who served in name only. In 1940, Cubans elected him president. The Constitution prevented him from being reelected in 1944, but in 1952 Batista again overthrew the government.

Cuba prospered under Batista, but he was a dictator, and most Cubans continued to live in poverty. In 1953, a young lawyer named Fidel Castro started a revolution against Batista. He and many of his followers were imprisoned. On his release, Castro formed a revolutionary group.

Revolution and Communist rule

Castro and his fellow rebels launched guerrilla attacks on the government. On Jan. 1, 1959, Batista was forced to flee the country, and Castro became premier of Cuba. Many former political officials and army officers were tried and executed. Many other Cubans fled the country.

Castro's government established the first Communist state in the Western Hemi-

Castro's takeover

On July 26, 1953, Fidel Castro and his supporters attacked the Moncado Army Barracks in Santiago de Cuba. Castro was caught and imprisoned. Released in 1955, he went to Mexico but returned to Cuba in 1956. He and his followers formed a guerrilla band in the Sierra Maestra to launch surprise attacks on the government. The revolt succeeded in 1959, and Batista fled the country.

Jan. 1, 1959, Batista flees. **Jan. 2, 1959,** Ché Guevara enters Havana. **Jan. 8, 1959,** Castro enters Havana.

HAVANA (LA HABANA)

Caibarién

Pinar del Río

Playa Larga

Cienfuegos

Sancti Spíritus

Bahía de Cochinos (Bay of Pigs)

April 17–19, 1961, United States sponsors invasion at Bay of Pigs.

CARIBBEAN SEA

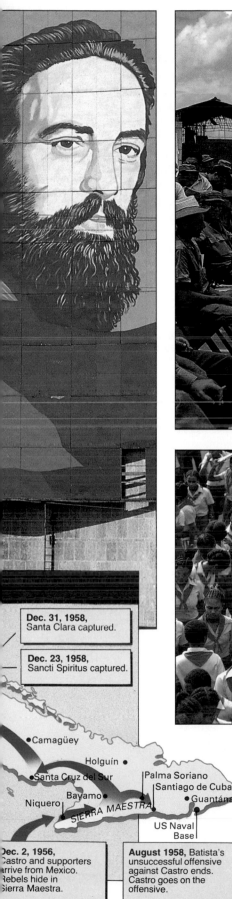

A huge portrait, *far left,* of Fidel Castro (right) and his fellow revolutionary leader Ché Guevara (left) is displayed in Havana's Plaza de la Revolución.

Fidel Castro, *above,* addresses a rally at Santiago de Cuba, where he was arrested in 1953 for attacking a military barracks.

The Ethiopian School, *above,* on the Isle of Youth is an example of Cuba's ties with other socialist countries. Castro has tried to aid revolution in Latin America and Africa.

Dec. 31, 1958, Santa Clara captured.

Dec. 23, 1958, Sancti Spiritus captured.

• Camagüey

Holguín •

•Santa Cruz del Sur

Palma Soriano

Santiago de Cuba

Bayamo

Niquero

• Guantánamo

SIERRA MAESTRA

US Naval Base

Dec. 2, 1956, Castro and supporters arrive from Mexico. Rebels hide in Sierra Maestra.

August 1958, Batista's unsuccessful offensive against Castro ends. Castro goes on the offensive.

sphere. In 1959 and 1960, it seized U.S.-owned farms and businesses. Castro turned to the Soviet Union for support. In 1961, the United States ended diplomatic relations with Cuba.

In April 1961, Cuban exiles tried to invade Cuba at the Bay of Pigs. They failed when the United States did not send troops to support them.

In 1962, the United States began a naval blockade of Cuba when it learned that the Soviet Union was shipping nuclear missiles and materials to build launch sites on the island. Cuba had asked for such aid from the Soviet Union because it feared an attack by the United States. The Cuban missile crisis brought the world close to nuclear war. The tension ended when the Soviets removed the weapons—over Castro's protest. Relations between the United States and Cuba have since remained strained.

Cuba Today

Cuba is one of the most beautiful islands in the Greater Antilles. Cubans call it the *Pearl of the Antilles*. It lies about 90 miles (140 kilometers) south of Florida, and along with more than 1,600 smaller islands, it forms the Republic of Cuba.

The land

Cuba has a varied and magnificent landscape. Towering mountains and rolling hills cover about a fourth of the island. The rest of Cuba consists mainly of gently sloping land, grassy plains, and wide, fertile valleys. Its coastline is marked with deep bays, sandy beaches, and colorful coral reefs.

Three mountain ranges rise from the island—the Sierra de los Organos in the northwest, the Sierra de Trinidad in the central region, and the Sierra Maestra in the southeast. Heavy pine forests cover the Sierra Maestra.

The rich cropland and pastureland between the mountain ranges consists mainly of red clay. Parts of the coastline are bordered by lowlands and swamps.

Cuba's 2,100-mile (3,380-kilometer) coastline is indented with about 200 harbors. Most of these harbors have narrow entrances to the sea, so the ships they shelter are protected against wind and waves. The most important harbors are Havana and Nuevitas on the north coast and Cienfuegos, Guantánamo, and Santiago de Cuba on the south coast.

Coral islands and reefs lie off the coast. The largest of the more than 1,600 islands that surround the Cuban mainland is Isla de la Juventud (the Isle of Youth).

Lying within the northern tropics, Cuba has a semitropical climate. Cool ocean breezes from the northeast in the summer and warm breezes from the southeast in the winter give the island a mild climate throughout the year. However, Cuba lies within a hurricane area. These violent windstorms frequently hit the island, especially its western half, during August, September, and October.

The government

According to the Constitution of Cuba, the country is a socialist state and a republic. Cuba is not, however, a democratic republic, in which the people elect leaders to represent them. Cuba is actually a dictatorship, controlled by Fidel Castro and the Communist Party of Cuba, which is the only party allowed. Cuba's Constitution calls the Communist Party "the highest leading force of the society and of the state." The party, headed by Castro, has about 400,000 members.

The legislature of Cuba is the National Assembly of People's Power. Local assemblies

---

FACT BOX

CUBA

COUNTRY

Official name: Republica de Cuba (Republic of Cuba)
Capital: Havana
Terrain: Mostly flat to rolling plains, with rugged hills and mountains in the southeast
Area: 42,803 sq. mi. (110,860 km²)

Climate: Tropical; moderated by trade winds; dry season (November to April); rainy season (May to October)
Main rivers: Cauto, Salado, San Pedro, Caunao, Zaza
Highest elevation: Pico Turquino, 6,578 ft. (2,005 m)
Lowest elevation: Caribbean Sea, sea level

GOVERNMENT

Form of government: Communist state
Head of state: President of the Council of State and the Council of Ministers
Head of government: President of the Council of State and the Council of Ministers
Administrative areas: 14 provincias (provinces), 1 municipio especial (special municipality)

Legislature: Asemblea Nacional del Poder Popular (National Assembly of People's Power) with 601 members serving five-year terms
Court system: Tribunal Supremo Popular (People's Supreme Court)
Armed forces: 65,000 troops

PEOPLE

Estimated 2002 population: 11,268,000
Population growth: 0.39%
Population density: 263 persons per sq. mi. (102 per km²)
Population distribution: 75% urban, 25% rural
Life expectancy in years:
Male: 74
Female: 79
Doctors per 1,000 people: 5.3
Percentage of age-appropriate population enrolled in the following educational levels:
Primary: 100
Secondary: 79
Further: 19
Language spoken: Spanish

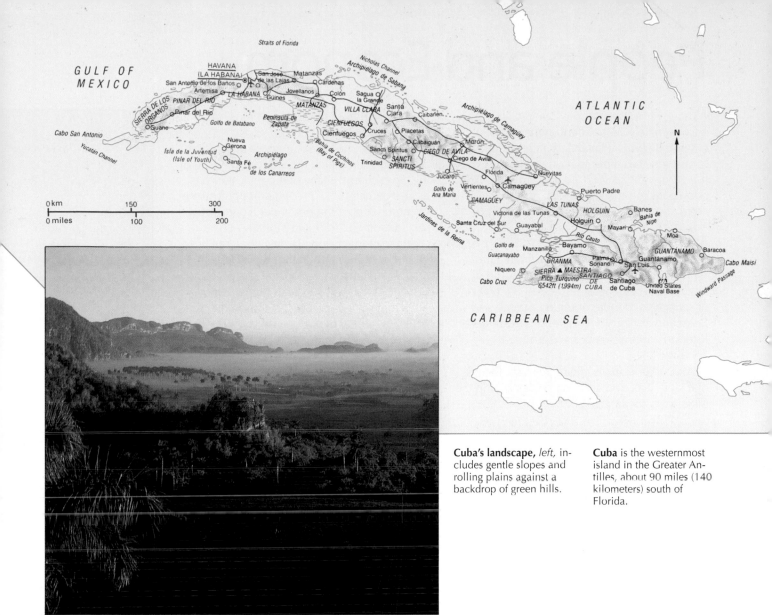

Cuba's landscape, *left,* includes gentle slopes and rolling plains against a backdrop of green hills.

Cuba is the westernmost island in the Greater Antilles, about 90 miles (140 kilometers) south of Florida.

Religions:
  Roman Catholic
  Jehovah's Witnesses
  Jewish
  Santeria

ECONOMY

Currency: Cuban peso

Gross domestic product (GDP) in 2001: $25.5 billion U.S.

Real annual growth rate (2001): 3%

GDP per capita (2001): $2,300 U.S.

Balance of payments (2001): N/A

Goods exported: Sugar, nickel, tobacco, shellfish, medical products, citrus, coffee

Goods imported: Petroleum, food, machinery, chemicals

Trading partners: Russia, Netherlands, Spain, Canada, Venezuela

TECHNOLOGY

Radios per 1,000 people: 353

Televisions per 1,000 people: 250

Computers per 1,000 people: 10.7

---

elect deputies to the National Assembly for five-year terms.

The National Assembly in turn elects 31 of its members to the Council of State. One of the 31 members elected by the National Assembly becomes the president of the Council of State—the most powerful person in the Cuban government. Today, Fidel Castro is president of the Council of State. This position puts him in firm control over Cuba.

In 1994, tension between the United States and Castro's regime increased as thousands of desperate Cubans attempting to emigrate to the United States were detained at the Guantanamo U.S. naval base in Cuba. Refugees were picked up by U.S. authorities as they attempted to cross the Straits of Florida in small boats and makeshift rafts. The crisis was triggered by U.S. President Bill Clinton's efforts to end an "open arms" immigration policy with Cuba. Officials of both countries negotiated a settlement to the crisis.

People and Economy

About 11 million people live in Cuba, and approximately 75 per cent of them live in the cities and towns. Havana, the capital and largest city, has a population of almost 2 million. Many of the rural people are poor. Few people live on the smaller islands off the coast.

Ancestry

According to the Cuban government, about 75 per cent of the people are white and of Spanish descent. Most of the rest are blacks or *mulattoes,* people of mixed African and European ancestry. However, many of those listed as white actually have a mixed ancestry.

Almost all Cubans speak Spanish, the official language. Some people, especially in the cities, also speak English.

The economy

According to the Constitution of Cuba, the country is a socialist state and a republic. In a socialist state, the government owns the land, businesses, and other means of production.

The Cuban government plans and controls the country's economy. It owns all industries, banks, and small businesses. The government also owns more than 70 per cent of the farmland, though the remaining 30 per cent is privately owned.

The government has two major goals for the country—economic development and economic and social equality. However, the economy has been developing slowly. In the early 1960's, the government began a program to industrialize the country. It was only partly successful because the country lacked the funds and raw materials necessary to launch successful new manufacturing enterprises.

The government then shifted its emphasis to agriculture, especially sugar production. But droughts, hurricanes, and mistakes in government planning have limited its success in this area also.

The Cuban government controls all agriculture, even that on privately owned land. Private farms may not be larger than 166 acres (67 hectares). Landowners receive financial help from the state and must sell their crops to the government.

The government also operates many large state farms, on which the workers are paid by the government. Many of these farms were estates owned by U.S. companies before the Communist government under Fidel Castro seized them in 1959 and 1960.

Sugar cane has long been Cuba's main crop. It is grown throughout the island, though the largest crops come from eastern Cuba.

Tobacco, the second most important crop, is grown mainly in northwestern Cuba. Other farm products include bananas, cassava, citrus fruits, coffee, pineapples, potatoes, rice, and tomatoes. Cattle raising and milk production have increased because of the government's farm program.

Before the Castro revolution, U.S. companies owned most Cuban industries. Almost all the factory equipment and raw materials came from the United States. After the Communist government took over these indus-

A Cuban boy helps lay bricks and mortar. The Cuban government has built much badly needed housing, but not enough to meet the demands of the population.

Day care for young children, *right,* is provided to make women available for Cuba's work force. Older children must go to school for six years. The government runs the schools, and education is free.

tries, Cuba began to rely mainly on the Soviet Union, Spain, and some Eastern European countries for its industrial needs.

The country's chief industry is food processing, especially of sugar, dairy products, and flour. Other manufactured products include cement, farm tools, fertilizer, iron and steel, paper, rum, shoes, textiles, tobacco products, and wood products.

Mining is a growing industry in Cuba, which has deposits of nickel ore, limestone, chromium, copper, and silver. The government owns all the mines and mineral reserves.

Cuba's fishing industry is also growing rapidly. The government owns a large fleet of fishing boats, and it has organized fishing cooperatives in which the members share in the profits.

Farmworkers, *above,* wear wide-brimmed straw hats to protect them from the sun. Members of the armed forces also help clear farmland and harvest sugar cane. Cuban men must serve three years in the armed forces or volunteer for three years of farm work.

Salsa band members, *right,* play popular Cuban music. The government supports the arts.

Daily Life

Life in Cuba today is very much influenced by the socialist government. Before the Castro revolution in 1959, the Cuban government used much of the nation's economic resources to help make Havana a luxurious and popular tourist center. But little was done to improve the lives of the Cuban people, particularly those in rural areas.

Castro's government turned attention from Havana to the countryside. One of the goals of the socialist government is economic and social equality, and the government has made great progress toward this goal. Today, Cuba spends large sums of money on housing and food for rural people and provides free education and medical care for all its people.

Cuba has a serious housing shortage. In the cities, many people live in crowded, run-down buildings, with two or more families often sharing an apartment. In the countryside, many people live in thatch-roofed huts with cement floors. The government has built much new housing, but not enough. Rent for government-built housing is set at 6 to 10 per cent of a family's income.

Many kinds of food are scarce in Cuba. To help make sure that even the poorest have enough to eat, the government has created a system of food rationing. People are provided with coupons allowing them to buy limited amounts of foods at very low prices. Beans, beef, milk, potatoes, and rice are all sold this way. Except for beef, additional amounts of the same foods may be purchased at much higher prices. Therefore, people who can afford it are able to eat more.

The government also provides one or two free meals a day to schoolchildren and to some workers. Hot lunches often consist of rice, beans, and meat.

Cuban law requires children to go to school for at least six years. The government controls the schools, and education is free.

The government also has set up various adult education programs. During the early 1960's, students were recruited to teach illiterate Cubans how to read and write. Later, other education projects were established. As a result, a great number of adults have completed elementary school, and many go to night school or job-training classes. More than 95 per cent of Cuban adults are literate today.

A strong sea wall protects Havana from the heavy swells of the Atlantic Ocean. Almost 2 million people live in the city, once one of the world's luxury tourist centers.

Havana's treelined avenues and impressive buildings, *right,* are a reminder of its past. Because the government has invested much more in rural areas, Havana now has a housing shortage.

Cuba has a good road system, but few Cubans have automobiles. There are more than 50 people for each car in the country. Most Cubans travel by bus.

Telephone and telegraph lines connect the major Cuban cities. Many homes do not have a telephone, but the government has installed free public telephones in many cities. On average, there is 1 radio for every 5 people and 1 television set for every 13 people. About 15 daily newspapers are published.

The government controls all Cuban newspapers and radio and television broadcasts. However, Florida is only 90 miles (140 kilometers) away, and the Cuban people can pick up radio and TV broadcasts from the United States. Radio Martí, a U.S. government radio station that broadcasts programs to the Cuban people, began operating in Miami, Florida, in 1985.

Cubans have a strong love for their country and their traditions. The government also encourages extreme patriotism in the people. Throughout the country, posters and neon lights display the revolutionary motto *Patria o*

The Bodeguita del Medio, *above,* once a favorite haunt of American writer Ernest Hemingway, is still a noisy, friendly club. Cuban music is popular both on the island and in other parts of the world.

Cannons still line the harbor of Havana, *left,* which was founded by the Spaniards in 1519. At one time, cannons were used to protect the town from raiding pirates.

Muerte, Venceremos (Fatherland or Death, We Shall Conquer).

Most Cubans are Roman Catholic, but few attend church services. People who attend religious services cannot obtain good jobs or join the Communist Party. The government has taken over almost all the church schools and forced many priests to leave the country. It has also banned two religious groups—Jehovah's Witnesses and Seventh-Day Adventists.

The Cuban government strongly supports the arts and sponsors free ballets, plays, and other cultural events. Most Cubans enjoy singing and dancing, especially Cuban folk music and the country's traditional dances. Cubans are also enthusiastic sports fans who enjoy baseball, basketball, swimming, and track and field.

Cyprus

Greek legend tells how Aphrodite, the goddess of love and beauty, sprang from the foam of the sea and was carried by the waves and sea breezes to the Isle of Cyprus. There she was prepared and dressed to meet the assembly of gods.

This small island country, in the northeastern corner of the Mediterranean Sea, lies about 40 miles (64 kilometers) south of Turkey and 60 miles (97 kilometers) west of Syria. It is the third-largest island in the Mediterranean Sea (after Sicily and Sardinia). Geographically, the island is part of Asia, but its history and culture have long been linked to European civilization.

Early history

The remains of a Neolithic settlement at Khirokitia are evidence that the island was settled as long ago as 6000 B.C. Mycenaean settlers gave the island a Greek identity in the 1200's B.C. Before the birth of Christ, Cyprus had been conquered by the Assyrians, Egyptians, Persians, Greeks, and Romans.

The island was part of the East Roman (Byzantine) Empire from 395 until King Richard the Lion-Hearted of England sold the island to the Lusignans, a French family, who ruled there for about 300 years. The Ottoman Turks ruled Cyprus from the 1570's until they were forced to turn the island over to the British in 1878. Cyprus became a crown colony of the United Kingdom in 1925.

Independence and conflict

In the 1950's, Archbishop Makarios led a Cypriot campaign for *enosis* (union with Greece). After terrorist attacks by a Greek Cypriot secret organization called EOKA, the British declared a state of emergency on the island. In 1959, Greek and Turkish leaders meeting in Zurich, Switzerland, agreed that Cyprus should be an independent state. The United Kingdom accepted the agreement and granted Cyprus its independence on Aug. 16, 1960. Archbishop Makarios became president of the new state.

In 1963, disagreements over changes in the Cypriot Constitution proposed by President Makarios led to renewed conflict between the Greeks and the Turks. The Turks feared that Makarios' changes would eliminate many of the provisions safeguarding their rights, and fighting broke out. In 1964, the United Nations sent a peacekeeping force to maintain order. In 1967, a new crisis developed when the two groups clashed again.

Between 1967 and 1974, some progress was made toward agreement between the two sides. But after President Makarios was

FACT BOX

COUNTRY

Official name: Republic of Cyprus
Capital: Nicosia
Terrain: Central plain with mountains to north and south; scattered but significant plains along southern coast
Area: 3,571 sq. mi. (9,250 km²)

Climate: Temperate, Mediterranean with hot, dry summers and cool winters
Main rivers: Pedieos, Serakhis, Ezouza, Dhiarrizos, Kouris
Highest elevation: Olympus, 6,401 ft. (1,951 m)
Lowest elevation: Mediterranean Sea, sea level

GOVERNMENT

Form of government: Republic
Head of state: President
Head of government: President
Administrative areas: 6 districts

Legislature: Greek area: Vouli Antiprosopon (House of Representatives) with 80 members serving five-year terms
Turkish area: Assembly of the Republic or Cumhuriyet Meclisi (Assembly of the Republic) with 50 members serving five-year terms)
Court system: Supreme Court
Armed forces: 10,000 troops

PEOPLE

Estimated 2002 population: 798,000
Population growth: 0.6%
Population density: 223 persons per sq. mi. (86 per km²)
Population distribution: 64% urban, 36% rural
Life expectancy in years:
Male: 74
Female: 79
Doctors per 1,000 people: N/A
Percentage of age-appropriate population enrolled in the following educational levels:
Primary: N/A
Secondary: N/A
Further: N/A

overthrown by Cypriot national guard forces in 1974, Turkey invaded the island, and new fighting erupted. Turkish forces captured large areas of the northeast, and thousands of Greek Cypriots fled to southwestern Cyprus.

A cease-fire in August 1974 ended the fighting, and Makarios returned as president later in the year. But the Turkish Cypriots refused to recognize the Cypriot government. In 1975, they declared the northeast part of the island, which they held, an autonomous territory within Cyprus, and in 1983, they declared it independent.

This territory, now called the "Turkish Republic of Northern Cyprus" by the Turkish Cypriots, has a president, a Council of Ministers (Cabinet), and a Legislative Assembly, with 50 members elected to 5-year terms. Since 1974, representatives of the Greek and Turkish Cypriots, and of Greece and Turkey, have frequently met to discuss the continuing problem, without success.

Cyprus is a scenic island of colorful folk traditions, beautiful beaches, and historic art and architecture. However, a military barrier, called the Attila line, has divided the Greek-speaking south from the Turkish-held north since 1974.

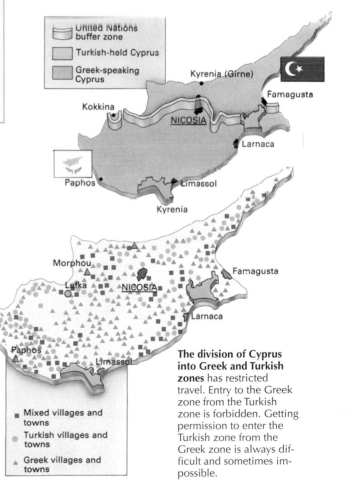

The division of Cyprus into Greek and Turkish zones has restricted travel. Entry to the Greek zone from the Turkish zone is forbidden. Getting permission to enter the Turkish zone from the Greek zone is always difficult and sometimes impossible.

Languages spoken:
- Greek
- Turkish
- English

Religions:
- Greek Orthodox 78%
- Muslim 18%
- Maronite
- Armenian Apostolic

TECHNOLOGY

Radios per 1,000 people: N/A

Televisions per 1,000 people: N/A

Computers per 1,000 people: N/A

ECONOMY

Currency: Greek area: Cypriot pound; Turkish area: Turkish lira

Gross domestic product (GDP) in 2001:
Greek area: $9.1 billion U.S.
Turkish area: $1.1 billion U.S.

Real annual growth rate (2001):
Greek area: 3.0%
Turkish area: 1.0%

GDP per capita (2001):
Greek area: $15,000 U.S.
Turkish area: $7,000 U.S.

Balance of payments (2001): N/A

Goods exported: Greek area: citrus, potatoes, grapes, wine, cement
Turkish area: citrus, potatoes, textiles

Goods imported: Greek area: consumer goods, petroleum and lubricants, food and feed grains
Turkish area: food, minerals, chemicals, machinery

Trading partners: Greek area: United Kingdom, United States, Russia
Turkish area: Turkey, United Kingdom, European Union

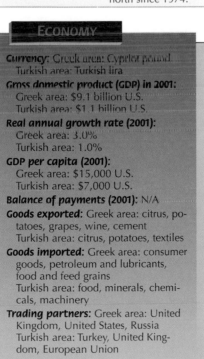

321

Tourism

Scenic beauty and an average of 340 days of sunshine a year attract many visitors to the island paradise of Cyprus, making tourism an important part of the economy. The island boasts a wealth of ruins from ancient times, as well as magnificent Gothic art and architecture. Golden, sandy beaches attract sunbathers, while the snow on Mount Olympus invites skiing enthusiasts.

Political tension on Cyprus has slowed the island's economic progress. The division of the island into Greek and Turkish zones hurt the tourism trade during the 1970's, but tourism has been revived in the Greek area since then.

Landscape

The Troodos Mountains extend along the southwest region of the island, while the Kyrenia Mountains stretch along the northern coast. Extensive pine forests cover parts of the Troodos, and one valley near the city of Paphos has about 40,000 cedars. The mountains also have rich deposits of asbestos and chromite.

Between the island's two mountain ranges lies the Mesaoria Plain. The fertile soil and mild climate of the plain yield two annual harvests of fruits and vegetables. Agricultural production makes a major contribution to the island's economy. Wheat and barley are grown in the eastern plain, while citrus fruits, olives, and almonds are grown in the west.

A mix of cultures

Tourists visiting Cyprus encounter a mix of cultural and ethnic groups, reflecting the island's long history of invasion. About 80 per cent of the island's people are Greek, and most of the rest are of Turkish origin. The island is also home to a number of British nationals, most of whom work at the two British Sovereign bases. Groups of Armenians, Maronites, and Lebanese refugees also live on Cyprus.

In the cities, Cypriots wear modern, Western-style clothing, but in the rural areas, many Cypriot men wear the traditional decorated vests and baggy black trousers called *vrakas*. The women wear long skirts and short blouses called *sarkas*.

Historic sites

The romance and legend of Cyprus' past come vividly to life in Paphos, the island's most important town during Roman times. The picturesque harbor and defensive wall of the old port at Paphos were built by Alexander the Great. Near the harbor, the mosaic pavements of the Villa of Dionysus are among the most beautiful in the Mediterranean area.

At the village of Kouklia (Palea Paphos) are the remains of the Sanctuary of Aphrodite, where pilgrims worshiped the goddess in ancient times. In the ancient city of Kourion, archaeologists have uncovered ruins dating

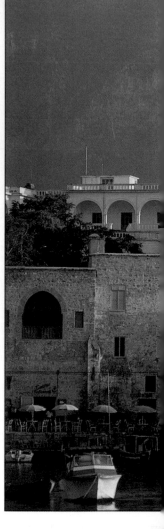

Extensive forests cover the rugged slopes of the Troodos Mountains in southwestern Cyprus, where the island's highest peak, Mount Olympus, rises to 6,401 feet (1,951 meters).

from the 400's B.C. Fine pavement mosaics, baths, and a Temple of Apollo are all that survived after an earthquake destroyed the city.

A few miles east of Kourion stands the massive Kolossi Castle, built in 1210 by the Knights of St. John. From the castle's towers, visitors may enjoy an extraordinary view of the rolling plains between the Troodos Mountains and the city of Limassol, where Richard

Boats are often moored in the Turkish-occupied port of Kyrenia, *left,* a resort on the north-central coast.

On the hill of Throni, outside the capital city of Nicosia, soldiers guard a portrait of President Archbishop Makarios (1913-1977) in front of his tomb. In the 1950's, Makarios led the Greek Cypriot campaign for independence from British rule.

The setting sun casts a golden glow over Petra tou Romiou. The legendary goddess Aphrodite is said to have emerged from the Mediterranean Sea off this rocky point. Ancient pilgrims sailed to Cyprus to worship at the nearby Sanctuary of Aphrodite.

Fishers at the south coastal port of Limassol, *above,* prepare freshly caught octopus for market. Like Larnaca to the northeast, Limassol is a major port as well as a bustling center of industry and commerce.

the Lion-Hearted married Berengaria of Navarre.

In the interior of the island, the capital city of Nicosia has an old section surrounded by a huge ring of Venetian walls. Inside the walls stands the Gothic St. John's Cathedral, seat of the Greek Orthodox Archbishop of Cyprus.

In the Turkish-occupied section of Nicosia, the Gothic St. Sophia's Cathedral, built in the 1200's, is now the Selimiye Mosque. The Turks also occupy the port of Famagusta. An interesting landmark on the seaward side of this city is a fortress featuring Othello's Tower, said to have been the scene of Shakespeare's tragedy. Not far from Famagusta lies the site of the ancient city of Salamis. Once a shipping center for the island's busy copper trade, it was destroyed by an earthquake in the A.D. 300's. The ruins of a large theater, a Temple of Zeus, an aqueduct, and other structures still stand today.

Czech Republic

The Czech Republic is a landlocked nation in the heart of central Europe, bordered by Poland to the north, Slovakia to the east, Hungary and Austria to the south, and Germany to the west. Its scenic landscape ranges from rugged mountains and rolling hills to dense forests and fertile plains. Prague, the nation's capital and largest city, has been called the "City of a Hundred Spires" because of its many churches.

A new nation

The Czech Republic was formerly a part of Czechoslovakia, which was established in 1918 when the Czech and Slovak people united to form a single nation. In mid-1992, the Czech and Slovak republics began discussions on whether to split the two republics. Czechoslovakia officially broke up into two separate nations—the Czech Republic and Slovakia—on Jan. 1, 1993, in a peaceful "divorce" engineered by Czech and Slovak leaders in 1992.

The Czech Republic consists of two historic regions—Bohemia and Moravia. The first known inhabitants of what is now the Czech Republic were the Boii, a Celtic tribe that lived in Bohemia during the 300's B.C. After the A.D. 400's, Slavic tribes settled in Moravia, and the Czechs settled in Bohemia.

These tribes joined together to form the Greater Moravian Empire, which once covered much of central Europe. However, the empire fell in 900, and Bohemia became a semi-independent kingdom within the Holy Roman Empire. Moravia became part of the territory ruled by the Duke of Bohemia.

In 1620, Bohemia lost its self-governing powers and was divided into three provinces—Bohemia, Moravia, and Silesia—ruled by the Habsburgs of Austria. The Habsburgs forced the Czechs to adopt the German language and culture.

In 1867, Austria and Hungary formed a monarchy called Austria-Hungary, which lasted until the end of World War I (1914-1918). During this period, Czech and Slovak leaders worked together to form an independent nation. After the collapse of Austria-

Hungary in 1918, Czechoslovakia was proclaimed an independent country. In 1948, Czechoslovakia became a Communist state.

Although the Czechs and Slovaks were united under a single flag, the two groups followed separate paths and maintained their own traditions. Since the Slovaks were mainly farming people with very little political experience, the Czechs took control of the new nation's economy and government.

Despite their cultural differences, the Czechs and the Slovaks united to seek political reform in the late 1980's. Working together, the two groups brought about the fall of Communism and the return of democratic government to their country.

When Czechoslovakia was dissolved in 1993, the Czechs and Slovaks cooperated to divide the assets of the country, and most problems were settled through peaceful negotiations. Leaders of both former republics agreed to coordinate defense and foreign policies, and possibly to share embassies in smaller countries. The Czechs and Slovaks also planned to maintain close trade contacts and to guarantee the free movement of labor and capital across their borders.

The Czech people

Most of the people living in the Czech Republic are Czechs. The republic's official language is Czech, a Slavic language that shares characteristics with other Eastern European tongues.

Through the years, the Czech culture was influenced by the Germans. For example, Czech cooking is similar to that of Austria and Germany, and the Czechs enjoy beer with their meals.

Most present day Czechs live in apartments in the cities and wear Western-style clothing. But some of them still enjoy dressing in colorful folk costumes on special occasions.

The Czech people enjoy one of the highest standards of living in Eastern Europe. Many families have such luxury items as television sets, refrigerators, and cars.

Czech Republic Today

November 1989 marked the beginning of dramatic political changes for the Czech people. These changes were triggered by the decline of Communist power in Czechoslovakia and the trend toward greater democracy in Eastern European countries during the late 1980's.

On Nov. 17, 1989, about 50,000 people took part in antigovernment demonstrations in Prague—the largest public protest in Czechoslovakia for 20 years. The police broke up the demonstration, and rumors that a student had been killed fueled a series of demonstrations that increased in size with each passing day.

The continuing demonstrations were not opposed by police, and a new opposition group, known as Civic Forum, called for a return to democracy. Civic Forum was supported by the majority of the people as well as by the Czechoslovak Socialist Party and the Czechoslovak People's Party. In early December, a new Federal Government was announced, but it was denounced by the Civic Forum because most of its ministers had been members of the previous administration. In addition, it included only five non-Communists.

After a mass demonstration of about 200,000 people in Prague, a new, interim Federal Government was formed—a govern-

The resort town of Mariánské Lázně in western Bohemia enjoyed great renown in the days of the Austro-Hungarian Empire, when it was known as Marienbad. Today, many people come to bathe in its more than 40 mineral springs or drink the waters—an activity that first became popular in the early 1800's. Mariánské Lázně lies in the heavily populated Bohemian Mountains, a region of large coal and uranium ore deposits and dense forests.

FACT BOX

COUNTRY

Official name: Ceska Republika (Czech Republic)
Capital: Prague
Terrain: The west consists of rolling plains, hills, and plateaus surrounded by low mountains; the east consists of very hilly country

Area: 30,450 sq. mi. (78,866 km²)
Climate: Temperate; cool summers; cold, cloudy, humid winters
Main rivers: Elbe, Morava, Vltava
Highest elevation: Snezka, 5,256 ft. (1,602 m)
Lowest elevation: Elbe River, 377 ft. (115 m)

GOVERNMENT

Form of government: Parliamentary democracy
Head of state: President
Head of government: Prime minister
Administrative areas: 73 okresi (districts), 4 mesta (municipalities)

Legislature: Parlament (Parliament) consisting of the Senat (Senate) with 81 members serving staggered two-, four-, and six-year terms and the Poslanecka Snemovna (Chamber of Deputies) with 200 members serving four-year terms
Court system: Supreme Court, Constitutional Court
Armed forces: 58,200 troops

PEOPLE

Estimated 2002 population: 10,215,000
Population growth: -0.08%
Population density: 335 persons per sq. mi. (130 per km²)
Population distribution: 77% urban, 23% rural
Life expectancy in years:
Male: 71
Female: 78
Doctors per 1,000 people: 3.0
Percentage of age-appropriate population enrolled in the following educational levels:
Primary: 104*
Secondary: 82
Further: 26
Language spoken: Czech

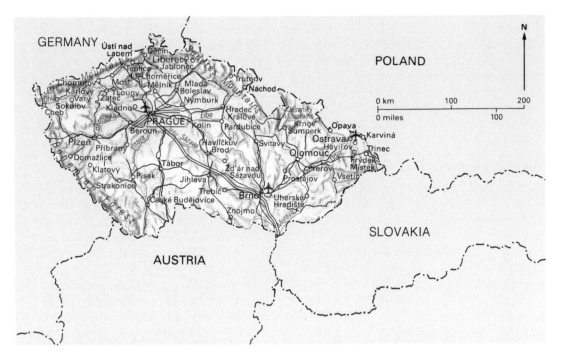

The Czech Republic came into existence on Jan. 1, 1993, when the Czech and Slovak Republic was officially dissolved. In geographical area, it represents about two-thirds of the now-defunct federation.

Religions:
 Atheist 39.8%
 Roman Catholic 39.2%
 Protestant 4.6%
 Orthodox 3%

Enrollment ratios compare the number of students enrolled to the population which, by age, should be enrolled. A ratio higher than 100 indicates that students older or younger than the typical age range are also enrolled.

TECHNOLOGY

Radios per 1,000 people: 803

Televisions per 1,000 people: 508

Computers per 1,000 people: 122

ECONOMY

Currency: Koruna

Gross national income (GNI) in 2000: $53.9 billion U.S.

Real annual growth rate (1999–2000): 2.9%

GNI per capita (2000): $5,250 U.S.

Balance of payments (2000): -$2,236 million U.S.

Goods exported: Machinery and transport equipment, other manufactured goods, chemicals, raw materials and fuel

Goods imported: Machinery and transport equipment, other manufactured goods, chemicals, raw materials and fuels, food

Trading partners: Germany, Slovakia, Austria

ment with a non-Communist majority that also included seven supporters of Civic Forum. In addition, the Federal Assembly voted to change the Constitution, deleting the sections that guaranteed the Communist Party's leading role.

Meanwhile, Gustáv Husák, leader of the Communist Party, resigned as president, and at the end of December, he was replaced by playwright Václav Havel, leader of the Civic Forum. During this "velvet revolution," the word *Socialist* was removed from the nation's official name.

Under the new government, civil liberties, such as freedom of religion, speech, and the press, were restored. In 1992, the government also made a dramatic move toward establishing a free market economy by offering shares of stock in the 1,446 companies it owned.

By mid-1992, Czech and Slovak leaders began discussions on whether to separate Czechoslovakia into two separate nations, although a majority of the people opposed it. In July of that year, Havel resigned his post, stating that he did not want to preside over the breakup of his country.

On Jan. 1, 1993, Czechoslovakia was broken up into two countries—the Czech Republic and Slovakia. Assets of the former Czechoslovakia were divided in a ratio of two to one in favor of the Czech side. Havel returned as president in February.

Prospects for economic growth in the new republic appeared strong, as the country continued its transition to privatization. Prague remained a busy retail and service center, while investment of foreign capital was expected to further boost the economy.

History

The ancestors of the Czech people settled in what is now the Czech Republic in about A.D. 500. During the 800's, these Slavic tribes banded together to form the Great Moravian Empire. Beginning in the late 800's, the Magyars (Hungarians) invaded the Great Moravian Empire, and in time they destroyed it.

The rise of Bohemia

After the fall of the Great Moravian Empire, Bohemia developed into a powerful, semi-independent kingdom of the Holy Roman Empire. By the 1100's, Bohemia included Moravia and parts of Austria and Poland. In the 1200's, many German craft workers and merchants settled in Bohemian towns.

Bohemia reached its cultural and political peak under Charles IV, who ruled from 1346 to 1378. Charles was crowned Holy Roman Emperor in 1347, and Prague—the city in which he was born—became the empire's leading city. Beginning in the late 1400's, a series of weak Polish kings ruled Bohemia, and Czech nobles became more powerful.

In 1526, Bohemia came under the control of the Austrian Habsburgs, who were Roman Catholic. Meanwhile, the Reformation gave birth to Protestantism in Europe, and in 1618, a group of Czech Protestant nobles revolted against Habsburg rule. They elected a Protestant king of Bohemia. The revolt touched off the Thirty Years' War.

The Bohemians were defeated by the Habsburgs in 1620, and Bohemia lost most of its self-governing powers. Bohemia and Moravia began to industrialize in the late 1700's, and many Czech peasants moved to urban areas to work in factory jobs. By the mid-1800's, the Czechs had replaced the Germans as the largest population group in the cities and towns of Bohemia and Moravia. Nationalistic feelings began to develop among the Czechs, and several revolutionary leaders called for Czech self-government.

An etching entitled *The Defenestration of Prague* illustrates Czech Protestants throwing Roman Catholic officials from a window of Prague Castle in 1618.

c. A.D. 500 Ancestors of the Czechs settle in Bohemia and Moravia.

800's Slavic tribes unite to form the Great Moravian Empire.

c. A.D. 900 Bohemia develops into a powerful central European nation ruled by Přemyslid family.

1347 Charles IV of Bohemia becomes Holy Roman Emperor.
1348 Prague University is founded.

1415 Religious reformer John Hus is found guilty of heresy and is burned at the stake.
1419–1436 The Hussite Wars bring turmoil to Bohemia.
1526 The Habsburgs take control of Bohemia.

1618 A Czech revolt touches off the Thirty Years' War.
1620 The Habsburg Army defeats the Czechs in the Battle of White Mountain, and Bohemia loses its self-governing powers.

Mid-1800's Czech nationalistic feelings grow, and a movement for self-government takes shape.
1867 Austria and Hungary unite as the country of Austria-Hungary.

1918 The Czechs and Slovaks form Czechoslovakia as an independent nation.
1938 Munich Agreement awards the Sudeten territory to Germany.
1939 German armies occupy Czechoslovakia.
1945 Soviet troops free most of Czechoslovakia, while U.S. troops liberate parts of Bohemia.
1948 Communists take over the government.
1968 The Prague Spring, a period of liberal reform, ends with the invasion of Czechoslovakia by Warsaw Pact troops.
1969 Gustáv Husák is appointed president after Alexander Dubček is removed from office.
1989 Communist regime collapses, and Husák is replaced by Václav Havel.
1991 Soviet Union withdraws its troops from Czechoslovakia.
1992 Havel resigns as president as Czech and Slovak leaders prepare to dissolve the Czechoslav federation.
1993 The Czech Republic is formally established on Jan. 1; Havel is returned to power as president of the new republic by parliamentary vote.
1999 The Czech Republic joined the North Atlantic Treaty Organization.

John Hus (1369?-1415) was a Bohemian religious reformer.

Bedřich Smetana (1824-1884), *far left,* was the first major nationalist composer of Czechoslovakia.

Václav Havel (1936-   ), a Czech dramatist, was inaugurated as president of the Czech Republic in February 1993.

A young Czech hammers at the armor of a Soviet tank during the invasion of Czechoslovakia in 1968. The Soviet Union and its Eastern European allies sent troops to crush the Czechoslovak movement toward democracy known as the *Prague Spring.*

A painted ceiling depicting the great thinkers of ancient times decorates the Philosophical Hall of the Strahov Library near Prague Castle. This historic building on *Hradčany* (Castle Hill) houses many of the nation's artistic treasures.

Surrounded by his fellow dignitaries, Václav Havel takes the oath of office in an inauguration ceremony held February 2, 1993. Havel was elected the first president of the newly independent Czech Republic after stepping down as president of Czechoslovakia shortly before the federation was dissolved.

During World War I (1914-1918), opposition activity increased in Bohemia. Although the Habsburg government arrested many revolutionary leaders, two leading Czech nationalists—Tomáš G. Masaryk and Eduard Beneš—fled to Paris, where they formed the Czechoslovak National Council to organize foreign support for an independent state made up of Czechs and Slovaks.

Unity of Czechs and Slovaks

When Austria-Hungary collapsed after World War I, Czechoslovakia became an independent democratic republic consisting of Bohemia, Moravia, and Slovakia. In 1919, Ruthenia, a region east of Slovakia, became part of Czechoslovakia.

Tension between minority groups weakened the new nation, and in the 1930's, German dictator Adolf Hitler encouraged the Sudeten Germans, who lived in the Sudeten Mountains of Czechoslovakia, to demand self-rule. He threatened to declare war on Czechoslovakia if this demand was not met. In 1938, under the terms of the Munich Agreement, Czechoslovakia was forced to give up the Sudeten territory to Germany.

In 1939, German troops invaded Czechoslovakia, and Bohemia and Moravia became a German protectorate, while Slovakia became a separate republic under German control. By 1945, Allied troops had freed Czechoslovakia from the Germans. During the years that followed, Czechoslovakia fell under Communist rule, and in 1948, the Communists forced the president of Czechoslovakia to form a new government consisting entirely of Communists.

In 1968, the Communist Party appointed Alexander Dubček as party leader. Under Dubček, the government introduced a program of liberal reforms, known as the *Prague Spring,* but the Soviet Union and other Eastern European nations, fearing that the reforms would weaken Communist control, invaded the country in August 1968. Dubček was removed from office in 1969, and the government remained under tight Soviet control until the democratic revolution of 1989.

Prague

Prague, situated on both banks of the Vltava River, is the capital and largest city of the Czech Republic. It is also an important center of culture and learning. One of central Europe's oldest and most beautiful cities, Prague is often called the *Golden City*—its picturesque stone castles set amid rolling hills could be the setting for a fairy tale.

Because Prague escaped massive bombing during World War II (1939-1945), the beauty and historic significance of many of its old buildings and churches are virtually unrivaled throughout Europe. Many historic events took place in Prague, including the uprising that triggered the Thirty Years' War in 1618, and the Soviet invasion of 1968, when armored tanks rolled through the city's streets, snuffing out the brief Prague Spring.

Early history

According to legend, Prague was founded about A.D. 800 by Princess Libuše, who had a vision of a glorious city while standing on a rocky ledge above the east bank of the River Vltava. The royal Palace of Vyšehrad was built on that spot in the 800's. However, the original settlement of Prague took place on the opposite bank of the river. At the end of the 900's, the first Czech kings built a massive hilltop citadel on *Hradčany* (Castle Hill), which dominates the city's skyline.

The commercial district of *Staré Město* (Old Town) developed across the river from Hradčany, at the intersection of important trade routes. German colonists settled in this section starting in the early 1200's. A large and flourishing Jewish community in this district was confined—beginning in the 1200's—inside a walled ghetto. The walls were pulled down in the mid-1800's, but one of the ghetto's original synagogues has survived.

In 1257, south of Hradčany and within the outer wall of the citadel, King Otakar II founded the Lesser Town of Prague—later known as the *Malá Strana,* or Lesser Quarter. Many beautiful old palaces line the narrow, winding streets of Malá Strana.

Waltzing couples in a Prague park reflect the graceful, elegant atmosphere of the Czech Republic's historic capital. The city was probably founded in the A.D. 800's and later served as the residence of Bohemian kings.

High above the Charles Bridge, the spires of St. Vitus' Cathedral crown Prague's *Hradčany* (Castle Hill). The Hradčany is also the site of Prague Castle, which now serves as an art museum and the official residence of the Czech Republic's president.

In 1348, Charles IV established the *Nové Město* (New Town), which extends south of the Staré Město and down to Vyšehrad. Today, the Nové Město is Prague's business district, featuring Wenceslas Square—actually a wide boulevard lined with hotels and shops.

The golden age

Prague soon grew into an important trading center, and in time it became the residence of the Bohemian kings. Charles IV, who also ruled the Holy Roman Empire, built many impressive buildings in the city.

Under Charles IV, Prague emerged as a cultural center of international renown. In 1348, the king founded Charles University, the oldest university in central Europe, and his court included the Italian poet Petrarch. The French architect Matthias of Arras and German architect Peter Parler

transformed St. Vitus' Cathedral into an architectural wonder.

During the 1600's, religious wars and conflict between the Habsburgs and the Czech nobility caused great damage to the city. The triumph of the Habsburgs in the Thirty Years' War was followed by an ambitious rebuilding campaign that gave the city its present appearance. Unlike the neighboring cities of Vienna, Austria, and Budapest, Hungary, which boast wide boulevards and huge apartment blocks, the old center of Prague remains unchanged from days gone by.

Street vendors supply Prague residents with fresh vegetables, *above.* Although the population has increased only slightly since World War II, Prague has a housing shortage. Many people live in crowded city apartments.

Houses along the streets of Malá Strana, *below left,* recall Bohemia's golden age. Many other buildings in Prague, constructed during the 1900's, are now in poor condition.

Prague, *map below,* is divided into two sections by the Vltava River. Largely untouched by war, Prague is home to many artistic and architectural treasures. The Staré Město (Old Town), Prague's historic center, contains the Old Town Hall. Wenceslas Square links the Staré Město with the Nové Město (New Town), which dates from the 1800's. Hradčany dominates the left bank of the Vltava River.

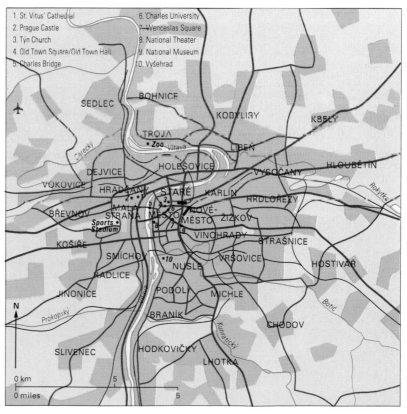

1. St. Vitus' Cathedral
2. Prague Castle
3. Týn Church
4. Old Town Square/Old Town Hall
5. Charles Bridge
6. Charles University
7. Wenceslas Square
8. National Theater
9. National Museum
10. Vyšehrad

Art and Politics

The line between art and life is a thin one in the Czech Republic—a country whose president is a noted playwright. Since before World War I (1914-1918), Czech writers have used wit and imagination to reveal many truths about politics, authority, and the human condition. During the years of Communist rule, when freedom of expression was greatly restricted, their writings challenged the system, poking fun at its often absurd ways.

Hašek's immortal Schwejk

In the days before World War I, the writings of Jaroslav Hašek subtly attacked Austrian rule of the Czech people through a shabbily dressed character named Schwejk. In Hašek's tales, Schwejk is thrown out of the army as an imbecile, but is drafted after the outbreak of World War I. Although he appears stupid, Schwejk succeeds in ridiculing and disrupting the whole military establishment.

To Hašek, Schwejk was a man whose humble achievements were ultimately more important than those of the greatest military figures, and the character became a hero of modern literature. Hašek himself was a colorful personality who enjoyed practical jokes. On one occasion, he identified himself as a "spy" in the guest register of a leading Prague hotel. Within moments, soldiers surrounded the hotel, only to find that the "spy" was none other than Hašek. When asked why he did it, Hašek replied that he was simply testing the efficiency of the Austrian secret service.

After World War I (1914-1918), the scholar and statesman Tomáš Masaryk became the first president of the newly independent state of Czechoslovakia. Masaryk's government gave enormous support to the arts, but the Germans squelched all freedom of expression during their occupation of the country in World War II. After the war, the Communist rulers put equally tight restrictions on the arts, severely punishing anyone who dared to oppose them.

The Czech tradition

Czech films combine humor and social comment in Menzel's *Closely Watched Trains* (1966), *above,* and Milos Forman's *The Firemen's Ball* (1967). Both films satirize authority and small-town life.

Tomáš Masaryk became the first president of the newly independent state of Czechoslovakia in 1918. Masaryk was a scholar and philosopher who did not enter politics until he was almost 40 years old. His academic background and the encouragement he gave to the arts reflect the traditional Czech connection between politics and the arts. Chief among the writers who used humor to ridicule government failings was Jaroslav Hašek. His beloved character, Schwejk, who outwitted the hard-hearted military authorities of World War I, was a model for later comedic characters such as Sergeant Bilko, a hero of American television comedy. When the Communists took over the Czech state in 1948, this tradition of ridiculing authority continued in the works of such writers as Bohumil Hrabal, whose novel, *I Served the King of England,* was published underground in the late 1950's. Jazz, officially dismissed by the Nazis and the Communists as a symbol of moral decay, became a Czech symbol of liberty and inspired Josef Skvorecky's highly influential 1960's novella, *The Bass Saxophone.*

In November 1989, crowds of students took to the streets of Prague and other Czechoslovakian cities, *above,* beginning the movement that came to be known as the "velvet revolution." While it involved some confrontation with government forces, *right,* the movement was largely peaceful. Artists, writers, and even rock musicians played a key role in the mass uprising. The velvet revolution brought down the Communist system in Czechoslovakia, paving the way not only for a democratic government system and free market economy, but also for a new freedom of expression for Czech writers and artists.

During the Prague Spring of 1968, those who disagreed with Communist policies spoke out against the government in massive demonstrations that were later crushed by Soviet troops.

Václav Havel, *above,* lifts his glass to celebrate the triumph of democracy with Alexander Dubček, whose policies led to the Prague Spring. Dubček died in late 1992.

The coming of Prague Spring

The bureaucratic absurdities of Czechoslovakia's Communist leaders provided rich subject matter for Czech writers, whose sense of humor helped them cope with the rigid authorities. However, many fine writers were rarely published during those years because their work did not conform to official policy.

Novelists, playwrights, musicians, and filmmakers joined forces in the 1960's to create a mood of optimism and vitality. Prague's Theater at the Balustrade, where Václav Havel's plays were first performed, became a rallying point for Czechs who disagreed with Communist policies. The new spirit culminated in the Prague Spring of 1968.

Gifted filmmakers brought the great Czech spirit of expression to worldwide attention. Jiri Menzel's film, *Closely Watched Trains,* won an Academy Award for Best Foreign Film of 1966. The film, based on a novella by Bohumil Hrabal, told the story of a young railway employee coming of age during the last days of World War II.

Many talented people were forced to leave Czechoslovakia after the Soviet invasion of 1968, but though they were officially silenced, the arts continued to play a major role in political developments. Charter 77 — a manifesto of individual liberties signed by nearly all the country's remaining intellectuals and cultural figures — was developed in 1977 in protest of the imprisonment of an antiauthoritarian rock band called The Plastic People of the Universe.

The Magic Lantern Theater in Prague literally provided the stage for Czechoslovakia's "velvet revolution" in 1989. Founded in 1958, the theater was famous for its innovative plays and films and became a meeting place for Czechoslovakia's artists and writers. In December 1989, Václav Havel and Alexander Dubček emerged in triumph from its backstage rooms to proclaim the return of democracy to Czechoslovakia. Havel served as president of Czechoslovakia from 1989 to 1992. He stepped down briefly during the breakup of the country before becoming president of the Czech Republic.

Environment

Although the Czech Republic is completely landlocked, two important rivers link the country to the Black and North seas. The Elbe River, one of the major commercial waterways of central Europe, rises in the western part of the republic and flows westward through Germany before emptying into the North Sea. And the Oder River rises in the Sudeten Mountains and flows northward to the Black Sea.

The Czech Republic can be divided into five major land regions. These are the Bohemian Mountains, the Sudeten Mountains, the Bohemian Basin, the Bohemian-Moravian Highlands, and the Moravian Lowlands.

Mountains and forests

The Bohemian Mountains, which rise in the extreme west of the country, include the Ore Mountains in the northwest and the Bohemian Forest in the southwest. Many people come to bathe in the mineral springs of the Ore Mountains. The mountain peaks—many rising more than 2,500 feet (762 meters) above sea level—make the region a popular skiing destination.

The Bohemian Mountain region contains large deposits of coal and uranium ore, making it a major center for the Czech Republic's mining and manufacturing industries. Tourists enjoy wandering along the region's forest paths—a route taken by highway robbers long ago. The thickly wooded hills of the Bohemian Forest are an important source of lumber and wood products.

The higher and more rugged Sudeten Mountains in the north-central part of the Czech Republic define the country's border with Poland. This heavily populated region includes industrial cities and towns as well as farming areas, forests, and resorts.

South of the Sudeten Mountains lies the Bohemian Basin, a low-lying area of plains and rolling hills. The numerous rivers and streams that rise in the surrounding highlands flow into the basin, providing water for this fertile region, where farmers grow

Plzeň, situated in the western part of the republic, ranks as one of the nation's major industrial centers, *right*. Its factories manufacture automobiles, buses, machinery, military equipment, and trucks, while breweries produce world-famous beer.

A craft worker in Karlovy Vary (Karlsbad) inscribes a design onto a glass bowl. Northern Bohemia has been a leading center of the glass industry since the 1600's.

The picturesque town of **Mikulov** lies on the edge of the Moravian Lowlands. One of the Czech Republic's leading industrial and mining centers lies to the northeast, around the city of Ostrava.

potatoes, rye, sugar beets, wheat, and other crops. Major rivers include the Vltava, which flows northward toward Prague, and the Elbe, which flows westward across the basin.

Farms and factories

The Bohemian Basin is also home to some of the Czech Republic's major industrial cities. Kladno, for example, ranks as a leading center of steel production, while factories in Prague manufacture motorcycles and products for heavy industry.

The Bohemian-Moravian Highlands cover most of southern Bohemia—a region of low hills and plateaus. Numerous small towns and villages are scattered throughout this area, which consists mainly of farmland.

The densely populated Moravian Lowlands extend across the eastern part of the Czech Republic. Fertile farmland covers the Morava River Valley, where farmers raise livestock and grow such crops as corn, potatoes, rye, sugar beets, and wheat.

The Moravian Lowlands also have the nation's most important coal fields. One of the Czech Republic's leading industrial and mining centers is situated around the city of Ostrava.

Brno, an important industrial city near the country's southeastern border with Slovakia, is the Czech Republic's second largest city and the chief city of Moravia. Founded in the 1800's, Brno is a manufacturing center that produces automobiles, chemicals, iron and steel, leather goods, machinery, and textiles.

A street vendor in Prague offers for sale fresh fruits and vegetables grown in the surrounding countryside. The city lies in the Bohemian Basin, where some of the country's most fertile farmland can be found.

The rugged cliffs of these mountains in Bohemia, *below,* rise in dramatic contrast to the rolling hills beyond them. The Bohemian and Sudeten mountains cover much of the northern Czech Republic.